SHAKESPEARE'S MORAL COMPASS

EDINBURGH CRITICAL STUDIES IN SHAKESPEARE AND PHILOSOPHY
Series Editor: Kevin Curran

Edinburgh Critical Studies in Shakespeare and Philosophy takes seriously the speculative and world-making properties of Shakespeare's art. Maintaining a broad view of 'philosophy' that accommodates first-order questions of metaphysics, ethics, politics and aesthetics, the series also expands our understanding of philosophy to include the unique kinds of theoretical work carried out by performance and poetry itself. These scholarly monographs will reinvigorate Shakespeare studies by opening new interdisciplinary conversations among scholars, artists and students.

Editorial Board Members
Ewan Fernie, Shakespeare Institute, University of Birmingham
James Kearney, University of California, Santa Barbara
Julia Reinhard Lupton, University of California, Irvine
Madhavi Menon, Ashoka University
Simon Palfrey, Oxford University
Tiffany Stern, Shakespeare Institute, University of Birmingham
Henry Turner, Rutgers University
Michael Witmore, The Folger Shakespeare Library
Paul Yachnin, McGill University

Published Titles
Rethinking Shakespeare's Political Philosophy: From Lear to Leviathan
Alex Schulman
Shakespeare in Hindsight: Counterfactual Thinking and Shakespearean Tragedy
Amir Khan
Second Death: Theatricalities of the Soul in Shakespeare's Drama
Donovan Sherman
Shakespeare's Fugitive Politics
Thomas P. Anderson
Is Shylock Jewish?: Citing Scripture and the Moral Agency of Shakespeare's Jews
Sara Coodin
Chaste Value: Economic Crisis, Female Chastity and the Production of Social Difference on Shakespeare's Stage
Katherine Gillen
Shakespearean Melancholy: Philosophy, Form and the Transformation of Comedy
J. F. Bernard
Shakespeare's Moral Compass
Neema Parvini

Forthcoming Titles
Making Publics in Shakespeare's Playhouse
Paul Yachnin
Derrida Reads Shakespeare
Chiara Alfano
The Play and the Thing: A Phenomenology of Shakespearean Theatre
Matthew Wagner
Shakespeare and the Fall of the Roman Republic: Selfhood, Stoicism and Civil War in Julius Caesar and Antony and Cleopatra
Patrick Gray
Conceiving Desire: Metaphor, Cognition and Eros in Lyly and Shakespeare
Gillian Knoll
Shakespeare and the Truth-Teller: Confronting the Cynic Ideal
David Hershinow
Revenge Tragedy and Classical Philosophy on the Early Modern Stage
Christopher Crosbie

For further information please visit our website at edinburghuniversitypress.com/series/ecsst

SHAKESPEARE'S MORAL COMPASS

◆ ◆ ◆

NEEMA PARVINI

EDINBURGH
University Press

Edinburgh University Press is one of the leading university presses in the UK. We publish academic books and journals in our selected subject areas across the humanities and social sciences, combining cutting-edge scholarship with high editorial and production values to produce academic works of lasting importance. For more information visit our website: edinburghuniversitypress.com

© Neema Parvini, 2018, 2020

Edinburgh University Press Ltd
The Tun – Holyrood Road,
12(2f) Jackson's Entry,
Edinburgh EH8 8PJ

First published in hardback by Edinburgh University Press 2018

Typeset in 12/15 Adobe Sabon by
IDSUK (DataConnection) Ltd

A CIP record for this book is available from the British Library

ISBN 978 1 4744 3287 0 (hardback)
ISBN 978 1 4744 3288 7 (paperback)
ISBN 978 1 4744 3289 4 (webready PDF)
ISBN 978 1 4744 3290 0 (epub)

The right of Neema Parvini to be identified as the author of this work has been asserted in accordance with the Copyright, Designs and Patents Act 1988, and the Copyright and Related Rights Regulations 2003 (SI No. 2498).

CONTENTS

Acknowledgements	vi
Series Editor's Preface	vii

Part I: Conflicting Moral Visions

1. Navigating Shakespeare's Moral Compass	3
2. The Constrained Vision of Evolutionary Ethics	35
3. Moral Philosophy in England during the Time of Shakespeare	71
4. The Reformation, Capitalism and Ethics in England during the 1590s and early 1600s	139

Part II: Shakespeare's Moral Compass

5. Past Reflections on Shakespeare and Morality	181
6. Authority	201
7. Loyalty	224
8. Fairness	246
9. Sanctity	262
10. Care	280
11. Liberty	295
Bibliography	305
Index	335

ACKNOWLEDGEMENTS

I'd like to thank Kevin Curran for encouraging this project, and Michelle Houston and the rest of the team at Edinburgh University Press for having the vision to launch this excellent and exciting series on Shakespeare and Philosophy. I am also grateful to colleagues who read sections of and made many helpful suggestions on this book, especially Jonathan Haidt, Patrick Gray, Joseph Carroll, Brian Boyd, James Knapp, Evelyn Gajowski, Jyotsna Singh, Will McKenzie, Michael Bristol and Ria Chatterjee. Thank you to Wendy Lee for tremendous copy-editing work, and to Rebecca McKenzie and James Dale for seeing this through to production. Much love also to my parents for their continued support, and especially my mother for her thoughtful comments. Finally, thank you to Sarah Frazer for being such a great partner; your love, patience and understanding, not to mention your attention to detail in proof reading, are much appreciated.

SERIES EDITOR'S PREFACE

Picture Macbeth alone on stage, staring intently into empty space. 'Is this a dagger which I see before me?' he asks, grasping decisively at the air. On one hand, this is a quintessentially theatrical question. At once an object and a vector, the dagger describes the possibility of knowledge ('Is this a dagger') in specifically visual and spatial terms ('which I see before me'). At the same time, Macbeth is posing a quintessentially *philosophical* question, one that assumes knowledge to be both conditional and experiential, and that probes the relationship between certainty and perception as well as intention and action. It is from this shared ground of art and inquiry, of theatre and theory, that this series advances its basic premise: *Shakespeare is philosophical.*

It seems like a simple enough claim. But what does it mean exactly, beyond the parameters of this specific moment in *Macbeth*? Does it mean that Shakespeare had something we could think of as his own philosophy? Does it mean that he was influenced by particular philosophical schools, texts and thinkers? Does it mean, conversely, that modern philosophers have been influenced by *him*, that Shakespeare's plays and poems have been, and continue to be, resources for philosophical thought and speculation?

The answer is yes all around. These are all useful ways of conceiving a philosophical Shakespeare and all point to lines of enquiry that this series welcomes. But Shakespeare is philosophical in a much more fundamental way as well. Shakespeare is philosophical because the plays and poems actively create new worlds of knowledge and new scenes of ethical encounter. They ask big questions, make bold arguments and develop new vocabularies in order to think what might otherwise be unthinkable. Through both their scenarios and their imagery, the plays and poems engage the qualities of consciousness, the consequences of human action, the phenomenology of motive and attention, the conditions of personhood and the relationship among different orders of reality and experience. This is writing and dramaturgy, moreover, that consistently experiments with a broad range of conceptual crossings, between love and subjectivity, nature and politics, and temporality and form.

Edinburgh Critical Studies in Shakespeare and Philosophy takes seriously these speculative and world-making dimensions of Shakespeare's work. The series proceeds from a core conviction that art's capacity to think – to formulate, not just reflect, ideas – is what makes it urgent and valuable. Art matters because, unlike other human activities, it establishes its own frame of reference, reminding us that all acts of creation – biological, political, intellectual and amorous – are grounded in imagination. This is a far cry from business-as-usual in Shakespeare studies. Because historicism remains the methodological gold standard of the field, far more energy has been invested in exploring what Shakespeare once meant than in thinking rigorously about what Shakespeare continues to make possible. In response, Edinburgh Critical Studies in Shakespeare and Philosophy pushes back against the critical orthodoxies of historicism and cultural studies to clear a space for scholarship that confronts aspects of literature that can be neither reduced to nor adequately explained by particular historical contexts.

Series Editor's Preface

Shakespeare's creations are not just inheritances of a past culture, frozen artefacts whose original settings must be expertly reconstructed in order to be understood. The plays and poems are also living art, vital thought-worlds that struggle, across time, with foundational questions of metaphysics, ethics, politics and aesthetics. With this orientation in mind, Edinburgh Critical Studies in Shakespeare and Philosophy offers a series of scholarly monographs that will reinvigorate Shakespeare studies by opening new interdisciplinary conversations among scholars, artists and students.

Kevin Curran

Part I

Conflicting Moral Visions

CHAPTER 1

NAVIGATING SHAKESPEARE'S MORAL COMPASS

Introduction

Shakespeare's Moral Compass is an attempt to uncover and define the moral framework that binds and blinds the characters of the most famous body of plays in world literature. I write at a time when some feel that Western civilisation is at a moment of crisis. It is a moment in which many of us are taking stock and looking for meaning. It is a moment in which it somehow feels apposite to look, as so many previous generations have looked, to the great literature of the past for some insight, and perhaps even for some guidance. Certain commentators worry that many people in Europe and North America appear to have lost 'the "tragic sense of life". They have forgotten what the World War II generation so painfully learnt: that everything you love, even the greatest and most cultured civilizations in history, can be swept away by people who are unworthy of them.'[1] Indeed, in drawing on modern psychological studies, as I do throughout this book, in some sense I prove the idea that 'it has taken modern science to remind us what our grandparents knew'.[2] What did they know about human morality? What did Shakespeare know about it?

In recent years, studies of Shakespeare's plays have concerned themselves with everyday objects and 'matter' rather than with questions of philosophy or moral value. As ideology critique has fallen out of fashion, scholars and critics have turned their attentions from thinking to living: it matters less what Shakespeare and his contemporaries thought and believed, and rather more how they prepared and ate their meals. How did they sleep? How did they arrange their furniture? What did their typical wardrobe contain? These and other such fascinating topics have dominated the past ten years of Shakespeare scholarship. At its best, this work has made us seriously rethink some of our ideas about literature in the early modern period,[3] but at its worst it has been a lapse into workaday positivism – an unwitting winding back of the clock, as if the new historicists had never heard of Hayden White and the cultural materialists had decided that Raymond Williams and Louis Althusser were not worth worrying about after all.[4] In their introduction to *Shakespeare and Renaissance Ethics* (2014), a recent book that has bucked this dominant trend, Patrick Gray and John D. Cox draw attention to the increasingly unreflective literal-mindedness of much of this work:

> Studying Shakespeare and ethics has been discouraged ... by the recent appearance of a new positivism. This interest seems to have been born of the desire to avoid high-flying theoretical controversy, but it is also indebted to the taking up of materialistic premises into a new set of common assumptions.... In contrast to 'Theory', the local history of specific objects seems reassuring, because it is 'scientific'. It eschews risky 'big ideas' in favour of tangible, quantifiable, and easily identified evidence.... In short, the pendulum of critical momentum, having swung too far in the direction of abstract theorizing, may now be at risk of swinging too far in the opposite direction, that of materialist detail.... A diet of minutiae is too ascetic;

literary criticism lives and breathes, properly speaking, in
the intersection, the connection, between the abstract and
the concrete, the universal and the particular.[5]

William James separated issues into 'living or dead ...
momentous or trivial'.[6] In focusing so squarely on early
modern living, these positivist studies have ended up concentrating on issues that are actually dead and trivial. Did
Shakespeare use a knife and fork to eat? Probably, yes.[7] It's a
dead, trivial question with a single answer. I remain entirely
unconvinced that it is the job of literary criticism to answer
such questions; they are best left to the museum curator and
antiquarian historian. By contrast, this book can be seen as
part of a slowly building move to bring literature to bear
on philosophical questions, what Stanley Stewart has called,
provocatively, 'the Litrification of Philosophy'.[8] I want to ask
the sorts of probing questions that brought us to read literature in the first place. How can we characterise the moral
vision of Shakespeare's plays? This is a living, momentous
question – much more suited to the task of literary criticism than the recent museum work – and it will take me the
remainder of this book to attempt an answer.

I started writing this book during the summer of 2016
in the aftermath of the historic 'Brexit' vote (the UK's withdrawal from the European Union), a few weeks after Michael
Gove was widely seen has having stabbed his long-time friend
and associate Boris Johnson in the back by putting himself
in the running to be prime minister while denouncing his
ally. The move drew instant comparisons with Shakespeare's
more Machiavellian characters as well as his plays – most
obviously *Julius Caesar*.[9] In the event, Gove would pay the
price, as he was sacked from the cabinet by the new Prime
Minister, Theresa May, while Johnson was elevated to Foreign Secretary. The episode illustrates two things: first, ethics
is still a 'living' issue of real concern to real people; second,

Shakespeare's plays are seen by the general public as being directly relevant and comparable to real-life happenings. The fact that Gove's betrayal might be compared to that of Marcus Brutus at all also suggests an underlying similarity in the moral values at stake in both the play and our own time. We might be living in a very different moment from Ancient Rome or Shakespeare's London, but we can still recognise treachery when we see it.

Where do these moral values come from? Peter Kreeft observes:

> Looking at history, we can see that pre-modern societies saw these values as objective, and as universal, absolute, and unchanging, and it wasn't until the advent of the modern Western society that philosophers began to claim them to be subjective, meaning that they are culturally relative, changing and man-made. These two viewpoints continue today and are highly critical of one another.[10]

Until fairly recently, it was generally the case that responses to Kreeft's questions would split down the political lines of left and right: those on the conservative right incline to the pre-modern view that morality is absolute and unchanging, while those on the liberal left – and especially those in the humanities – have strongly inclined to the view that it is relative, changing and man-made. However, as Clancy Martin points out, this dichotomy has recently been disturbed by developments in the sciences:

> Scientific research and evolutionary theory is increasingly showing that we may actually be naturally inclined toward a universal set of moral intuitions that we might collectively call the good. It turns out that the latest scientific research shows that we have a kind of baseline sense for morality that transcends the relativity of cultural, social, or historical position.[11]

I will elaborate on some of these developments shortly.

This living, momentous and ultimate question of the origins of moral values generates three smaller and more specific (though no less living or momentous) ones: first, in their moral philosophy, were the early moderns closer to the ancients or to modern Western society? That is, did they think morality was objective or subjective? Second, through his depictions of characters and their relationships *in situ*, does Shakespeare tend towards one of these views more than the other? Third, what moral values in particular did Shakespeare foreground through representation in his plays? It is the aim of this book to answer all three of these questions.

This book is divided into two parts. In Part I, I seek to develop a comprehensive understanding of morality in Shakespeare's time. In Chapter 2, I will situate Moral Foundations Theory in its broader frameworks of philosophy, politics and evolutionary ethics. The long Chapter 3 will provide the historical and philosophical frameworks in which we can seriously consider my questions in an informed way. It maps the moral landscape of England during the time in which Shakespeare was writing by tracing the influence of four Hellenistic approaches to moral philosophy (virtue ethics in the Aristotelian–Thomist tradition, Stoicism, scepticism, Epicureanism). Chapter 4 complicates the picture further by considering the impact of the Protestant Reformation and the challenge posed by John Calvin to the synthesised humanist moral systems that had been developing during the Renaissance. It also considers the impact of the rise of capitalism, which is broadly coincident with that of Protestantism. Building on this historical and philosophical understanding, Part II focuses on moral foundations in Shakespeare's plays. Chapter 5 focuses on what previous generations of critics have had to say about Shakespeare and morality. Chapters 6 to 11 each centre on one of six moral foundations (authority, loyalty, fairness, sanctity, care and liberty), which I will explain further in the following section.

The remainder of the present chapter divides into two sections. In the first, I will outline some recent developments in thinking about morality derived from evolutionary psychology, which have broadly been given the name 'Moral Foundations Theory' (MFT). In the second, I will refine my thoughts on literary character and cognition, before expanding on how I intend to use them to approach the question of morality in Shakespeare's plays. For the purposes of clarity, I have provided summaries in bullet-point form at the end of each section.

I

Moral Foundations Theory

'Jesus died for somebody's sins but not mine': so begins Patti Smith's 'Gloria' from her seminal album *Horses* (1975),[12] at once an audacious rejection of faith and a statement of cultural and moral relativism. The speaker rejects Christian salvation, while at the same time acknowledging its possibility for believers. The verse ends with an assertion of property rights: 'My sins my own / They belong to me, me.' Insomuch as one would expect an urbane and educated Westerner from the late twentieth century to believe that there is neither an absolute, universal morality nor an original, collective sin, Smith's speaker is undeniably a product of her time and place. The repetition of 'me' is marked and suggests an individualistic and subjective moral system defined mainly by the self: *my* sin, therefore *my* values and *my* ethical code. It is a modern, self-centred view of ethics that has come to typify the so-called 'Me' Generation to which Smith belongs (and indeed its children). In such a moral system, the primacy of self-determination outstrips any sense of social responsibility. As another of its popular voices sang a decade earlier, 'I'm free to do what I want any old time.'[13] A modern, Western individual is far more likely to bridle at the feeling of their own value system being judged than to feel a sense of shame for their 'sins' (as externally defined by, for example, traditional Christian ethics), which – as in Smith's song – can be worn almost as badges of pride. There is a general distaste for the 'old' values, such as respect for and trust in authority or the idea that we should avoid sensual pleasures because they are 'sinful', and a corresponding valorising of individual liberty and expression, and, indeed, pleasure-seeking, without apparent guilt or consequence.

In his influential book, *The Righteous Mind* (2012) – which will inform the present study, Jonathan Haidt calls individuals such as Patti Smith's speaker 'WEIRD': that is, 'Western, educated, industrial, rich, and democratic'. According to Haidt:

> [WEIRD] societies are statistical outliers on many psychological measures, including measures of moral psychology. . . . The WEIRDer you are, the more you perceive a world full of separate objects, rather than relationships. . . . The moral domain is unusually narrow in WEIRD cultures, where it is largely limited to the ethic of autonomy (i.e., moral concerns about individuals harming, oppressing, or cheating other individuals). It is broader – including the ethics of community and divinity – in most other societies, and within religious and conservative moral matrices within WEIRD societies.[14]

Modern Western liberal morality is distinguished from the moral systems of almost all other known cultures by its intense focus on the self: the basic unit of analysis is not the group, family or community, but rather the individual. This is even true of utilitarianism, which ostensibly makes its calculations for the greater good of the group, because in those calculations individuals become discrete data points – 'separate objects' – which are taken to be autonomous and self-serving rather than bound by social or familial relations.

This is a key realisation when considering the issue of Shakespeare and morality: English society of the 1590s and early 1600s was pre-industrial, non-democratic and mostly uneducated, and religion played a much more significant role in daily life – it can scarcely qualify as 'WEIRD'. One would expect, therefore, to find the broader moral domain that Haidt describes. This domain consists of the six moral foundations around which I have structured Part II of this book. These are described as follows:

1. **Authority / subversion:** This foundation was shaped by our long primate history of hierarchical social interactions. It underlies virtues of leadership and followership, including deference to legitimate authority and respect for traditions.
2. **Loyalty / betrayal:** This foundation is related to our long history as tribal creatures able to form shifting coalitions. Loyalty underlies virtues of patriotism and self-sacrifice for the group. It is active any time people feel that it's 'one for all, and all for one'.
3. **Fairness / cheating:** This foundation is related to the evolutionary process of reciprocal altruism. It generates ideas of justice, rights, and autonomy.
4. **Sanctity / degradation:** This foundation was shaped by the psychology of disgust and contamination. It underlies religious notions of striving to live in an elevated, less carnal, more noble way. It underlies the widespread idea that the body is a temple that can be desecrated by immoral activities and contaminants (an idea not unique to religious traditions).
5. **Care / harm:** This foundation is related to our long evolution as mammals with attachment systems and an ability to feel (and dislike) the pain of others. It underlies virtues of kindness, gentleness and nurturance.
6. **Liberty / oppression:** This foundation is about the feelings of reactance and resentment people feel toward those who dominate them and restrict their liberty. Its intuitions are often in tension with those of the authority foundation. The hatred of bullies and dominators motivates people to come together, in solidarity, to oppose or take down the oppressor.[15]

According to Haidt and others, these six foundations are innate in human moral thinking, and therefore universal. This is not to say that everyone responds equally to all six foundations – indeed, Western liberals tend to respond only to care, fairness and liberty and are somewhat blind to the other three (more on this in the next chapter) – but rather that we each have the capacity to respond to them. Haidt makes an analogy to taste receptors on the tongue: we all have the capacity to taste sweet, salty or sour foods, but that does not mean that we all must necessarily *like* the taste of those foods. Gary Marcus makes another analogy – that the brain is like a book, which at birth already has a rough draft written in outline, even though no chapters are complete: 'Nature provides a first draft, which experience then revises. . . . "Built-in" does not mean unmalleable; it means "organized in advance of experience".'[16] As Scott M. James elaborates, 'We do not come into the world as blank slates, as many commonly assume . . . our heads are full of psychological *adaptations*.'[17]

Culture can mediate, mould and shape our natural tendencies, but there is a limit to the extent to which this is possible:

> [O]ne of the deathblows to behaviorism was the demonstration that animals have constraints on learning: some pairings of stimuli and responses are so heavily prepared that the animal can learn them on a single training trial, while other associations go against the animal's nature and cannot be learned in thousands of trials. Virtue theories would thus be improved if they took account of the kinds of virtues that 'fit' with the human mind and of the kinds that do not. Virtues are indeed cultural achievements, but they are cultural achievements built on and partly constrained by deeply rooted preparednesses to construe and respond to the social world in particular ways.[18]

Incidentally, this echoes a passage in Aristotle's *Nicomachean Ethics*:

> Virtue, then, being of two kinds, intellectual and moral, intellectual virtue in the main owes both its birth and its growth to teaching (for which reason it requires experience and time), while moral virtue comes about as a result of habit, whence also its name (*ēthikē*) is one that is formed by a slight variation from the word *ethos* (habit). From this it is also plain that none of the moral virtues arises in us by nature; for nothing that exists by nature can form a habit contrary to its nature. For instance the stone which by nature moves downwards cannot be habituated to move upwards, not even if one tries to train it by throwing it up ten thousand times; nor can fire be habituated to move downwards, nor can anything else that by nature behaves in one way be trained to behave in another.[19]

Virtues can be socially constructed and learned, but they must still work by activating the innate moral 'modules' or taste receptors. We cannot go against our natures; our sense of virtue in part derives from this. Historically, in moral philosophy, this has been called 'natural law'.

However, it is important that we do not commit the naturalistic fallacy and mistake *is* for *ought*. Just because nature pushes us in a certain direction, it does not follow that it is therefore morally justified.[20] Nor does it follow that culture must follow the dictates of nature, even if it is constrained by it. As Daniel Dennett puts it,

> no matter how potent cultural forces are, they always have to act on the materials genetic forces have shaped for them, and will go on shaping, but they can just as readily *redirect* or *exploit* or *subvert* those genetically endorsed designs as *attenuate* or *combat* them.[21]

In Richard Dawkins's famous line 'We, alone on earth, can rebel against the tyranny of the selfish replicators.'[22] The relationship between nature and culture thus may take the form of being mutually assured, in mutual tension, a complex set of checks and balances, or some other configuration. As I will explore in this book, it is quite possible that the moral signals an individual receives from their natural intuitions might diverge sharply and even contradict the signals received from culture. Indeed, often in Shakespeare's plays, ethical decision-making takes place in the ambiguities and uncertainties of this space between moral intuition and cultural script.

When it comes to morality, the area in which human nature has been most keenly felt in recent scientific studies is in questions of altruism. This is a subject tackled in Richard Dawkins's *The Selfish Gene* (1976), which argues that animals, including humans, are capable of selflessness in the service of their 'selfish genes' – that is, to ensure the survival of a particular set of genes. Dawkins does not see scope for altruism outside of this except in cases of *quid pro quo* arrangements of mutual benefit, also known as reciprocal altruism.[23] Following Charles Darwin's idea of group selection, and utilising concepts from Émile Durkheim's *The Elementary Forms of Religious Life* (1915),[24] Haidt argues (*contra* Dawkins) that while humans are naturally selfish, they are also naturally *groupish*: 'I mean that our minds contain a variety of mental mechanisms that make us adept at promoting our *group's* interests, in competition with other groups. We are not saints, but we are sometimes good team players.'[25] According to Haidt, individuals can temporarily look beyond their own self-interests in a sort of momentary transcendence to become part of an organism larger than themselves. This effect is somewhat tribal in nature and cannot extend to 'all of humanity'; its effectiveness and possibilities for existence necessarily depend on competition between different groups. There is no small degree of disagreement over this among evolutionists; I will return to this in Chapter 2, but for now the crucial point for us is that, no matter its exact constitution, evolutionists are agreed that there *is* an underlying human nature (that is mostly selfish), which both constrains and shapes moral decision-making.

In addition, Haidt and other advocates of MFT argue that moral thinking is primarily intuitive and instinctual, rather than deliberative: the intuition comes first and strategic reasoning follows. Moral reasoning is most often *post hoc*: a justification for a snap judgement made on the spur of the moment. His favourite metaphor is that of the elephant (intuition) and the rider (reasoning):

> When human beings evolved the capacity for language and reasoning at some point in the last million years, the brain did not rewire itself to hand over the reins to a new and inexperienced charioteer. Rather, the rider (language-based reasoning) evolved because it did something useful for the elephant.... The rider is skilled at fabricating post-hoc explanations for what the elephant has just done, and it is good at finding reasons for whatever the elephant wants to do next.... Reason is the servant of the intuitions. The rider was put there in the first place to serve the elephant.[26]

It is clear that the elephant is the one in control, with the rider acting more like a little defence lawyer. The rider seldom questions the elephant because of the heuristic of confirmation bias: 'We make our judgements rapidly, and we are dreadful at seeking out evidence that might disconfirm those initial judgements.'[27] Here it is important to make two points clear: first, following the work of the neuroscientist Antonio Damasio and the dual-process theory of Daniel Kahneman and Amos Tversky,[28] MFT views emotions and intuitions as cognitive processes – that is, a *part* of thinking rather than a distinct category in opposition to it. The two cognitive systems – the elephant and the rider, or intuitions and reasoning – are complementary and mostly work together rather than being at odds. Second, we must not conflate intuitions into emotions. Emotions are a kind of information processing; as Richard Lazarus and Craig A. Smith put it, they 'are the product of *transactions* or *relationships* between the person and the environment'.²⁹ Emotions represent one type of intuition, perhaps the strongest, but they are seen to be at a heightened level to which most intuitions do not reach. Intuitions are rapid and automatic, we make them constantly, and most of the time they do not flare up into 'full-blown emotions'.³⁰

This set of positions puts MFT at odds with at least two different traditions of thought: first, any moral system based on rationalist philosophies that give primacy to reason alone, which would include thinkers as diverse as Plato, the Stoics, Immanuel Kant (deontology) and Jeremey Bentham (utilitarianism), as well as the moral psychologist Lawrence Kohlberg, whose work MFT challenges;³¹ and second, any socially deterministic mode of thinking that denies human nature and gives exclusivity to the structuring forces of culture, which would include various varieties of Marxism, Michel Foucault and the anthropology of Clifford Geertz, as well as their inheritors, including the 'new materialism'. I will elaborate on this when discussing the 'conflict of visions' between constrained (tragic) and unconstrained (utopian) views of humanity in Chapter 2.

MFT's chief antecedent in the philosophical tradition would be David Hume, who argued, of course, that 'Reason is, and ought only to be the slave of the passions.'³² Thus, in the late eighteenth century, its insights came naturally to those influenced by Hume, such as the New England Federalists. For example, here is Fisher Ames, a US Congressman and Founding Father, recognising that politics is driven primarily by emotion rather than reason:

> Politicians have supposed, that man really is what he should be; that his reason will do all it can, and his passions and prejudice no more than they ought; whereas his reason is a mere looker-on; it is moderation, when it should be zeal; it is often corrupted to vindicate, where it should condemn; and is a coward or a trimmer, that will take hush-money.³³

This is a near-perfect description of Haidt's elephant and rider written over two centuries before *The Righteous Mind*.

There is also something of Aristotle's virtue ethics in MFT, which its advocates view as 'the most psychologically sound approach to morality', because 'such theories fit more neatly with what we know about moral development, judgment, and behavior than do theories that focus on moral reasoning or on the acceptance of high-level moral principles such as justice'.[34] Here 'virtues' (such as loyalty, honesty and so on) are learned social skills that become so ingrained and habitual that they become almost second nature – that is, they can start to function on the level of intuitions. I will note in passing that in this view, moral virtues are behaviours (or habits of action) rather than fixed character traits (I will expand on this in Chapters 2 and 3).

In this book, I am using MFT primarily as a framing mechanism and starting point. I am supposing, at the most general level, that Shakespeare and the other members of his culture were *pre-wired* to respond to the six different moral foundations it outlines in whatever way, although the specifics of those responses are subject to and in tension with their cultural upbringing, which includes a diverse and complex mix of different ideas (see Chapters 3 and 4). My concern is primarily with how Shakespeare's plays and the characters that populate them respond to each of these moral foundations. We do not typically think of Shakespeare as a moralistic writer; his plays – distinguished as they are by their polyvocality – can scarcely be thought of as being morally didactic or instructive. William Hazlitt's remarks on this are still broadly convincing:

> Shakespeare was in one sense the least moral of all writers; for morality (commonly so called) is made up of antipathies; and his talent consisted in sympathy with human nature, in all its shapes, degrees, depressions, and elevations. The object of the pedantic moralist is to find out the bad in everything:

his was to show that 'there is some soul of goodness in things evil'. . . . In one sense, Shakespeare was no moralist at all: in another, he was the greatest of all moralists. He was a moralist in the same sense in which nature is one. He taught what he had learnt from her. He showed the greatest knowledge of humanity with the greatest fellow-feeling for it.[35]

I am not sure that Hazlitt is right that Shakespeare always sees 'some soul of goodness' in his characters; that makes his plays perhaps more optimistic than they often are, and I suspect the optimism is Hazlitt's rather than Shakespeare's. For now it is enough to note that, in my scepticism here, I am not suggesting that Shakespeare has a dim view of humanity or that he is necessarily pessimistic, but rather that Hazlitt pushes the analysis too far. It certainly does not hold true for every character. Where is the 'soul of goodness' in a character like Oswald from *King Lear*? This is not to mention his great villains such as Iago, Richard III, or Goneril and Regan. In emphasising the obviously humane side of Shakespeare, Hazlitt seems to ignore him at his blackest and bleakest – let us say *Titus Andronicus* or *Timon of Athens* – which one might argue are visions of nihilism and misanthropy, respectively. However, this remains to be seen and the issue as to whether or not Hazlitt is right is one of the recurring themes of this book. I will return to this basic theme at numerous junctures, especially in Part II (Chapters 5–11). But, whatever the case, Hazlitt is right to say that Shakespeare has an extraordinary capacity for empathy in his characterisation – he will not write anyone off entirely, not even the villains – and this renders futile any attempt to locate a single moralistic voice in his plays. Despite that, however, one expects to find patterns of moral response across his works, and the sharp focus on each moral foundation should make these patterns easier to find. By this study's conclusion, I hope to have defined a six-point 'moral compass' derived by the responses we find in Shakespeare's plays.

> **In summary**
> - Moral Foundations Theory claims that human beings are 'pre-wired' to respond to six moral foundations: authority / subversion, loyalty / betrayal, fairness / cheating, sanctity / degradation, care / harm and liberty / oppression.
> - It argues that we experience these responses as near-automatic moral intuitions, and that most moral reasoning is *post hoc* justification.
> - Culture mediates our moral responses, but is limited in its scope by the raw materials of nature.
> - Most cultures in history have been rooted in all six moral foundations, but modern Western cultures are statistical outliers in that they lean very strongly on the foundations of care / harm and liberty / oppression.
> - Part II of this book is structured around Shakespeare's treatment of the six moral foundations outlined above.

II

Literary Character, Morality and the Cognitive Reading of Shakespeare's Plays

As well as being at odds with cultural historicism in various forms, MFT also somewhat complicates the assumptions of recent studies of Shakespeare that have focused on the history of emotion. Following the so-called 'affective turn', these studies tend to view emotions as the post-linguistic playing out of a learned 'cultural script'.[36] As I have made clear, MFT sees language as coming after and being in the service of intuitions and emotions. MFT does not deny that culture strongly mediates moral responses, but it does insist that moral intuitions are at base instinctual; in Jonathan Haidt's phrase, 'morality is universal, yet culturally variable'.[37] James A. Knapp – to my knowledge the only Shakespeare scholar to devote any serious attention to MFT before the present study – gives a concrete example of what this might mean in practice:

> [T]hough the moral categories invoked to judge a particular action are different in different cultural settings, the concept of a universal moral sense remains intact: an honor killing is a moral act for the brother who is moved by the category of purity ['sanctity / degradation' in the definitions outlined above], while it is immoral for the outside observer moved by an appeal to [protect from] harm.[38]

One culture might lean more heavily on the moral foundation of sanctity / degradation and another more heavily on that of care / harm, but the point is that the raw materials of these categories are fundamental and felt intuitively rather than learned. Knapp continues: 'Haidt is clear that we have the ability to override the initial intuition, and that one way to do so is to use moral reasoning to consider the situation.'[39] Implicitly, therefore, I would suggest that the more one applies reasoning to a situation, the more one starts to challenge the natural intuition through cultural learning. We can see this in action in *Hamlet*: clearly, Hamlet has an intuition about what he must do, but he insists on reasoning through every decision and so dramatises *in situ* the tension between first-level moral instincts and culturally learned ethical reasoning (we must not forget he was training to be a lawyer).[40] Haidt's point, however, is that *most* of the time, we do not go down the same agonising path as Hamlet; we simply make a judgement and act on it, and then make our justifications or excuses after the fact. Hamlet's case of painstakingly weighing up all options in a rational manner is the exception rather than the rule. It requires a greater mental effort to overturn initial moral intuitions than it does to follow them, and most of the time we follow them.

There is in this, therefore, an implied tension between what an individual *should do*, as dictated by the cultural scripts of their social conditioning (which, by their very nature, have been derived *post hoc* and rationally), and what an individual *actually feels* in any given moment in which ethical decision-making is required. Knapp has suggested that we can see this play out in Shakespeare:

> Literary characters are notorious for their moral reasoning prior to action, and Shakespeare's characters would seem to be no exceptions, a fact that would seem to suggest that Shakespeare's interest was with his characters' facility with moral reasoning rather than their innate moral sense. But I want to suggest the opposite – that Shakespeare's representation of moral agency focuses on the way moral conviction wells up in his characters against established moral principles and in tension with the calm domain of moral reasoning. [His concern] is less with adjudicating human action according to a set moral code and more with examining the lived experience of moral agents.[41]

He is surely right that Shakespeare's literary purpose is seldom, if ever, to push a particular moral doctrine; he is an exceptionally undidactic writer. I would suggest that this idea of 'lived experience', of analysing characters in situations that we can imagine as real (or at least alluding to reality), provides us with a situated way of thinking about ethics that exceeds what is possible in the abstract and rational world of pure philosophy and, indeed, most psychology.

I want to pause briefly on the significance of Knapp's idea of moral conviction 'welling up' in Shakespeare's characters, because it presents a challenge to the way modern psychologists of character and morality (as distinct from those who advocate MFT) have been thinking about both categories. It seems to me that Shakespeare's characters are often more fluid and more dynamic than the personality trait-mapping models on which that strand of psychology rests.[42] Through this 'welling up' of feeling, Shakespeare often brings us up against the limits of scientific attempts to codify human behaviour. The unpredictability and changeability of Shakespeare's characters, therefore, pose a rebuttal to the idea of fixed personality traits. Even the most nuanced models available, such as Christian B. Miller's 'Mixed Trait Framework', provide an essentially static view of character. Shakespeare's characters seem to exceed the stability that such models would assume, and one reason for this is because the plays are what psychologists would call inherently 'situationist': that is to say, the complex simulations that Shakespeare imagines in the pressured situations of his plays contain too many moving parts, too many variables, for psychologists to be able to map or reproduce in their experiments. The situatedness of Shakespeare's plays shows us *in action* how people react in changing circumstances; sometimes those circumstances are even transformational. Shakespeare's understanding of character is truly experiential – supposed traits are put to the test even as they are introduced. As an immediate example, we might think of Angelo in *Measure for Measure*: it is not long after Duke Vincentio describes him as 'a man of stricture and firm abstinence' (I, iii, 12) that he sets about stunningly disproving that assessment at nearly every turn. Perhaps Angelo was never the man that the Duke thought he was, or perhaps his supposed traits had never been tested by experience. Angelo finds himself in changed circumstances and reacts in a way that few, probably not even himself, could have predicted. Even if some psychologists, such as Miller, accept that 'most people do not have *any of the virtues* to any degree, although a few might possess one or more of them' and, by the same token, that 'Most people do not have *any of the vices* to any degree, although a few might possess one or more of them,' they still assume at a basic level that people conform to their personality traits.[43] To my mind, if we accept the insights of MFT, this seems a fundamentally wrong-headed and unrealistic way to approach moral thinking. The 'welling up' that

Knapp finds in Shakespeare is much closer to how we actually make moral decisions than any idea of personality traits. Character traits, it seems to me, are a *post hoc* description of a response. Macbeth is not a cruel man but he undoubtedly *becomes* cruel; we describe his behaviour as cruel only after he does cruel things – this is quite distinct from the logic of the personality trait, which says 'this person is cruel, therefore they do cruel things'. Shakespeare's characterisation, at its most engaging and dynamic, does not function on the level of fixed traits; rather, he gives us the process of *becoming* – the spontaneous welling up of feelings that characters almost need to invent new language to describe.

In 2015, I published a short book called *Shakespeare and Cognition: Thinking Fast and Slow through Character*, in which I argued for the central importance of character as a unit for literary analysis.[44] In this line of thought, I have been influenced by Michael D. Bristol's recent work on moral agency,[45] as well as by Harry Berger, Jr, and A. D. Nuttall.[46] In that book, to use Berger's phrase, I proposed 'a modified character and action approach',[47] in which the modification comes from an understanding of human thought processes updated by modern cognitive psychology. In this present book, I want to build on that approach by taking advantage of the unique opportunity for moral thinking that literature – and Shakespeare in particular – afford. Of course, that literature provides us with opportunities to consider moral quandaries *in situ* is not a new idea – as Patrick Gray and John D. Cox put it succinctly, 'not new, but . . . also not current'[48] – but it is one that is being considered again with increasingly renewed vigour across the discipline, including beyond Shakespeare studies. One recent volume, *Fictional Characters, Real Problems: The Search for Ethical Content in Literature* (2016), edited by Garry L. Hagberg, ranges across genres and periods, and collects a number of suggestive essays about the fruitful intersections between literature and ethics, several of which stress the central importance of character. In one such essay, Eileen John does well to remind us that although characters are not real people, we still feel as if we have a stake in their fictive lives:

> [F]ictional characters are in a way representationally excessive and fantastic. They serve as occasions for more, and more intense, representational activity than do most real people. But they are also manifestations of ordinary activity, of putting into words how people and their lives are found to be, and we have strong interests at stake in this activity.[49]

I think this is an important recognition: literary characters are not real people but they allow us to consider aspects of reality. We must, however, expect not verisimilitude – perhaps the pipe-dream of a perfected naturalism – but rather an exaggerated, heightened, even extreme and distorted version of reality. It is also important to recognise that most leading characters are hardly going about their everyday lives: we usually glimpse them at a moment of *crisis*, in abnormal conditions.

Shakespeare specialises in crisis. The imagined worlds of his plays place their characters in highly pressured and extreme situations and then demand that they *react* to those situations. Shakespeare has a habit of taking a situation and then adjusting the variables to see what might happen if just one or two details are altered. Think, for example, of the pressure he exerts on the friendship of Helena and Hermia in *Midsummer Night's Dream* through the simple device of Puck applying the love potion to Lysander and then Demetrius. Was the friendship between Helena and Hermia actually contingent on Hermia being the one who had the attention of the men? We might think of many other examples: Macbeth's encounter with the weird sisters; Lear's outburst at and subsequent banishment of Cordelia; Duke Frederick's sudden banishment of Rosalind in *As You Like It*; Duke Vincentio's apparently arbitrary decision to delegate his power temporarily to Angelo in *Measure for Measure*; Shylock's outrageous condition for the loan to Bassanio (namely, a pound of Antonio's flesh) in *The Merchant of Venice*; Richard II's double banishment of Bolingbroke and Mowbray; and so on and so forth. These are all classic 'set-ups' for the necessary dramatic action to occur – in most cases, without them there would be no play and the plot would collapse – but I would like to take them out of their literary context for a moment and imagine them as *game-like scenarios*. The characters are players in a game with established rules; Shakespeare intervenes and changes the rules and then looks on as his characters scramble to react to those changes. Of course, Shakespeare also has control over *how* they react but I am imagining him as a writer who in some sense lets the characters take on a 'life of their own'. He was able to use his considerable creative powers as a conduit for the imagined consciousness of another. In fact, as Lynn Enterline has shown brilliantly, this is exactly the sort of mental exercise he would have learned from an early age through training in classical *imitatio*.[50]

Terence Cave's enormously provocative *Thinking with Literature: Towards a Cognitive Criticism* (2016) calls for critics to 'give priority to the kinds of question that literature itself poses, since those questions might well challenge some of the positions and perspectives put forward by other disciplines' while recognising 'that literature does what the human mind (cognition) does best – it specialises in cognitive fluidity, the tangled connectivity and capacity for improvisation that enable it to engage with a world in "decoupled" mode'.[51] 'Decoupling' is a term borrowed from Jean-Marie Schaeffer, which describes a complex process by which we are able to respond to and become immersed in fiction (we might say 'suspension of disbelief'), without invoking our natural defence mechanisms against deception.[52] We do not mistake fiction for reality but we also do not process it as lies. In Cave's phrase, 'pretence is a weapon; shared pretence is a game.'[53] I want to suggest that to watch or read a Shakespeare play is to share in a pretence, and therefore to participate in a game.

So, there are, in fact, two games going on: one played between the characters and the other by the audience. The first game is being played between the characters struggling to adapt to new rules that have placed them *in extremis*. But since the audience cannot possibly participate in that, what sort of game are they playing? When I teach the *Henry IV* plays, I ask my students to perform a mock trial for Falstaff. There is a prosecution and a defence. One student plays Falstaff, who must prepare for the trial in consultation with his defence team. Each team is also allowed to call a single witness (played by one of themselves) who – after swearing on *The Complete Works* ('I swear to tell the truth, and nothing but the truth, so help the Bard') – will face cross-examination. In my experience of putting on this mock trial over several years, successive classes have, without fail, taken the exercise extremely seriously, perhaps partly owing to the increased stakes of competition. I want to suggest that it is precisely in this sort of little game that *every* attentive audience or reader of a Shakespeare play is participating. We watch how the characters perform in their game and simultaneously evaluate their performance as judge and jury, as if they were in a mock trial. As the players engage in their game, we almost automatically assess how they are playing it; we make a judgement. In the history plays, for example, Shakespeare gives us many different players of the political game: ideologues, Machiavellian schemers, naïfs, populists, elitists, brutal tyrants, selfish self-preservationists, and selfless servants to the commonwealth. We see who wins, who loses, and why: we can see who played the game well and who did not.[54] But the political is subsumed by the ethical: we judge these characters not simply by how well they perform in the political arena but also in moral terms. The question is not only 'was he a good king?' but also 'was he a good man?' This being Shakespeare, regardless of the king in question, the answer is likely to be complex and debatable rather than simple and binary. We do not judge only on the character as a whole but on their actions as well. Whenever a character acts on a decision, we ask automatically 'was that the right thing to do?' Sometimes ostensibly good characters make catastrophic decisions. Henry VI, in general, is perhaps the most obvious example: a terrible king in terms of his political decisions, who was none the less quite a good man.

Our near-automatic judgements on these questions are what Michael D. Bristol has called 'vernacular intuitions'.[55] Assuming competence enough to understand Shakespeare's language, they do not require special scholarly training. Bristol mentions his sister's vernacular intuitions at one point; I am reminded of a time when I watched a production of *Measure for Measure* with my mother. She was utterly disgusted at Claudio's behaviour in III, i, when he begs his sister, Isabella, to save his life by sleeping with Angelo and violating her vows as a novice nun. It was a genuine, visceral reaction: perhaps my mother was responding to the moral foundation of sanctity / degradation. Many other modern viewers of the play, perhaps moved instead by the foundation of care / harm, actually have the opposite reaction: they cannot believe that Isabella could be so callous as to let her brother die for the sake of a religious principle. In either case, the scenario is provoking a moral intuition. This works so effectively because, in most cases, Shakespeare does not appear to judge himself: he provides the raw materials for judgements to be made but asks the audience to make them. In *Shakespeare's Philosophy: Discovering the Meaning Behind the Plays* (2006) – a work that is stunningly out-of-step with workaday Shakespeare scholarship – Colin McGinn recognises this:

> The sense in which [Shakespeare] is a great moralist is that he is an expert recorder of nature in its moral aspect. And not merely a disinterested recorder: for Shakespeare is a moral being, like the rest of us. As he records, he also evaluates; or better, he provides us with the materials with which to evaluate. All he needs to do is accurately describe; it is left to the audience's moral sense to supply the moral assessment. . . . His task is essentially *cognitive*: he must

share his knowledge of moral psychology with the audience, leaving the evaluative part to them.[56]

This, I think, is the difference between morality in Shakespeare's plays and in philosophy. An average philosopher may define their ethics and tell you what to think, a great philosopher may outline a moral framework and tell you how to think, but Shakespeare does neither; instead, he throws complex, game-like moral situations at the members of the audience and asks them to figure it all out for themselves. As Bristol says, he 'delineates the question of how to live a good life in all its messy uncertainty'.[57]

The process of moral judgement McGinn and I have been describing is what happens near-automatically when, in Bristol's words, 'smart, well-educated people who are interested in Shakespeare' (but who are not academics who specialise in Shakespeare or literature) engage with the plays.[58] It is important to be aware of this process because for the remainder of this book I wish to attempt to suspend it entirely while being alert to it in other critical responses to date: that is to say, this is not a reader-response study about my own 'vernacular' moral intuitions about various scenarios in Shakespeare's plays. I want to gain an understanding of how Shakespeare represents (or, in McGinn's terms, 'describes') morality in his plays by tracing the extent to which characters react to or invoke particular moral foundations. To do this properly, it is necessary to put my own moral judgements on hold – not only for fear of anachronism, but also because I do not want my own moral compass 'contaminating' the one that will derive from Shakespeare's plays. It is almost a cliché to point out that:

> Whoever writes about Shakespeare, writes to some extent about himself or herself. Lawyers, Marxists, Freudians, Feminists and others often give in to the temptation to put their special interest above all else, and end up sifting through Shakespeare's plays in search of echoes of their own preoccupation.[59]

My special interest is in discovering how Shakespeare frames and thinks about moral issues. To be clear, this is not a book that is concerned with putting characters on trial and asking if what they did at a given moment was ethically right or wrong. The 'moral compass' in its title is not mine or yours but Shakespeare's, as expressed by his characters and their relationships *in situ*. My concern is with how Shakespeare represents and develops his own nuanced understandings of the six moral foundations: authority, loyalty, sanctity, fairness, liberty and care. In order to do this, it is important to develop a deepened historical and cultural understanding of moral philosophy in Shakespeare's time and place, which I will provide in Chapters 3 and 4.

In summary

- Lived moral intuitions are often in tension with the official, fully rationalised moral doctrines or 'cultural scripts'.
- Shakespeare's characters are dynamic and in the process of *becoming* rather than conforming to a set of fixed personality traits, and in this way they exceed trait-based accounts of human character provided by one branch of modern psychology.
- An approach to morality in literature must be centred on characters and their actions.
- Shakespeare often throws characters into crisis by tweaking some aspect of their circumstances and forcing them to 'react' under pressure; in this way, they are like game scenarios in which the rules have been altered. His ethics, therefore, are always situated and experiential.
- Audiences and readers of Shakespeare's plays are invited to make moral judgements of characters' actions and do so near automatically.
- This study will not engage in making its own moral judgements of characters and their actions, but rather will focus on how Shakespeare depicts the six moral foundations (authority, loyalty, sanctity, fairness, liberty and care) and develops his own nuanced versions of them.

Notes

1. Douglas Murray, *The Strange Death of Europe: Immigration, Identity, Islam* (New York and London: Bloomsbury, 2017), p. 3. See also Pascal Bruckner, *The Tyranny of Guilt: An Essay on Western Masochism*, trans. Stephen Rendall (Princeton: Princeton University Press, 2012); and the philosophy of John Gray, especially *Straw Dogs: Thoughts on Humans and Other Animals* (London: Granta, 2003) and *The Silence of Animals: On Progress and Other Modern Myths* (New York and London: Penguin, 2013).
2. David Goodhart, *The Road to Somewhere: The Populist Revolt and the Future of Politics* (London: Hurst & Co., 2017), p. 28.
3. See Jonathan Gil Harris, *Sick Economies: Drama, Mercantilism, and Disease in Shakespeare's England* (Philadelphia: University of Pennsylvania Press, 2003); Jonathan Gil Harris, *Untimely Matter in the Time of Shakespeare* (Philadelphia: University of Pennsylvania Press, 2008); Natasha Korda, *Shakespeare's Domestic Economies: Gender and Property in Early Modern England* (Philadelphia: University of Pennsylvania Press, 2002); Margareta De Grazia, Maureen Quilligan, and Peter Stallybrass (eds), *Subject and Object in Renaissance Culture* (Cambridge: Cambridge University Press, 1996); and Ann Rosalind Jones and Peter Stallybrass, *Renaissance Clothing and the Materials of Memory* (Cambridge: Cambridge University Press, 2001).
4. For my in-depth analysis of this trend see Neema Parvini, 'The Legacy of New Historicism', in *Shakespeare and New Historicist Theory* (New York and London: Bloomsbury Arden Shakespeare, 2017), pp. 117–30; and 'The Scholars and the Critics: Shakespeare Studies and Theory in the 2010s', *Shakespeare*, 10:2 (2014), pp. 212–23.
5. Patrick Gray and John D. Cox, 'Introduction: Rethinking Shakespeare and Ethics', in *Shakespeare and Renaissance Ethics*, ed. Patrick Gray and John D. Cox (Cambridge: Cambridge University Press, 2014), pp. 10–11.
6. William James, *The Will to Believe, Human Immortality, and Other Essays in Popular Philosophy* (1897; New York: Dover Publications, 1956), p. 9.

7. Catherine Simpson, 'Shakespeare's World in 100 Objects: Number 74, a Knife and Fork Set', *Finding Shakespeare* (18 April 2003), <http://findingshakespeare.co.uk/shakespeares-world-in-100-objects-number-74-a-knife-fork-set> (last accessed 1 July 2016).
8. Stanley Stewart, *Shakespeare and Philosophy* (New York and London: Routledge, 2010), p. 175.
9. See Roy Greenslade, 'Newspapers Draw on Shakespeare to Report Gove's Knifing of Johnson', *The Guardian* (1 July 2016), <https://www.theguardian.com/media/greenslade/2016/jul/01/newspapers-draw-on-shakespeare-to-report-goves-knifing-of-johnson/> (last accessed 7 July 2016).
10. Peter Kreeft, *Ethics: A History of Moral Thought* (Charlotte Hall, MD: Recorded Books, 2003), p. 7.
11. Clancy Martin, *Moral Decision Making: How to Approach Everyday Ethics* (Chantilly, VA: The Great Courses, 2014), pp. 4–5.
12. Patti Smith, 'Gloria', on *Horses* (New York: Arista, 1975).
13. The Rolling Stones, 'I'm Free', on *Out of Our Heads* (London: Decca, 1965).
14. Jonathan Haidt, *The Righteous Mind: Why Good People Are Divided by Religion and Politics* (New York: Random House, 2012), p. 129.
15. Definitions taken from: <http://moralfoundations.org/> (last accessed 7 July 2016).
16. Gary Marcus, *The Birth of the Mind: How a Tiny Number of Genes Creates the Complexities of Human Thought* (New York: Basic Books, 2004), pp. 34, 40.
17. Scott M. James, *An Introduction to Evolutionary Ethics* (Oxford: Wiley–Blackwell, 2011), p. 19.
18. Jonathan Haidt and Joseph Craig, 'Intuitive Ethics: How Innately Prepared Intuitions Generate Culturally Variable Virtues', *Daedalus*, 133:4 (Fall 2004), p. 63.
19. Aristotle, *The Nicomachean Ethics*, ed. Lesley Brown (Oxford: Oxford University Press, 2009), p. 23.
20. James, *An Introduction to Evolutionary Theory*, pp. 23–7; see also Daniel C. Dennett, *Darwin's Dangerous Idea: Evolution*

and the Meanings of Life (New York and London: Penguin, 1995), pp. 467–93.
21. Dennett, *Darwin's Dangerous Idea*, p. 472, emphasis in original.
22. Richard Dawkins, *The Selfish Gene*, 4th edn (1976; Oxford: Oxford University Press, 2016), p. 260.
23. See Ibid. pp. 239–44. The seminal paper on reciprocal altruism is Robert L. Trivers, 'The Evolution of Reciprocal Altruism', *The Quarterly Review of Biology*, 46:1 (March 1971), pp. 35–57. See also Daniel J. Kruger, 'Evolution and Altruism: Combining Psychological Mediators with Naturally Selected Tendencies', *Evolution and Human Behavior*, 24 (2003), pp. 118–25.
24. See Émile Durkheim, *The Elementary Forms of Religious Life* (London: George Allen & Unwin, 1915).
25. Haidt, *The Righteous Mind*, p. 221, emphasis in original.
26. Ibid. pp. 53–4.
27. Ibid. p. 55. I outlined confirmation bias and other heuristics in more detail in 'Key Concepts: Dual-Process Theory, Heuristics and Biases', in *Shakespeare and Cognition: Thinking Fast and Slow Through Character* (New York and London: Palgrave, 2015), pp. 12–22.
28. See Antonio Damasio, *Descartes' Error: Emotion, Reason and the Human Brain* (New York: Putnam, 1994); and Daniel Kahneman, *Thinking Fast and Slow* (New York and London: Penguin, 2011).
29. Craig A. Smith and Richard S. Lazarus, 'Emotion and Adaptation', in *Handbook of Personality: Theory and Research*, ed. L. A. Pervin (New York: Guildford Press, 1990), p. 632, emphasis in original.
30. Haidt, *The Righteous Mind*, p. 53.
31. See Lawrence Kohlberg, *The Psychology of Moral Development: The Nature and Validity of Moral Stages* (*Essays on Moral Development, Vol. 2*) (New York: Harper & Row, 1984). Kohlberg's model, which outlines six stages of moral development, posits an essentially rationalist view of moral reasoning in which the least advanced stage (stage one) is egocentrically concerned with direct punishment, the level at which young children operate, and the most advanced stage

(stage six) is reasoned through an abstract and universal system akin to Kantian ethics.
32. David Hume, *A Treatise of Human Nature* (1739; New York: Dover Publications, 2003), p. 295.
33. Fisher Ames, *Works of Fisher Ames: Compiled by a Number of His Friends* (Boston, MA: T. B. Wait & Co., 1809), pp. 226–7.
34. Haidt and Craig, 'Intuitive Ethics', p. 62. For a systematic fusion of Aristotle, Hume and Darwin, which in many ways prefigures Moral Foundations Theory, see Larry Arnhart, *Darwinian Natural Right: The Biological Ethics of Human Nature* (Albany: State University of New York Press, 1998).
35. William Hazlitt, *The Characters of Shakespear's Plays* (1817; London: J. M. Dent & Sons, 1912), pp. 246–7.
36. For a representative cross-section of work carried out in this vein, see Lynn Enterline, *Shakespeare's Schoolroom: Rhetoric, Discipline, Emotion* (Philadelphia: University of Pennsylvania Press, 2012); Richard Meek and Erin Sullivan (eds), *The Renaissance of Emotion: Understanding Affect in Shakespeare and His Contemporaries* (Manchester: Manchester University Press, 2015); and R. S. White, Mark Houlahan and Katrina O'Loughlin (eds), *Shakespeare and Emotions: Inheritances, Enactments, Legacies* (New York and London: Palgrave Macmillan, 2015).
37. Jonathan Haidt, 'The New Synthesis in Moral Psychology', *Science*, 316:5827 (18 May 2007), p. 998.
38. James A. Knapp, *Image Ethics in Shakespeare and Spencer* (New York and London: Palgrave Macmillan, 2011), p. 17.
39. Ibid. p. 22.
40. I have made a reading of the play along these lines previously; see Neema Parvini, '"And Reason Panders Will": Another Look at Hamlet's Analysis Paralysis', in *Shakespeare and Cognition*, pp. 52–62.
41. James A. Knapp, 'A Shakespearean Phenomenology of Moral Conviction', in *Shakespeare and Moral Agency*, pp. 33, 38.
42. For a critique of one such model – the Five-Factor model of personality advocated by Paul T. Costa and Robert R. McCrea – through a reading of Othello, see Parvini, 'Iago, Othello and Trait Ascription Bias', in *Shakespeare and*

Cognition, pp. 36–51. For an outline of the model, see Paul T. Costa and Robert R. McCrea, 'Four Ways Five Factors are Basic', *Personality and Individual Differences*, 13:6 (1992), pp. 653–65.

43. Christian B. Miller, *Character and Moral Psychology* (Oxford: Oxford University Press, 2014). On 'Situationism', see pp. 85–106. For an overview of his 'Fixed Trait Framework', see pp. 41–2.
44. See Parvini, 'Why Characters Matter in Shakespeare's Plays', in *Shakespeare and Cognition*, pp. 1–11.
45. See especially Michael D. Bristol, 'Is Shakespeare a Moral Philosopher', in Bristol, *Shakespeare and Moral Agency*, pp. 1–14; 'Macbeth the Philosopher: Rethinking Context', *New Literary History*, 42:4 (Autumn 2011), pp. 641–62; and 'Confusing Shakespeare's Characters with Real People: Reflections on Reading in Four Questions', in *Shakespeare and Character Theory, History, Performance and Theatrical Persons*, ed. Paul Yachnin and Jessica Slights (New York and London: Palgrave Macmillan, 2009), pp. 21–40.
46. Of A. D. Nuttall's work, see especially *A New Mimesis: Shakespeare and the Representation of Reality* (1983; New Haven, CT: Yale University Press, 2007) and *Shakespeare: The Thinker* (New Haven, CT: Yale University Press, 2007).
47. Harry Berger, Jr, *Making Trifles of Terrors: Redistributing Complicities in Shakespeare*, ed. Peter Erikson (Stanford: University of Stanford Press, 1997), p. 25.
48. Gray and Cox, 'Introduction', p. 1.
49. Eileen John, 'Caring About Characters', in *Fictional Characters, Real Problems: The Search for Ethical Content in Literature*, ed. Garry L. Hagberg (Oxford: Oxford University Press, 2016), p. 46.
50. See Enterline, *Shakespeare's Schoolroom*, especially pp. 120–52.
51. Terence Cave, *Thinking with Literature: Towards a Cognitive Criticism* (Oxford: Oxford University Press, 2016), pp. 155–6.
52. Jean-Marie Schaeffer, *Why Fiction?*, trans. Dorrit Cohn (1999; Lincoln: University of Nebraska Press, 2010), especially pp. 159–62.
53. Cave, *Thinking with Literature*, p. 71.

54. For a sustained reading of the histories I made along these lines see Neema Parvini, *Shakespeare's History Plays: Rethinking Historicism* (Edinburgh: Edinburgh University Press, 2012), pp. 122–73.
55. Bristol, 'Is Shakespeare a Moral Philosopher?', p. 11.
56. Colin McGinn, *Shakespeare's Philosophy: Discovering the Meaning Behind the Plays* (New York: Harper Collins, 2006), p. 179, emphasis in original.
57. Bristol, 'Macbeth the Philosopher', p. 659.
58. Bristol, 'Is Shakespeare a Moral Philosopher?', p. 10.
59. Daniel J. Kornstein, 'A Comment on Prof. Halper's Reading of *Measure for Measure*', *Cardazo School of Law*, 13:2 (Fall 2001), p. 265.

CHAPTER 2

THE CONSTRAINED VISION OF EVOLUTIONARY ETHICS

I

A Conflict of Visions

'Before Kingdoms change, men must change'[1]
'To know the state, first we must know the ethical man'[2]

In *The Cave and the Light* (2013), Arthur Herman argues that 'the struggle for the soul of western civilization' has been primarily a philosophical one between Aristotelian empiricism, which lends itself to realism, and Platonist rationalism, which lends itself to idealism and 'the utopian impulse'.[3] The supreme articulation of this idea is found in Thomas Sowell's *A Conflict of Visions* (1987), a book of rare clarity, which argues that modern political struggles boil down to two very different visions of humanity: the constrained vision and the unconstrained vision.[4] Later, in *The Blank Slate* (2002), Steven Pinker recast these in perhaps more poetic terms: the tragic vision and the utopian vision.[5] The political scientist Larry Arnhart prefers to call them the 'realist' and 'utopian' visions.[6] The constrained (or empiricist, or tragic, or realist) vision sees the limit of human potential in its very nature. Humans have essentially unchanging characteristics that constrain what can and cannot be expected of them. They are primarily selfish, greedy and driven by self-interest, although they retain some capacity for cooperation. In this view *'man is an individual*, an individual born with a natural sociability ... but also a desire to protect his own natural rights and his own self-interest'.[7] In this tradition, we find an extensive line of thinkers; Sowell names Thomas Hobbes, Thomas Malthus, Adam Smith, Alexander Hamilton, Edmund Burke, Oliver Wendell Holmes, F. A. Hayek and Milton Friedman. Scholars of the early modern period would also surely add Niccolò Machiavelli to that list. In fact, it seems to me that the constrained vision was broadly dominant in Western thought until at least John Locke. As we shall see in Chapters 2 and 3, we can see variants of the constrained vision in Aristotle, Epicurus, Cicero, Seneca, Augustine of Hippo and John Calvin. These thinkers all, to a certain extent, recognise that we have baser instincts that cannot be helped, and so, in this vision, moral codes and laws emerge naturally from the ancient wisdom of experience. In this view, cultural rituals, governments and institutions are necessary checks and balances to help curb the baser instincts and save humans from themselves. This line of thought is encapsulated by Russell Kirk, discussing Edmund Burke:

> Pride, ambition, avarice, revenge, lust, sedition, hypocrisy, ungoverned zeal, disorderly appetites – these vices are the actual causes of the storms that trouble life. 'Religion, morals, laws, prerogatives, privileges, liberties, rights of men, are the *pretexts*' for revolution by sentimental humanitarians and mischievous agitators who think that established institutions must be the source of our afflictions. But the human heart, in reality, is the fountain of evil.[8]

There are no solutions, only trade-offs. There is no hope, for example, of somehow stopping people from being selfish or greedy, so organisations must devise incentives to lure them into more positive behaviours. By the same token, the government must ensure that the disincentives for committing crime are strong enough to make the costs outweigh the benefits.

In this vision, social processes are so irreducibly complex that their mechanisms are beyond the understanding of any single individual, and develop over centuries. Because of this, those who hold the constrained vision make no real distinction between intellectuals and the general populace. They do not greatly elevate the wisdom of the elites over the wisdom of the people, which is inherent in the social processes we have developed over the centuries. As Kirk puts it, 'the individual is foolish, but the species is wise; prejudices and prescriptions and presumptions are the instruments which the wisdom of the species employs to safeguard man against his own passions and appetites'.[9] No one can engineer solutions to provide better outcomes for the whole because no one's understanding of these processes can possibly be good enough to predict their possible consequences. It is for this reason that they focus instead on incentives.

Against all of this, we can contrast the unconstrained (or rationalist, or utopian) vision. In this vision, there are virtually no natural limits on what human beings can achieve because human behaviour is contingent on its social and environmental conditions, which can be transcended through our powers of reason. This means humans are 'perfectible' in a way that is seen to be impossible by those who hold the constrained vision. Indeed, Edmund Burke was 'contemptuous of the notion of human perfectibility'.[10] This is what Pinker calls 'The Blank Slate'. This view of the world is encompassed in Jean-Jacques Rousseau's phrase 'man is born free, and everywhere he is in chains'.[11] According to this vision, the main thing holding humanity back from achieving its full potential is not its nature, but rather its bad old institutions and other such social contrivances. If only we could get those institutions right, if only we could somehow reconfigure society in such and such a way, then the problems that have dogged human history till now would go away, and the rest would follow. The unconstrained vision 'insists that inherited institutions are diseased and oppressive, traditional values dissembling and dishonest; and it therefore proposes to supplant them with an infinitely more just and benign way of life'.[12] As Roger Scruton puts it,

> the most important point to notice is that it is [a vision] that *allows nothing to stand in its way*. No existing custom, institution, law, or hierarchy; no tradition, distinction, rule or piety can trump [the vision] . . . . Everything that does not conform to . . . [its] goal must be pulled down and built again, and the mere fact some custom or institution has been handed down and accepted is no argument in its favour.[13]

In a memorable passage, speaking of the differences between the constrained and unconstrained visions, Sowell writes,

> The issue is not as to whether changes have occurred in human history, but whether these are, in effect, changes of costumes and scenery or changes of the play itself. In the constrained vision, it is mostly the costumes and scenery that have changed; in the unconstrained vision, the play itself has changed, the characters are fundamentally different, and equally sweeping changes are both likely and necessary in the future.[14]

In the tradition of the unconstrained vision, Sowell names William Godwin, Jean-Jacques Rousseau, Thomas Paine, Thorstein Veblen, George Bernard Shaw, Laurence Tribe and John Kenneth Galbraith. As I suggested, scholars of the early modern period would surely take it back to John Locke. Of course, we can trace back the idea of the *tabula rasa* much further to Aristotle and then the Ancient Stoics such as Zeno of Citium, and later some residue of this finds its way into

Avicenna and Thomas Aquinas. Remarkably, Aristotle can be found near the start of both lists – although, as per Herman, the tradition of rationalist, utopian thinking surely owes more to Plato than it does to his student, even if Plato's own vision was pessimistic.[15] It is this broadly unconstrained, utopian view of the world that has today come to dominate both the political left and the academy – especially in Shakespeare studies and the discipline of English literature more broadly. 'The mind, in this view, is basically passive – it is a basin into which, as a person matures, the local culture is gradually poured; if the mind sets any limits at all on the content of culture, they are exceedingly broad.'[16] This belief in the unrestrained malleability of humans wedded to a faith reason alone begets a remarkable faith in the philosopher kings of Plato's *Republic* and their prescriptions for a rationally planned society. The central logic of utopian thinking almost always has as its solution to the problems of the world a belief that we should follow the teachings of a great sage, be it Jean-Jacques Rousseau, Karl Marx, Vladimir Lenin or any number of more recent theorists; the solution invariably emanates from the font of their special insights and *a priori* authority.

But when Sowell speaks of these 'visions', it is not in the sense of 'a dream, a hope, a prophecy, or moral imperative, though each of these things may ultimately derive from some particular vision', but rather as an intuitively felt root cause.

> Here a vision is a sense of *causation*. It is more like a hunch or a 'gut feeling' than it is like an exercise in logic or factual verification. These things come later, and feed on the raw material provided by the vision.[17]

In other words, logic and the seeking of verification are often *post hoc* rationalisations. As in MFT, intuition comes first and strategic reasoning follows. Because of the greatly contrasting first principles of the two visions, they differ on some very fundamental issues. In the cases of equality, power and justice, for example, their very definitions are completely different. In the constrained vision, equality means equality of rights or opportunity, power is diffuse and held by the people, and justice is understood as fairness of process. These are largely the principles that underpin the 'unwritten' British constitution and the many checks and balances that Alexander Hamilton ensured were written into the United States constitution. In the unconstrained vision, meanwhile, equality means equality of outcome, power is held and exercised by specific groups with specific interests, and justice is understood – as with equality – as fairness of outcome. It is not difficult to see these ideas underpinning, for example, socialism or modern notions of social justice, what Sowell would later dub 'the quest for cosmic justice'.[18]

In drawing from MFT, and from evolutionary psychology more broadly, this book aligns itself with the constrained vision. Studies in evolutionary psychology have widely corroborated the constrained vision and repudiated the unconstrained vision, for which there is little concrete evidence beyond wishful thinking. To admit that human beings have discernible natural characteristics that limit their range of possible behaviours is to subscribe to the constrained vision. Sowell notes that:

> Virtually no one believes that man is 100 percent unconstrained and virtually no one believes that man is 100 percent constrained. What puts a given thinker in the tradition of one vision rather than the other is not simply whether he refers more to man's constraints or to his untapped potential, but whether, or to what extent, constraints are built into the very structure and operation of a theory.[19]

The six moral foundations serve to constrain the range of possible moral intuitions, even if (ironically) a certain set of moral responses (see 'WEIRD' in Chapter 1) lead many people to believe in the unconstrained vision. Like Pinker in *The Blank Slate*, Jonathan Haidt references Sowell's *A Conflict of Visions* in *The Righteous Mind*.[20] In an interview with *The Wall Street Journal*, he made his position explicit: 'as a moral psychologist, I had to say the constrained vision is correct'.[21] In a paper on the ethics of the emerging political paradigm of globalisation versus nationalism, Haidt provided a useful summary of Sowell's argument in the form of a table:[22]

Unconstrained Vision	Constrained Vision
Human nature is malleable and can be improved – perhaps even perfected – if social conditions are improved. Anything is possible, if the artificial constraints placed on human beings can be removed. We must therefore free people from the petty tribal loyalties that cause mistrust and war.	Human beings need external structures or constraints in order to behave well, cooperate, and thrive. These external constraints include laws, institutions, customs, traditions, nations, and religions. These constraints are built up slowly and organically in local communities, but they can be destroyed quickly by radical reformers who don't understand their value.

It is important to note that the distinction between the constrained and the unconstrained vision should neither be seen as a simple shorthand for political right versus left, nor be mistaken for the old binary between nature and nurture. In the case of political persuasions, even though the logic of much thinking on the left follows the unconstrained vision, it is possible for someone who broadly holds the constrained vision to find themselves, by various circumstances, aligned to the left, and the same is true for those on the right who hold the unconstrained vision. The role of culture – and, more fundamentally, one's structures of beliefs and values (that is, 'cultural scripts') – is central in both visions. The crucial difference is that, in the unconstrained vision, culture itself is put at such a premium that in many cases it shapes not only beliefs but also the very possibility of what *can* be thought; culture itself becomes the ultimate constraint. In the constrained vision, however, culture serves primarily to promote desirable behaviours by providing incentives and, by the same token, discourages undesirable behaviours through disincentives. This is to say that, although human beings must be taught how to speak, read and write, and to follow certain cultural rules, certain instinctual moral intuitions are prior to cultural laws.

One can see this latent assumption in modern economics, in the tradition of Adam Smith. Consider, for example, Milton Friedman, who finds human beings acting according to their desires and their own moral instincts, regardless of whatever laws might be in place:

> There's a fundamental economic law which has never been contradicted: if you pay more for something, there will tend to be more of that something available. If the amount you're willing to pay for anything goes up, somehow or other somebody will supply more of that thing. We have made immoral behaviour far more profitable. We have in the course of changes in our society been establishing greater and greater incentives on people to behave in ways that most of us regard as immoral. . . . When the only laws are those laws which everybody regards as right and valid they have great moral force. When you make laws which people separately do not regard as right and valid, they lose their moral force. Is there anybody in here who has a *moral* compunction to speeding? I'm not saying you may not have a *prudential* compunction to speeding, you may be afraid to get caught, but does it seem to you immoral to speed? Maybe, if so, you're in a small minority. I've never yet found anybody who regarded it immoral to violate the

exchange rate regulations of a foreign country. Here are people who would never dream for a second of stealing a nickel from their neighbour, who have no hesitancy in manipulating their income tax returns so as to reduce their income tax returns by thousands. Why? Because one set of laws have a moral value that people recognise independent of the government having passed these laws, the other set do not appeal to people's moral instincts.[23]

He provides a concrete example from US history:

Prohibition of liquor, which was attempted as you know, had disastrous effects on the climates of law obedience and morality. Something which had been legal – to buy and drink alcoholic beverages – became illegal. And you converted law abiding citizens into bootleggers overnight.[24]

We can see in this sentiment the same logic as that used by Sir Toby in *Twelfth Night* when confronted by Malvolio: 'Dost thou think because thou art virtuous there shall be no more cakes and ale?' (II, iii, 107–8). And again in *Measure for Measure* when Pompey protests to Escalus about Angelo's punitive new anti-prostitution laws: 'If you head and hang all that offend that way but for ten year together, you'll be glad to give out a commission for more heads' (II, i, 234–6). In the real world, attempts to curb our instincts by the blunt imperative of legal dictates usually fail in such a way as to make them seem farcical.

Hence in modern-day Iran, where the fundamentalist Islamic government attempts to enforce laws not too dissimilar to those enacted by Angelo, rates of porn distribution and prostitution have ironically sky-rocketed.[25] Even if you make every attempt to stop them by force or coercion, individuals still show a very strong pattern of following their own interests, based on the incentives for doing so. The utopian vision that society or culture 'produces' individuals is therefore shown to be demonstrably untrue. In every case, the dictate triggers the psychological phenomenon of 'reactance', known to the layperson as 'reverse psychology' – that is, a natural urge to do directly the opposite of what has been forbidden.[26] While these dictates were both examples from the political right, one might easily find examples from the left. Let us not forget either that the likes of Michel Foucault, like many on the radical left at the time, supported the Iranian Revolution.[27] It is a testament to the strength of the unconstrained vision, insulated from evidence, that this has neither been a source of embarrassment for them, nor made any dent in their reputations.

In the constrained vision, individuals pursuing their own separate interests none the less end up benefiting the 'whole' of society through the product of their labour. So Adam Smith writes in *The Wealth of Nations* (1776):

> He generally, indeed, neither intends to promote public interest, nor knows how much he is promoting it. . . . he intends only his own security; and by directing that industry in such a manner as its produce may be of the greatest value, he intends only his own gain; and he is in this, as in many other cases, led by an invisible hand to promote an end which was no part his intention. Nor is it always the worse for society that it was no part of it. By pursuing his own interests he frequently promotes that of the society more effectually than when he really intends to promote it.[28]

Here, unplanned social benefits are the by-product of individual self-interest. A factory owner may be thinking only of pennies and pounds, but in the process ends up employing a lot of other people, and his factory is making a product that people presumably want enough to pay for it. Here, the owner, the worker and the consumer are all driven by their own interests and yet they are all benefiting in some way:

the factory owner turns a profit, the worker is paid for their time and labour, and the consumer has a product they want. This is in sharp contrast to the Marxist view of the economy, which, rather than seeing individual agency and mutually beneficial relationships of exchange, sees instead only power and exploitation.

The utopian aspect of the Marxist vision (Sowell lists it as a 'hybrid') assumes that if one removes individual property rights, then 'self-interest' – which capitalists following Smith assume is natural – will fall away and be replaced by a concern with the common good. The fact that, to date, there have been more than five dozen failed socialist states,[29] and the fact that this utopian vision failed to materialise in any of them, should be all the evidence required to see that, whatever the rights and wrongs of capitalism, Smith's vision of human nature was none the less closer to the truth than that of Marx. Of course, those holding a utopian vision above empirical reality will find ever more ingenious ways to explain away failed predictions. As Sowell says,

> One of the more remarkable feats of those with the [unconstrained] vision ... has been the maintenance of their reputations in the face of repeated predictions that have been wrong by miles.... In each case, the utter certainty of their predictions has been matched by the utter failure of the real world to cooperate – and by the utter invulnerability of their reputations.[30]

Sowell discusses the predictions of John Kenneth Galbraith and Paul Ehrlich, but fast-forward to the present-day and he might just as well be talking about any of the numberless pundits who spoke with certainty that the United Kingdom would vote to remain in the European Union and that Hillary Clinton would defeat Donald Trump to become president of the United States. How many of them saw any serious dent to their reputations? To advocates of MFT, such as Jonathan Haidt, there is nothing remotely surprising about this: whatever the facts of a given matter, the rider – strategic reasoning – will work overtime to justify the proclamations of the intuitive elephant. In the conflict of visions, systemic and routine confirmation bias prevails.[31] If we know this, is there any wonder that we live in a post-truth moment characterised by blind partisanship and 'fake news' on both sides of the political divide? The right, as well as the left, can be prone to utopian visions: I have touched already on prohibition laws and the Iranian Islamic revolution, but think also of Donald Rumsfeld's neo-conservative dream of dropping American-style democracy on to Iraq and expecting it to take root.

Likewise, despite evidence of a growing consensus regarding evolutionary ideas across twenty-two disciplines,[32] we can also see a hostility to science, perhaps our last bastion of empiricism, on both sides of the political divide. In the United States, both evangelical Christians and radical feminists have been notable for their fierce opposition to evolutionary ideas.[33] Leftist thinkers such as Jean-François Lyotard and Michel Foucault told us for decades to distrust science, while Marxists such as Louis Althusser declared their own form of ideology critique 'scientific knowledge'.[34] Whenever a political group holds its utopian vision above empirical reality, you can expect that group to find ways of claiming that the scientific method is in some way ideological. Thus, in the Soviet Union, when accepted scientific consensus failed to cooperate with socialism, Josef Stalin supplanted it with Lysenkoism, named after the thoroughly debunked pseudo-science of Trofim Lysenko.[35] My view is that the denial or bastardisation of science for political ends is almost always dangerous, and this is something of which we must be acutely aware when navigating the fiercely contested waters of evolutionary psychology.

The Constrained Vision of Evolutionary Ethics [47

In 1978, when Edward O. Wilson wrote his double Pulitzer Prize-winning masterpiece, *On Human Nature*, Marxists moved swiftly to denounce it as 'unscientific', as they had done with his previous book, *Sociobiology: The New Synthesis* (1975). Writing in 2004, Wilson reflected,

> the fashionable mood in academia was revolutionary left. Elite universities invented political correctness, enforced by peer pressures and the threat of student protest. Marxism and socialism in this ambience were all right. Communist revolutions were all right. The regimes of China and the Soviet Union were, at least in ideology, all right. Centrism was scorned outside the dean's office. Political conservatives, stewing inwardly, for the most part dared not speak up. Radical professors, the heroes on campus, repeated this litany: The Establishment failed us, the Establishment blocks progress, the Establishment is the enemy. Power to the people it was, but with an American twist. Because ordinary working people remained dismayingly conservative throughout this sandbox revolution, the new proletariat in the class struggle had to be the students.[36]

If any of this sounds familiar, it is because similar 'revolutionary' forces have strengthened their death-grip in some areas of the humanities in the past three decades. The Berkeley campus at the University of California has become a symbol of their authoritarianism. Should it be any news to us that the far left is prone to tyranny? At the time of writing, the endemic of 'no-platforming' speakers with whom certain students disagree has reached the point where even the Democrat firebrand Bernie Sanders was moved to defend the outspoken conservative Ann Coulter's right to speak.[37] Haidt has been a vocal critic of this anti-intellectual and authoritarian streak in the radical left:

> Aristotle often evaluated a thing with respect to its 'telos' – its purpose, end, or goal. The telos of a knife is to cut.

> The telos of a physician is health or healing. What is the telos of university? The most obvious answer is 'truth' – the word appears on so many university crests. But increasingly, many of America's top universities are embracing social justice as their telos, or as a second and equal telos. But can any institution or profession have two teloses (or teloi)? What happens if they conflict? . . . I believe that the conflict between truth and social justice is likely to become unmanageable. Universities will have to choose, and be explicit about their choice, so that potential students and faculty recruits can make an informed choice. Universities that try to honor both will face increasing incoherence and internal conflict.[38]

The academy will increasingly struggle to serve two masters. It is very much 'a conflict of visions' between an empiricism concerned with describing reality and a utopian rationalism concerned only with a righteous quest for a cosmic justice that can never be achieved. Where the truth is inconvenient to their ends, radical political groups, like religious groups, will almost always seek to silence or defame them, as they did throughout the twentieth century. Although Haidt describes the left as primarily responding to the moral foundations of care, fairness and liberty (for example, WEIRD), it seems to me that when groups cluster around a utopian vision, they develop new forms of sanctity, authority and loyalty. It is not difficult to see, for example, how for some – of which the Antifa group offer the most extreme and violent example – 'diversity' has become an almost quasi-religious sacred creed. It is a kind of purity test. If this test is failed (sanctity), the sinner will be 'de-platformed' and punished (authority), and cast out for their betrayal as an unrepentant heathen (loyalty). As we will see in Chapter 4, when I consider the European Reformation and the rise of puritanism, it is a pattern characteristic of resistance groups driven by an ideological vision.

Both Sowell and Haidt note that there is a significant difference between how those with the constrained and unconstrained visions deal with disagreements. Those with the constrained vision are much more likely to see their unconstrained opponents as well-meaning but dangerously misguided and perhaps naïve or idealistic people, who often end up doing more harm than good. For those holding the unconstrained vision, however, it is often insufficient to see those who disagree as being simply wrong; in many cases they must also *morally* condemn them. This is because it is 'not simply a vision of the world and its functioning in a causal sense, but is also a vision of themselves as and of their moral role in that world. *It is a vision of differential rectitude.*'[39] Perhaps because of this '*the localization of evil* is one of the hallmarks of the unconstrained vision'.[40] Once it is clear who the bad people are, then the moral crusader has a focal point on which to fixate their righteous indignation. Once this compulsion in some people towards *moral* condemnation is understood, our current 'outrage culture' looks almost like an inevitability. Anthony Walsh puts it bluntly:

> Unconstrained visionaries seem to believe that if apparently intelligent and well-educated individuals research race and sex differences, or oppose programs they believe could improve the lives of the less fortunate, they must be evil racists or sexists, or some other hissing epithet.[41]

One of the aims of this book is to show how a writer like Shakespeare, with his extraordinary capacity for empathy and his singular unwillingness to write anyone off, can teach us all how to be a little more understanding of where another person with a different point of view – perhaps a different vision of the world, a different moral compass – might be coming from.

> **In summary**
> - Political and ideological struggles across the centuries can be characterised as 'a conflict of vision' following the scheme described in Thomas Sowell's (1987) book of the same name.
> - The constrained vision sees human nature as fundamentally unchanging and hence an ultimate 'constraint' on what can realistically be expected from human beings. Accordingly, there are no solutions, only trade-offs; individuals need incentives to encourage naturally good behaviour and disincentives to discourage naturally bad behaviour. Society must erect institutions to help curb humanity's 'baser instincts'.
> - The unconstrained vision sees human nature as having no fixed characteristics, and hence as free from natural constraints, as being 'perfectible'. Accordingly, there are permanent solutions; individuals need only change society and the rest will follow.
> - Moral Foundations Theory holds the constrained vision, and in following it, so does this book.
> - The unconstrained vision has no truck with empirical reality; it is insulated from evidence. Through confirmation bias, those who hold it will look only for evidence that confirms their existing beliefs and systematically ignore facts inconvenient to its narrative. Although the constrained vision derives from empirical knowledge, those who hold it can also be guilty of confirmation bias.
> - Those who hold the unconstrained vision see themselves as being morally superior to others, and accordingly seek to condemn and, in the worst cases, silence others.
> - One of this book's aims is to show how we might learn to be more understanding of one another's differences of opinion from Shakespeare's remarkable capacity for empathy.

II

Evolutionary Ethics

While there can be little doubt that the constrained vision is closer to empirical reality than the unconstrained vision, evolutionary studies none the less vary in how they characterise human nature, and as such have reproduced their own version of the 'conflict of visions'. The effort to understand morality from a biological perspective started with Charles Darwin himself in *The Descent of Man* (1871). Unfortunately, it was not long after this that Darwin's ideas were hijacked by 'survival-of-the-fittest' Social Darwinists such as Herbert Spencer and William Graham Sumner. While enormously popular in their day, Spencer and Sumner had fallen out of fashion by the 1930s. The first years of the twentieth century would also see Darwin pressed into service for a utopian vision, where the unconstrained idea of human perfectibility reached its most terrifying conclusion in eugenics. In Britain, Francis Galton believed that aspects that make up human character, such as moral virtues or dispositions, were hereditary traits. In Germany, such thinking resulted in atrocity. Perhaps understandably, research into the relationship between ethics and biology was considered taboo until the mid-1970s and the pioneering work of Edward O. Wilson, especially his books *Sociobiology: The New Synthesis* (1975) and *On Human Nature* (1978), which built on earlier studies by W. D. Hamilton and Robert Trivers.[42] Wilson argued that to find 'a new morality based on a more truthful definition of man, it is necessary to look inward, to dissect the machinery of the mind and to retrace its evolutionary history'.[43]

The central moral dilemma for biologists and evolutionists is perhaps summed up best by Adam Smith in *The Theory of Moral Sentiments* (1759):

> How selfish soever man may be supposed, there are evidently some principles in his nature, which interest him in the fortune of others, and render their happiness necessary to him, though he derives nothing from it except the pleasure of seeing it.[44]

If human beings are naturally selfish, why should they take pleasure in the fortune of others? If we are self-interested, why are people sometimes moved to help each other when there is no obvious gain in doing so? Darwin himself was puzzled by this. He noted that human beings are unique among all animals in caring for weaker members of a society, even at the apparent detriment to survival:

> With savages, the weak in body or mind are soon eliminated; and those that survive commonly exhibit a vigorous state of health. We civilised men, on the other hand, do our utmost to check the process of elimination; we build asylums for the imbecile, the maimed, and the sick; we institute poor-laws; and our medical men exert their utmost skill to save the life of every one to the last moment. There is reason to believe that vaccination has preserved thousands, who from a weak constitution would formerly have succumbed to small-pox. Thus the weak members of civilised societies propagate their kind. No one who has attended to the breeding of domestic animals will doubt that this must be highly injurious to the race of man. It is surprising how soon a want of care, or care wrongly directed, leads to the degeneration of a domestic race; but excepting in the case of man himself, hardly any one is so ignorant as to allow his worst animals to breed.[45]

For Darwin this impulse to help the less fortunate and 'helpless is mainly an incidental result of the instinct of sympathy, which was originally acquired as part of the social instincts, but subsequently rendered . . . more tender and more widely diffused'. He sees this instinct 'extending to men of all races, to the imbecile, maimed, and other useless members of society, and finally to the lower animals'. He argues that the more mankind nurtures this natural sympathy, the more the standard of morality will 'rise higher and higher'. Indeed, he thinks that 'the standard of morality has risen since an early period in the history of man'. Thus, for Darwin, it is in us to be nicer to each other, which he views as a mark of 'civilized man'.[46] This is, of course, the morality of care and harm.

Although Darwin's consideration of morality in *The Descent of Man* is couched in the racially and culturally insensitive language typical of his period, when considering various indigenous peoples from Africa, the Americas and

Australia he none the less recognises their moral capacities, even if these often seem constrained by groupishness:

> As barbarians do not regard the opinion of their women, wives are commonly treated like slaves. Most savages are utterly indifferent to the sufferings of strangers, or even delight in witnessing them. It is well known that the women and children of the North-American Indians aided in torturing their enemies. Some savages take pleasure in cruelty to animals, and humanity is an unknown virtue. Nevertheless, besides family affections, kindness is common, especially in sickness, between members of the same tribe, and is sometimes extended beyond those limits. Mungo Park's touching account of the kindness of the negro of the interior to him is well known. Many instances could be given of the noble fidelity of savages towards each other, but not to strangers; common experience justifies the maxim of the Spaniard, 'Never, never trust an Indian.'[47]

One might imagine that the natives had similar expressions about the Spaniards, but it is clear from Darwin's account that the so-called savages *do* possess the 'natural sympathy' he ascribes to 'civilized man', under the right conditions. What is interesting here is that Darwin starts to spot other types of morality beyond that of care and harm. For example, he spots the moral foundation of authority in Native American stoicism:

> As soon as a tribe has a recognised leader, disobedience becomes a crime, and even abject submission is looked on as a sacred virtue. . . . The American savage voluntarily submits to the most horrid tortures without a groan, to prove and strengthen his fortitude and courage; and we cannot help admiring him [. . .].[48]

And that of sanctity:

> As soon, however, as marriage, whether polygamous, or monogamous, becomes common, jealousy will lead to the inculcation of female virtue; and this, being honoured, will spread to the unmarried females. How slowly it spreads to

the male sex, we see at the present day. Chastity eminently requires self-command, therefore it has been honoured from a very early period in the history of civilized man. As a consequence of this, the senseless practice of celibacy has been ranked from a remote period as a virtue.[49]

He goes on to reveal that his own understanding of morality is, in Haidt's term, 'WEIRD' – that is, primarily concerned with the individual, rather than with the community or in-group. Like most Western liberals, he downplayed the moral foundations of authority, sanctity and loyalty. Thus, according to Darwin, 'savages' regard actions as 'good or bad, solely as they obviously affect the welfare of the tribe – not that of the species, nor that of an individual member of the tribe'.[50] In this sentence, Darwin drew the key battle-lines of contemporary evolutionary ethics. Did morality develop primarily to serve the survival of the tribe (or group), the whole species or the individual? Plainly, Darwin saw tribal morality as being at a more primitive stage of development to moralities that foreground the whole species or the individual – it is something that he has in common with the globalists of today who are so quick to condemn the deplorable nationalists. But is it true that there is such a hierarchy of progress between the moral foundations? It seems unlikely.

Before continuing, it is important to note that Darwin's assumption that the differences between people around the world stem from genetic difference is not simply something we cannot countenance because it is politically distasteful to modern sensibilities; it is also flatly untrue. On this score, biology does not provide us with an adequate answer because there are no meaningful or significant evolutionary differences between European, Native American, African or Asian peoples. Cultural differences between historic peoples around the world are much more readily understood in terms of geographical differences. Many indigenous cultural practices lead directly from the relationship between people and the land. Excellent and meticulous studies by Fernand Braudel, Jared Diamond, David S. Landes, Thomas Sowell, Ian Morris and Francis Fukuyama demonstrate, almost beyond doubt, that at both a local and a continental level, geography accounts for technological and military development,[51] the structure of political order,[52] and the types of characteristics valued by the culture.[53] Hence, we find striking similarities between disparate sets of mountain peoples from around the globe, as distinct from coastal peoples, or jungle-dwelling peoples in the tropics.[54] As Braudel argues, 'In understanding Black Africa, geography is more important than history ... [because] climate accounts for the alternation of vast areas of grass and trees which inevitably involve different ways of life.'[55] Diamond argues that, given the lopsided nature of historical conquests, 'it *seems* logical to suppose that history's pattern reflects innate differences in people themselves', but in actuality 'there is no hint of any intellectual *dis*advantage' in the tribes and civilisations that for one reason or another were colonised by others.[56] The evidence overwhelmingly suggests that, despite typical variations in physical and mental abilities within groups, biologically speaking, people everywhere are essentially the same in their natural capacities, even if not wholly identical. People vary much more within groups than between groups.[57] Perhaps Thomas Hobbes put it best:

> Nature hath made men so equal, in the faculties of the body and mind; as that though there be found one man sometimes manifestly stronger in body, or of quicker mind than another; yet when all is reckoned together, the difference between man, and man, is not so considerable, as that one man can thereupon claim to himself any benefit, to which another may not pretend, as well as he. For as to the strength of body, the weakest has strength enough to kill the strongest, either by secret machination, or by confederacy with others, that are in the same danger with himself.[58]

Even in the realm of natural advantages between individuals, there are built-in checks and balances. Indeed, the moral foundations that bind – authority, loyalty, fairness and sanctity – evolved partly as a natural counterweight to individual egoists.

The task of evolutionary psychology, then, is not to account for the differences between cultural groups, which is explained in large part by geography, but rather, as Wilson suggested, to gain a more accurate picture of the underlying common humanity. As I mentioned in Chapter 1, the key dispute in evolutionary ethics since the 1970s has centred on questions of altruism versus selfishness, and group selection versus kin selection. In *The Righteous Mind*, Haidt's shorthand metaphor is that 'we are selfish and we are groupish ... 90 percent chimp and 10 percent bee',[59] by which he means that, in the clear majority of cases, human beings, like chimpanzees, are self-interested, but nevertheless retain a certain capacity for cooperation and altruism to protect the 'hive' or in-group. For some, this allows for rather too much altruism, and for others too little. At the polar ends of this dispute we find in the corner of altruism and group selection (or 'multi-level selection'), among others, Edward O. Wilson, David Sloan Wilson, Elliott Sober and Leo Buss, and, in the corner of selfishness and kin selection, among undoubtedly a greater number of others (because it is the orthodox position), Richard Dawkins, Steven Pinker, Daniel Dennett, David M. Buss, Robert Wright, and John Tooby and Leda Cosmides.[60] To make matters more complicated, both groups found common enemies in Stephen Jay Gould, Niles Eldredge and Richard Lewontin, who stood against the entire enterprise of sociobiology and its successor, evolutionary psychology, arguing that their conception of humanity is too limited. As per the unconstrained vision, Gould, Eldredge and Lewontin emphasised cultural and ideological causes through their conception of 'species selection' and the related idea of 'punctuated equilibrium'. Just as Sowell lost patience with those holding the 'vision of the anointed', so Gould's opponents came to see him as an ideologue more concerned with an anti-capitalist progressive political agenda than with the truth: 'his essays become revealed as mini-theatricals carefully staged for purposes of self-aggrandizement rather than for the careful and charitable pursuit of the truth'.[61] As Daniel Dennett puts it, 'Gould has gone from revolution to revolution. So far his declarations of revolution have all been false alarms, but he has kept on trying, defying the moral of Aesop's fable about the boy who cried wolf.'[62]

These are vast disagreements, which, across the decades, have raged sufficiently to be dubbed 'The Darwin Wars'.[63] As such, I cannot hope to do their complexity justice here beyond offering the briefest of sketches. At the heart of the dispute is a disagreement over levels of causation. When successful evolutionary adaptations occur in animal species, do they take place at the level of the entire species, or at the level of the in-group, or, rather, at the level of the individual animal and its offspring? I have put the three options in Table 2.1.

Table 2.1

| Species Selection (macro-level) |
| Group Selection (in-group-level, 'multi-level') |
| Kin Selection (gene-level) |

We need not concern ourselves with species selection, which has been largely debunked; the key debate is currently between kin selection and group selection, which, in lay terms, is a contrast between 'the "dog-eat-dog" view of nature and a new emphasis on "the bright side of biology"'.[64] To take examples from the extreme ends, for Dawkins evolution is like survival in the tough world of Chicago gangsters, in which the 'predominant quality to be expected in a successful gene is ruthless selfishness'. In this view, evolution is an explanation rather than a moral justification: 'I am saying how things have evolved. I am not saying how we humans morally ought to behave.' While this ruthlessly selfish view of nature may seem unpalatable, 'unfortunately, however much we may deplore something, it does not stop it being true'. Because of this, in Dawkins's view, 'we must *teach* our children altruism, for we cannot expect it to be part of their biological nature'.[65] In sharp contrast, the primatologist Frans de Waal, who has built his career on providing evidence for empathy and a sense of fairness among the primates and even among other animals, argues that humans 'are group animals: highly competitive, sensitive to injustice, sometimes warmongering, but mostly peace loving'.[66] It is interesting that, despite ostensible appearances, it is de Waal who attributes more of our behaviour to nature, and Dawkins who gives the greater scope for a cultural perspective. Indeed, in *The Selfish Gene*, he grants quite extraordinary powers to cultural 'memes' that start to approach the unconstrained vision.[67]

Although David Sloan Wilson has advocated passionately for group selection, through the 1970s, 1980s and 1990s it was largely dismissed as a heterodox, fringe position among biologists, except where their arguments helped them fend off Gould and the claims made by species selection. This is the case, for example, in Dennett's *Darwin's Dangerous Idea* (1995).[68] Elsewhere, such as in *The Moral Animal* (1994) by Robert Wright, the idea was given short shrift.[69] The heart of the dispute is that advocates of kin selection claim that they can explain away virtually any evolutionary trait as having developed for the benefit of the gene rather than for the benefit of the group. Thus, Steven Pinker argues:

> The recent surge of interest in group selection has been motivated by two empirical phenomena. One is eusociality in insect taxa such as bees, ants, and termites, whose worker or soldier castes forgo their own reproduction and may sacrifice their lives to benefit their fellows, as when a bee dies when

stinging an invader. E. O. Wilson notes that a self-sacrificing insect benefits the colony, and concludes that eusociality must be explained by selection among colonies. But most other biologists point out that the sacrificer benefits the queen (her sister or mother), who founds a new colony when she reproduces, so the simplest explanation of eusociality is that the genes promoting self-sacrifice were selected because they benefited copies of themselves inside the queen.[70]

In virtually all cases, they argue that apparently selfless and altruistic behaviour can be put down to either nepotism or reciprocity.

> Individuals give alarm calls not to protect their group but to protect their genes. . . . Females control the number of eggs laid or babies born not to aid the population regulation and save the group from extinction, but rather to optimize the number of offspring that survive and reproduce.[71]

Jonathan Haidt has followed David Sloan Wilson and others in rejecting – or at the very least complicating – this claim, based on new empirical evidence from studies conducted since the 1970s. Their charge, which has gathered momentum since the turn of the twenty-first century, is that while kin selection is undoubtedly true in some cases, it cannot explain away instances where stronger individuals, bullies or egoists, are subdued to confer long-term group advantages afforded by cooperation. For example, William Muir has found that when breeding chickens for egg production, if you select only the most productive hens – who tend to be more aggressive and dominant – the total number of eggs goes down because of the increased levels of aggression, which result in killings and cannibalisation. By using group selection – that is, breeding all the hens in the cage, not simply the most productive ones – the death rate fell from 67 per cent to just 8 per cent, and the total number of eggs produced jumped from 91 to 237 in just three generations.[72] Haidt suggests that similarly rapid development can occur in human societies, and this might be one reason why religions have persistently developed in cultures around the world. Religion helps to promote in-group social cohesion, curbs the most aggressive and dominant characters, and greatly increases the capacity for cooperation and hence the social productivity of a society. In outlining the positive functions of religion in this way, Haidt offends Richard Dawkins, and his allies Daniel Dennett, Sam Harris and the late Christopher Hitchens – together the 'four horsemen of new atheism', on two counts. He not only returns to group selection, a concept Dawkins strongly opposes, but also gives an evolutionary rationale for religion. This is an argument first outlined in David Sloan Wilson's *Darwin's Cathedral* (2002), in which he compares religious organisations to 'a social insect colony' and outlines the many group advantages that they have conferred on human groups over the centuries.[73]

Accordingly, in *The Moral Landscape* (2010), Sam Harris criticised Haidt on two grounds: first, that the six moral foundations might all be collapsed into different manifestations of care / harm, since the others are all ultimately about reducing harm in the long run,[74] and second, that his defence of religion is wrong-headed because it can be shown to cause more harm than good, and also by the fact that it simply is not true. For Harris, morality must have a basis in scientific truth.[75] We need not concern ourselves with the lengthy exchanges between Harris and Haidt on this matter. The underlying difference between them comes down to the central dichotomy in Arthur Herman's *The Cave and the Light*: Harris is a rationalist trying to derive truth through pure reason, while Haidt is an empiricist simply describing things as they can be observed. In other words, Harris is subscribing to the unconstrained, utopian vision: implicitly he imagines a world where human beings are no longer groupish or tribal, where the social functions traditionally provided for by religious institutions are no longer needed. Even though he is an atheist himself, Haidt sees no such possibility, and it seems to me that the weight of evidence is entirely on his side. One need only think of the recent history of conflicts around the world to see that the groupish and tribal element of humanity remains constant, whether we have religion or not.

Joshua Greene has been another prominent critic of Haidt. In *Moral Tribes* (2014), while he agrees with many of the core arguments of *The Righteous Mind*, like Harris, he ultimately has a problem with the emphasis Haidt places on intuitionism.

> My first important disagreement with Haidt concerns the role of reason, of manual mode, in moral psychology. I believe that manual-mode thinking has played an enormously important role in moral life, that it is, once again, our second moral compass. Haidt disagrees. He thinks that moral reasoning plays a minor role in moral life, a conclusion neatly expressed by the title of his famous paper 'The Emotional Dog and Its Rational Tail'.[76]

Greene's basic problem is that Haidt's prescription – to try to negate self-righteous indignation by understanding where your political adversary might be coming from (that is, by understanding the underlying moral foundations to which they are responding) – does not tell us what to do next. As Greene puts it, 'it's one thing to acknowledge that one's opponents are not evil. It's another thing to concede that they're right, or even half-right.'[77] Ultimately, though, this comes down to a political disagreement. As I have discussed, Haidt (a self-described liberal) argues that liberals ('WEIRD' people) are blind to three out of the six moral foundations, and so effectively are morally colour-blind. All Greene can offer here is 'One might say, as Haidt does, that liberals have narrow moral tastes. But when it comes to moral foundations, less may be more. Liberals' moral tastes, rather than being narrow, may instead by more refined.'[78] To take this stance, he invokes rationalist Enlightenment values. Note that this is the same argument that Darwin made when comparing various Native American and African tribes to

Victorian England. Some readers may very well agree with that argument instinctively; after all, this is how moral intuitions work, and if you are a liberal, you might prefer to see your moral tastes as 'refined' rather than 'blind'. However, it seems to me that Greene seeks to make this argument almost exclusively because Haidt's evidence does not fit with, as Thomas Sowell would put it, the vision of the anointed. We need to check whatever our own moral impulses might be and study the evidence without partisanship. To this end, I think it is perfectly transparent that Harris takes issue with Haidt because his work seems to defend religion, which he does not like, and that Greene takes issue with it because it seems to defend conservatives, who he does not like. Both are examples of partisanship: Harris and Greene each defend their own team (atheists for Harris, liberals for Greene) from claims that *feel* as if they pose an existential threat. As Sowell predicted, even when faced with hard evidence, and even in the sciences, those who hold utopian visions will prefer to keep their 'differential rectitude' rather than accept the facts.[79] They will invariably find some issue with those who describe things as they are, and not how they should be.

The evolutionary critic, Joseph Carroll, provides a more substantial critique of Haidt on two grounds. First, the 'open-ended' suggestion that there might be more moral foundations discovered beyond the six outlined in *The Righteous Mind* reveals a 'weak theoretical structure' that would be 'better grounded ... within human life history theory'. Second, Carroll criticises the residue of the sociologist, Émile Durkheim, in Haidt's conception of corporate social identity because it sits oddly next to the claim that moral foundations have an evolutionary root. For Carroll, this is 'a split-level version of human identity', which suggests 'a basic failure to overcome an original belief in the primacy of individuals as a unit of selection'.[80]

> In reality, we are never an asocial species. We are always a species in which social identity is integral to individual identity. Haidt has not developed an integrated view of

human nature. He has simply shoved together two anomalous pieces: the egoistic isolate that makes up, supposedly, 90 percent of human motives and the superorganism that makes up the other 10 percent.[81]

Carroll raises some valid concerns here, which push up against the limits of what is currently known at the cutting edge in this field. The current study aims to provide a robust starting point for those wishing to foster fruitful dialogue between the latest research from evolutionary psychology and literary texts. If further moral foundations are found, it will be an exciting opportunity for further research. The 'split-level' view of humanity of which Carroll complains is mirrored in this book's discussion of moral foundations on the one hand, and 'cultural scripts' on the other. As a literary critic (as opposed to a biologist or evolutionary psychologist), I do not find the fact that these two aspects of humanity are in obvious tension to be especially troubling, particularly if one considers that the constrained vision posits that culture needs to protect humanity from its darkest impulses. Thus, I see no reason to believe that human identity should be 'integrated'. Indeed, if group selection functions in the way Haidt, David Sloan Wilson and others describe, it makes perfect sense that the structures, institutions and rituals produced by the 'superorganism' should be at odds with the individual egoist. In situations when a moral decision is required, the superorganism and the individual will invariably pull in different directions. If a loved one is murdered, the twenty-first-century cultural script tells us to report it to the police, but many individuals will likely experience the welling up of emotions pushing them towards revenge and retaliation. As Carroll says, social identity is always important, and this might ultimately push the individual to perform the cultural script, but on other occasions the 'egoistic isolate' will win out. Both the cultural scripts (group-level) and the individual emotional drive (kin-level) have an ultimate evolutionary root and, despite their apparent lack of integration and probable collision course, they are both aspects of humanity. Accordingly, one of the key concerns in Part II of *Shakespeare's Moral Compass* is whether the playwright's moral thinking tends towards the superorganism or the individual.

> ### In summary
> - In *The Descent of Man* (1871), Charles Darwin argued that human morality is found in our 'natural sympathy', and that the most civilised societies are those that show the greatest kindness to their weakest members.
> - After Darwin, there has been a split in evolutionary psychology between those, such as Richard Dawkins, who believe that evolution is primarily driven by the ruthlessly self-interested reproduction of genes, which can explain even apparently selfless and altruistic behaviours, and those, such as Edward O. Wilson, who believe such behaviours develop because they confer group advantages.
> - Following David Sloan Wilson, Jonathan Haidt argues that group selection helps explain the development of religious organisations, which promote social cohesion and cooperation. Sam Harris has criticised this view because (in his view) religion has caused more harm than good and is based on false beliefs.
> - Joshua Greene has also criticised Haidt because he believes that ('WEIRD') liberals are not morally lacking but rather 'morally refined'.
> - This book rejects the criticisms of both Harris and Greene because they are plainly born of a desire to protect rationalist utopian visions from empirical evidence.
> - Joseph Carroll has criticised Haidt's *The Righteous Mind* for failing to integrate moral foundations as experienced on an individual level and human groupishness. This book argues that there is no need for integration because the fundamental tension between these two aspects of humanity is central to understanding moral thinking.

Notes

1. Line from the TV series *Jesus of Nazareth*, dir. Franco Zeffirelli (UK and Italy: ITC Films, 1977).
2. Russell Kirk, *The Conservative Mind: From Burke to Eliot*, 7th edn (1953; Washington, DC: Gateway Editions, 2016), p. 28.
3. Arthur Herman, *The Cave and the Light: Plato versus Aristotle and the Struggle for the Soul of Western Civilization* (New York: Random House, 2013), p. 67.
4. See Thomas Sowell, *A Conflict of Visions: Ideological Origins of Political Struggles*, rev. edn (1987; New York: Basic Books, 2007).
5. Steven Pinker, *The Blank Slate: The Modern Denial of Human Behaviour* (New York and London: Penguin, 2002). Note that Sowell himself had coined the term 'tragic vision' in a later book, *The Vision of the Anointed: Self-Congratulation as Social Policy* (New York: Basic Books, 1995).
6. Larry Arnhart, 'Darwinian Conservativism', in *Darwinian Conservativism: A Disputed Question*, ed. Kenneth C. Blanchard, Jr (Charlottesville, VA: Imprint Academic, 2009), p. 6.
7. Herman, *The Cave and the Light*, p. 364, emphasis in original.
8. Kirk, *The Conservative Mind*, p. 36.
9. Ibid. pp. 37–8.
10. Ibid. p. 35.
11. Jean-Jacques Rousseau, *'The Social Contract', and Other Political Writings*, ed. and trans. Victor Gourevitch (Cambridge: Cambridge University Press, 1997), p. 41.
12. Clinton Rossiter, *Conservativism in America: The Thankless Persuasion*, 2nd edn (1955; New York: Vintage Books, 1962), p. 11.
13. Roger Scruton, *Fools, Frauds and Firebrands: Thinkers of the New Left* (New York and London: Bloomsbury, 2015), p. 4.
14. Sowell, *A Conflict of Visions*, p. 78.
15. Note that there are some complications in my expanded schema, and these are loose tendencies as opposed to fixed rules. For example, John Locke was an empiricist after Aristotle; despite his belief in the *tabula rasa*, his vision is none

the less broadly 'constrained' by human sense perceptions and he thus set a limit on the possibility of human understanding (see Herman, *The Cave and the Light*, pp. 362–4; Sowell, *A Conflict of Visions*, pp. 19, 79). Furthermore, although I have listed Augustine and Calvin as holding the constrained vision, it is common knowledge that both were influenced much more by Plato than by Aristotle.

16. Robert Wright, *The Moral Animal: Why We Are the Way We Are* (London: Abacus, 1994), pp. 5–6.
17. Sowell, *A Conflict of Visions*, p. 82, emphasis in original.
18. Thomas Sowell, *The Quest for Cosmic Justice* (New York: Simon & Schuster, 1999), p. 7. This book completes a trilogy, following *A Conflict of Visions* and *The Vision of the Anointed*, in which Sowell greatly elaborates on the implications of the two visions in politics, economics and social policy.
19. Sowell, *A Conflict of Visions*, p. 34.
20. Haidt, *The Righteous Mind*, p. 372n.
21. Quoted in Holman W. Jenkins, Jr, 'Jonathan Haidt: He Knows Why We Fight', *The Wall Street Journal* (29 June 2012).
22. Jonathan Haidt, 'The Ethics of Globalism, Nationalism and Patriotism', *Minding Nature*, 9:3 (September 2016), pp. 18–24.
23. Milton Friedman, 'Is Capitalism Humane?', lecture delivered at Cornell University, Ithaca, NY (27 September 1977).
24. Ibid.
25. Larry Getlin, 'Inside Modern Iran, where Porn and Prostitution are Rampant', *New York Post* (30 August 2014) , available at <https://nypost.com/2014/08/30/inside-modern-iran-where-porn-and-prostitution-are-rampant/> (last accessed 21 October 2016). 'It is said that, after the Koran, Plato's *Republic* was the favourite book of the founder of Iran's Islamic Republic, Ayatollah Khomeini' (Herman, *The Cave and the Light*, p. 67n).
26. See Sharon S. Brehm and Jack W. Brehm, *Psychological Reactance: A Theory of Freedom and Control* (New York and London: Academic Press, 1981).
27. See Janet Afary and Kevin B. Anderson (eds), *Foucault and the Iranian Revolution: Gender and the Seductions of Islamism* (Chicago: Chicago University Press, 2005).

28. Adam Smith, *The Wealth of Nations*, ed. Edwin Cannan (1776; New York: Modern Library, 2000), p. 485.
29. See Thomas J. DiLorenzo, *The Problem with Socialism* (Washington, DC: Regnery Publishing, 2016), pp. 15–30. See also Scruton, *Fools, Frauds and Firebrands*, pp. 5–7.
30. Sowell, *The Vision of the Anointed*, pp. 65–6.
31. See Kahneman, *Thinking Fast and Slow*, pp. 80–1; Parvini, *Shakespeare and Cognition*, pp. 12–22.
32. Joseph Carroll, John A. Johnson, Catherine Salmon, et al., 'A Cross-Disciplinary Survey of Beliefs about Human Nature, Culture, and Science', *Evolutionary Studies in Imaginative Culture*, 1:1 (2017), pp. 1–32.
33. For an excellent exploration of the relationship between various forms of feminism and evolutionary theory, see Patricia Adair Gowarty (ed.), *Feminism and Evolutionary Biology: Boundaries, Intersections, and Frontiers* (New York and London: Chapman & Hall, 1997).
34. See Jean-François Lyotard, *The Postmodern Condition: A Report on Knowledge*, trans. Geoff Bevington and Brian Massumi (Manchester: Manchester University Press, 1984), pp. 23–4; Michel Foucault, *The Order of Things: Archaeology of the Human Sciences* (1966; London: Routledge, 2002), pp. 375–420; Louis Althusser, 'Philosophy as a Revolutionary Weapon', in *Lenin and Philosophy and Other Essays*, trans. Ben Brewster (1971; New York: Monthly Review Press, 2001), pp. 85–126.
35. See Michael D. Gordin, 'How Lysenkoism became Pseudoscience: Dobzhansky to Velikovsky', *Journal of the History of Biology*, 45:3 (Fall 2012), pp. 443–68; and Sergei Prozorov, *The Biopolitics of Stalinism: Ideology and Life in Soviet Socialism* (Edinburgh: Edinburgh University Press, 2016).
36. E. O. Wilson, *On Human Nature*, rev. edn (1978; Cambridge, MA: Harvard University Press, 2004), p. xv.
37. Matt Vespa, 'Sanders Slams UC Berkeley's Anti-Free Speech Zealots: "It's a Sign of Intellectual Weakness"', *Townhall* (23 April 2017), <https://townhall.com/tipsheet/mattvespa/2017/04/23/sanders-slams-uc-berkeleys-antifree-speech

-zealots-its-a-sign-of-intellectual-weakness-n2317054> (last accessed 27 April 2017).
38. Jonathan Haidt, 'Why Universities Must Choose One Telos: Truth or Social Justice', (21 October 2016), <http://heterodoxacademy.org/2016/10/21/one-telos-truth-or-social-justice/> (last accessed 25 April 2017).
39. Sowell, *The Vision of the Anointed*, p. 5, emphasis in original.
40. Sowell, *A Conflict of Visions*, p. 160, emphasis in original.
41. Anthony Walsh, *Science Wars: Politics, Gender, and Race* (New Brunswick, NJ: Transaction Publishers, 2013), p. 155.
42. See W. D. Hamilton, 'The Genetic Evolution of Social Behaviour', *Journal of Theoretical Biology*, 7:1 (1964), pp. 1–52; Robert L. Trivers, 'The Evolution of Reciprocal Altruism', *The Quarterly Review of Biology*, 46:1 (March 1971), pp. 35–57.
43. Wilson, *On Human Nature*, p. 4.
44. Adam Smith, *The Theory of Moral Sentiments*, ed. Ryan Patrick Henley (1759; New York and London: Penguin, 2010), p. 8.
45. Charles Darwin, *The Descent of Man: Selection in Relation to Sex* (1871; New York and London: Penguin, 2004), p. 159.
46. Ibid. pp. 159, 149, 134.
47. Ibid. p. 142.
48. Ibid. pp. 142–3.
49. Ibid. p. 143.
50. Ibid. p. 143.
51. See Jared Diamond, *Guns, Germs, and Steel: The Fates of Human Societies* (New York and London: W. W. Norton & Co., 1997); Ian Morris, *Why the West Rules – For Now* (London: Profile Books, 2010).
52. See Francis Fukuyama, *The Origins of Political Order: From Prehuman Times to the French Revolution* (London: Profile Books, 2011).
53. See David S. Landes, *The Wealth and Poverty of Nations: Why Some Are So Rich and Some So Poor* (New York: W. W. Norton & Co., 1998).
54. See Thomas Sowell, *Migrations and Cultures: A World View* (New York: Basic Books, 1996), pp. 1–49.

55. Fernand Braudel, *A History of Civilizations*, trans. Richard Mayne (1987; New York and London: Penguin, 1993), p. 120.
56. Diamond, *Guns, Germs, and Steel*, pp. 13, 24, emphasis in original.
57. For a robust discussion of this complex, and often vexed, topic see Andrew M. Colman, 'Race Differences in IQ: Hans Eysenck's Contribution to the Debate in the Light of Subsequent Research', *Personality and Individual Differences*, 103 (2016), pp. 182–9.
58. Thomas Hobbes, *Leviathan*, ed. J. C. A. Gaskin (1651; Oxford: Oxford University Press, 2008), 1.13.1, p. 82.
59. Haidt, *The Righteous Mind*, p. 369.
60. For a neat summary of the dispute, see David Sloan Wilson, 'Richard Dawkins, Edward O. Wilson, and the Consensus of the Many', *This View of Life* (1 January 2015), <https://evolution-institute.org/article/richard-dawkins-edward-o-wilson-and-the-consensus-of-the-many/> (last accessed 25 April 2017). See also Edward O. Wilson, *On Human Nature*, pp. 149–68; and Dawkins, *The Selfish Gene*, pp. 239–44.
61. John Tooby and Leda Cosmides, 'Letter to the Editor of *The New York Review of Books* on Stephen Jay Gould's "Darwinian Fundamentalism" (12 June 1997) and "Evolution: The Pleasures of Pluralism"' (26 June 1997), <http://cogweb.ucla.edu/Debate/CEP_Gould.html> (last accessed 26 April 2017).
62. Dennett, *Darwin's Dangerous Idea*, pp. 264–5.
63. See Andrew Brown, *The Darwin Wars: The Scientific Battle for the Soul of Man* (London: Simon & Schuster, 1999).
64. Maurizio Meloni, 'Moralizing Biology: The Appeals and Limits of the New Compassionate View of Nature', *History of the Human Sciences*, 26:3 (2013), p. 83.
65. Dawkins, *The Selfish Gene*, pp. 5, 181, emphasis in original.
66. Frans de Waal, *The Age of Empathy: Nature's Lessons for a Kinder Society* (New York: Harmony Books, 2009), p. 5.
67. See Dawkins, *The Selfish Gene*, pp. 245–60.
68. Dennett, *Darwin's Dangerous Idea*, pp. 453–60.
69. Wright, *The Moral Animal*, pp. 186–8.

70. Steven Pinker, 'The False Allure of Group Selection', *Edge* (6 June 2012), <https://www.edge.org/conversation/steven_pinker-the-false-allure-of-group-selection> (last accessed 16 May 2017).
71. Marc D. Hauser, *Moral Minds: How Nature Designed Our Universal Sense of Right and Wrong* (New York: HarperCollins, 2006), p. 360.
72. W. M. Muir, 'Group Selection for Adaptation to Multiple-Hen Cages: Selection Program and Direct Responses', *Poultry Science*, 75 (1996), pp. 447–58.
73. David Sloan Wilson, *Darwin's Cathedral: Evolution, Religion, and the Nature of Society* (Chicago: University of Chicago Press, 2002), p. 1.
74. Incidentally, this is not necessarily the case. There are countless cases in history of people risking their lives to escape oppression, and in such cases the moral foundation of liberty outweighs the ultimate harm of death. Likewise, consider Darwin's stories about tribal Native Americans enduring 'horrid tortures' for the sake of courage and fortitude; here, the moral foundations of authority and loyalty outweigh harm.
75. Sam Harris, *The Moral Landscape: How Science Can Determine Human Values* (London: Bantam Press, 2010), pp. 85–91, 180–1.
76. Joshua Greene, *Moral Tribes: Emotion, Reason, and the Gap Between Us and Them* (London: Atlantic Books, 2014), pp. 335–6.
77. Ibid. p. 336.
78. Ibid. p. 339.
79. Sowell, *The Vision of the Anointed*, p. 5.
80. Joseph Carroll, 'Evolutionary Social Theory: The Current State of Knowledge', *Style*, 49:4 (2015), pp. 529–30.
81. Ibid. pp. 531–2.

CHAPTER 3

MORAL PHILOSOPHY IN ENGLAND DURING THE TIME OF SHAKESPEARE

Introduction

In this chapter, I aim to provide a broad overview of the sorts of thinking about ethics that were swirling around during the period in which Shakespeare lived and wrote. I say 'swirling around' for two reasons: first, because I do not think we can make any easy assumptions about the extent to which the philosophical and theological debates of the day carried into everyday life; second, because this is a particularly complicated phase in the history of ethics to navigate. In the early modern period we are dealing with 'a dizzying moment in the history of heterodoxy', in which the 'sudden presence' of newly rediscovered and reinterpreted ideas from the Hellenistic schools competed for primacy at practically the same moment as the Church was facing its largest major schism since 1054.[1] Perhaps as a symptom of this,

> many early modern philosophers were extremely (and sometimes overly) eclectic and their influences were not always straightforward: what looks to us as Stoic in an author could just as well be Epicurean . . . or a mixture of ancient sources, or a modern variant generally influenced by ancient schools without strong commitment to one school.'[2]

Shakespeare's moment in particular – the 1580s to the 1610s – was a time when the intellectual world was still reeling from the twin effects of High Renaissance humanist philosophy and the Protestant Reformation, but had not yet formulated coherent responses to them as the next few decades would, in the form of thinkers such as Francis Bacon, René Descartes, Thomas Hobbes, John Locke and Benedict de Spinoza. It is a moment that histories of moral philosophy have a habit of skipping over: for example, Henry Sidgwick's classic *Outlines of the History of Ethics for English Readers* (1886) does not seem to know what to do with the late sixteenth century and so essentially jumps from Martin Luther to Hugo Grotius's *De jure belli ac pacis* ('On the Law of War and Peace') (1625).[3] It is a move repeated by Bertrand Russell in his towering *History of Western Philosophy* (1946), in which he complains, 'Philosophically, the century following the Reformation is a barren one.'[4] Likewise, in the most comprehensive history of ethics published to date, *The Development of Ethics* (2011), Terence Irwin gets as far as the Reformation, and from the second half of the 1500s can find room only for Francisco Suárez (1548–1617), a theistic natural law theorist in the Thomist tradition.[5] In short, we can characterise Shakespeare's time only as one that took on board a diverse mix of competing philosophical discourses around ethics but did not settle on any one of them and did not significantly add anything new. If the period produced a great moral philosopher, our likeliest candidates are figures who were not philosophers in the conventional sense at all and who did not 'write philosophy': Michel de Montaigne and, in fact, Shakespeare himself.

With this said, I think it is prudent to remember that Shakespeare was not a trained philosopher and therefore to assume that he did not read the vast majority of the philosophical material that I will reference below. The question of what Shakespeare read is, of course, vexed. We must remember that he was, first and foremost, a man of the theatre with significant commercial interests and time commitments; he was a living and working playwright and actor who, as we know, had not attended university. To draw on Ben Jonson's endlessly quoted phrase yet another time: he had 'small Latin, and less Greek'.[6] In 1949, Gilbert Highet put it less charitably: 'He can only string a few schoolbook Latin words together.' Highet believed, with some justification, that Shakespeare loved the classics, but supplemented what he been taught at school 'by reading translations'.[7] He echoes Richard Farmer, who put this more memorably in 1767:

> He remembered perhaps his *school-boy* learning to put the *hig, hag, hog*, into the mouth of Sir *Hugh Evans*; and might pick up in the course of his conversation a familiar word or two in French or Italian: but his *Studies* were most demonstrably confined to *Nature* and *his own Language*.[8]

Leonard Barkan characterises Shakespeare's reading as 'more middle-brow than high-brow; heterodox; philosophically not of the avant-garde; anglo-centric in certain ways'.[9] Therefore, I have generally thought it sensible to assume that if particular philosophical works written in Latin had not been translated into English, Shakespeare almost certainly had not read them. Furthermore, even if certain works had been translated into English, in the absence of direct textual evidence I have erred on the side of assuming that Shakespeare – being busy and probably not possessing the time or the inclination to seek out scholarly works of theology or philosophy – had not read them. But this does not mean, I must stress, that he did not feel the influence of ideas in the cultural ether. It is also, lest we forget, not paramount to have read the work of a particular thinker in order to get the gist of their general stance. If I might draw an analogy in the twenty-first century, for example, how many people outside specialists in political and economic theory have actually sat down and read Milton Friedman's *Capitalism and Freedom* (1962)?[10] I would warrant relatively few; yet, such has been its influence and consequences that we broadly know its arguments and positions – they are ideas that have been 'swirling around' our historical moment.

Renaissance philosophers and theologians saw morality as consisting of three distinct branches following Aristotle: ethics, *Oeconomics* (which was a work then ascribed to Aristotle, which we now believe was written by his student, Theophrastus) and politics. Morality therefore had three domains: 'the individual man was the subject of ethics; the home and its inhabitants were the subject of oeconomics; and the state was the subject of politics'.[11] In this book, I am primarily concerned with the first of these: ethics.

In her still-valuable study *Shakespeare's Tragic Heroes: Slaves of Passion* (1930), Lily B. Campbell begins her account of the fundamental ideas found in 'Moral Philosophy in Shakespeare's Day' by signalling the early-modern indebtedness to previous ages:

> That there was little new in these ideas no one can deny, for they represent something like a composite picture of the works of the most revered ancients and the most influential Schoolmen. Hippocrates, Galen, Aristotle, Plato, Plutarch, Cicero, Quintilian, Seneca, Hesiod, Thomas Aquinas, Augustine – these are the names which are mingled with others of less frequent recurrence in the list of authorities for philosophical ideas throughout the century.[12]

In order to understand the intellectual milieu around ethics in England during the late sixteenth and early seventeenth centuries, it is necessary to trace the four philosophical traditions from antiquity that would strongly influence moral philosophy across Europe in the Renaissance and early modern periods. The first, and most prominent, is Aristotelian virtue ethics. This was revived and reworked in the thirteenth century by the Christian scholastics, most notably Thomas

Aquinas, whose work itself was revived and reworked by Catholic theologians such as Jean Capréolus and Cardinal Cajetan during the fifteenth and early sixteenth centuries. The second tradition that made itself felt during the years of the Renaissance is that of Stoicism, especially Seneca and earlier philosophers whose arguments are summarised in Cicero, such as Zeno of Citium and Chrysippus. The revival of Stoicism in 1580s and 1590s was known as 'neostoicism', a movement led by the Flemish scholar Justus Lipsius, and popularised by the charismatic French lawyer Guillaume du Vair, and which, in England, influenced Joseph Hall. A third tradition to consider is that of scepticism, for which, again, Cicero provides the key sources: particularly his *Academica* (*'On Academic Scepticism'*), which summarises earlier thinkers of the New Academy, such as Arcesilaus and Carneades. Another important influence on Renaissance scepticism was the work of Sextus Empiricus, which unarguably made a greater impact in the fifteenth and sixteenth centuries than it did in the second or third centuries when he lived and wrote. The early modern revival of interest in scepticism is seen most obviously in Francisco Sanches's *Quod nihil scitur* (*'That Nothing Is Known'*) and the essays of Michel de Montaigne. Finally, there is the perennially unpopular figure of Epicurus, caricatured and reviled by the other schools in Hellenistic Greece and generally frowned on in Renaissance Europe. Epicureanism was primarily transmitted through Diogenes Laërtius's *The Lives and Opinions of Eminent Philosophers*, after its translation into Latin in 1430, and Lucretius's poem *De rerum natura* (*'On the Nature of Things'*), after its rediscovery in 1417, and there is an argument to be made that its natural successor was, in fact, Niccolò Machiavelli, a thinker who became reviled in his own right. Although Machiavelli is a political theorist rather than a moral philosopher, his radical assault on Christian ethics in *The Prince* warrants special attention. In the following four sections, I will give some consideration to all four strains of moral thought – virtue ethics, Stoicism, scepticism and Epicureanism – while keeping the question of the possibility of Shakespeare's exposure to these ideas in focus. Each section will follow the same structure:

1. Outline of the basic ethical ideas at stake in the philosophical tradition.
2. Tracing of the impact of this thinking in the late 1500s in England.
3. Consideration of some evidence of this impact in Shakespeare's plays.

After this, in the next chapter, I will consider the impact of both the Protestant Reformation and capitalism on moral thinking in Shakespeare's time.

I

Virtue and Vices: The Aristotelian–Thomist Tradition

As David N. Beauregard has gone to great lengths to show, the prevalent mode of morality in Shakespeare's time was a Christian version of Aristotelian virtue ethics as mediated by Thomas Aquinas.[13] Ethics was seen predominantly through the prism of virtues and vices: broadly speaking, cultivate the former by making them habitual, which will *de facto* help one resist temptation of the latter. The most influential ethical texts in the period after the Bible,[14] therefore, were Aristotle's *Nicomachean Ethics* and Aquinas's *Summa Theologiae*. I will return to the question of the influence of both writers in England during the late 1500s, and of Shakespeare's possible familiarity with them, but first let us consider the ideas at stake in the ethics of both Aristotle and Aquinas.

As was customary in classical ethics, both Aristotle and Aquinas define the ultimate end as, in Cicero's phrase, the *summum bonum*, or 'the highest good'. For Aristotle, this was *eudaimonia*, a word that has no direct English translation. It combines both happiness and a kind of flourishing, and is achieved through excellence of character (moral virtues), which can be brought about by habit of action. Aristotle's ethics are thus egocentric because the agent's personal happiness, contentment and fulfilment are seen as the highest ends: *eudaimonia* is an end in itself and is the highest good. In distinguishing between moral virtues and intellectual virtues (wisdom, knowledge and reason), Aristotle departed from rational deontologists, such as Plato, who maintained that the highest good consisted in reason, pure contemplation of the Idea, which brings us closer to the supreme good: namely, God. The Stoics, meanwhile, saw the essence of the highest good not in *eudaimonia* but in virtue itself, which can be achieved only through reasoned action. The question of what constitutes the *summum bonum* is thus a matter of emphasis: on *eudaimonia* (Aristotle), on reason (Plato) or on virtue (Stoicism). In his Christianisation of Aristotle, Aquinas, in a sense, synthesised and harmonised these different approaches, by blending *eudaimonia* (or 'happiness'), reason and virtue into each other. The highest good in Aquinas is, of course, God, and it can be reached only in the afterlife: when we experience true happiness it is because we are closer to God, who is the rightful object of reason, and who is the author of our very capacity for virtue. For Aquinas, these three categories all presuppose one another as aspects of blissful possession: there can be no happiness that does not presuppose God because he is its ultimate source; there can be no rational argument that does not have God as its end because to deny God in Aquinas's proof is irrational; and there can be no virtuous act that does not admit the nature of God because virtue is the highest achievement of which human beings are capable, and God created us. Therefore, because happiness, reason and virtue amount to aspects of the same thing, Aquinas always maintains that virtues must be treated as ends in themselves, never as means to some ultimate end. To put it crudely, an individual must not act virtuously in the hope of some imagined reward (such as entry to Heaven), but rather do so for virtue's own sake.

I should note that MFT, from which I have drawn in this study, in many ways comes out of the virtue ethics tradition. Consider this passage from Aristotle:

> Anger seems to listen to reason to some extent, but to mishear it, as do hasty servants who run out before they have heard the whole of what one says, and then muddle the order, or as dogs bark if there is but a knock at the door, before looking to see that it is a friend; so anger by reason of the warmth and hastiness of its nature, though it hears, does not hear an order, and so it springs to take revenge.[15]

And how about this from St Thomas?

> For the formal principle of virtue by which we speak now is value in accord with reason. This can be considered in two ways. First, as lying in a judgement of reason; in this way there is one principle virtue, called *prudence*. Secondly, according as reason puts its order into something else, either into what we do, and then we have *justice*, or into what we feel, and then we need two virtues. . . . For the need of putting the rule of reason into our emotions rises from their resistance to reason, and so need a curb, which we name *temperance*. Or they may make us shirk a course of action dictated by reason, through fear of dangers or hardships. Then a person needs to be steadfast and not run away from what is right; and for this *courage* is named.[16]

Both Aristotle and Aquinas recognise that ethical decision-making must always in some sense work with or against natural instincts and intuitions in the individual, which manifest themselves as emotions or 'passions'. We can recognise in this the moral intuitions of MFT and correspondingly James A.

Knapp's 'welling up' of moral conviction in Shakespearean characters. Both philosophers appear to be aware that reason is fighting an uphill struggle for primacy over gut-instinctual intuitions, which it sometimes cannot win. Tillyard argues that 'The battle between Reason and Passion, the commonplace of every age, was peculiarly vehement in the age of Elizabeth.'[17] His assumption that it has been 'the commonplace of every age' is one that we should not dismiss easily because the overwhelming evidence suggests that this recurring theme across different periods in history is a universal symptom of human experience, precisely because this *is* the way we process thought. 'Every age' has made the distinction between emotions and reasoning – what Cicero, drawing on Chrysippus, called 'The Twofold Division of the Mind'[18] – because they are two different cognitive processes. Think of the way, for example, in modern vernacular English or American English we might say 'I lost it' when getting angry. It is a momentary loss of the reasoning function: the rider has failed to keep the unruly elephant in check, which is now crashing about wildly. We can recognise – just as Aristotle, Aquinas and Shakespeare before us – that is a distinctive feature of human behaviour. I will return to this later in my discussion of Seneca's Stoicism.

The recognition that we have such instinctual tendencies, for both Aristotle and Aquinas, is foundational to ethics: we must know what we are in order to know how to act: 'before philosophers could even begin considering how to train man's character, they first had to understand his nature'.[19] As the great historian of philosophy, F. C. Copleston, explains,

> Aquinas emphasized the place and function of reason in moral conduct. He shared with Aristotle the view that it is the possession of reason which distinguishes man from the animals, to whom he is in many ways similar. It is reason which enables him to act deliberately in view of a consciously apprehended end and raises him above the level of purely instinctual behaviour.[20]

I do not think the advocates of MFT would disagree on this point. Theirs is a psychological model that accounts for how we think when making day-to-day moral decisions, rather than an ethics trying to answer the eternal question of how to live the good life. I also do not think that either Aristotle or Aquinas believes that moderating the passions with reason is easy. Neither do they think that passions are always necessarily bad; rather, they condemn, to return to Copleston, 'unhealthy upsurges of emotion, unregulated by reason and tending to lead man into acts contrary to right reason'.[21] It is easy to see why G. K. Chesterton called this 'the philosophy of common sense'.[22]

Before moving on, it is worth mapping Aquinas's conception of virtues and vices, which is surely the most robust account available in Christian theology. The *Summa* consistently conforms to the structure of scholastic disputation: each question begins with several objections before a brief statement from a chosen authority that contradicts the objections (*sed contra*, 'on the contrary'). Aquinas draws on a great many sources for these contrary statements but most often leans on the Bible, 'the Philosopher' (Aristotle), 'The Theologian' (Augustine) or 'The Master' (Peter Lombard). After this argument from authority, Aquinas then proceeds to reply to each objection one by one. Because of this adherence to the scholastic system of argument, Aquinas's ethical system is incredibly rigorous and fully realised. He follows both Ambrose and Augustine in expanding Plato's four cardinal virtues (prudence, temperance, fortitude and justice) by adding St Paul's three theological virtues of faith, love and hope: the 'former, as acquired virtues, lead to natural happiness, but the latter, the theological virtues, as being infused by God (*virtues infusae*), lead to supernatural happiness'.[23] There are thus seven heavenly virtues, which each has various precepts, parts, gifts or associated acts, and corresponding vices. This is a complex and intricate system and any summary necessarily risks reduction. I have listed the seven heavenly virtues below and attempted to note the various correspondences:

1. Faith, which requires and bestows knowledge and understanding.
2. Hope, which bestows fear (which can be good or bad; in this case it is the fear of God and therefore good) and is opposed to despair and presumption.
3. Charity, which bestows wisdom, requires love, joy, peace and mercy, and is opposed to hatred and the vices of sloth and envy.
4. Prudence, which bestows (good) counsel, and is opposed to imprudence, negligence and false resemblance.
5. Justice, which bestows piety, and is opposed to a great many things including crimes of all sorts, back-biting, derision, perjury, lying, dissimulation and hypocrisy, boastfulness, flattery, disobedience and covetousness.
6. Fortitude, which bestows courage, magnanimity (opposed to presumption, ambition and vainglory) and pusillanimity (opposed to deficiency). It is also opposed to (bad, 'disordered') fear, (foolish) fearlessness and daring.
7. Temperance, which bestows abstinence, sobriety and chastity, and is opposed to gluttony, drunkenness and lust.[24]

Aquinas's writing around these seven virtues is not insignificant, comprising the entirety of the *Secunda Secundae*; the Blackfriars edition takes up seventeen volumes, with several virtues getting a book or two each. These categories are, of course, not unique to Aquinas, even though he synthesised and codified them more systematically than any other Christian thinker before or since. Aquinas's *Summa* represents 'an encyclopedic bringing together and harmonizing' of thinking around virtues and vices from Aristotle to the thirteenth century – encompassing even Islamic thinkers such as Avicenna and Al-Ghazali, and the Jewish philosopher Maimonides – which was inherited by the Renaissance.[25] Even if the specific configurations of the virtues and vices we encounter in literature might differ slightly from Aquinas's codification, his comprehensiveness offers a good starting point. As I hope to have shown in the list above, Aquinas considers many more than seven virtues and, indeed, more than seven vices, but the heavenly virtues each represent a type of node around which 'lesser' virtues and vices cluster.

This can lead to some confusion around exactly which vices count as cardinal sins and which do not. For example, even though Gregory the Great folded 'vainglory' into pride when defining his seven deadly sins in 590,[26] Aquinas still devotes a whole question to it; however, he seems to define it as 'the desire of glory' rather its typical associations with excessive pride in one's achievements.[27] The word persists into the sixteenth century and is used extensively in early modern English. Shakespeare, for example, uses it three times: in *Troilus and Cressida* (III, iii, 258–9), *Cymbeline* (4.1.7) and *Henry VIII* (III, i, 126). However, it seems to have been downgraded into being just a common vice rather than a cardinal sin; for example, when Christopher Marlowe depicts the allegorical figures of the seven deadly sins in *Doctor Faustus* (*A-Text*, 2.3.108),[28] it is the embodiment of pride rather than vainglory who appears.

We must also be aware that Aquinas's seven heavenly virtues (combining the four cardinal virtues and three theological virtues) are not the same as the seven contrary virtues, as first depicted in Prudentius's *Psychomachia*.[29] The seven contrary virtues are those specifically designed to combat the seven cardinal sins. These are as follows:

> Humility versus Pride
> Kindness versus Envy
> Abstinence versus Gluttony
> Chastity versus Lust
> Patience versus Wrath
> Liberality versus Greed
> Diligence versus Sloth

Aquinas accounts for each of these in the *Summa*, even though they are not listed as such. But these seven virtues and vices far from exhaust Aquinas's account. We might also add:

Knowledge and Understanding versus 'Blindness of mind'
Hope versus Despair
Hope versus Presumption
Charity versus Hatred
Peace versus Discord / War / Strife / Sedition
Beneficence versus Scandal
Wisdom versus Folly
Prudence versus Imprudence / Negligence
Prudence versus Carnal Prudence ('Prudence of the Flesh')
Friendliness / Affability versus Flattery / Quarrelling
Obedience versus Disobedience
Honesty versus Lying / Dissimilation and Hypocrisy / Boasting
Gratitude versus Ingratitude
Perseverance versus Effeminacy ('Softness') / Pertinacity
Sobriety versus Drunkenness
Temperance versus Insensibility / Intemperance
Clemency versus Cruelty
Meekness versus Anger
Studiousness versus Curiosity

There are more, no doubt. As is traditional in Catholic thinking, Aquinas distinguishes between two categories of sin: venial and mortal. The former is a forgivable – in Aquinas's phrase, 'reparable'[30] – lesser sin that does not necessarily require repentance before death – which is to say that it does not require sacramental confession – while the latter is much more serious, leading to damnation in Hell if the sinner is unrepentant. On some vices he is not entirely clear as to their status as sin; for example, he argues that curiosity 'may be sinful' if the knowledge sought results in bad ends.[31] Curiosity, as a minor vice, can lead to much greater sins. For example, by following curiosity in the pursuit of knowledge we can succumb to pride, a cardinal sin that itself begets many other vices. Aquinas's advice on most of these matters, therefore, is to err on the side of caution; his is a system of moderation that is akin to Aristotle's 'Golden Mean'.

John Wylkinson translated the *Ethics* into English for R. Grafton in 1547 and there is direct evidence that Shakespeare had some familiarity with it, mentioning Aristotle in connection with moral philosophy twice in *Troilus and Cressida*.[32] There is also an echo of the *Ethics* in *King Lear*, when Lear, upon seeing Poor Tom, exclaims, 'Thou art the thing itself' (III, iv, 96–7); Aristotle uses the phrase 'a thing itself'.[33] Aquinas's works, meanwhile, could be readily bought at the booksellers in St Paul's churchyard.[34] Despite this, there is some reason to doubt that Shakespeare read the *Summa*: a work of over 3,500 pages, which, in its modern Blackfriars edition, takes up sixty volumes, and which was not translated into English until 1911. That said, he seems at least conceptually familiar with the Thomistic framework,[35] which was widely disseminated in the period through mediated forms such as Thomas Wright's *The Passions of the Minde in Generalle* (1604) and Sir Walter Raleigh's 'A Treatise of the Soul'.[36]

However, I think we must caution against too readily asserting any centrality for Aquinas, as perhaps Beauregard does in his, at times, narrow focus. It is important to be aware that Aquinas was idiosyncratic among the scholastics, and hardly a typical thinker in his own period. As Peter Adamson makes plain:

> [I]f one were to choose the 13th century thinker whose ideas had most influence in the following century then Duns Scotus, Henry of Ghent – or, for that matter, Albert the Great – would be at least as plausible choices as Aquinas. His emergence as the most indispensable thinker of the middle ages was a slow one and owes something to

Renaissance authors like John Cabrol ['Jean Capréolus'], the fifteenth-century author of a work called *Defences of the Theology of Thomas Aquinas*, and later, in the sixteenth century, the great exponent of Aquinas, Cardinal Cajetan [Thomas de Vio].[37]

Scotus, Henry of Ghent and Albert the Great (who was Aquinas's mentor) were all, in some respect, influenced in their moral thinking by Aristotle, whose complete works had only recently been translated into Latin – his centrality is not in question. But Aquinas's teachings were not canonised by papal authority until Leo XIII in 1879,[38] and we must remember that the Renaissance humanists had a strong distaste for his style of medieval Scholasticism, preferring the more literary dialogues found in Plato or Cicero. None the less, it is true to say – as will be evident throughout my discussion of ethics across all traditions below – that we find Aquinas embedded in the works of practically every major theologian of the period, Catholic or Protestant.

Capréolus (1380–1444) – dubbed by some 'the Prince of Thomists'[39] – was a French Dominican friar who trained in the Order in Paris, but spent most of his life teaching in Toulouse. Cajetan (1469–1534), also a Dominican, lectured at various universities during the 1490s in Northern Italy, most notably in Padua and Milan, before moving to Rome in 1501 to carry out administrative business; he was made a cardinal in 1517 and spent the remainder of his life, until his death in 1534, battling the Protestant Reformation. He travelled to Germany to confront Martin Luther in 1518, and was later a vocal opponent of Henry VIII's attempts to annul his marriage to Catherine of Aragon.[40] While it is unlikely that he would have had knowledge of Capréolus, Shakespeare may well have been aware of Cajetan, not only because of his involvement in Henry VIII's attempted divorce, but also because there is a possible allusion to his altercations with

Luther in *Romeo and Juliet* when Sampson says 'I'll bite my thumb at them' (I, i, 42). Joseph Hunter seems to have been the first to spot this in 1845:

> It ought to have been added in the notes that this is a trait of Italian manners. Thus [Thomas] Fuller, in his *Abel Redivivus* [1651] . . . after relating a conversation between Luther and the messenger of Cardinal Cajetan, says, 'at this the messenger, *after the Italian manner*, *biting his thumb*, went away'.[41]

Although Fuller was writing after Shakespeare, Cajetan's three days in Augsburg were famous across Europe, and it is possible that the detail of the thumb-biting was well disseminated in both Catholic and Protestant circles.

Pausing on a figure like Cajetan illustrates that moral philosophy in early modern England was almost entirely bound up with matters of religion, and we cannot gloss over this by trying to maintain the modern distinction between philosophy and theology. In this period, 'ethics and theology were entangled through institutional structures' and therefore 'the boundaries between ethics and theology' are not 'very clear'.[42] Moral thinking is, in a sense, muddied by both religious upheaval (the Reformation, Protestantism in general) and political realities, which is to say that the official state religious doctrines of England at any given moment might not necessarily reflect the reality of moral thinking 'on the ground'.

Both Capréolus and Cajetan were considered scholastic revivalists, and this revival was taking place in parallel with (and in reaction to) the emergence of Renaissance humanism in France and Italy, but not *necessarily* in England, where Erasmus's repudiation of medieval Scholasticism was gaining purchase at the same time: for example, in the work of Thomas More, who saw Aquinas's incorporation of ideas from Aristotle and others as one of 'corrupting novelties' that had taken Christianity away from the original inspiration of God.[43] Someone like Thomas Wyatt, who had travelled to Italy, had certainly read the work of Cajetan (and translated some of his psalms),[44] but this was an elite discourse, requiring technical knowledge of Latin, French or Italian, and confined to the courts and universities. We cannot, therefore, draw a straight line from Aristotle to Aquinas to 'Renaissance champions' such as Cajetan and expect that this thinking naturally trickled down to the general populace in any straightforward way. We also cannot overlook the fact that this thinking was primarily taking place abroad and not in England. David A. Lines has shown that while Aristotelian ethics formed a core part of university training in England (just as in France, Spain and Italy), the country seems to have produced scant mediations on the subject itself:

> What is astounding . . . is the dearth of works on the *Ethics* produced in England. We know of only one prolusion for the fifteenth century and of the commentaries by John Case, William Temple, and Cuthbert Tunstall for the sixteenth.[45]

Of the writers that Lines names, as a philosophical interpreter of Aristotle, John Case (c. 1556–1600) was undoubtedly the most influential and important, his *Sphaera civitatis* ('*The Sphere of State*') (1588) becoming compulsory reading for students at Oxford by 1590.[46] Sir William Temple (1555–1627; not to be confused with his more famous grandson of the same name) was a logician who worked as a secretary for Robert Devereux, the Earl of Essex, before which he served as the Master of Lincoln Free School and after which he became Provost of Trinity College, Dublin; his work was admired by Philip Sidney. Cuthbert Tunstall (1474–1559), meanwhile, was the Bishop of Durham under Henry VIII, exiled from his original bishopric of London after opposing the divorce from Catherine of Aragon. These authors all wrote their key ethical studies in Latin and they were not translated into English. Therefore, it seems unlikely to me that Shakespeare himself would have been familiar with any of these works, although it is possible he had a general awareness of each of the men themselves. There is an echo of Case in Perdita and Polixenes's disputation on art and nature in *The Winter's Tale* (IV, iv, 86–97), but it is not clear that Case is the source.[47] William Temple was still in Essex's services during the Essex Rebellion of 1601, but claims to have had no knowledge of the plot. We cannot know for sure whether he was present during the Lord Chamberlain's Men's special performance of *Richard II* on the eve of the rebellion, where he might feasibly have encountered Shakespeare in person. In a letter to Robert Cecil, he claims to have been kept in the dark about the rebellion. In the previous weeks, he had been employed primarily as a messenger, and so was not close to Essex's person during this time, which suggests that his presence at the performance was unlikely.[48] Even though Tunstall does not appear in *Henry VIII*, in writing that play, Shakespeare, along with John Fletcher, demonstrates a good working knowledge of the key religious and political figures of the period and it is not unreasonable to think that they would have known about his political exile to Durham.

If Shakespeare was unlikely to have read Capréolus, Cajetan, Case, Temple or Tunstall, even if he had heard of some of them by reputation, it is also stands to reason that Italian works providing Thomist reinterpretations of Aristotelian ethics, such as Donato Acciaiuoli's *Expositio super libros ethicorum* ('Exposition on the Books of Ethics') (1481),[49] were not on his intellectual radar either. In short, I am suggesting that while Shakespeare possessed some knowledge of both Aristotle and Aquinas, he did not engage significantly with the burgeoning body of scholarly work around them – he was a playwright, not Richard Hooker.

In fact, Hooker, perhaps the most famous English theologian of the period, probably deserves special mention. E. M. W. Tillyard famously used his *Of the Laws of Ecclesiastical Polity* (1594–7) as the basis for his argument that Shakespeare and his contemporaries believed strongly in the Great Chain of Being. Indeed, in a characteristic moment of overstatement, for Tillyard, 'It is what everyone believed in Elizabeth's days.'[50] Hooker's writings on the relationship between the Church and State were deeply indebted to Aquinas's idea of law and justice.[51] And the cosmic order that Tillyard outlines in *The Elizabethan World Picture* (1952) is not dissimilar to Aquinas's model, though Tillyard seems to de-emphasise his influence, instead foregrounding St Paul, the Platonic–Augustinian tradition, and the physiology of Hippocrates and Galen, which he argues underpinned the Elizabethan belief in the four passions (pleasure, pain, desire and fear) and four humours (melancholic, phlegmatic, choleric and sanguine). For Aquinas, there were, in fact, eleven passions. Lily B. Campbell provides a neat summary:[52]

Concupiscible	*Irascible*
Love and Hatred	Hope and Despair
Desire and Aversion	Courage and Fear
Joy (or Pleasure) and Sadness (or Grief)	Anger

As Campbell and Beauregard argue, this idea of there being eleven passions, following Aquinas, was popular in Shakespeare's time. But others, such as Rolf Soellner, have insisted that Shakespeare, being a well-known fan of Cicero and Seneca, followed the Stoics in maintaining only four.[53]

Even allowing for qualifications about the extent and centrality of his influence, in the *Summa* Aquinas essentially provides us with an index to the full lexicon of ethical language as it was still being used in 1590s and early 1600s, and extensively in Shakespeare's plays. We can see it in virtually any passage that touches virtues or vices that we care to pluck out. To choose one almost at random, here is Helena in *All's Well That Ends Well*:

> Yet these fixed evils sit so fit in him
> That they take place when virtue's steely bones
> Looks bleak i'th' cold wind withal. Full oft we see
> Cold wisdom waiting on superfluous folly. (I, i, 98–101)

'Evils' here seems to trigger in Shakespeare's imagination its opposite, 'virtue', which in turn triggers a single instance of 'wisdom' and, as per Aquinas, its opposite, 'folly'. Aquinas thus provides a skeleton key with which to unlock the ways in which Shakespeare and his audiences would have understood how various virtues and acts are connected, and indeed how they are juxtaposed with specific vices.

In summary

- The prevalent mode of morality in Shakespeare's time was a Christian version of Aristotelian virtue ethics as mediated by Thomas Aquinas.
- Aristotle views the highest good as the achievement of *eudaimonia*, a combination of happiness and flourishing achieved by excellence in virtue, whereas for Aquinas the highest good is God, which necessarily assumes a combination of virtue, reason and *eudaimonia*, as each by nature implies the other.
- Both Aristotle and Aquinas draw a distinction between reason and emotion, and recognise that the emotions do not always respond to reason and can be difficult to control. In this way, their thinking bears some striking similarities with Moral Foundations Theory.

- In his *Summa Theologiae*, Aquinas systematically outlines the seven heavenly virtues, which act as nodes for many other acts and virtues. He also outlines eleven passions, and many vices, which are subdivided into venial and mortal sins.
- Shakespeare is likely to have read Aristotle and have had some familiarity with the key tenets of Aquinas, but is not likely to have read Jean Capréolus, Cardinal Cajetan, John Case, William Temple or Cuthbert Tunstall because they wrote their key works almost exclusively in Latin as part of an elite discourse.
- Aquinas codifies ideas that were deeply embedded in both medieval and early modern culture, and therefore provides a useful guide to the ethically charged language that we find in Shakespeare's plays.

II

'Inward Government': Stoicism, the Will and the Self

Let us turn now to the Stoics, who were transmitted to the early modern period chiefly by Cicero and Seneca. As I have mentioned, the Stoics believed that the highest (and, indeed, *only*) good consisted in virtue. For them, however, unlike in Aristotle or Aquinas, where action can cultivate habitual virtue, it is possible to achieve virtue only through reason, which is seen as being consistent with the laws of nature and the universe. The actual virtues and vices are not dissimilar from what we saw in Aristotle or Aquinas but the basis for their application is very different. The Stoics were hard materialists, who believed that there was nothing incorporeal in the universe and that matter is ordered by an absolute law of logic. To 'live according to nature', therefore, is to live a rational life. Cicero gives us a good flavour of how the early Stoics proceeded in their rational arguments for virtues in *Tusculanae Disputationes* ('*Tusculan Disputations*'), 'perhaps the most celebrated guide to Stoic philosophy in the sixteenth century':[54]

[A1] Anyone who is courageous is also confident.
[A2] Moreover, anyone who is confident does not become greatly frightened.
[A3] But anyone who is subject to distress is also subject to fear,
[A4] distress is incompatible with courage.
[A5] But no one is wise who is not also courageous.
[A6] Therefore, the wise person will not be subject to distress.

Furthermore,

[B1] Anyone who is courageous must also be great in spirit.
[B2] A person great in spirit must also be indomitable.
[B3] The indomitable person must be able to disregard the circumstances of human life as matters beneath his notice.
[B4] But no one can disregard things that are capable of causing him distress.
[B5] Therefore, the courageous man cannot ever be distressed.
[B6] But everyone who is wise is courageous.
[B7] Therefore, the wise person is not subject to distress.[55]

Thus, the early Stoics relied primarily on syllogism to advance their arguments. In this way, it can appear rather abstract and divorced from real-world practical application. We can see from the above that it is good to be wise and courageous, and bad to be distressed, but there are no real guidelines for how to achieve wisdom or courage. It is an 'all or nothing' proposition.

In their ethics, the Stoics held to two central tenets: first, that the passions – irrational emotions – are mostly always bad because they steer us from the path of reason. As Cicero puts it, they saw emotions as a 'sort of wild lack of self-control'.[56]

Second, they held that everything external to virtue is indifferent – although, somewhat inconsistently, both its founder, Zeno of Citium, and its most influential exponent, Chrysippus, maintain, *contra* Aristo of Chios, that some indifferent things are preferable to others. Here is Cicero on Zeno in *Academica* ('*On Academic Scepticism*'):

> Well, Zeno was not at all the sort of person to hamstring virtue, as Theophrastus had. Quite the reverse: his position was that everything belonging to the happy life depends on virtue alone. He admitted nothing else into the category of goods, and gave the name 'honourable' to the uniform, unique, and only good there was. But, though everything else was neither good nor bad, he claimed that some of these indifferent things were in accordance with nature and others contrary to nature – and in between the latter two he added a further class of intermediates. He taught that those in accordance with nature were worthy of selection and assigned them a degree of value, and the reverse for the opposite class, while those that were neither he left in the intermediate class, to which he ascribed no practical weight at all. But among those worthy of selection or disselection some were assigned considerable value or disvalue; he called the former 'preferred' and the latter 'dispreferred' indifferents.[57]

Thus we get a sort of 'indifference' index ranking things from preferable to undesirable. For example, health is considered to be morally indifferent, but it is preferable to be healthy than to be ill. Cicero himself appears to have thought this absurd, as he outlines in *De Finibus Bonorum et Malorum* ('*On Moral Ends*') in his dialogue with the Stoic, Cato the Younger:

> At least Aristo's [principles] are straightforward; yours are convoluted. Ask Aristo whether he thinks the following are goods: freedom from pain, wealth, health. He will say no.

> Well then, are their opposites evils? Similarly, no. Now ask Zeno the same question, and his reply will be the same. In our astonishment, we ask both philosophers how it will be possible to live a life if we think it makes no difference to us whether we are well or ill, free from pain or in agony, able to stave off cold and hunger or not. Aristo says we will live great and glorious lives, doing whatever we think fit, without sorrow, desire or fear.
>
> 'What does Zeno say?' That Aristo's doctrine is a monstrosity; no life can be lived by such a rule. His own view is that there is a huge, an utterly immense, gap between morality and immorality, but that between all other things there is no difference whatsoever. So far, this is still the same as Aristo. Hear the rest and choke back your laughter if you can.[58]

Cicero is arguing that Zeno's insistence that his 'preferred' categories of indifference are still indifferent is logically contradictory and guilty of mere word-play, or, as he puts it, borrowing a phrase from Accius, 'false-speaking trickery'. He rejects Stoicism in its strictest form, as preached by Aristo, because, when 'you do away with concern for one's health, care of one's household, public service, the conduct of business and the duties of life[, u]ltimately morality itself, which you regard as everything, must be abandoned'.[59] He also disregards Stoicism in its more accepted modified form – as in Zeno or Chrysippus – because, in his view, they are merely reproducing Aristotle's ethics using different words. He therefore sees no real difference between Aristotelian ethics and Stoicism.

Even in these few passages from Cicero that I have quoted, we can see the Roman rhetorical flourishes that were so popular with Renaissance readers, which stand in sharp contrast to the dry, academic style of Aquinas's scholastic disputations. Sixteenth-century taste, with its deep appreciation of rhetoric, was predisposed to prefer dialogues to scholastics, but Cicero's prose tended towards expansion and complexity rather than rhetorical flair; for that, the early modern reader could turn instead to Seneca. As Tobias Reinhardt tells us,

> Seneca is the main representative of so-called Silver Latin prose. The hallmark of his style is a clipped, paratactic way of writing, which depends for its effect on particular stylistic devices like parallelism, antithesis, and the pointed and brilliant one-liner, the epigram or *sententia*.[60]

It is fair to say that this rhetorical flashiness accounts for the enormous popularity of Seneca in early modern England. Indeed, 'during this period, Seneca prevails over Cicero as a stylistic model'.[61]

Seneca, far from sharing Cicero's antipathy towards the Stoics, identified as one as part of the 'Roman Stoa', a Roman revival of Stoicism during the first and second centuries that was at its apex during the reign of Marcus Aurelius c.161–180. Here is Seneca taking Aristotle to task for his apparent defence of anger in his dialogue *De Ira* ('*On Anger*'):

> Aristotle stands as the defender of anger and forbids that it be cut out of us: it is, he says, the spur to virtue, and, if the mind is robbed of it, it cannot defend itself and becomes lazy and indifferent to great endeavours. And so we must first of all prove how loathsome and savage a thing anger is, and set before the eyes what a monster a man is when he rages against another man, with what violence he rushes on to wreak destruction, while bringing it on himself, and seeks to wreck what can only be sunk if he, too, sinks in the process. So, tell me, will someone call a man sane who, as if caught up in a tempest, does not walk but is driven along, and takes as his master a furious demon, a man who does not entrust his revenge to another but executes it himself, and so becomes a savage in thought and deed, the executioner of those persons he holds most dear and destroyer of the things whose loss will soon make him weep? Is this a

passion that anyone can assign as a helper and companion to virtue, when it makes havoc of the resolutions essential to virtue achieving anything?[62]

Seneca plainly does not think that anger is a good thing, but then – if you recall the passage I quoted earlier – neither does Aristotle. The key difference is that Aristotle saw anger, and other emotions, as flaring up in spite of our efforts to control them with reason. They are in some sense involuntary, or rather undeliberate – that is, 'not chosen' – but Seneca, conforming to a core Stoic doctrine, maintains that an emotion such as anger involves the assent of the moral agent and therefore is only ever a voluntary act.

For Seneca, the question of self-control comes down to one of his key concepts: the will. Consider his remedy for anger:

> Do battle with yourself: if you have the will to conquer anger, it cannot conquer you. Your conquest has begun if it is hidden away, if it is given no outlet. Let us conceal the signs of it, and as far as is possible let us keep it hidden and secret. This will cost us a great deal of trouble (for it is eager to leap out and inflame the eyes and alter the face), but if it is allowed to display itself outside ourselves, it is then on top of us. In the lowest recess of the heart let it be hidden away, and let it not drive, but be driven. Moreover, let us change all its symptoms into the opposite: let the expression on our faces be relaxed, our voices gentler, our steps more measured; little by little outer features mould inner ones.[63]

This psychological notion of a struggle within the self, of the will battling with a passion such as anger, is characteristically Senecan and is missing in Aristotle and the earlier Stoics, but it is present in Aquinas, who inherited the concept from Augustine.[64] In Aristotle, as we saw, anger is something that a person experiences and, once it takes hold, reason is not enough to extinguish its flames. Seneca's moral compass, meanwhile, is one of near-total self-determination; as he puts it elsewhere, 'Whatever can make you a good man is there in you. What do you need to be a good man? Willpower.'[65] Thus we can see in Seneca's ethics something approaching the sort of advice we might find in modern self-help books. His emphasis is always on mental self-improvement and self-shaping. Seneca also seems to us much more practical and realistic than the early Stoics such as Zeno, who, as we have seen, seemed in their abstract way to wish for an impossible utopia of perfect sages but offered few guidelines for achieving it. In contrast, Seneca lived in the real world. For example, the lines I have just quoted come from a letter he writes in a quiet moment while everyone else is attending a boxing match. There is, just as in Shakespeare, a real situatedness in Seneca's treatment of morality, and we can appreciate why aspects of his version of Stoicism might have been attractive to people in late sixteenth-century England.

Unsurprisingly, therefore, just as Beauregard has made strides to claim Shakespeare for the Aristotelian–Thomist tradition, Charles and Michelle Martindale have tried to show that he was influenced by Stoicism, rejecting claims that he was hostile to it.[66] As they point out, he was certainly aware of the tradition; for example, as in *Taming of the Shrew*, when Tranio says, 'while we do admire / This virtue and this moral discipline / Let's be no stoics nor no stocks, I pray' (I, i, 29–31). Likewise in *Hamlet*, when Horatio says, 'Give me a man / That is not passion's slave' (III, ii, 71–2). According to the Martindales, Stoicism was admired by many in the period:

> [T]he treatise *De Constantia* by Julius Lipsius (1547–1606) was a major influence from the date of its publication in 1584. The cultivation of detachment, of freedom from passion, led to an admiration for people whose attitudes were unwavering in viewpoint, attitude or mood, who despised the vicissitudes of Fortune, showed equanimity in the face of death, disregarded the changing fashions of the world

and possessed an unshakable inner serenity. This idea of personality – repellent to many today – could be presented as something moving or thrilling.[67]

With its emphasis on self-control, Stoicism was fundamentally compatible with Christianity, especially in its Augustine form. The 'accepted view' is that English Stoicism 'reached a height of popularity and influence during the age of Shakespeare'.[68]

In Thomas James's preface to Guillaume du Vair's *The Moral Philosophie of the Stoicks* (1598), a French treatise that he had 'englished for the benefit of them which are ignorant of that tongue', he wrote:

> Christians may profit by the Stoicks . . . Philosophie in generall is profitable vnto a Christian man, if it be well and rightly vsed: but no kinde of philosophie is more profitable and neerer approching vnto Christianitie (as S. *Hierome* saith) then the philosophie of the Stoicks.[69]

One example of a Christian following James's advice can be found in the works of Joseph Hall (1574–1656), whose advocacy of Stoicism was such that Thomas Fuller, in his *History of the Worthies of England* (1662), reported that he 'was commonly called our English Seneca'. Fuller gives a pithy assessment of his output: 'very good in his *Characters*, better in his *Sermons*, best of all in his *Meditations*'.[70] Although, as Fuller suggests, his best-known work is *Mediations and Vowes* (1605), we can get a better measure of his moral vision in *Two Guides to a Good Life* (1604), in which he gives us a clear view of his conception of virtue:

> Virtue, is a proportion and vprightnesse of life agreeable to reasonne, and consisteth in mediocritie, as Vice doth in excesse or defect: It is neither subject to Fortune, sclander, sicknesse, ol[d]-age, aduersitie, or tyrannie. Of vertues there are two kindes, contemplatiue and morrall: contemplatiue, which is a quiet and setled beholding of all those good things

gathered together by reason, and approoued by iudgement: and morrall, which consisteth in the practise and dispersing of those good thinges to the benefite of humane societie; so that it is not sufficient to thinke well, but to doe well. And the bodie of vertue is of that nature, that it must be complet, not found of one lim[b], and lame of another.[71]

We can see here how Hall has taken key aspects of traditional Stoicism – seeing virtue in reason and contemplation, demanding total rather than partial virtue – and blended them with elements of the Aristotelian–Thomist tradition, such as seeing vice in excess and virtue in positive action.

Hall departs from the Stoics in his view of the passions, in that he does not see them as being necessarily bad:

> I would not bee a Stoick to haue no Passions; for that were to ouerthrow this inward gouernme[n]t, God hath erected in me; but a Christian, to order those I haue: and for that I see that as in commotions, one mutinous person drawes on more, so in passions, that one m[a]kes way for the extremitic of another (as excesse of loue causes excesse of grie[f]e, vpon the losse of what we loued): I will doo as wise Princes vse, to those they misdoubt for faction, so holde them downe, and keepe them bare, that their very impotencie & remisnesse [s]hall affoorde me security.[72]

Hall's idea of an 'inward government' and a 'holding down' of excessive and extreme emotions echoes Seneca's belief in the power of the will. There is in this too, just as in Seneca, an admission that we have to live in the real world.

It is evident, then, how deeply Stoicism touched England in the 1590s and early 1600s – undoubtedly part of the moral fabric during this period, it held 'considerable currency'[73] – and indisputably it is registered in Shakespeare's plays. But as we have seen so far, this fabric has the quality of a patchwork quilt rather than a uniform cloth. In a thinker like Joseph Hall we find, as befitting the manner of Renaissance eclecticism, a mingling of ideas from different traditions.

> **In summary**
> - The Ancient Stoics, such as Zeno of Citium and Chrysippus, see virtue as its own end, which could be achieved only through reason.
> - Accordingly, they view all passions as bad and seek to live by reason alone.
> - They argue that everything outside of virtue is morally indifferent, although, contrary to Aristo, they maintain that some things – for example, good health – are preferable to others.
> - Cicero sees this as contradictory and argues that it is mere word-play; in his view the Stoics reproduced Aristotelian virtue ethics using different language.
> - Seneca updates and adds to the early Stoics by being more situated in lived experience (and therefore more realistic); he adds the concept of the will, which can be used to battle against strong emotions, such as anger.
> - Seneca argues that virtue can be achieved through sheer willpower; his is an inward philosophy of self-control and self-determination.
> - Joseph Hall, who wrote at the same time as Shakespeare, takes elements from the Ancient Stoics, Seneca, Aristotle and Aquinas; his ethics represent a kind of Renaissance eclecticism.
> - Stoicism was thus, in various ways, embedded in the ethical milieu of England in the 1590s and early 1600s.

III

'Suspension of Judgement': The Revival of Scepticism

I will turn now to consider another powerful philosophical current in the period: scepticism. Although scepticism seems generally more concerned with epistemology than with ethics, it is directly relevant to us in at least two ways: first, even though it rejects most known moral systems, it is itself a covert form of ethics. It might appear to maintain that there is no single answer to the question 'what is the best

Moral Philosophy [101]

way to live?', but it does, in fact, provide one: most of its exponents argue that the sceptical life results in a form of tranquillity (*ataraxia*), in contrast to the perpetual mental turmoil of dogmatism.[74] In this way, it has an ethical end: the best way to live is to achieve *ataraxia*. Second, it is relevant because it is possible that, in their apparent refusal to judge, Shakespeare's plays themselves implicitly endorse a sceptical outlook. In this section, I will explain the key tenets of Academic scepticism as mediated by Cicero, Pyrrhonian scepticism as mediated by Sextus Empiricus, and the 'new scepticism' of the late 1500s as represented by Michel de Montaigne, before considering again whether Shakespeare can be aligned with this philosophical approach to ethics.

In antiquity, after Arcesilaus took over Plato's Academy c.266 BC there was a prolonged period of Academic scepticism in the mainstream of Greek philosophy. The Academic sceptics enjoyed nothing more than attacking the key arguments of the Stoics, to whom they were entirely opposed. Once again, we can count on Cicero, who tended to side with the sceptics against the Stoics, for an account. Here he is, in reply to his interlocutor Lucullus:

[1] If the wise person ever assents to anything, he will sometimes hold an opinion;
[2] but he will never hold an opinion;
[3] so he won't ever assent to anything.

Arcesilaus approved this argument, since he supported the first and second premises. Carneades sometimes gave as his second premise the concession that the wise person would sometimes assent; and from this it followed that the wise person would hold opinions (a conclusion you won't accept, and rightly, in my view). But the Stoics, with Antiochus in agreement, thought that the first premise – if the wise person were to assent, he would hold opinions – was false: they thought that he could distinguish false from true and inapprehensible from apprehensible impressions.[75]

The debate between the Stoics and Academics is largely epistemological: it is concerned with the question of what can be known. The Stoics hold that true knowledge is possible, whereas the Academics argue that there is always reason to doubt and therefore it is impossible. Because true knowledge is not possible, for the Academic the only wise course of action is what Cicero calls, following Carneades, the 'suspension of all assent', or judgement, also known as *epokhê*.[76] Although the Academics admit probabilities for the practical purpose of living, in the final analysis they can be sure of nothing – not even of that very fact.

Scepticism somewhat fell out of fashion during the medieval era. Generally, Scholasticism was not predisposed to epistemological questions, although there are some traces of scepticism; for example, in William of Ockham.[77] The ideas of Pyrrho of Elis (360–270 BC), the mysterious founder of scepticism, 'were practically unknown in the Middle Ages'.[78] But this was to change in 1562, when Henri Estienne translated the major work of Sextus Empiricus (160–210), *Outlines of Pyrrhonism*, which simultaneously summarised Pyrrho's thinking while offering an alternative strand of scepticism to that known from the Academics, and somewhat side-lining as the chief source Cicero's *Academica*, and Diogenes Laërtius's *The Lives and Opinions of Eminent Philosophers* (which had been available in Latin since the 1430s).[79] A translation of Sextus's *Against the Professors* by Gentian Hervant followed in 1569. These translations were to have an explosive impact in the 1570s. Widely read among the literary and intellectual elites in Europe, the Pyrrhonian form of scepticism was first used as a weapon of argumentation in the theological wars during the period of the Counter-Reformation by both Catholics and Protestants. The intellectual foundations of European thought had been rocked by several seismic events: the discovery of the New World, Nicolaus Copernicus's advances in astronomy, Martin Luther and the outbreak of Protestantism, the dissemination of Machiavelli's *The Prince* and, as we have seen, the revival of many competing systems of ancient thought. As Richard H. Popkin puts it:

> In such a ferment – with the intellectual world losing its established footing, on all sides and with competing claims and beliefs on all sides – the revival of ancient Greek scepticism was an attempt to focus the problems, pose a universal 'sceptical crisis', and force men like Francis Bacon and René Descartes to look for new foundations for the entire intellectual world.[80]

In 1576 came the publication of two key works of the 'new scepticism': Frances Sanches's *Quod nihil scitur* ('*That Nothing is Known*') and Michel de Montaigne's *An Apology for Raymond Sebond*. For our purposes, Montaigne is more directly relevant to Shakespeare than Sanches.

However, before moving to Montaigne, let us take a look at how Sextus Empiricus moves beyond the Academic sceptics. The first and most striking way is that Sextus – perhaps because he was a practicing physician – is content to take certain things for granted: let us say, for example, the appearance of one's own hand. In the strictest sense, a sceptic in Sextus's vein would say, 'it seems to me that I have a hand' – the observation ends with the description. Sextus is not ambiguous about this:

> When we say that Sceptics do not hold beliefs, we do not take 'belief' in the sense in which some say, quite generally, that belief is acquiescing in something; for Sceptics assent to the feelings forced upon them by appearances – for example, they would not say, when heated or chilled, 'I think I am not heated (or: chilled)'. Rather, we say that they do not hold beliefs in the sense in which some say that belief is assent to some unclear object of investigation in the sciences; for Pyrrhonists do not assent to anything unclear.[81]

They do not reject 'what is apparent'. The problem starts when these things begin to be explained. And, for Sextus, scepticism consists in attacking the explanations given for such phenomena by philosophers and scientists, which he consistently labels as 'Dogmatists', who 'in the proper sense of the word think they have discovered the truth'.[82]

Sextus – just like the Academic sceptics – advocates the suspension of judgement, but following Aenesidemus, who revived Pyrrho in the first century, outlines ten modes through which Pyrrhonists conclude that this is the only course of action; then, following Agrippa the Sceptic, he offers 'the five grounds of doubt'. He offers a truly exhaustive account; I will do my best to summarise these modes as succinctly as possible:

The Ten Modes

1. From differences among animals.
2. From differences among human beings.
3. From differences among the senses.
4. Contrasting circumstances.
5. Contrasting positions, distances and places.
6. Contrasting mixtures.
7. Contrasting qualities and compositions.
8. From relativity.
9. According to constant or rare occurrence.
10. Contrasting ways of life, customs, laws, myths and dogmatic assumptions.[83]

Paul Woodruff provides a neat summary:

> The first seven Modes show the relativity of perceptual appearances in various ways; these are summed up in the Eighth Mode, Relativity, which may also go beyond the seven to argue for the relativity of all things. The Ninth and Tenth modes deal with issues of value.[84]

We can recognise in this something approaching modern cultural relativism; however, in moral terms, we should not mistake it for the liberal value of pluralism, described by Isaiah Berlin, in which individuals are faced with difficult choices between ultimate ends (that foreclose alternative ends).[85] To assent to value pluralism entails admitting that there are, in fact, (valid) absolute claims, which the sceptic would *de facto* deny; faced with such a choice, the sceptic should make no choice. I think this distinction is important to grasp. Modern cultural relativism is implicitly a doctrine of toleration that accepts that others will believe in whatever they will (think back to my quotation from Patti Smith in Chapter 1), but the Pyrrhonist overtly doubts any such belief and, if true to their philosophy, will necessarily be moved to argue against it. This is not to say that the Pyrrhonist is intolerant of others (despite their indifference to any form of settled or dogmatic position), but rather that we should not anachronistically see their relativism as a mark of toleration.

Next, here the five doubts of Agrippa:

The Five Modes

1. The mode deriving from dispute.
2. The mode throwing one back *ad infinitum* (infinite regress).
3. The mode deriving from relativity.
4. The hypothetical mode.
5. The reciprocal (circular) mode.[86]

It might seem here that we are not a long way from Descartes – surely this is the mental toolkit he uses in *Discourse on the Method* (1637) – but this would be to misrecognise the difference between the Pyrrhonists and their most extreme successor. For Sextus, true to the foundations of scepticism, these modes are enough to resolve in the 'tranquillity' of suspension of judgement: 'those who make no determination about what is good and bad by nature neither avoid nor pursue anything with intensity; and hence they are tranquil'.[87] Scepticism is thus an end in itself but, for Descartes, it is only a means, the vehicle by which he arrives at his famous *cogito ergo sum*, a new 'foundation' for knowledge.[88] Furthermore, the force and intensity of Cartesian scepticism are the very opposite of tranquil; they are disquieting. Thus, we can see how Cartesian scepticism 'is methodologically (rather than ethically) conceived',[89] and by the same token Pyrrhonism is ethically rather than methodically conceived. As I pointed out in the introduction to this section, scepticism – at least as practised by both the Academics and the Pyrrhonists – is a form of ethics.

Let us move forward now to Shakespeare's time. Before we get to the looming figure of Montaigne, we must pause to ask a question: was Shakespeare familiar with Sextus Empiricus or, indeed, with the concept of scepticism at all? As with most questions pertaining to Shakespeare's reading, we do not know for sure, and the answer depends on who you ask. Graham Bradshaw, famously hostile to historicism, simply sidesteps the question in his still brilliant and broadly convincing *Shakespeare's Scepticism*.[90] For Sarah Hutton, apparently free of the agenda that a thesis can often impose, 'the writings of Sextus Empiricus do not appear to have been well known in Tudor England'.[91] John D. Cox, meanwhile, points out that 'Shakespeare does not use the word "skeptic" or its derivatives . . . It seems unlikely that a poet so sensitive to words would have ignored "skeptic" had he known it and understood its importance.'[92] For those who want to make Shakespeare's plays 'exhibit the effects of a potent philosophic skepticism verging upon nihilism', as Millicent Bell does, we can perhaps detect a touch of hope for the playwright's closer personal connection:

> Those meetings at the Mermaid Tavern in which Shakespeare lifted a tankard with Ben Jonson and others, including Raleigh, may be only legend, but Shakespeare could have seen Raleigh's translation of the *Hypotyposes* of Sextus Empiricus. It was circulating – also in manuscript – as early as 1591, when one of the 'university wits' Shakespeare undoubtedly knew, Thomas Nashe, read it. The clever young men who caught the latest word on the wind would have been eager to get a look at Montaigne – a writer who knew Sextus but went beyond him in brilliance and daring – as soon as the translation was heard of.[93]

Whether or not Shakespeare had read Sextus Empiricus or knew the word 'scepticism', two things are not in doubt. The first is that, as many critics including A. C. Bradley, A. P. Rossiter, Graham Bradshaw, Millicent Bell, Hugh Grady, Andy Mousely and John D. Cox have pointed out, his plays often enact the 'suspension of judgement'; he often gives us the arguments but always gives us reasons to doubt them, and then does not take sides or give us the satisfaction of didactic resolution.[94] Of this, as per the second section of Chapter 1, I am entirely convinced. This does not mean that Shakespeare was a fully card-carrying sceptic, however – as we have seen, his plays also strongly register both virtue ethics and stoicism. It is possible to see the 'suspension of judgement' as part of his *mimesis*. The second is that Shakespeare read Montaigne, whose works were translated by John Florio in 1603, and the evidence for this is incontrovertible, registered as it is in plays such as *King Lear* and *The Tempest*. Some have tried to push the date of Shakespeare's reading back to 1600 or even earlier on the grounds that Florio's manuscripts were in circulation well before publication.[95]

In Montaigne, I think we find something missing in earlier sceptics: namely, a natural sympathy for the human condition. According to Diogenes Laërtius, such was Pyrrho's indifference to the world around him that he would not even move out of the way of wagons, or change his direction if he was near the edge of a cliff; his followers would have to intervene to save him.[96] It is difficult to imagine Montaigne carrying on in this way. As we have seen, in its pursuit of *ataraxia*, there is an ethical charge to Pyrrhonian scepticism, but I think in Montaigne the moral force is coming from a quite different place:

> Presumption is our natural and original infirmity. *Of all creatures man is the most miserable and frail, and therewithal the proudest and disdainfulest.* Who perceiveth and seeth himself placed here, amidst their filth and mire of the world, fast tied and nailed to the worst, most senseless,

and drooping part of the world, in the vilest corner of the house, and farthest from the heavens'-cope, with those creatures, that are the worst of the three conditions. And yet dareth imaginarily place himself above the circle of the moon, and reduce heaven under his feet. It is through vanity of the same imagination, that he dare equal himself to God, that he ascribeth divine conditions unto himself, that he selecteth and separateth himself from out of the rank of other creatures.... How knoweth he by the virtue of his understanding the inward and secret motions of beasts? By what comparison from them to us doth he conclude the brutishness ascribed unto them?

When I am playing with my cat, who knows whether she have more sport in dallying with me, than I have in gaming with her? We entertain one another with mutual apish tricks, if I have my hour to begin or to refuse, so hath she hers.[97]

Although this is recognisably an argument derived from scepticism, note the morally charged language here. He accuses mankind of vices that we saw in Aquinas: pride, vanity and presumption. There is, therefore, also a corresponding appeal to humility and magnanimity. At some level this is an assent to the belief that pride, vanity and presumption are undesirable qualities. I do not think that we can call Montaigne a true sceptic in the Pyrrhonian sense because, even in expressing his scepticism, he seems unable to exercise the suspension of judgement, and in this case moral judgement. Indeed, he seems aware of this himself: 'I see the Pyrrhonian philosophers, who can by no manner of speech express their general conceit; for they had need of a new language. Ours is altogether composed of affirmative propositions.'[98] Montaigne's suspension of judgement – similar to the polyvalent perspective of Shakespeare's drama – comes not in the particular instance of any statement, but rather, as Zahi Anbra Zalloua has argued to convincing effect,[99] in the formal contradictions of the essay taken as a whole, in its refusal of coherent structure, in its rambling digressions and apparent inability to come to any resolution.

Readers of Shakespeare will have already noted the striking similarity of the Montaigne passage I quoted to Isabella's speech in *Measure for Measure*:

> But man, proud man,
> Dressed in a little brief authority,
> Most ignorant of what he's most assured –
> His glassy essence – like an angry ape
> Plays such fantastic tricks before high heaven
> As makes the angels weep, who with our spleens
> Would all themselves laugh mortal. (II, ii, 118–24)

Although I am not the first to point out the similarity of the sentiments expressed by Montaigne and Shakespeare in these passages – a distinction that it seems we can attribute to Elizabeth Robbins Hooker in 1902[100] – I have not been able to find any commentary on the close proximity of the 'apish tricks' in Florio's Montaigne to Shakespeare's 'angry ape' that 'plays such fantastic tricks'. Whether this likeness is because Shakespeare wrote Isabella's speech with Montaigne's essay fresh in his mind, or simply by dint of coincidence, I think it is self-evident that the two writers have a natural affinity: an apparent love of bombastic rhetorical strategies undercut by the refusal to offer the certainty of final resolution; they share an inbuilt sense of sceptical doubt that serves to strip away the surety of the single narrow reading.[101] For Bertrand Russell, this is a consequence of their historical moment:

> And so the curiosity of the Renaissance.... Such a cataract of new facts overwhelmed men that they could, at first, only be swept along with the current.... Montaigne and Shakespeare are content with confusion: discovery is delightful, and system is its enemy.[102]

Here, I think, Russell gets it both right and wrong. He is surely correct that the sceptical disposition we find in the late 1500s and early 1600s is the result of a vast confluence of competing systems of ideas and philosophical discourses all bearing down on a moment in history in which traditional certainties had been shattered, and orthodoxies challenged in ways that were previously unthinkable. But I am not sure that 'content with confusion' is the right way to put it; rather, Montaigne and Shakespeare have every reason to be uncertain, and every reason to doubt all of the absolutist discourses ('dogmas') that different groups are trying to sell them.

In summary

- The Academic sceptics, such as Arcesilaus and Carneades, argue that true knowledge is impossible because there is always a reason to doubt.
- Because of this, they maintain that the wisest course of action is *epokhê* (the suspension of judgement, the refusal to have opinions), which achieves *ataraxia* (tranquillity).
- The Pyrrhonian sceptics (named after their founder, Pyrrho of Ellis), meanwhile, accept 'what seems apparent', but will not assent to any explanations derived from dogmatism.
- The Pyrrhonists develop a number of 'modes' with which to cast doubt on any argument. These include relativising the apparent reliability of sense perceptions in various ways, and the apparent certainty of cultural norms and doctrines; demonstrating how most arguments, when pressed hard enough, can either be disputed, or else succumb to infinite regress, relativity, unfounded hypothesis or circularity.
- Michel de Montaigne, influenced by the Pyrrhonists after reading Sextus Empiricus, uses various sceptical modes to attack the hubris of mankind and the edifices it has built up around itself.
- Montaigne is an influence on Shakespeare, even though scholars disagree over the extent of this. They share a similarity in that both writers demonstrate a sceptical 'suspension of judgement' in their works.

IV

Epicureanism: From Lucretius to Machiavelli

During my account of ethics in Shakespeare's time thus far, I have scarcely mentioned the influence of one of the major Hellenistic schools: that of Epicurus (341–270 BC), whose ideas were transmitted to the Renaissance, in part, by Lucretius's poem *De rerum natura* ('*On the Nature of Things*') (56 BC), which had been rediscovered in 1417. For Epicurus, the *summum bonum*, or highest good, is not *eudaimonia* (as in Aristotle), virtue (as in Stoicism) or in the suspension of judgement (as in scepticism), but in pleasure. Here pleasure is, in fact, the *only* good. As in scepticism, the ultimate end for Epicurus's ethics is achieving *ataraxia*, a state of tranquillity – or rather, imperturbability, the absence of mental disturbances as well as physical pain (*aponia*) – but the means of reaching it are different.

Epicureanism should not be misunderstood, as it so frequently has in the popular conception across history, as hedonistic pleasure-seeking, but rather, as is more often the case, the careful avoidance of pain. For example, while we get a modicum of sensual pleasure from eating rich foods, doing so can result in indigestion and therefore greater pain, and so Epicurus advocates basic consumption: 'content with water and plain bread', stretching to some cheese if he needs to entertain a feast.[103] Seneca, adapting Epicurus, argued:

> For water and barley groats or a crust of barley bread is not a pleasant thing but it is the greatest pleasure to be able to find pleasure even in these foods and to have brought oneself to the level which no unjust act of fortune can snatch away.[104]

A meagre crust of bread when we are very hungry can bring greater pleasure than the richest of foods eaten every day. In this way, Epicureanism 'was not designed to stimulate the appetite to desire more but rather to train it to be satisfied with less'.[105]

Likewise, while power gives pleasure by bestowing a certain amount of self-satisfaction for those who wield it, the combined weight of responsibility and expectation induces greater anxieties (a threat to *ataraxia*), and so Epicurus advocates avoiding political and public offices. To use his phrase, 'The wise man will not go into public life, unless something interferes.'[106] Thus, according to Diogenes, 'from an excess of modesty, [Epicurus] voided affairs of state'.[107] So it is too, with wealth: riches can help one seek pleasure, but the prospect of its loss produces a greater amount of anxiety – this is something we can readily recognise today, in the pithy phrase of the late rapper, The Notorious B.I.G.: 'Mo' Money, Mo' Problems'.[108] Epicurus thus cautions against the accumulation of wealth and advocates instead living on moderate means. Again, in his phrase, 'Happy poverty is an honourable condition.'[109] In each case, we can see that a true Epicurean, far from living a life of hedonistic excess, instead tends to exercise restraint and moderation. Epicurus reasoned that exposure to great pleasures – which might be facilitated by power or wealth – has the potential to create in us needs that cannot be fulfilled. We moderns can readily recognise this notion of a 'created need' in advertising; as Bob Dylan once wrote, 'Advertising signs they con / You into thinking you're the one / That can do what's never been done / That can win what's never been won.'[110]

Such are the austerity and moderation of the Epicurean life that it is somewhat surprisingly reminiscent of its rival school, Stoicism. Indeed, Seneca seemed to think that many aspects of Epicureanism and Stoicism are compatible and thereby incorporated Epicurus's teachings into his version of Stoicism, even though the two schools were seen to be fundamentally at odds. He justified drawing on Epicurus many times on the basis that 'it is my custom to visit the opposite camp, not as a deserter but as a spy'.[111] He saw it as a form of philosophical 'plundering'. Just because he was not an Epicurean, it did not mean that Epicurus did not sometimes speak the universal truth: 'You may perhaps ask me why I take so many fine sayings from Epicurus rather than our own school. But why do you think these sayings belong to Epicurus and are not common to us all?'[112] Ironically, Seneca quotes Epicurus far more often than he does the founder of Stoicism, Zeno. For Seneca, the wisdom of Epicurus seems to falter only at the final hurdle: in insisting that virtue should be pursued for the pleasure it brings, rather than as an end in itself.

Epicurus's ethical teachings drew the ire of the other schools, and later Christians, because of three controversial beliefs: first, he maintained that the gods, having achieved *ataraxia*, are entirely indifferent to human life, and would not deign to concern themselves with our affairs by intervening in them. It follows, therefore, that we need not have anxiety about the gods because they are not 'watching'. Second, there is therefore no divine plan for the universe: which is to say, Epicurus opposed the notion of providence. Third, he argued that we should not fear death because there is nothing after death (annihilation). Since we cannot experience death, we have no reason to fear it. There is also no afterlife, so the only thing that matters is what we do on Earth. In Book III of *De rerum natura*, Lucretius offers over forty arguments against fearing death. For Lucretius, the fear of death is at the root of many of mankind's ills: 'This man it persuades / To break bonds of friendship and another / To violate honour' (3.40–2). It causes people to 'make wealth for themselves / And heap up riches, murder upon murder / Piling in greed' (3.70–2). If only we could free ourselves of the crippling fear of death, which we cower from 'like children in the dark' (3.87),[113] we would conquer the most nagging and constant of all anxieties and finally reach *ataraxia*.

The insistence on a non-interventionist God in a non-providential universe, and especially the refusal of the afterlife, led to 'the widespread and persistent conviction' among Christians that Epicurus 'and his disciples were atheists'.[114] It was for this that Dante placed Epicureans in the sixth circle of Hell in *The Inferno*: 'Epicurus and his followers have their cemetery in this part, who make the soul die with the body' (10.13–14).[115] But this did not mean that all Renaissance philosophers *de facto* dismissed Epicurus out of hand; Petrarch, for example, said he was 'a philosopher unpopular with the multitude but considered great by the wise men'.[116] Some, who actually deigned to read Epicurean writings, tried to think seriously through his ethics. Agostino Nifo conducted one of the most vehement critiques of Epicureanism in *De Amore Liber Secundus* ('*The Second Book of Love*') (1549):

> Epicurus thus offered something for everyone: he prohibited the indolent from participating in politics, the slothful from exercising and the cowardly from fighting; the irreligious were told that there was no divine providence; and the miserly were taught that they could live on bread and water.[117]

Nifo thus attacks Epicurus through the Thomist prism of virtues and vices: his is a system that rewards vice, so how can it be virtuous? Viewed cynically, as Cicero was also inclined to view him, Epicurus provides convenient and robust excuses for those so inclined to evade responsibility, 'the worst kind of intellectual evasion'.[118]

Lorenzo Valla had a more charitable view and pitted the Epicureans in a winning effort against the Stoics in his dialogue *De vero falsoque bono* ('*Of the True and False Good*') (1431) on the simple grounds that they are more realistic about how human beings really are. Here is his Epicurean speaker, Maffeo Vegio, replying to the advocate for the Stoics:

Now, to go back to your argument, Catone, the primary reason that it dissatisfies is that you Stoics, unhappy and inflexible as you are, desire that nothing should exist that is not wicked and vile; you measure everything by a hollow wisdom that is in all respects fixed and complete. Thus, while you take joy in flying prodigiously and in striving toward the higher regions, your wings melt (not being natural to you but artificial and made of wax), and like the foolish Icarus [who flew too close to the sun] you fall into the sea. Truly, what kind of farfetched subtlety is it to describe the wise man in such a way that, by your own admission, no example can be found among us men, and to declare that he alone is happy, that he alone is friendly, good, and free?'[119]

Even though the austere adjudicating monk ends by condemning both schools for not being Christian, he rules in favour of the Epicureans because their idea that people are by instinct naturally pleasure-seeking is much more realistic than the Stoics, who seek to eschew emotion. Valla saw in this honest view of human nature a compatibility with Christian notions of virtues and vices: Christianity accepts that no one is perfect and that we are drawn to earthly pleasures, but preaches (*contra* Epicurus) that 'we must abstain from the pleasure here below if we want to enjoy the one above'.[120] Just as we have seen other thinkers in the Renaissance blend and synthesise disparate ethical systems, in Valla we get what Lynn S. Joy calls 'a sophisticated amalgam of Epicurean and Christian belief'.[121]

Before moving on, I want to consider one last vital aspect of Epicurus's thinking, which, although not strictly speaking a part of his ethics, is none the less important to grasp: I am talking about his materialism and conception of the cosmos, which to our eyes can seem breath-taking in its apparent anticipation of modern molecular theory. Following the pre-Socratic philosopher Democritus (c.460–370 BC), Epicurus was a hard materialist and an atomist, who conceived of an infinite corporeal universe made up of an infinite number of tiny atoms 'beyond all calculation' that have somehow been compelled to act together. Let us consider a passage quoted by Diogenes:

> Now, of bodies, some are combinations, and some the elements out of which these combinations are formed. These last are indivisible, and protected from every kind of transformation; otherwise everything would be resolved into non-existence. They exist by their own force, in the midst of the dissolution of the combined bodies, being absolutely full, and as such offering no handle for destruction to take hold of. It follows, therefore, as a matter of absolute necessity, that the principles of things must be corporeal, indivisible elements.[122]

According to Epicurus, therefore, matter cannot be created or destroyed. Readers of Shakespeare will no doubt be reminded of Lear: 'Nothing will come of nothing. Speak again' (I, i, 88). Because they cannot be broken down into anything smaller and cannot be destroyed, corporeal entities are thus 'full elements', but being so must therefore reside in something that is specifically *not* matter: namely, an emptiness or void:

> The universe is infinite. For that which is finite has an extreme, and that which has an extreme is looked at in relation to something else. Consequently, that which has not an extreme, has no boundary; and if it has no boundary, it must be infinite, and not terminated by any limit. The universe then is infinite, both with reference to the quantity of bodies of which it is made up, and to the magnitude of the vacuum; for if the vacuum were infinite, the bodies being finite, then, the bodies would not be able to rest in any place; they would be transported about, scattered across the infinite vacuum for want of any power to steady themselves,

Moral Philosophy [117]

or to keep one another in their places by mutual repulsion. If, on the other hand, the vacuum were finite, the bodies being infinite, then the bodies clearly could never be contained in the vacuum.[123]

An infinite number of atoms are therefore contained by an infinite vacuum.

Although seemingly a long way away from his talk of cheese and crusty bread, this conception of the universe does, in fact, have an impact on Epicurean ethics. It seemed to Epicurus that even atoms in an infinite void needed some means of being compelled to move, and hence he determined that this was achieved by weight – this seems similar to how we understand gravity, but Epicurus thought that atoms were compelled only downwards, rather than towards each other (which was Isaac Newton's breakthrough). This appeared to render the universe deterministic, which seemed at odds with the human free will and agency apparent from lived experience, and so – in a move that seems to apprehend Chaos Theory – Epicurus reasoned that sometimes atoms randomly 'swerve' to create the conditions necessary for free will. Here is a hostile Cicero on this:

> Epicurus realised that if atoms were borne downwards by their own weight, free will would be out of the question, because the movements of the atoms would be fixed and inevitable. So he devised a means of avoiding such determinism . . . he stated that when the atom was borne directly downwards by the force of gravity, it swerved ever so slightly. This explanation is tawdrier than his inability to defend his thesis would have been.[124]

Lucretius has a more sympathetic rendering:

> While atoms move by their own weight straight down
> Through the empty void, at quite uncertain times
> And uncertain places they swerve slightly from their course.

> You might call it no more than a mere change of motion.
> If this did not occur, then all of them
> Would fall like drops of rain down through the void,
> There would be no collisions, no impacts
> Of atoms upon atom, so that nature
> Would never have created anything.[125] (217–23)

This provides the proof that human beings and even animals are able to use their will to compete with external deterministic forces: 'Though men are driven / By an external force, compelled to move / Often in headlong rush against their will, /Yet in our breasts there's something that has the power / To fight against this force and resist it' (276–80).[126] If we think back to Seneca's idea of the will, we can see how the Roman Stoics built on this idea, and some have argued that it lies at the heart of our modern concepts of liberty and self-determination.

The past decade has seen the publication of two significant studies that argue for the central importance of Lucretius's notion of the will to the Renaissance transformation from medieval to early modern. The first is Alison Brown's *The Return of Lucretius to Renaissance Florence* (2010), which contends that Lucretius and Epicureanism have been underrepresented in previous accounts of the philosophical boiling pot of the 1400s and 1500s.[127] The second is Stephen Greenblatt's Pulitzer Prize-winning *The Swerve: How the World Became Modern* (2011), which, somewhat more dramatically, claims that Lucretius's poem lays the 'foundations on which modern life has been constructed'.[128] Aimed at a popular audience, and under the spotlight that such a major award brings, Greenblatt's thesis has come under much scrutiny for its caricatured account of the medieval period being one of monastic self-flagellation.[129] In giving short shrift to rigorous, sensitive and nuanced thinkers of the period, such as Thomas Aquinas, Greenblatt's version of an unyieldingly dogmatic medieval period is essentially a fiction. Aquinas was aware of the Epicureans and treated them with seriousness. For example, *In decem libros ethicorum Aristotelis ad Nicomachum: expositio* ('*Commentary on Aristotle's Nicomachean Ethics*') he points out:

> Even the Epicureans, who considered pleasure the highest good, carefully cultivated the virtues. They did so, however, on account of pleasure, that is, for fear their pleasure would be hindered by means of contrary vices. The vice of gluttony, for instance, causes bodily suffering through excessive eating; because of theft a man is thrown into prison. So different vices are an impediment to pleasure in different ways. Since then the ultimate end is exceedingly delectable, they who make pleasure the highest good intensely love the life of pleasure.[130]

Here we can see how he diligently takes the time and space to note Epicurus's arguments without necessarily condemning them wholesale – hardly the words of the closed-minded and dogmatic thirteenth-century monk we might imagine. As I have stressed throughout this chapter, I think it is important for us to avoid making hyperbolic claims about philosophical currents in general, especially when dealing with eras marked by their eclecticism and heterodoxy, which we undoubtedly are in both the Renaissance and the early modern periods.

Greenblatt is surely right to say, as he does in a brief response to John Monfasani's review, that 'something significant happened in the Renaissance'. I would prefer, though, to view the recovery of Lucretius's poem as one small part of the wide and wildly eclectic re-appropriation of Ancient philosophy that the period saw – which is to say, there is good reason to doubt any single claim to centrality for any single text or philosophy. I think it is fair to say that both Brown and Greenblatt, in the pursuit of their respective agendas, have somewhat overstated the centrality, importance and influence of Lucretius for Renaissance and early modern thinkers in the fifteenth or sixteenth century, although the influence of Epicurean ideas in England during the seventeenth century, especially after 1650, is beyond doubt.[131] Both Brown's and Greenblatt's accounts are sharply at odds with the view that we get from authorities in the History of Philosophy, such as Jill Kraye, who argues:

> For most medieval and Renaissance moral philosophers, Epicureanism was the unacceptable face of classical ethics. Of the four major ancient philosophical schools, Epicureanism had the worst reputation and the least influence. . . . Renaissance authors continued to rely on Cicero and Seneca for information about Epicureanism. But in addition to these traditional sources, two new texts became available in the early fifteenth century. By far the more important of these was Diogenes Laertius' *Lives of the Philosophers*, book X of which contains three letters by Epicurus and a list of his principal doctrines. . . . The other newly rediscovered text was Lucretius' *De rerum natura*. Virtually unknown since the ninth century, this poetic exposition of Epicurean philosophy was discovered in 1417 and gradually entered the repertoire of classical authors cited and studied by humanists. Although admired for the artistry of his poetry, Lucretius never attained the popularity and canonical status of Horace, Virgil and Ovid, precisely because of his commitment to unacceptable Epicurean doctrines.[132]

Accordingly, for the vast majority of ordinary people in Shakespeare's time, Epicureanism was a byword for hedonism, especially of the sensual pleasures associated with gluttony, drunkenness and lust, and summarily dismissed without being read. This is registered in Shakespeare, as Don Cameron Allen noted in 1944: '[Robert] Greene and [Thomas] Nashe lived according to what was thought to be the creed of Epicurus, but united in assailing the philosopher as an advocate of gluttony and license. With this opinion Shakespeare agreed.'[133] Allen picks up on two lines in Shakespeare suggesting this: 'Then fly, false thanes / And mingle with the English epicures' (*Macbeth*, V, iii, 7–8), and 'Epicurism and lust / Makes it more like a tavern or a brothel' (*King Lear*, I, iv, 208–9). As Mary Floyd-Wilson has pointed out, Shakespeare does not have in mind 'Epicureanism in its complex form as a philosophical classical position', but depends instead on 'a popular conception of epicures as degenerately self-indulgent and directly opposed to the tempered and controlled stoic'.[134] It could also be an in-joke of sorts to his contemporary audience, a reference to his old forebears, the 'University Wits' – Thomas Nash, Robert Greene and possibly Christopher Marlowe too[135] –who, as Allen mentions, were known to be Epicureans. Back in 1848, in his *An Inquiry into the Philosophy and Religion of Shakspere*, W. J. Birch speculated that Shakespeare probably learned much of what he knew about philosophy, and Epicureanism in particular, from them:

> They were followers of Lucretius and Epicurus in philosophy, and they were Epicureans, unfortunately, in the modern sense of the word. They all died early from the effects of dissipation. Greene was taken ill, and died a month after a drunken feast with his friend Nash. . . . They were nearly all University Men, and Shakespeare may have derived much of his learning, philosophy and idiosyncrasies from his acquaintance with them.[136]

But this, I think, may be to assume too much of Greene's own reading. In *Planetomachia* (1585), a work that, on the face of it, owes something to Lucretius, he does not mention Lucretius at all, and makes only one fleeting reference to 'this Epicurean herd, dim-witted and born to eat up the earth's produce',[137] which seems to echo Petrarch's line about Epicurus reducing men to 'an animal good, the senses'.[138] Even Greene's view of Epicureanism seems to be a form of received humanist wisdom.

In another of his popular books, *Will in the World: How Shakespeare became Shakespeare* (2004), Greenblatt imagines that Greene was, in fact, Shakespeare's inspiration for Falstaff: 'The deeper we plunge into the tavern world of Falstaff – gross, drunken, irresponsible, self-dramatizing and astonishingly witty . . . – the closer we come to the world of Greene.'[139] It seems clear that Shakespeare, at some level, had a fascination with the popular conception of the Epicurean life, as he may have seen manifest first-hand in a figure like Greene. But this appears to have little, if anything, to do with the actual teachings of Epicurus. Allen maintains that no one read Epicurus seriously in England for at least another fifty years, until 'after the Restoration', when 'there is a definite change in the English attitude' and 'Epicurus becomes quotable and worth reading.'[140]

Ada Palmer's pioneering work on marginalia in Renaissance copies of Lucretius's *De Rerum Natura* gives us a unique insight into how the poem was actually read in Europe in the 1500s.[141] As she has shown, in restoring various ancient texts, including that of Lucretius, the Renaissance humanists had a broad agenda that assumed that reading the classics would have a positive, restorative and moralising effect:

> Humanism was supposed to produce virtuous men, who would imbibe in childhood the loyalty, nobility, courage, and patriotism which made ancient Rome strong, and without which the modern world was wracked by corruption, petty ambition, and cowardly self-interest. The beauty of ancient rhetoric was supposed to arm authors and orators to inspire virtue in others, especially princes. This humanism did not value learning only for learning's sake but had a very practical agenda, to repair Europe through the education of its elite. As my findings demonstrate, the specific methods of reading taught by this humanist agenda, with its focus on moral concerns and repairing Europe along

classical lines, preserved and circulated the radical content of classical texts, even while only a tiny sliver of the humanists responsible for this transmission were demonstrably interested in the radical content.[142]

As we have seen throughout this chapter, Renaissance thinkers – much like their Roman forebears – tended towards eclecticism and synthesis. They were prone to borrow from disparate, sometimes even diametrically opposed, Hellenistic schools, to form hybrid moral systems blending Plato, Aristotle, Stoicism, scepticism and Epicureanism with Christianity. It is clear that Epicurus was in this more general mix, but his more controversial ideas, such as those traditionally considered atheist or those on atomism, were paid little heed; they were 'obscure and stigmatized in the same period'.[143]

In fact, there was only one Renaissance reader who paid any significant attention to the atomist passages – those that contain the idea of 'the swerve', made to do so much work by Greenblatt: Niccolò Machiavelli. Indeed, Machiavelli had transcribed *De rerum natura* by his own hand and it had a profound effect on his thinking.[144] As Paul Rahe argues, 'by 1517 or so, if not well before, Machiavelli had made Lucretius' repudiation of religion and his rejection of natural teleology his own'.[145] Machiavelli's knowledge of Epicureanism arguably underpins three aspects of his thinking: his hard materialism, his concept of fortune (that the nature of reality is fundamentally chaotic) and his rather dim and cynical view of human motives. Consider this passage in *Discourses on Livy* (1531):

> Besides this, human appetites are insatiable, for since from nature they have the ability and the wish to desire all things and from fortune the ability to achieve few of them, there continually results from this a discontent in human minds and a disgust with the things they possess.[146]

We can see here how Machiavelli inherits the Epicurean view that people are naturally inclined to seek out pleasure and that they have free will, but this takes on a fundamentally ambitious character that brings humans up to the limits of an unpredictable world, which they cannot control. Humans are thus in a perpetual state of anxiety because their desire can never be fulfilled. Unlike Epicurus, whose entire moral system can be seen as a kind of therapeutic coping mechanism to help people live a life freed from such anxieties, Machiavelli proposes no real solutions. Rather, he insists that we must recognise the reality of the situation; we cannot try to avoid or hide from 'every type of filth' because human vices exist in every age.[147] It is on this recognition, of course, that Machiavelli builds his amoral political consequentialism in *The Prince* (1532): 'For a man who wants to practice goodness in all situations is inevitably destroyed, among so many men who are not good.'[148]

The nature of human desire in Machiavelli has at times a palpably capitalist character, an idea to which I will return in the next chapter, as he seems to think that people value property and possessions more than the lives of others. In a letter to Giovanni de' Medici (the future Pope Leo X) in 1512, he writes:

> Men feel more grief at a farm that is taken away from them than at a brother or father put to death, because sometimes death is forgotten, but property never. The reason is evident: everybody knows that a brother cannot rise from the dead because of a change in regimes, but there is a good possibility of regaining a farm.[149]

He echoes this later in *The Prince*: 'Men are quicker to forget the death of a father than the loss of an inheritance.'[150] Again, we can see some root traces of Epicureanism here: property produces both avarice and loss aversion, and death is annihilation.

In England and elsewhere, of course, like Epicurus, Machiavelli was reduced to caricature.[151] Vilified and despised, Machiavellianism was seen as a byword for evil, both on stage and in print. However, as Michael J. Redmond has demonstrated, Shakespeare's contemporaries could scarcely hide their excitement and fascination with the forbidden Florentine. Despite loud displays of disapproval, a political writer such as Barnable Barnes still could mask 'his clear preference for Machiavelli' over other Italian Renaissance humanists such as Francesco Guicciardini. Barnes evokes Guicciardini as a historical authority while attacking Machiavelli at length, but his superficial treatment of the former is in sharp contrast with the careful and meticulous treatment of the latter. For Redmond, this belies a 'furtive enthusiasm' for Machiavelli in the period that is made manifest in the prologue of Christopher Marlowe's *Jew of Malta*, in which the stage Machiavel boasts:[152]

> Admir'd I am of those that hate me most:
> Though some speak openly against my books,
> Yet will they read me, and thereby attain
> To Peter's chair; and, when they cast me off,
> Are poison'd by my climbing followers.
> I count religion but a childish toy,
> And hold there is no sin but ignorance. (9–15)

Machiavelli thus asserted influence even as he was reviled; he was actively being read. And, regardless of whether he had encountered his works directly, Shakespeare appears to have shared a profound interest in Machiavellian ideas, which are so recognisable in his plays. Just as in the case of Montaigne, there has been no shortage of book-length studies that consider Machiavelli's possible influence on Shakespeare's thinking.[153] Thus, alongside Shakespeare the sceptic, we can file Shakespeare the pragmatic realist.

> **In summary**
> - For Epicurus, the highest and only good is pleasure and, at the same time, the absence of pain and anxieties (the state of *ataraxia* or tranquillity).
> - Epicurus argues that we should live moderately because excesses, while pleasurable, can result in greater pain and anxiety. For example, rich foods can cause indigestion, while plain foods only satiate hunger. We should shun wealth, power and political influence because they each create additional (unfulfilled) desires and produce anxieties.
> - Epicurus was considered an atheist by Renaissance thinkers because he rejected three ideas that would later become central to Christian theology: the concept of an interventionist God, the concept of Divine Providence and the concept of an afterlife.
> - His ethics are underpinned by his atomist cosmology, which finds its most articulate expression in Lucretius's *De rerum natura* ('On the Nature of Things'). In this conception, atoms are naturally drawn downwards by their own weight but sometimes randomly 'swerve', and so chance and free will enter into the universe.
> - Recent studies by Alison Brown and Stephen Greenblatt have claimed a centrality for Lucretius's poem in the early modern period that it plainly did not have, and Epicurean ideas were somewhat limited in their impact.
> - The popular conception of Epicurus in early modern England was that of a hedonist who lived in pursuit of sensual pleasures, and this is the context in which Epicureanism is most widely used by Shakespeare and his contemporaries.
> - Machiavelli, however, was profoundly influenced by Epicureanism, and though he was vilified and seen as a byword for evil, early modern English writers, including Shakespeare, seem fascinated by his amoral and pragmatic realist view of politics.

Coda

This chapter has shown that Shakespeare wrote during a time in which there were many competing ethical systems.

These were inherited from Ancient Greece by way of Roman mediation (chiefly through Cicero, Seneca and Lucretius) and were being re-appropriated and synthesised to be compatible with Christian thought. Even if Shakespeare did not encounter much of this material directly, we can see versions of each of the major approaches to ethics – Aristotelian–Thomist virtue ethics, Stoicism, scepticism, and Epicureanism – registered in his plays, although, in the spirit of Renaissance eclecticism, they do not finally endorse any of them. In Part II, when we come to consider each of the six moral foundations outlined by modern cognitive psychology, we will be doing so through the kaleidoscope lens of this complex cultural moment. Before doing so, however, in the next chapter, we must complicate our vision yet further by taking on board the radical moral interventions of both the Protestant Reformation and capitalism.

Notes

1. Ada Palmer, *Reading Lucretius in the Renaissance* (Cambridge, MA: Harvard University Press, 2014), p. 20.
2. Aaron Garrett, 'Seventeenth-Century Moral Philosophy: Self-Help, Self-Knowledge and the Devil's Mountain', in *The Oxford Handbook of the History of Ethics*, ed. Roger Crisp (Oxford: Oxford University Press, 2013), p. 232.
3. See Henry Sidgwick, *Outlines of the History of Ethics for English Readers* (1886; Cambridge: Cambridge University Press, 2011), pp. 155–60.
4. Bertrand Russell, *History of Western Philosophy* (1946; New York and London: Routledge, 2004), p. 482.
5. Terence Irwin, *The Development of Ethics, Vol. 2: From Suarez to Rousseau* (Oxford: Oxford University Press, 2011), pp. 1–69.
6. Ian Donaldson (ed.), *Ben Jonson* (Oxford: Oxford University Press, 1985), p. 464.
7. Gilbert Highet, *The Classical Tradition: Greek and Roman Influences on Western Literature* (1949; Oxford: Oxford University Press, 1976), pp. 199, 200.

8. Richard Farmer, *An Essay on the Learning of Shakespeare: Addressed to Joseph Cradock, Esq.* (Cambridge: W. Thurlbourn & J. Woodyer, 1767), p. 49; emphasis in original.
9. Leonard Barkan, 'What did Shakespeare Read?', in *The Cambridge Companion to Shakespeare*, ed. Margareta de Grazia and Stanley Wells (Cambridge: Cambridge University Press, 2001), p. 40.
10. Milton Friedman, *Capitalism and Freedom* (Chicago: University of Chicago Press, 1962).
11. Jill Kraye, 'Moral Philosophy', in *The Cambridge History of Renaissance Philosophy*, ed. Charles B. Schmitt, Quentin Skinner, Eckhard Kessler and Jill Kraye (Cambridge: Cambridge University Press, 1988), p. 303.
12. Lily B. Campbell, *Shakespeare's Tragic Heroes: Slaves of Passion* (1930; London: Methuen, 1961), p. 47.
13. See David N. Beauregard, *Virtue's Own Feature: Shakespeare and the Virtue Ethics Tradition* (Newark: University of Delaware Press, 1995).
14. For accounts of biblical allusions in Shakespeare, see Steven Marx, *Shakespeare and the Bible* (Oxford: Oxford University Press, 2000). See also Patricia Parker, *Shakespeare from the Margins: Language, Culture, Context* (Chicago: Chicago University Press, 1996), which, while not ostensibly about biblical allusions in Shakespeare, has a notably keen eye for them.
15. Aristotle, *The Nicomachean Ethics*, p. 128.
16. Thomas Aquinas, *Summa Theologiae (Vol. 23: Virtue)* [1a2ae. 55–67], ed. W. D. Hughes (London: Eyre & Spottiswoode, 1969), question 61, article 2, p. 121.
17. E. M. W. Tillyard, *The Elizabethan World Picture* (1942; London: Vintage, 1959), p. 75.
18. Cicero, *Cicero on the Emotions: Tusculan Disputations 3 and 4*, trans. Margaret Graver (Chicago: University of Chicago Press, 2002), p. 43.
19. Kraye, 'Moral Philosophy', p. 306.
20. F. C. Copleston, *Aquinas* (New York and London: Penguin, 1955), p. 212.
21. Ibid. p. 213.
22. G. K. Chesterton, *St. Thomas Aquinas* (London: Hodder & Stoughton, 1933), p. 171.

23. Friedrich Uberweg, *History of Philosophy: From Thales to the Present Time*, Vol. 1: *History of the Ancient and Medieval Philosophy*, trans. Geo. S. Morris (New York: Charles Scribner's Sons, 1890), p. 451.
24. See Thomas Aquinas, *Summa Theologiae: Secunda Secundae* (*Vols 31–47*) [2a2ae1–189], (London: Eyre & Spottiswoode, 1969), questions 1–189. In compiling this list, I found it useful to consult Stephen J. Pope, 'Overview of the Ethics of Thomas Aquinas', in *The Ethics of Aquinas*, ed. Stephen J. Pope (Washington, DC: Georgetown University Press, 2002), pp. 30–53. This website, which creates a fully hot-linked version of the *Summa*, is also very useful: <http://www.newadvent.org/summa/3.htm> (last accessed 9 September 2016). There have also been sterling efforts to make Aquinas's imposing work more accessible and manageable for modern readers, the best of which are Peter Kreeft, *The Summa of the Summa* (San Francisco: Ignatius Press, 1990); and Brian Davies, *Thomas Aquinas's Summa Theologiae: A Guide and Commentary* (Oxford: Oxford University Press, 2014).
25. Shawn R. Tucker, *The Virtues and Vices in the Arts: A Sourcebook* (Eugene, OR: Cascade Books, 2015), p. 111.
26. Ibid. p. 102.
27. See Thomas Aquinas, *Summa Theologiae* (*Vol. 42: Courage*) [2a2ae.123–40], ed. Anthony Ross and P. G. Walsh (London: Eyre & Spottiswoode, 1969), question 132, articles 1–5, pp. 142–59. The quotation is taken from p. 142.
28. Christopher Marlowe, *Doctor Faustus and Other Plays*, ed. David Bevington and Eric Rasmussen (Oxford: Oxford University Press, 1995).
29. See Tucker, *The Virtues and Vices in the Arts*, pp. 78–84.
30. Thomas Aquinas, *Summa Theologiae* (*Vol. 27: Effects of Sin, Stain and Guilt*) [1a2ae.86–9], ed. T. C. O'Brien (London: Eyre & Spottiswoode, 1969), question 88, article 1, p. 47.
31. Thomas Aquinas, *Summa Theologiae* (*Vol. 44: Well-Tempered Passion*) [2a2ae.155–70], ed. Thomas Gilby (London: Eyre & Spottiswoode, 1969), question 167, article 1, p. 203.
32. See W. R. Elton, 'Aristotle's *Nicomachean Ethics* and Shakespeare's *Troilus and Cressida*', *Journal of the History of Ideas*, 58:2 (April 1997), pp. 331–7.

33. Aristotle, *The Nicomachean Ethics*, p. 8. Margarita Pascucci has also picked up on the allusion, and to good effect, in *Philosophical Readings of Shakespeare: 'Thou Art the Thing Itself'* (New York and London: Palgrave Macmillan, 2013), p. 187.
34. David N. Beauregard, 'Shakespeare and the Passions: The Aristotlean–Thomistic Tradition', *The Heythrop Journal*, 54:6 (2013), p. 913.
35. Beauregard, *Virtue's Own Feature*, pp. 51–7; see also Steve Sohmer, *Shakespeare's Mystery Play: The Opening of the Globe Theatre 1599* (Manchester: Manchester University Press, 1999), p. 204, in which he argues that Feste's invented name, 'Quinapulus', is an oblique reference to Aquinas.
36. Beauregard, 'Shakespeare and the Passions', pp. 913–14.
37. Peter Adamson, 'Everybody Needs Somebody – Aquinas on Soul and Knowledge', *History of Philosophy Without Any Gaps*, 244 (3 January 2016), <http://historyofphilosophy.net/aquinas-soul-knowledge> (last accessed 9 September 2016).
38. Russell, *History of Western Philosophy*, p. 418.
39. Romanus Cessario, *Short History of Thomism* (Rome: Catholic University of America Press, 2005), p. 61.
40. Information taken from Thomas Jeschke, 'John Caprelous', pp. 606–8, and Benjamin Hill, 'Thomas of Vio (Cajetan)', in *Encyclopedia of Medieval Philosophy: Philosophy Between 500 and 1500, Vol. 1*, ed. Henrik Lagerlund (New York and London: Springer, 2011), pp. 1295–300.
41. Joseph Hunter, *New Illustrations of the Life, Studies, and Writings of Shakespeare, Vol. 2* (London: J. B. Nichols and Son, 1845), p. 134.
42. David A. Lines, 'Humanistic and Scholastic Ethics', in *The Cambridge Companion to Renaissance Philosophy*, ed. James Hankins (Cambridge: Cambridge University Press, 2007), p. 311.
43. Richard Marius, *Thomas More: A Biography* (1984; Cambridge, MA: Harvard University Press, 1999) p. 69; for a discussion of More and Erasmus, see pp. 79–97.
44. See William T. Rossiter, *Wyatt Abroad: Tudor Diplomacy and the Translation of Power* (Cambridge: D. S. Brewer, 2014),

p. 156. For an accessible introduction to the works of Cajetan, see F. C. Copleston, *The History of Philosophy, Vol. 3: The Late Medieval and Renaissance Philosophy, Part II: The Revival of Platonism to Suarez* (Westminster, MD: Newman Press, 1952), pp. 155–9.
45. Lines, 'Humanistic and Scholastic Ethics', p. 312.
46. Charles B. Schmitt, *John Case and Aristotelianism in Renaissance England* (Montreal: McGill-Queen's University Press, 1983), p. 89.
47. Ibid. p. 199.
48. See Paul E. J. Hammer, 'Lord Henry Howard, William Temple, and the Earl of Essex', *Huntington Library Quarterly*, 79:1 (Spring 2016), pp. 41–62.
49. For an excellent discussion of this work, see Risto Saarinen, *Weakness of Will in Renaissance and Reformation Thought* (Oxford: Oxford University Press, 2011), pp. 54–62.
50. See Tillyard, *The Elizabethan World Picture*, p. 12.
51. See Copleston, *The History of Philosophy: Vol. 3*, pp. 135–8.
52. Campbell, *Shakespeare's Tragic Heroes*, p. 69.
53. Rolf Soellner, 'The Four Primary Passions: A Renaissance Theory Reflected in the Works of Shakespeare', *Studies in Philology*, 5:4 (October 1958), pp. 549–67.
54. Christopher Tilmouth, *Passion's Triumph of Reason: A History of the Moral Imagination from Spencer to Rochester* (Oxford: Oxford University Press, 2007), p. 18.
55. Cicero, *Cicero on the Emotions*, pp. 8–9.
56. Cicero, *On Academic Scepticism*, trans. Charles Brittain (Indianapolis: Hackett, 2006), p. 102.
57. Ibid. p. 101.
58. Cicero, *On Moral Ends*, ed. Julia Annas, trans. Raphael Woolf (Cambridge: Cambridge University Press, 2004), p. 113.
59. Ibid. p. 112.
60. Tobias Reinhardt, 'Introduction', in Seneca, *Dialogues and Essays*, trans. John Davie (Oxford: Oxford University Press, 2007), p. xxiii.
61. Francisco Citti, 'Seneca and the Moderns', in *The Cambridge Companion to Seneca*, ed. Shadi Bartsch and Alessandro Schiesaro (Cambridge: Cambridge University Press, 2015), p. 304.

62. Seneca, 'On Anger', in *Dialogues and Essays*, p. 20.
63. Ibid. p. 29.
64. For an excellent discussion of this topic, see Charles H. Kahn, 'Discovering Will from Aristotle to Augustine', in *The Question of 'Eclecticism': Studies in Later Greek Philosophy*, ed. John M. Dillon and A. A. Long (Berkeley: University of California Press, 1988), pp. 234–59. For a concentrated account of Seneca's concept of the will and the self, see Brad Inwood, 'The Will in Seneca', in *Reading Seneca: Stoic Philosophy at Rome* (Oxford: Oxford University Press, 2005), pp. 132–56.
65. Seneca, 'Letter 80', in *Selected Letters*, trans. Elaine Fantam (Oxford: Oxford University Press, 2010), p. 142.
66. See Charles Martindale and Michelle Martindale, 'Shakespeare's Stoicism', in *Shakespeare and the Uses of Antiquity: An Introductory Essay* (New York and London: Routledge, 1990), pp. 165–89. See also David Bevington, 'Is Man No More Than This? Shakespeare's Ideas on Scepticism, Doubt, Stoicism, Pessimism, Misanthropy', in *Shakespeare's Ideas: More Things in Heaven and Earth* (Oxford: Blackwell, 2008), pp. 143–67.
67. Martindale and Martindale, 'Shakespeare's Stoicism', p. 168.
68. John Freehafer, 'Stoicism and Epicureanism in England, 1530–1700', *PLMA*, 88:5 (October 1973), p. 1180. See also William Bouwsma, 'The Two Faces of Humanism: Stoicism and Augustinianism in Renaissance Thought', in *A Usable Past: Essays in European Cultural History* (Berkeley: University of California Press), pp. 19–73.
69. Thomas James, in Guillaume du Vair, *The Moral Philosophie of the Stoicks*, trans. Thomas James (London: Felix Kingston, 1598), pp. 5–6.
70. Thomas Fuller, *The History of the Worthies of England who for Parts and Learning have been Eminent in the Several Counties: Together with an Historical Narrative of the Native Commodities and Rarities in Each County* (London: Thomas Williams, 1662), p. 130.
71. Joseph Hall, *Two Guides to a Good Life. The Genealogy of Vertue and the Nathomy of Sinne. Liuely Displaying the Worth*

of One, and the Vanity of the Other (London: W. Iaggard, 1604), p. 6.
72. Joseph Hall, *Meditations and Vowes, Diuine and Morall. Seruing for Direction in Christian and Ciuill Practise. Deuided into Two Bookes* (London: John Porter, 1605), pp. 99–100.
73. Jill Kraye, 'Philologists and Philosophers', in *The Cambridge Companion to Renaissance Humanism*, ed. Jill Kraye (Cambridge: Cambridge University Press, 1996), p. 152.
74. See Richard Bett, 'Scepticism and Ethics', in *The Cambridge Companion to Ancient Scepticism*, ed. Richard Bett (Cambridge: Cambridge University Press, 2010), pp. 181–94.
75. Cicero, *On Academic Scepticism*, pp. 39–40.
76. Ibid. p. 46.
77. On this topic, see Mauricio Beuchot, 'Some Traces of the Presence of Scepticism in Medieval Thought', in *Scepticism in the History of Philosophy*, ed. Richard H. Popkin (Kluwer: Dordrecht, 1996), pp. 37–43.
78. David Pirillo, 'Philosophy', in *The Cambridge Companion to the Italian Renaissance*, ed. Michael Wyatt (Cambridge: Cambridge University Press, 2014), p. 274.
79. The most authoritative and detailed accounts of the history of the reception of Sextus Empiricus's works are Charles B. Schmitt, 'The Rediscovery of Ancient Skepticism in Modern Times', in *The Skeptical Tradition*, ed. Myles Burnyeat (Berkeley: University of California Press, 1983), pp. 225–51; Luciano Floridi, 'The Diffusion of Sextus Empiricus's Works in the Renaissance', *Journal of the History of Ideas*, 56 (1995), pp. 63–85; and Richard H. Popkin, *The History of Scepticism from Erasmus to Spinoza* (Berkeley: University of California Press, 1979), pp. 18–41.
80. Richard H. Popkin, 'Introduction', in *The Philosophy of the 16th and 17th Centuries*, ed. Richard H. Popkin (London: Collier–Macmillan, 1966), pp. 8–9.
81. Sextus Empiricus, *Outlines of Scepticism*, ed. Julia Annas and Jonathan Barnes (Cambridge: Cambridge University Press, 2000), p. 6.
82. Ibid. pp. 8, 3.

83. Ibid. pp. 12–40.
84. Paul Woodruff, 'The Pyrrhonian Modes', in *The Cambridge Companion to Ancient Scepticism*, ed. Richard Bett (Cambridge: Cambridge University Press, 2010), p. 214.
85. See Isaiah Berlin, *Four Essays on Liberty* (Oxford: Oxford University Press, 1969), pp. 214–15. Note, in *Shakespeare's History Plays: Rethinking Historicism*, pp. 166–9, I argue that Shakespeare reaches a position akin to value pluralism in 2 and 3 *Henry VI*. Robin Headlam Wells recognises the distinction between Sextus's scepticism and value pluralism in *Shakespeare's Humanism* (Cambridge: Cambridge University Press, 2005), pp. 50–66.
86. Sextus Empiricus, *Outlines of Scepticism*, pp. 40–1.
87. Ibid. p. 10.
88. René Descartes, *Discourse on the Method of Correctly Conducting One's Reason and Seeking Truth in the Sciences*, trans. Ian Maclean (Oxford: Oxford University Press, 2008), p. 15.
89. Duncan Pritchard, 'Doubt Undogmatized: Pyrrhonian Scepticism, Epistemological Externalism and the "Metaepistemological" Challenge', *Principia*, 4:2 (2010), p. 194.
90. Graham Bradshaw, *Shakespeare's Scepticism* (Ithaca, NY: Cornell University Press, 1987).
91. Sarah Hutton, 'Platonism, Stoicism, Scepticism and Classical Imitation', in *A Companion to English Renaissance Literature and Culture*, ed. Michael Hattaway (Oxford: Blackwell, 2000), p. 52.
92. John D. Cox, *Seeming Knowledge: Shakespeare and Skeptical Faith* (Waco, TX: Baylor University Press, 2007), p. 2.
93. Millicent Bell, *Shakespeare's Tragic Skepticism* (New Haven, CT: Yale University Press, 2003), pp. 1, 19.
94. See A. C. Bradley, *Shakespearean Tragedy: Lectures on Hamlet, Othello, King Lear, Macbeth* (London: Macmillan, 1905), p. 55; A. P. Rossiter, *Angels With Horns: Fifteen Lectures on Shakespeare* (1961; New York: Longman, 1989), especially pp. 44–51; Bradshaw, *Shakespeare's Scepticism*; Bell, *Shakespeare's Tragic Skepticism*; Hugh Grady, *Shakespeare, Machiavelli, and Montaigne: Power and Subjectivity*

from Richard II to Hamlet (Oxford: Oxford University Press, 2002), pp. 109–25; Andy Mousely, *Re-Humanising Shakespeare* (Edinburgh: Edinburgh University Press, 2007), pp. 22–32; John D. Cox, *Seeming Knowledge: Shakespeare and Skeptical Faith.*

95. See Stephen Greenblatt, 'Shakespeare's Montaigne', in Michel de Montaigne, *Shakespeare's Montaigne: The Florio Translation of the Essays, A Selection*, ed. Stephen Greenblatt and Peter G. Platt, trans. John Florio (New York: New York Review Books, 2014), pp. ix–xxxiii. For a more sceptical (pun not intended) take, see Margaret T. Hodgen, 'Shakespeare and Montaigne Again', *Huntington Library Quarterly*, 16:1 (November 1952), pp. 23–42.
96. Diogenes Laërtius, *The Lives and Opinions of Eminent Philosophers*, trans. C. D. Younge (London: Henry G. Bohn, 1853), p. 402.
97. Michel de Montaigne, *Shakespeare's Montaigne*, p. 142.
98. Ibid. p. 159.
99. See Zahi Anbra Zalloua, *Montaigne and the Ethics of Skepticism* (Charlottesville, VA: Rookwood Press, 2005), especially pp. 1–19.
100. Elizabeth Robbins Hooker, 'The Relation of Shakespeare to Montaigne', *PMLA*, 17:3 (1902), p. 326.
101. For a sustained consideration on the many parallels between them, see Peter Holbrook (ed.), *The Shakespearean International Yearbook: 6: Special Section, Shakespeare and Montaigne Revisited* (Aldershot: Ashgate, 2006) – a publication with no fewer than sixteen contributors offering perspectives on this topic.
102. Russell, *History of Western Philosophy*, p. 476.
103. Diogenes Laërtius, *The Lives and Opinions of Eminent Philosophers*, p. 428.
104. Seneca, 'Letter 18', in *Selected Letters*, p. 34.
105. Kraye, 'Moral Philosophy', p. 375.
106. Quoted by Seneca, 'On the Private Life', in *Moral and Political Essays*, ed. John M. Cooper and J. F. Procopé (Cambridge: Cambridge University Press, 1995), p. 174.

107. Diogenes Laërtius, *The Lives and Opinions of Eminent Philosophers*, p. 427.
108. The Notorious B.I.G., 'Mo' Money, Mo' Problems', on *Life After Death* (New York: Bad Boy Records, 1997).
109. Quoted by Seneca, 'Letter 2', in *Selected Letters*, p. 4.
110. Bob Dylan, 'It's Alright Ma (I'm Only Bleeding)', on *Bringing It All Back Home* (New York: Columbia Records, 1965).
111. Seneca, 'Letter 2', in *Selected Letters*, p. 4.
112. Seneca, 'Letter 9', in Ibid. p. 15.
113. Lucretius, *On the Nature of the Universe*, trans. Ronald Melville (Oxford: Oxford University Press, 1997), pp. 71–2.
114. Kraye, 'Moral Philosophy', p. 382.
115. Dante Alighieri, *The Divine Comedy of Dante Alighieri, Vol. 1: Inferno*, ed. Robert M. Durling (Oxford: Oxford University Press, 1996), p. 155.
116. Francesco Petrarch, *Letters on Familiar Matters, Vol. 1: Books I–VIII*, ed. Aldo S. Bernardo (New York: Italica Press, 2005), 1.1, p. 7.
117. Translation in Ibid. p. 379.
118. Jamie Mayerfield, *Suffering and Moral Responsibility* (Oxford: Oxford University Press, 1999), p. 137.
119. Lorenzo Valla, 'Of the True and False Good', in *The Renaissance in Europe: An Anthology*, ed. Peter Elmer, Nick Webb and Roberta Wood (New Haven, CT: Yale University Press, 2000), p. 78.
120. Ibid. p. 85.
121. Lynn S. Joy, 'Epicureanism in Renaissance Moral and Natural Philosophy', *Journal of the History of Ideas*, 53:4 (October to December 1992), p. 576.
122. Diogenes Laërtius, *The Lives and Opinions of Eminent Philosophers*, p. 439.
123. Ibid. p. 439.
124. Cicero, *The Nature of the Gods*, ed. P. G. Walsh (Oxford: Oxford University Press, 2008), pp. 26–7.
125. Lucretius, *On the Nature of the Universe*, p. 42.
126. Ibid. p. 44.
127. Alison Brown, *The Return of Lucretius to Renaissance Florence* (Cambridge, MA: Harvard University Press, 2010).

128. Stephen Greenblatt, *The Swerve: How the World Became Modern* (New York: W. W. Norton, 2011), p. 77.
129. For two such reviews, see Jim Hinch, 'Why Stephen Greenblatt Is Wrong – and Why It Matters', *Los Angeles Review of Books* (1 December 2012), https://lareviewofbooks.org/article/why-stephen-greenblatt-is-wrong-and-why-it-matters/ (last accessed 12 December 2016); and John Monfasani, 'The Swerve: How the Renaissance Began', *Reviews in History* (July 2012), <http://www.history.ac.uk/reviews/review/1283> (last accessed 12 December 2016).
130. Thomas Aquinas, *Commentary on the Nicomachean Ethics*, trans. C. I. Litzinger, 2 vols (Chicago: Henry Regnery Company, 1964), chapter 5, paragraph 57.
131. See Thomas Franklin Mayo, *Epicurus in England (1650–1725)* (Dallas: Southwest, 1934).
132. Kraye, 'Moral Philosophy', pp. 374–6.
133. Don Cameron Allen, 'The Rehabilitation of Epicurus and His Theory of Pleasure in the Early Renaissance', *Studies in Philology*, 41:4 (January 1944), p. 1.
134. Mary Floyd-Wilson, 'English Epicures and Scottish Witches', *Shakespeare Quarterly*, 57:2 (Summer 2006), pp. 131–2.
135. On Marlowe as an Epicurean, see the classic Harry Levin, *The Overreacher: A Study of Christopher Marlowe* (London: Faber & Faber, 1952).
136. W. J. Birch, *An Inquiry into the Philosophy and Religion of Shakspere* (London: C. Mitchell, 1848), p. 3.
137. Robert Greene, *Robert Greene's Planetomachia*, ed. Nandini Das (Aldershot: Ashgate, 2007), p. 157.
138. Petrarch, *Letters on Familiar Matters*, 3.6, p. 128.
139. Stephen Greenblatt, *Will in the World: How Shakespeare Became Shakespeare* (New York: W. W. Norton, 2004), p. 216.
140. Allen, 'The Rehabilitation of Epicurus and His Theory of Pleasure in the Early Renaissance', p. 3.
141. See Palmer, *Reading Lucretius in the Renaissance*.
142. Ada Palmer, 'Reading Lucretius in the Renaissance', *Journal of the History of Ideas*, 73:3 (July 2012), p. 396.
143. Ibid. p. 396.

144. For a book-length study of the Epicurean influence on Machiavelli, see Robert J. Roecklein, *Machiavelli and Epicureanism: An Investigation into the Origins of Early Modern Political Thought* (Lanham, MD: Lexington Books, 2012). See also Alison Brown, 'Lucretian Naturalism and the Evolution of Machiavelli's Ethics', in *Lucretius and the Early Modern*, ed. David Norbrook, Stephen Harrison and Philip Hardie (Oxford: Oxford University Press, 2016), pp. 69–90.
145. Paul Rahe, 'In the Shadow of Lucretius: The Epicurean Foundations of Machiavelli's Political Thought', *History of Political Thought*, 28:1 (2007), p. 43.
146. Niccolò Machiavelli, *Discourses on Livy*, trans. Harvey C. Mansfield and Nathan Tarcov (Chicago: University of Chicago Press, 1996), book II, Preface, p. 125.
147. Ibid. p. 24.
148. Niccolò Machiavelli, *The Prince*, trans. James B. Atkinson (1976; Indianapolis: Hackett, 2008), chapter 15, p. 257.
149. Quoted in James B. Atkinson, 'Introduction', in Ibid. p. 62.
150. Ibid. chapter 17, p. 273.
151. Of course, this does not tell the full story of the complex relationship between Machiavelli and English readers in the 1500s. On this, see the classic Felix Raab, *The English Face of Machiavelli: A Changing Interpretation, 1500–1700* (London: Routledge & Kegan Paul, 1964); and, more recently, Alessandro Arienzo and Alessandra Petrina (eds), *Machiavellian Encounters in Tudor and Stuart England* (Farnham: Ashgate, 2013).
152. Michael J. Redmond, *Shakespeare, Politics, and Italy: Intertextuality on the Jacobean Stage* (New York and London, Routledge, 2009), pp. 88–9.
153. See Grady, *Shakespeare, Machiavelli and Montaigne*; John Rowe, *Shakespeare and Machiavelli* (Cambridge: D. S. Brewer, 2002); Andrew Moore, *Shakespeare Between Machiavelli and Hobbes: Dead Body Politics* (Lanham, MD: Lexington Books, 2016). See also my own *Shakespeare's History Plays*, especially pp. 122–73, in which I argue that Shakespeare's view of history and politics is broadly Machiavellian in both its pragmatism and its value pluralism.

CHAPTER 4

THE REFORMATION, CAPITALISM AND ETHICS IN ENGLAND DURING THE 1590s AND EARLY 1600s

Introduction

In my account of moral philosophy in Shakespeare's England so far, I have concentrated on traditions of thought inherited from antiquity and refracted through Renaissance humanism. I have painted a picture of four competing moral systems – Aristotelian–Thomist virtue ethics, neo-Roman Stoicism, scepticism and Epicureanism – which swirled around in the social milieu of England at the turn of the seventeenth century: a moment of uncertainty and confusion. In Diarmaid MacCulloch's phrase, 'if you study the sixteenth century, you are inevitably present at something like the aftermath of a particularly disastrous car-crash'.[1] Into this already messy scene, we must lob another Molotov cocktail. It comprises two parallel social currents with far-reaching consequences: on the one hand, the Reformation, and on the other, the rise of capitalism. In this chapter, I seek to assess their impact on moral ideas in Shakespeare's England. I will do this in two parts. First, I will summarise the most important ideas of the Reformation as they came to be understood in England, and discuss their moral ramifications. I will do this chiefly with reference to John Calvin's *Institutes of the Christian*

Religion (1559), William Perkins's *A Golden Chain* (1591) and Thomas Becon's *The Governance of Vertue* (1556). Second, I will turn to the question of how increasingly capitalistic modes of thinking in the period further complicate the picture. In so doing, I will consider the famous thesis of Max Weber's *The Protestant Ethic and the Spirit of Capitalism* (1905) before contemplating the moral implications of capitalist thinking in Giovanni Botero's *Treatise, Concerning the Causes of the Magnificencie and Greatnes of Cities . . .* (1606), John Wheeler's *A Treatise of Commerce* (1601) and Walter Raleigh's *A Cleare and Evident Way for Enriching the Nations of England and Ireland* (1650).

I

The Moral Thought of the Reformation

The seismic events of the Reformation dominated the 1500s in Europe and in England. These events encompass several enormous topic areas, including but not limited to Martin Luther and the German Reformation, Ulrich Zwingli and the Swiss Reformation, John Calvin and the Geneva Experiment, the Anabaptists and the Münster Rebellion, the Reformation in England, John Knox and the Reformation in Scotland, and the extent and efficacy of the Counter-Reformation. The far-reaching scale of these events is quite beyond the scope of this book, and one could stock a generous library with the studies written about each of them. My concern must remain restricted to a single question: what were the consequences of Protestantism for moral philosophy in England during the 1590s and early 1600s? In order to answer this, I will attempt to look beyond the specifics of political intrigue and cultural contingencies to define the general principles of Protestant thinking around moral questions – in other words, I attempt only to provide an intellectual history, and one that parses religious writings for moral rather than theological content. In drawing this distinction, I assume that moral questions concern the matter of how best human beings should live, whereas theological questions pertain to scriptural interpretation or religious practices. For example, there was a huge amount of ink – and indeed blood – spilled over the question of the sacraments, and the nature of the Eucharist in particular, 'which affirme that Christes naturall body and bloud, is carnally eaten and dronken in the lordes supper'[2]; I have treated such an issue as theological rather than moral, and therefore placed it beyond the scope of my study.

My task is made difficult by the fact that – unlike the Renaissance, which was arguably an intellectual development before it was a social one – the Reformation was propelled as much by political events, 'an explosion of different concerns',[3] as it was by theology. Any true understanding of this passage of history must look back to the Great Schism, which lasted from 1378 to 1417. During this period, which remains a source of embarrassment for the Catholic Church, there were rival popes in Rome (Urban VI [1378–89]; Boniface IX [1389–1404]; Innocent VII [1404–6]; Gregory XII [1406–15]) and Avignon (Clement VII [1378–94]; Benedict XIII [1394–1403]), who were little more than proxies for the Holy Roman Empire and France, respectively. By 1409, the election of yet a third pope (Alexander V [1409–10]; John XXII [1410–15]) made the situation, for all practical purposes, a farce. Denys Hay provides a concise summary of its consequences:

> These consequences were: a forced administrative division of the Church into regions largely corresponding with kingdoms; a sharp decline in the standing of the pope *vis-à-vis* princes; a doctrine that councils of the Church were in the last resort superior to popes; and a recognition of a divided Church in the concordats. ... Beyond that the Schism weakened the Church by putting it in the power of princes to choose which pope they would obey.[4]

All of these factors made 'churches more regional in spirit and more secular in their control'. The Church in many places had become flagrantly corrupt in its pursuit of money in exchange for tithes, burial services and, most notoriously, indulgences.[5] The clergy often did not perform their services adequately and 'were frequently absent from their parishes'.[6] 'Ignorant priests, vagabond friars and monks, and licentious nuns are not found everywhere and all the time, but they are all too common.'[7]

Dissidents who called for reform, such as John Wycliffe in England (1320s–1384), and Jan Hus in Prague (1369–1415), had been denounced as heretics and their writings banned by the Church; Hus was burned at the stake. Bishoprics had become the offices of territorial lords driven by land and power, and 'secured through dubious means . . . relying upon the family connections or the political or financial status of the candidates'.[8] This is embodied in a figure such as Luigi d'Aragona, the Cardinal of Aragon (1474–1519), who is depicted so memorably as a villain in John Webster's *The Duchess of Malfi* (1612–13). Perhaps the ultimate example is Roderic Borgia, Alexander VI (papacy 1492–1503), who openly kept mistresses and fathered children as pope and then used his office to create one of the most powerful families in Europe. In Barnabe Barnes's play *The Devil's Charter* (1606) – performed by Shakespeare's company, the King's Men[9] – he is portrayed as selling his soul to the devil in exchange for the papacy. The Church not only was corrupt, but also suppressed criticism through naked abuses of power and brutal methods of oppression. By the time Giovanni di Lorenzo de' Medici – to whose nephew, Lorenzo, Niccolò Machiavelli dedicated *The Prince* – became Pope Leo X in 1513 (the first of four popes from this powerful family), the situation was out of control. At the same time, there were increasing numbers of university-educated laymen who were reading vernacular translations of the Bible. In short, as the

Church had strayed furthest from its ostensible mission to continue the work of Jesus Christ, more people were reading the Bible for themselves than ever before. Viewed from this perspective, change – dramatic and violent change – was practically inevitable.

It came in the form of the Reformation, a complex series of events, which are typically marked as being triggered by Martin Luther's *Ninety-Five Theses* published in 1517, popularly imagined as being nailed to the doors of All Saints' church in Wittenberg. The Reformation began in earnest after Luther's return to Wittenberg in 1522 following his condemnation at the Diet of Worms a year earlier. Looking back to the medieval era, Shakespeare puts a list of popular anti-papal grievances into the mouth of King John:

> Though you and all the kings of Christendom
> Are led so grossly by this meddling priest,
> Dreading the curse that money may buy out,
> And by the merit of vile gold, dross, dust,
> Purchase corrupted pardon of a man,
> Who in that sale sells pardon from himself;
> Though you and all the rest, so grossly led,
> This juggling witchcraft with revenue cherish,
> Yet I alone, alone do me oppose
> Against the Pope and count his friends my foes. (*King John*, III, i, 88–98)

Here, King John alludes to the sale of indulgences. He argues that the clergymen who sell these pardons ironically end up condemning themselves to damnation because only God has the power to pardon sinners. The speech strikes a decidedly Lutheran note. We can see Shakespeare in the mid-1590s anachronistically reading Martin Luther's arguments against indulgences from the 1520s back into the 1210s.

Even from this brief account of the period from the Middle Ages to the 1500s, it is plain to see that the causes of the Reformation are as much structural and political as they are philosophical. If there is a moral impetus, it is first as a corrective to corruption and power, and only second as a corrective to the perceived corruptions of scholastic theology. Indeed, as Denys Hay says cryptically:

> [T]he really profound change in the moral climate of Europe in the sixteenth and seventeenth centuries – by which a belief in renunciation of the world was replaced by a belief in virtue of action in the world – owed, I think, little to the theologians either Protestant or Catholic. But that, as they say, is another story.[10]

We will get to that story in the second part of this chapter, which looks forward to capitalism. For now, I will briefly sketch the core tenets of Reformation belief with a view to their moral implications, which look backwards to the first five centuries of Christianity.

Theologically, the Reformation is best understood as a 'back to basics' purification of Christian thinking, which, in the view of the Reformers, had become corrupted by endless commentaries and scholastic disputations, and tainted by pagan philosophy – as we saw in the last chapter – especially that of Aristotle. They looked back to a time before these 'corruptions' to the early Church Fathers, especially Augustine of Hippo (395–430) and, to a lesser extent, Jerome (347–420) and Origen (184–254). During the 1400s, this process had already begun as the great synthesiser of classical and Christian ethics, Thomas Aquinas, came under attack from William of Ockham, Duns Scotus and the *via moderna*. University theology became preoccupied by debates over the primacy of the intellect over the will, or vice versa. The classical intellectualism of Aquinas insisted on the primacy of the intellect and the fundamentally hierarchical nature of the *logos*, which can be discerned through human reason and observation. In contrast, the voluntarism of Ockham and Scotus emphasised the primacy of the will and the personal nature of the *logos* (that is, Christ himself), which is not bound by logic or any cosmic order and, as such, cannot be accessed through human reason. If this is the case, classical teachings from Aristotle and others, which Aquinas draws on frequently, are fundamentally incompatible with Christianity. Furthermore, in some quarters, the teachings of Pelagius (360–418), a contemporary of Augustine, caused controversy. Pelagius was opposed both to the idea of original sin and to the idea of predestination; he emphasised the role of free will and human agency in salvation.[11] Pelagius was declared a heretic at the Council of Carthage, and accordingly Pelagianism came to be viewed as a form of heresy. Therefore, it was mainly applied as a pejorative label by critics rather than being self-affirmed. For example, one of the leading lights of the *via moderna*, Ockham, explicitly rejected Pelagius on the matter of original sin[12] but none the less insisted on the 'moral centrality of the agent'.[13] For later Reformers, this reflected the obscure and technical quibbling typical of the period, but nevertheless they continued the voluntarists' movement away from trying to reconcile classical philosophy with Christianity. Luther, for example, is strongly critical of Pelagius in his 'Disputation against Scholastic Theology'.[14] The Reformers followed Augustine in insisting on the fallenness of man: human beings are 'contaminated by sin from the moment of their birth . . . Augustine portrays sin as inherent to human nature.'[15]

In what follows, I will concentrate primarily on the theology of Calvin. This is chiefly because it was his ideas that were to have a greater influence than Luther's on Protestant England. The final version of Calvin's *Institutes of Christian Religion* (1559) was translated into English by Thomas Norton in 1561, and reprinted five times before 1600. Indeed, 'by the late 1590s . . . England's print culture and its book trade were flooded with Calvinist writings'.[16] 'The work of Luther', meanwhile, 'was much less read in England.'[17] 'Luther's ideas had only slight impact in England before Henry [VIII] – for his own, decidedly un-Lutheran reasons – turned against the pope.'[18] The Geneva Bible (1560) – compiled by Englishmen who were given sanctuary in Calvin's Geneva during the time of Mary Tudor's persecution of Protestants in the 1550s[19] – was in wide circulation after its first printing in 1576. Elizabeth I herself owned a copy and wrote of 'the pleasant fields of the holy scriptures' in its front cover. This was also, of course, the Bible that Shakespeare used.[20] It was effectively replaced, over time, by the King James Version, whose titular monarch had been raised in the Church of John Knox, who was one of the English exiles given sanctuary in Calvinist Geneva during the 1550s. Another Marian exile, John Foxe, whose *Actes and Monuments* (1563) – widely known as *The Book of Martyrs* – was so instrumental in the development of English puritanism, was also a staunch Calvinist. I will return to the theme of Protestantism during the reigns of Elizabeth I and James I in due course, but for now it is enough to note that its spiritual – as opposed to political or practical – supporters were Calvinists to whom Geneva seemed 'a far more clear and logical realization of evangelical aspirations than anything they had been acquainted with in England'.[21] I would include in their number John Bradford (1510–55, burned at the stake by Mary), Hugh Latimer (1487–1555, burned at the stake by Mary), John Foxe (1516–87), John Jewel, Bishop of Salisbury (1522–71), Thomas Becon (1511–67), William Perkins (1558–1602) and John Norden (1547–1625). The Church of England, even still, is best understood as a compromise between the political interests of successive monarchs from Henry VIII onwards, and the more purely theological interests of Puritans – this is the *via media* that would culminate in Elizabeth's reign and form the basis for Anglicanism. Its architects were, in succession, Thomas Cranmer (1489–1556, burned at the stake by Mary),[22] Archbishop of Canterbury under Henry VIII and Edward VI; Matthew Parker (1504–75), Archbishop of Canterbury under Elizabeth I; and the influential theologian Richard

Hooker (1554–1600). Calvinist disappointment in the English Reformation would be the ultimate cause of emigration to New England in the 1620s, the English Civil War of the 1640s, and perhaps more indirectly, the American War of Independence over a century later.

Before continuing, I should note that in asserting the primacy of the Calvinist influence in England during the late 1500s, I find myself at odds with some distinguished historians such as Peter White and Diarmaid MacCulloch, who in different ways somewhat downplay the influence of Calvin in England. White considers James I's doctrinal Calvinism to be a 'myth'.[23] MacCulloch, meanwhile, argues that the English connection with Zurich and Ulrich Zwingli's successor, Heinrich Bullinger, was more influential in the development of the Church of England.[24] This is true, I think, from the point of view of the establishment, especially if one takes (as MacCulloch seems to) Anglicanism as an endpoint. Against this general position, Nicholas Tyacke has argued that 'manifestly by the 1590s Calvinism was dominant in the highest reaches of the Established Church'.[25] His strongest evidence is that Calvinist writings were not censored in this period, while anti-Calvinist writings (such as works by the Arminianist Peter Baro, based at the University of Cambridge) were. It seems to me that although Calvinism was prevented from truly dominating the Church of England by moderate establishment figures, such as Archbishop Parker, and later by the High Anglicanism of Hooker, it none the less certainly had enough momentum during Elizabeth's reign to be an acceptable mainstream position for an ordained minister or bishop to hold. Furthermore, the weight of evidence that Calvin's ideas had a wide reach in the popular consciousness – the high frequency of Calvinist reprints, for example – is impossible to ignore.

I do not think it is controversial to posit that there was a political spectrum in Elizabethan England that encompassed conservative Catholic traditionalists, establishment *via media* centrists (influenced by Bullinger's Zurich) and more extremist Puritan reformers (influenced by Calvin's Geneva). It seems likely that the clear majority of regular Elizabethans would have found themselves somewhere along this spectrum, with some reason to believe that most were towards the conservative end.[26] I would also warrant that for the layperson – Shakespeare and most of his audience included – we should not expect a thorough understanding of theological debates at the cutting edge.[27] It is not difficult to imagine an Elizabethan who held strong anti-papal sentiments, especially after hearing the gory stories of Mary's persecution of Protestants, who, to all intents and purposes, was still broadly Catholic in his or her beliefs and practices. We can easily register such confused and contradictory positions in a play such as Christopher Marlowe's *Doctor Faustus*, which seems to reject Calvinism in adopting a broadly Catholic framework of forgiveness and redemption, yet openly mocks the papacy. In Chapter 8, I will return to this question when discussing Shakespeare's view of sanctity.

So what exactly were the ideas that fuelled all of this division? Following Augustine, John Calvin insisted on the three solas:

1. *Sola scriptura* ('by scripture alone'), the belief that we should take our religious beliefs exclusively by reading the Bible and not through later commentaries. In short, if a practice is not justified explicitly in the text itself, there are no grounds for believing in it.
2. *Sola fide* ('by faith alone'), the belief that Redemption through Christ cannot be achieved by any human 'works' but rather is granted by 'justification', which can only be received by faith.
3. *Sola gratia* ('by grace alone'), the belief, *à la* Augustine, that despite the unworthiness of humans, God in his benevolence may still grant them divine favour.

On *sola scriptura*, Calvin especially opposed 'speculations' beyond the biblical text that had gradually crept into the

Christian mythos. For example, let us consider the writings of Pseudo-Dionysus, an obscure Syrian monk of the late fifth century, who falsely claimed to be the biblical figure Dionysus the Areopagite, a judge who is converted by Paul (Acts 17: 34). It was Pseudo-Dionysus who first codified the hierarchies of angels in *De Coelesti Hierarchia* ('On the Celestial Hierarchy'); in fact, it is believed that he invented the word 'hierarchy'.[28] Because it was believed that he was a biblical figure, the Dionysian schema of angels gained much purchase and was given prominence by Peter Lombard, on whose *Sentences* it was a scholastic theologian's rite of passage to write commentaries. Thomas Aquinas cites Pseudo-Dionysus over 1,700 times and follows his ranking of angels into nine orders.[29] For this, Calvin has no time at all; he dismisses Dionysus, 'whoever he was', for being, for the most part, 'nothing but talk'. He cautions that 'the theologian's task is not to divert the ears with chatter'.[30] He goes on to show that there is scant textual evidence in the Bible for the advanced angelology we see in Pseudo-Dionysus and Aquinas, and likewise for the demonology that so enthralled medieval mystics.[31] For Calvin, these things devolve into superstition, and ultimately distract from worship of God alone because 'divine glory does not belong to the angels'. He has similar scorn for the cults of personality that arose around the Virgin Mary and the Catholic veneration of saints, in which 'stupidity has progressed to the point that we have here a manifest disposition to superstition'.[32] It is easy to see from this how there arose the Puritan opposition not only to idolatry but also to all manner of customs, rituals and feast days. Later, infamously, the Puritans under Oliver Cromwell banned Christmas – perhaps Malvolio's ultimate revenge on Sir Toby and the Lord of Misrule – 'thus the whirligig of time brings in his revenges' (*Twelfth Night*, V, i, 363).

However, for our purposes, it is the second and third *solas* – *sola fide* and *sola gratia* – that are of special interest. It is worth pausing on them because these concepts are particularly difficult to understand for the modern secular mind and the source of much confusion. We must grasp two crucial things here: first, that the word 'justification' does not correspond to our modern usage of the word. Alister McGrath provides a clear-sighted explanation: 'In everyday English, the word "justification" usually means either "a defense of an idea or a person," or "the process of alignment of margins in word processing or typesetting".' In its theological sense, however, 'it refers to the "rectification" of the relationship between humanity and God – the "putting right" of something that has become fractured, damaged, or distorted'.[33] This, in Calvin's view, is entirely out of our hands – human beings can do nothing to 'put right' the relationship; only God can do this by his 'grace'. We can see, therefore, that he is the agent, while human beings are the ones being acted upon. In his own words, 'the question is not how we may become righteous but how, being unrighteous and unworthy, we may be reckoned righteous'.[34]

The second principle of vital importance is that 'faith' is the passive acceptance of God's grace and not an active affirmation. In other words, 'praying harder' or otherwise making a great show of one's faith has no effect at all on God's grace. To do so would be to 'puff up our hearts with vainglory'. Rather, faith is a form of *readiness* to receive grace; it is 'obedience to the divine will'.[35] There is nothing you can 'do', one way or the other, to change the outcome of your judgement. Only God will decide who is permitted entry into Heaven. What is interesting, however, is that in this schema human beings still have agency to do good or evil works:

> For works righteousness is perfect obedience to [God's] law. Therefore, you cannot be righteous according to works unless you unfailingly follow this straight line, so to speak, throughout life. The minute you turn away from it, you slip into unrighteousness. From this it is apparent that righteousness does not come about from one or a few good works

but from an unwavering and unwearying observance of the divine will. But very different is the rule for judging unrighteousness. For a fornicator or thief is by one offence guilty of death because he has offended against God's majesty.[36]

There is thus a moral imperative not to do evil things – as defined by the Bible in the Ten Commandments and elsewhere; that imperative, however, is not defined by the possible outcome of one's final judgement but 'by faith alone'. To do something evil – murder, for example – is *de facto* to turn away from God and to deny his grace. For Calvin, it is vital that there should be no self-seeking motive for any decision. To put this plainly: if you are restraining yourself from sinful acts only because you are worried that you will be sent to Hell, that is not good enough. By the same token, if you are doing 'good works' only in the hopes that it will raise your moral stock in the eyes of God, think again. The reason *must* be because of your devotion and obedience to God's will because there is no other logical reason: the very categories of good and evil are defined only with reference to the Bible. Killing is wrong because God said it is wrong, not because it will get you into trouble or any other reason.

If this sounds a particularly zealous note, we should remember that, at the same time, Calvin urges that believers should not spend all of their time worrying about offending God because in his infinite wisdom he knows that human beings are flawed. In a compassionate passage, he envisions the relationship not as one of master and slave, but as a doting father who overlooks the faults in his son.

> Those bound by the yoke of the law are like servants assigned certain tasks for each day by their masters. These servants think they have accomplished nothing, and dare not appear before their masters unless they have fulfilled the exact measure of their tasks. But sons, who are more generously and candidly treated by their fathers, do not

> hesitate to offer them incomplete and half-done and even defective works, trusting that their obedience and readiness of mind will be accepted by their fathers, even though they have not quite achieved what their fathers intended. Such children ought we to be, firmly trusting that our services will be approved by the most merciful Father, however small, rude, and imperfect these may be.[37]

But this is not to be taken as a licence to misbehave, as it were, since 'its purpose is to encourage us to good'.[38] Thus he warns against complacency, nihilism or fatalism because – despite the insistence on *sola gratia* – there are still valid reasons to do good works and avoid doing evil ones, even if our best efforts are still deeply flawed. It is simply that these works do not affect the final judegment, and not that we should not care about them either way.

This line of thought leads logically to the doctrine of predestination because, since God already knows the outcome of his judgement on every sinner, it stands to reason that who is pardoned and who is damned has already been decided. We have no way of knowing how or why God will decide on his judgements and no means of affecting the outcome. From the human perspective, God's judgements must appear completely arbitrary (insomuch as they are inscrutable) and outside the control of the individual. McGrath, again, provides much clarity on this point:

> Why is it that some are more fortunate than others in life? Why does one person possess intellectual gifts denied to another? Even from the moment of birth, two infants may find themselves in totally different circumstances through no fault of their own: one may find a full breast of milk to suck and thus gain nourishment, while another may suffer malnutrition through having to suck a breast that is nearly dry. For Calvin, predestination is merely a further instance of a general mystery of human existence, in which some

are inexplicably favoured with material or intellectual gifts which are denied to others. It raises no difficulties which are not already presented by other areas of human existence.[39]

Read charitably, Calvin's view of predestination might be a great equaliser: whether you are rich, poor, clever or below average intelligence, you still have the same chance of being saved by God's grace.

Where does this leave morality? For Calvin, human morality is merely an extension of God's will: 'For God's will is so much the highest rule of righteousness that whatever he wills, by the very fact that he wills it, must be considered righteous.'[40] And so we are back to the circular logic of faith: the source of all goodness is God, so whatever God wills is always already good, and it is not for us to question this through reason or any other means. To do so is wicked. On the scale of MFT, then, we can see that Calvin rests very heavily on the moral foundations of authority and purity, and virtually not at all on liberty, care, fairness or loyalty (other than loyalty to God alone). It seems that, for Calvin, the *summum bonum* is the complete submission of the individual will to God's will (authority) as defined by the Bible, which is the only legitimate source of ethical guidance (sanctity). What you are left with is a more officious and strident, and rather less forgiving, version of Christianity that seems always to demand the abasement of the individual to duty, yet, at the same time, one that recognises the near-impossibility of ever achieving such a thing. If the scholastics such as Aquinas or Ockham, as well as the Renaissance humanists following any of the four ethical models outlined in Chapter 2 (Aristotelianism, Stoicism, scepticism and Epicureanism), were all marked by a deep-seated rationalism trying to overcome the emotions, Calvin in fact represents the reverse: a deep-seated emotionalism trying to overcome the human urge to rationalise.[41]

Calvin's ideas on predestination are given direct purchase in England by William Perkins in *A Golden Chain* (1591), in which he comes to seven conclusions:

I. The Predestination, and Reprobation of God, doe not constraine or inforce any necessitie upon the will of man.
II. God hath predestinated all men, that is, hee hath appointed and disposed all men, so as they might obtaine eternall salvation.
III. Man is neither by necessitie nor chance saved or condemned, but voluntarily.
IV. God hath Predestinated some, other hath he rejected.
V. Those whom God hath predestinated by his absolute predestination, which cannot be lost, they shall infallibly die in grace: But they which are predestinate by that predestination which being according to preset justice, may be lost by some mortall sinne which followeth, are not infallibly saved, but oftentimes such are condemned, & loose their crown & glory. Hence ariseth that position[n] of theirs, that hee which is justified may be a reprobate, and perish eternally. Therefore predestination is not certaine, seeing it may be lost.
VI. God alone doeth know the certaine and set number of them which are predestinate.
VII. There is one set number of them which are predestinate, or reprooved, and that can neither be encreased nor diminished.[42]

As we can see, at least on the matter of predestination, Perkins is a doctrinaire Calvinist, and there are few ideas here that one cannot find in the *Institutes*. By the 1590s, it is obvious that predestination was yet another set of moral ideas swirling around in the complex milieu of Elizabethan England.

To gain an idea of how this manifested itself in the moral thinking of English men and women influenced by Calvin, I will consider briefly the popular writings of Thomas Becon, whose *The Sick Man's Salve* (1561) 'was so popular that the

Stationer's Company kept it constantly in print till the seventeenth century'; there were at least twenty-nine editions.[43] Just as with Perkins, the influence of Calvin on a writer like Becon is obvious: he consistently adheres to *sola scriptura* by systematically providing examples from the Old and New Testaments for each of his arguments. He provides citations in the margin of chapter and verse, which were first numbered in the manner that we know today in the Geneva Bible. In *The Governance of Vertue* (1556), a book that 'was to remain very popular throughout the Elizabethan age and beyond',[44] he outlines a number of moral instructions. Most of these are entirely what one would expect from a sixteenth-century Christian of any stripe. He writes against a long list of sins: 'swearing', 'lying, slaundering and filthy or uncleane talke', 'pride or vayneglory', 'feasting glotony, and dronkennes', 'fornication and adultery', 'covetousnes' and so on.[45]

We can see the specifically Calvinist nature of his thinking only if we zoom in to look at a section in detail. Let us take, for example, the section 'Against Idleness':

> *Against Idlenes.*
> If Sathan moue the[e] vnto idelnes, which is the wel spring and rote of al vice, et before the eyes of thy mind both these sentences and examples of the holy scripture.
> *Sentences out of the olde Testament.*
> The Lord toke Adam, and put him into the garden of Eden, that he might dresse and kepe it. In the sweate of thy face shalt thou eat thy bread, vntil thou turnest into the earth, from whence thou wast taken. For dust thou art and into duste thou shalt bee turned agayne. A man is borne to labour, and a byrde to flye. Thou shalt eate the labour of thy hand.[46]

Becon cites three verses from the Old Testament:[47]

- Genesis 3: 19 – 'In the sweat of thy face shalt thou eat bread, till thou return to the earth, for out of it wast thou taken, because thou art dust, and to dust shalt thou return.'

- Job 5: 7 – 'But man is born unto travail, as the sparks fly upward.'
- Psalms 128: 2 – 'When thou eatest the labors of thine hands, thou shalt be blessed, and it shall be well with thee.'

Becon sees human toil as being as natural as the flying of birds. Because God commanded Adam to 'sweat' for his bread, it is morally good to work. Idleness, meanwhile, is the work of Satan.

For further evidence, Becon draws from Ezekiel 16: 49 and the New Testament. He points out that Jesus's disciples were all working men and women:

> Christ was a carpenter. The Apostles of Christe were fishermen. Paule laboured with his own hands ... Saint Luke was a Phisicion, and as some write a painter also. Aquila was a maker of tentes, of the which occupation saint Paule was. Simon S. Peters host was a tanner. Dorcas that vertuous woman made garmentes with her owne handes & gaue them to the poore people.[48]

Becon echoes Calvin's thinking about the 'calling' here, which is as strong an ethical statement as Calvin makes in the *Institutes*: 'The Lord's calling as a basis of our way of life'. Just as each of Christ's disciples had a day job, 'each individual has his own kind of living assigned to him by the Lord as a kind of sentry post so that he may not heedlessly wander about through life'.[49] We should not regard this emphasis on the inherent worth of professional work as something that would have been self-evident to any early modern Christian. As McGrath points out, 'we need to understand the intense distaste with which the early Christian tradition, illustrated by the monastic writers, regarded work'.[50] Thus, for example, although Thomas Aquinas considered sloth (or 'apathy') to be a mortal sin and one of the seven capital vices,[51] he none the less saw monastic withdrawal as being superior to the pursuit of a profession. In fact, he ordered the professions into a hierarchy based on inherent value to society (derived from philosophical investigation): 'Significantly, merchants and shopkeepers were rated not only lower than farmers and peasants, but also lower than artisans. The priesthood and other sacred callings were ranked highest.'[52] In drawing attention to the everyday professions of the disciples, we can see Becon arguing strongly against this line of thinking. Here we can see what Max Weber would later call the 'Protestant work ethic' in its nascent state, which I will discuss in the second part of this chapter.

Before I do so, I think it is worth pausing on Shakespeare's attitude towards puritanism, which seems – at least by his judicious standards – unusually hostile. This is, of course, entirely to be expected because, by the 1590s, 'puritan animus against theater was . . . of long standing and of increasing intensity'.[53] In May 1603, puritans got their way in persuading James I to forbid public performances on Sundays,[54] and, of course, by 1642 they would shut down the theatres completely. Thus, they represented a direct threat to Shakespeare's livelihood, and to the world in which he lived and operated. I do not think puritans rankle with Shakespeare because of any deeply held theological conviction on his part,[55] but rather because they deeply offend his sense of fun. As we saw in Chapter 2, he had a fascination with the 'Epicurean' university wits of the tavern. Our thoughts turn inevitably to *Twelfth Night*, in which Malvolio is identified as 'a kind of puritan' (II, iii, 130), which is seen by Sir Andrew and Sir Toby as sufficient cause to beat him. While we cannot align Shakespeare too closely with any of his characters, it seems to me that his plays sound a recurring note of human outrage against puritanical moralising. It is the same sort of reaction evoked by that most twenty-first-century of phrases, 'virtue signalling'.[56] We can spot it when Sir Toby says, 'Dost thou think because thou art virtuous, there shall be no more cakes and ale?' (II, iii, 106–7). Falstaff makes much the same argument in the play-within-the-play in *1 Henry IV*: 'If sack and sugar be a fault, God help the wicked. If to be old and merry be a sin, then many an old host that I know is damned. If to be fat be to be hated, then Pharaoh's lean kine are to be loved' (II, iv, 428–32). We see a similar logic in

Pompey's riposte to Angelo's puritanical order against prostitution in *Measure for Measure*:

> If you head and hang all that offend that way but for ten year together, you'll be glad to give out a commission for more heads. If this law hold in Vienna ten year, I'll rent the fairest house in it after threepence a bay. (II, i, 217–20)

All of these lines are spoken by comic characters who would have got a big laugh from the crowds at the Globe, but in them is the recognition that the puritans hold human beings to impossible moral standards that are generally unwelcome. We can also recognise a general disdain for the stickler or jobsworth. Even so, Shakespeare's instinct is towards empathy and understanding. He might bring Malvolio and Angelo down a peg or two but he does not destroy them.[57]

In summary

- Corruption and inadequate service in the Catholic Church were endemic by the 1520s, when Martin Luther started the European Reformation in earnest.
- The Reformation is best understood as a 'back-to-basics' return to studying the Bible and the early Church Fathers, especially Augustine of Hippo (395–430).
- Augustine stressed the ideas of original sin and predestination, which were especially influential on the Reformers.
- Of the various strands of the Reformation, the theology of John Calvin (1509–64) proved to have the most influence on Elizabethan England.
- Calvin, following Augustine, insisted on *sola scriptura* ('by scripture alone), *sola fide* ('by faith alone') and *sola gratia* ('by grace alone'), which lead logically to a belief in predestination. In short, this is the belief that human salvation can be achieved only through God's will and cannot be affected at all by human action (*sola gratia*). Since God is all-knowing, he already knows who will be saved (to Heaven) and who will be damned (to Hell). Our only recourse is to have faith (*sola fide*).

- Calvin's moral compass heavily emphasises the moral foundations of authority and sanctity (*sola scriptura*); Calvinists and puritans therefore tend to stress, above all else, a sense of duty to God at the expense of individual expression.
- The influence of Calvin's ideas about predestination on English thought can be seen in William Perkins's *A Golden Chain* (1591), which was wildly popular.
- It can also be seen in Thomas Becon's *The Governance of Vertue* (1556), which, among other things, stresses the importance of maintaining a strong work ethic and warns 'against idleness'.
- In his plays, William Shakespeare seems unusually hostile to puritanism. We can see this especially in *Twelfth Night*, *1 Henry IV* and *Measure for Measure*.

II

Capitalism and Ethics in Shakespeare's England

At the same time as the Reformation was carving a deep and divisive rift through Europe, there was a great flourishing of commercial and industrial activity that we recognise today as being capitalism in its nascent state and, with it, seemingly, a new attitude towards work, money and profits. Why did this happen shortly after the Reformation? Could it be that something in the mindset and moral character of people altered because of a change in their religious belief? It was this question that ultimately animated Max Weber's famous essay *The Protestant Ethic and the Spirit of Capitalism* (1905), which was translated in 1930 by the renowned American sociologist Talcott Parsons. In it, Weber argued that, by way of Calvin's doctrine of callings, the Protestant work ethic lies at the heart of modern-day capitalism and it was ultimately this that propelled the Industrial Revolution of the 1800s. This view found support in Ernst Troeltsch's *Protestantism and Progress* (1912). A few years after the English translation of Weber's essay, Robert K. Merton, a student of Parsons, published 'Science, Technology and Society in Seventeenth Century England' (1938), in which he outlined an argument, later known as 'the Merton thesis', that effectively extended Weber's argument to correlate Protestantism not only with capitalism but also with the rise of science.[58] Christopher Hill expanded the thesis further in *Intellectual Origins of the English Revolution* (1965), which was put to much scrutiny by Hugh Trevor-Roper in a lengthy review and then later a long essay, 'The Religious Origins of the Enlightenment' (1967). Trevor-Roper sought to challenge Hill's view that the puritans were 'the Moderns' and the Catholics (and, later, the English Cavaliers) 'the Ancients'.[59] More recently, Weber's thesis was revived in David S. Landes's magisterially sweeping *The Wealth and Poverty of Nations* (1998).[60]

Weber's thesis, often misread to be more reductive than it is, would find many opponents[61] – far too many to list here. I will note just six key objectors:

1. Werner Sombart, who argued in *The Jews and Modern Capitalism* (1911) that capitalism developed mainly because of the Jews being excluded from medieval guilds and pushed into usury.[62]
2. R. H. Tawney, whose still towering *Religion and the Rise of Capitalism* (1926) argued that Weber's thesis is too linear and simplistic, and that the practical consequences of the Reformation resulted in a moral travesty in which religion now justified trade, commercialism and ultimately self-interest, greed and profit.[63]
3. H. M. Robertson, who, in *Aspects of the Rise of Economic Individualism* (1933), insisted that the causes of capitalism were secular rather than religious and, in any case, predate the Reformation.[64]
4. The aforementioned Hugh Trevor-Roper, who, in a long essay, 'Religion, the Reformation and Social Change' (1967), locates the 'spirit' of capitalism not in Lutherism or Calvinism but in 'Erasmianism'. He argues that the developments of the Reformation

are a natural extension of Renaissance humanist thinking and are not *necessarily* Protestant in character.[65]
5. Fernand Braudel, who, in his masterpiece, *Civilization and Capitalism* (1993), argued along materialist lines that 'there are more things in the world than the Protestant ethic' and that Northern Europe overtook the Mediterranean after 1590 because of 'its lower wages, its increasingly unbeatable industry, its cheap transport, its fleet of coasters . . . this was a matter of pounds, shillings and pence, of competitive costs'.[66] Incidentally, this view is widely held by economists today.[67]
6. G. R. Elton, who, in his characteristically positivist approach to history, objected strongly to Weber's theoretical approach (as well as to Tawney's and Hill's) and argued that the Weber thesis was effectively a 'faith in despite of the facts', which are that the Protestant leaders were almost always moralistic and explicitly preached charity against profiteering and worldly success. 'It was not Calvinism that freed man from the restraints of the traditional moral concepts in economics, but emancipation from religion and theology in general which enabled men, pursuing the logic of palpable economic fact, either to ignore the thunders of the clergy or ultimately to persuade some clergy to come to terms.'[68]

Just as the tumultuous specifics of the Reformation across Europe are beyond my scope here, so too is the question of the ultimate causes of modern capitalism. For my purposes, a survey of the evidence shows that two things are beyond doubt: first, capitalism – or at least rampantly self-interested commercial activity – predates Protestantism; even as Weber says himself, it is 'as old as the history of man'.[69] However, before the late 1500s, it was 'allowed only sporadic manifestations'.[70] Second, despite all this disagreement, there is wide consensus that *something* in the moral temper of Europe, and England especially, changed during the 1500s.

In passing, I will add that, to my mind, the true spirit of capitalist thinking must have an entrepreneurial element as well as a work ethic. I do not think that Calvin provides much in the way of capitalist enterprise; we can find it instead in Niccolò Machiavelli, whose 'instrumental opportunism',[71] not to mention – as we saw in Chapter 2 – his emphasis on the self-interested nature of human beings and their capacity for free will and agency in the face of contingency, seems to me entirely in keeping with individualist capitalist enterprise. The march towards modern business ethics is more obviously found in Englishmen influenced by Machiavelli – Thomas Cromwell, William Camden, Walter Raleigh, Francis Bacon and, dare I say, possibly also William Shakespeare – than it is in those influenced by Calvin, even if Machiavelli tended to emphasise civic greatness and social order over profit-making.[72] I do not think it is too crude to suggest that a Machiavellian would make a fantastic entrepreneur (a calculated risk-taker and pragmatist who acts for self-gain), whereas a Calvinist would make an excellent factory worker (a dutiful employee whose anxiety about salvation ensures maximum productivity). Of course, both are necessary for capitalism to keep ticking along.

However, my aim is not to locate the spirit of capitalism but moral philosophy, that which lies in 'the unchartable realms of the mind'.[73] In this regard, Weber was surely correct that there was a general re-orientation of the self in the period towards what he calls 'practical rationalism'.[74] We may observe the parallel development of 'individualistic–civic English nationalism'. We see the rise of joint-stock companies, including the Merchant Adventurers of England, the Muscovy Company, the Levant Company and, of course – a name that would become synonymous with capitalism – the East India Company. With this development, we see both a renewed justification of the profit motive and an emphasis on individual enterprise. Before 1601, the only work published in English that overtly advertised business in its title was Shakespeare's *The Merchant of Venice*; by the end of that decade, books about business had become a burgeoning industry.⁷⁵ Their contents are revealing. Consider these statements from Giovanni Botero – notably, an Italian Jesuit and a Thomist who believed in natural law and strongly opposed Protestantism – whose *Treatise, Concerning the Causes of the Magnificencie and Greatnes of Cities* . . . was translated into English in 1606 by Robert Peterson:

> This Profit is of such power, to unite and tye men fast unto one place; as the other causes aforesayd, without this accompany them with all, are not sufficient to make any city great. . . . profite is the verie thing from whence, as from the principall cause, the greatnesse of citties growth. . . . There is not a thing of more importance to encrease a state, and to make it both populous of Inhabitants, and rich of all good things; than the industrie of men, and the multitude of Artes.⁷⁶

Botero stresses the positive effects of commercial growth. He sees profit as a force that can bring people together under a common goal, bound in industry, even if they are competitors. On this score, it would appear that he has been vindicated by modern scholarship.⁷⁷ Botero suggests that growth in one industry will lead to growth in other industries, which will make a city 'rich of all good things'. It is interesting that he mentions the 'Artes' here, which is almost certainly meant in the sense of 'learning' or education; Botero is making an unmistakably bourgeois link between commercial prosperity and education.

In *A Treatise of Commerce* (1601), John Wheeler, the secretary of the Merchant Adventurers of England, echoes this line of thinking:

> To conclude, all that a man worketh with his hand, or discourseth in his spirit, is nothing els but merchandise, and a trial to put in practice the Contracts . . . the which words in effect comprehend in them all negotiations . . .

> and are none other than mere matter of merchandise and Commerce. Now albeit this affection bee in all persons generally both high and low, yet there are of the notablest, and principallest, Traffiquers which are ashamed, and think scorn to be called Merchants: whereas indeed merchandise, which is used of proper vacation ... is not to be despised, or accounted base by men of judgement, but to the contrary, by many reasons and examples it is to be proved, that the estate is honourable.[78]

If you will recall from the first part of this chapter, Thomas Aquinas had placed merchants right at the bottom of his hierarchy of professions, below farmers, artisans and even peasants. In the Middle Ages, profit-seeking was tantamount to avarice, a damnable sin. Economic interests were secondary to seeking salvation for one's soul and understood as being antagonistic to that goal. Business transactions were by necessity, for the simple trade of goods and services, and not for any ends beyond that. Thus, there was a long-lasting stigma in Christian moral thought on commercial matters, especially on the question of usury (the charging of interest rates).[79] This persisted in the Elizabethan era: for example, in Thomas Wilson's *A Discourse Upon Usury* (1572). It is unsurprising, then, to find Wheeler somewhat embattled in his defence of merchants and the profit motive here, but rather telling that he feels so emboldened as to make it in the first place.

To all of this, Walter Raleigh adds a note of nationalistic competitiveness:

> No[t] so[ev]er a Dearth of, Wine, or Corn here, or other merchandise, but forth with the Emb[e]deners, Hamburgers and Hollanders, out of their Storehouses lade 50. 100 or more ships, dispersing themselves round about this Kingdom, and carry away great store of Coin and wealth for little Commodities, in those times of Dearth: by which means they suck our Commonwealth of their Riches, cut down our Merchants, and decay our Navigation, not with their Natural commodities which groweth in their own

Country, but the Merchandises of other Countries and Kingdoms. Therefore it is far more easie for us to serve our selves, hold up our Merchants, increase our Ships and Mariners, strengthen the Kingdome, and not only keep our money in our own Realm, (which other Nations still rob us of) but bring in their who carry ours away, and make the Bank of Coin and Storehouse to serve other Nations as well and far better cheap then they in England.[80]

Where Botero still thought on the level of the city, Raleigh thinks on the level of the nation-state. Raleigh is palpably angry about foreign traders making profits at England's expense. What is interesting, however, is that his anger apparently stems from the fact that England already has enough goods. It appears that because foreign merchandise is flooding the market, supply is outstripping demand and this is hurting local merchants both by competing directly and by keeping the price of their wares low. In a plan that would not be alien to President Donald Trump, Raleigh's solution is to fight the foreigners at their own game: increase English exports while adopting a form of protectionism at home. We can see in Raleigh's line of thought the burgeoning mercantilism that dominated European economic theory until Adam Smith's *The Wealth of Nations* (1776).[81]

The radical implications of the ideas outlined by Botero, Wheeler and Raleigh cannot be overestimated, and in them we can see the eventual and inevitable overthrow of the nobility by the bourgeoisie. Between them, they make at least three crucial theoretical moves:

1. Human industry and commerce are inextricably linked, and *this is natural*.
2. Profits and capital growth create a net benefit for society, and *this is good*.
3. Nation-states must therefore virulently protect their own interests (that is, ensuring capital growth) by out-manoeuvring other nations because *their gain is your loss*.

Today we can recognise in this line of thinking both utilitarianism and Machiavellian consequentialism, working backwards from the perceived positive ends of commerce to the means. What is interesting to me is the specifically moral dimension that this *post hoc* justification for commerce acquires. It is the birth of what Jonathan Haidt has called *homo economicus*.[82]

Weber was keenly aware of the fact that capitalism justified itself through this ethical rationalisation, 'a heroism', but he gives it a specifically puritanical edge:

> In fact, the *summum bonum* of this ethic, the earning of more and more money, combined with the strict avoidance of all spontaneous enjoyment of life, is above all completely devoid of any eudaemonistic, not to say hedonistic, admixture. It is thought of purely as an end in itself, that from the point of view of the happiness of, or utility to, the single individual, it appears entirely transcendental and absolutely irrational. Man is dominated by the making of money, by acquisition as the ultimate purpose of his life.[83]

Later, he continues:

> The Puritan wanted to work in a calling; we are forced to do so. For when asceticism was carried out of monastic cells into everyday life, and began to dominate worldly morality, it did its part in building the tremendous cosmos of the modern economic order. . . . In Baxter's view the care for external goods should only lie on the shoulders of the 'saint like a light cloak, which can be thrown aside at any moment'. But fate decreed that the cloak should become an iron cage.[84]

For Weber, the 'calling' in question takes a specifically Calvinist form, but rather than being an embrace of self-interest, humanistic agency and individualism (as per Machiavelli, Botero, Wheeler or Raleigh), it is in fact a denial of those things.

He views it as a 'tyranny', 'the most absolutely unbearable form of ecclesiastical control of the individual which could possibly exist'.[85] And I think this view is borne out in my discussion of Calvin in the first part of this chapter. It is possible that the unresolved tension between the buccaneering humanistic and individualist spirit of the Merchant Adventurers and the automaton-like 'worker ant' mentality that emerges from Weber's iron cage remains at the heart of capitalism. They are two countervailing forces, pulling in opposite directions, yet paradoxically towards the same ends. We can glimpse in these forces what Friedrich Nietzsche called 'a *master morality* and a *slave morality*'. The master morality '*creates values* . . . proud of the very fact that he has not been made for compassion' – this is Machiavelli, Raleigh, et al.[86] In contrast, the slave morality harbours 'a pessimistic suspicion towards the whole human condition [that] would find expression, perhaps a condemnation of man together with his condition'. Seeking solace in 'compassion' and 'the obliging helping hand', it is 'essentially a morality of usefulness' – this is Calvin.[87]

In closing, let us pause very briefly on the question of what Shakespeare might have made of this nascent capitalism. We know, for starters, that he made a lot of money himself from it. He was a joint stockholder in the Globe Theatre and the Lord Chamberlain's / King's Men. He bought property, illicitly hoarded grain, evaded taxes and bought the right to collect tithes.[88] It does not seem like too much of a stretch to say that Shakespeare was a type of capitalist. But do his plays endorse such ribald profiteering? Unsurprisingly, much has been made of this question, with critics mostly taking their cue from *The Merchant of Venice*, or else using Shakespeare to play out contemporary squabbles between Marxist socialism and free-market neo-liberalism.[89] As ever, Shakespeare is not a systematic thinker: he does not think on the level of economies and systems of value, but rather in the immediacy of the reduced human scale. In *The Moral Foundation of Economic Behaviour* (2011), David C. Rose argues that 'opportunism is the single greatest impediment to the development and operation of a market economy capable of producing a condition of general prosperity'. In a society in which no one can be trusted, and in which the fair rules of the market are not upheld, there are weak incentives for entrepreneurial behaviour because 'it is not rational to expect that contracts will be impartially enforced by courts when disputes arise'.[90] Rose is, of course, writing in the twenty-first century with over 400 years of economic theory from which to draw.

Shakespeare was writing as the first shoots of that economic theory were beginning to sprout, and almost 200 years before Adam Smith. It seems to me that Shakespeare imagines the capitalistic spirit primarily in terms of stolen moments of opportunism that reflect the zero-sum game of mercantilist economics: if you win, that means someone else is losing. But, characteristically, he operates on a human rather than national scale. Here, his own hoarding of grain at a time of shortage is instructive: other people were starving but their loss was Shakespeare's gain. And this spirit enters his plays in numerous 'stolen moments'. For example, in *1 Henry IV*, when Falstaff brings Hal the grave news of Percy's rebellion, he undercuts the seriousness of the message with the impish 'You may buy land now as cheap as stinking mackerel' (II, iv, 328–9). It is telling that where Hal's mind goes to women (he replies with a crude quip about the taking of virginity as a war spoil), Falstaff's goes to money-making. There is also something of this quick-witted opportunism in *Othello* when Iago swindles Roderigo into selling his lands to fund a trip to Cyprus (I, iii, 339–40).[91] We might also think of Edmund in *King Lear*, whose unscrupulousness in spotting an opening takes him from bastard to the Earl of Gloucester (III, v, 14) in the space of a couple of scenes, or, of course, the Macbeths, whose ruthless opportunism gains them the throne of Scotland. In every case, self-interested expediency equates to land and wealth at the expense of another economic agent. In every case, too, it is also clear that the gains are bought at a moral cost. Shakespeare registers both the emergent capitalism – or rather mercantilism – of early modern England, as embodied in the buccaneering spirit of a Walter Raleigh, and residual – which is to say, medieval or feudal – anxieties about the pursuit of self-interest above obligations to the common good as well as to salvation.

In summary

- In *The Protestant Ethic and the Spirit of Capitalism* (1905), Max Weber argued that John Calvin's doctrine of callings developed a 'Protestant work ethic', which lies at the heart of modern capitalism.
- Although many commentators have disagreed with Weber, he is right to suggest that there was a change of attitude towards both work and money-making during the 1500s.
- The 'spirit of capitalism' can be located as much in Niccolò Machiavelli as it can in John Calvin: if Calvin represents the work ethic of the capitalist employee, Machiavelli represents the entrepreneurial spirit of the capitalist enterprise.
- We can see this change of attitude in the writings of Giovanni Botero, John Wheeler and Walter Raleigh, who severally argue for a *natural* and inextricable link between human industry and commerce, the positive benefits of profits and capital growth (which are *good*), and the importance of outmanoeuvring rivals because their gain is your loss.
- There is an unresolved tension in capitalist ethics between the 'master morality' of Machiavellianism and the 'slave morality' of Calvinism.
- Shakespeare's plays register the cynical and self-interested opportunism of mercantilism but they do not wholly embrace it, instead resolving in moralistic caution.

Coda

In this chapter, which concludes Part I of *Shakespeare's Moral Compass*, I sought to complicate further the already complex picture of moral thinking in Shakespeare's England that I outlined in Chapter 3. There, four moral systems – virtue ethics in the Aristotelian–Thomist tradition, Stoicism, scepticism and Epicureanism – competed and intertwined in early modern England. Here, we have added at least two more modes of morality: puritanism (as influenced by John Calvin), and the ruthless dog-eat-dog mercantilism of early capitalism (as influenced by Niccolò Machiavelli).

Thus we are left with six major competing moral systems, which, by coincidence, is also the number of moral foundations I have inherited from Jonathan Haidt, outlined in Chapter 1, and around which Part II of this book is structured. As a reminder, these are authority, loyalty, sanctity, fairness, care and liberty. If MFT is to carry any weight, we need to assume that these six foundations are both universal and a fact of being: which is to say, where we will find human beings, we will also find these six foundations, which are felt intuitively. The moral systems I have been outlining in Chapters 2 and 3, however, are all *post hoc* rationalisations and attempts to codify and schematise this 'basic fact of being' in ways that are behaviourally instructive; they are – to use the phrase from Chapter 1 again – cultural scripts. In Part II, when considering Shakespeare's treatment of each of the six moral foundations, we will constantly have to keep in mind the various cultural scripts that may be in play at any given time. I am especially interested in the potential tension between these cultural scripts and the instinctive moral intuitions derived from human nature as they inform the myriad-minded playwright's moral compass.

Notes

1. Diarmaid MacCulloch, *All Things Made New: The Reformation and Its Legacy* (New York: Oxford University Press, 2016), p. 1.
2. Thomas Becon, *The Governance of Vertue* (London: John Day, 1556), p. 30.
3. MacCulloch, p. 2.
4. Denys Hay, 'The Background to the Reformation', in *The Reformation Crisis*, ed. Joel Hurstfield (London: Edward Arnold, 1965), pp. 12–13.
5. On indulgences, see E. G. Rupp, 'Luther and the German Reformation to 1529', in *The New Cambridge Modern History, Vol. 2: The Reformation*, ed. G. R. Elton (Cambridge: Cambridge University Press, 1958), pp. 75–6.
6. Alister E. McGrath, *Reformation Thought: An Introduction*, 4th edn (Chichester: Wiley-Blackwell, 2012), p. 2.
7. Hay, 'The Background to the Reformation', pp. 14, 18.
8. McGrath, *Reformation Thought*, p. 2.
9. See E. K. Chambers, *The Elizabethan Stage*, 4 vols (Oxford: Clarendon Press, 1923), vol. 3, pp. 214–15.
10. Hay, 'The Background to the Reformation', p. 20.
11. Rega Wood, 'Ockham's Repudiation of Pelagianism', in *The Cambridge Companion to Ockham*, ed. Paul Vincent Spade (Cambridge: Cambridge University Press, 1999), p. 351.
12. Ibid. pp. 350–74.
13. Peter King, 'Ockham's Ethical Theory', in *The Cambridge Companion to Ockham*, ed. Paul Vincent Spade (Cambridge: Cambridge University Press, 1999), p. 243. See also Marylin McCord Adams, 'The Structure of Ockham's Moral Theory', *Franciscan Studies*, 46 (1986), pp. 1–35.
14. Martin Luther, 'Disputation against Scholastic Theology', in *Martin Luther's Basic Theological Writings*, ed. Timothy F. Lull and William R. Russell, 3rd edn (1989; Minneapolis: Fortress Press, 2012), pp. 3–7.
15. McGrath, *Reformation Thought*, p. 66.

16. Russell M. Hillier, 'Hamlet the Rough-hewer: Moral Agency and the Consolations of Reformation Thought', in *Shakespeare and Renaissance Ethics*, ed. Patrick Gray and John D. Cox (Cambridge: Cambridge University Press, 2014), p. 161.
17. Ronald Bayne, 'Religion', in *Shakespeare's England: An Account of the Life and Manners of His Age*, 2 vols, ed. C. T. Onions and Sidney Lee (Oxford: Clarendon Press, 1916), vol. 1, p. 71.
18. Christopher Haigh, *English Reformations: Religion, Politics, and Society Under the Tudors* (Oxford: Clarendon Press, 1993), p. 12.
19. It should be noted that the Geneva Bible, as with the later King James Version, was based largely (over 75 per cent) on William Tyndale's pioneering translation of the 1520s. For an excellent and up-to-date discussion of this, see Naomi Tadmor, *The Social Universe of the English Bible: Scripture, Society, and Culture in Early Modern England* (Cambridge: Cambridge University Press, 2010), pp. 1–22.
20. See MacCulloch, *All Things Made New*, pp. 167–74; Bayne, 'Religion', pp. 75–6; Thomas Carter, *Shakespeare and the Holy Scripture with the Version He Used* (London: Hodder and Stoughton, 1905); H. R. D. Anderson, *Shakespeare's Books: A Dissertation on Shakespeare's Reading and the Immediate Sources of His Works* (Berlin: George Reimer, 1904), pp. 196–200; Steven Marx, *Shakespeare and the Bible* (Oxford: Oxford University Press, 2000).
21. Bayne, 'Religion', p. 56.
22. For a superb account of how the martyrdom of Cranmer was co-opted by both the puritan and more moderate factions of the English Reformation, see MacCulloch, *All Things Made New*, pp. 256–78.
23. Peter White, 'The Rise of Arminianism Reconsidered', *Past and Present*, 101 (November 1983), p. 39.
24. MacCulloch, *All Things Made New*, pp. 218–38.
25. Nicholas Tyacke, *Aspects of English Protestantism, c. 1530–1700* (Manchester: Manchester University Press, 2001), p. 160.
26. 'As virtually all historians now agree, Catholics – or at least religious conservatives – constituted a clear majority of the nation in Elizabeth's first years': Peter Marshall, 'Choosing

Sides and Talking Religion in Shakespeare's England', in *Shakespeare and Early Modern Religion*, ed. David Loewenstein and Michael Witmore (Cambridge: Cambridge University Press, 2015), p. 42.

27. See Neil G. Smith, 'Was Shakespeare a Theologian?', *Theology Today*, 21:4 (January 1965), pp. 417–32.
28. MacCulloch, *All Things Made New*, p. 27. See also Feisel G. Mohamed, *In the Anteroom of Divinity: The Reformation of the Angels from Colet to Milton* (Toronto: University of Toronto Press, 2008), especially pp. 3–15.
29. Kevin F. Doherty, 'St. Thomas and the Pseudo-Dionysian Symbol of Light', *The New Scholasticism*, 34 (1960), pp. 170–89.
30. John Calvin, *Institutes of the Christian Religion*, 2 vols, ed. John T. McNeil, trans. Ford Lewis Battles (1559; Philadelphia: Westminster Press, 1960), 1.14.4, p. 164.
31. For a longer discussion of Calvin on angels and demons, see Charles Partee, *The Theology of John Calvin* (Louisville, KY: Westminster John Knox Press, 2008), pp. 70–5.
32. Calvin, *Institutes*, 1.4.10, 3.20.22, pp. 170, 880.
33. McGrath, *Reformation Thought*, pp. 116–17.
34. Calvin, *Institutes*, 3.29.2, p. 834.
35. Ibid. 3.18.4, 3.18.10, pp. 825, 832.
36. Ibid. 3.18.10, pp. 833.
37. Ibid. 3.1.9.5, p. 837.
38. Ibid. 3.19.6, p. 838.
39. McGrath, *Reformation Thought*, pp. 127–8.
40. Calvin, *Institutes*, 3.23.2, p. 949.
41. For a study that has argued along these lines to good effect, see Bouwsma, 'The Two Faces of Humanism', pp. 3–60 and especially pp. 47–50.
42. William Perkins, *A Golden Chain, Or The Description of Theologie, Containing the Order of the Causes of Saluation and Damnation, According to God's Word* (London: Edward Alde, 1591), chapter 51, pp. 290–2.
43. Bayne, 'Religion', p. 72. Mary Hampson Patterson, *Domesticating the Reformation: Protestant Best Sellers, Private Devotion and the Revolution of English Piety* (Madison, NJ: Fairleigh Dickinson University Press, 2007), p. 101.

44. A. G. Dickens, *The Marian Reaction in the Diocese of York, Part II: The Laity* (York: St Anthony's Press, 1957), p. 12.
45. Becon, *The Governance of Vertue*, p. iv.
46. Ibid. pp. 78–9.
47. Biblical quotations are from Peter A. Lillback (ed.), *1599 Geneva Bible* (Dallas, GA: Tolle Lege Press, 2006).
48. Becon, *The Governance of Vertue*, p. 80.
49. Calvin, *Institutes*, 3.10.6, p. 724.
50. McGrath, *Reformation Thought*, p. 256.
51. Thomas Aquinas, *Summa Theologiae* (*Vol. 35: Consequences of Charity*) [2a2ae. 34–46], ed. Thomas R. Heath (London: Eyre & Spottiswoode, 1969), question 35, articles 1–4, pp. 21–36.
52. Jaume Aurell, 'Reading Renaissance Merchants Handbooks: Confronting Professional Ethics and Social Identity', in *The Idea of Work in Europe from Antiquity to Modern Times*, ed. Josef Ehmer and Catharina Lis (Farnham: Ashgate, 2009), p. 86.
53. David Bevington, 'The Debate about Shakespeare and Religion', in *Shakespeare and Early Modern Religion*, ed. David Loewenstein and Michael Witmore (Cambridge: Cambridge University Press, 2015), p. 24.
54. Margot Heinemann, *Puritanism and Theatre: Thomas Middleton and Opposition Drama during the Early Stuarts* (Cambridge: Cambridge University Press, 1980), p. 33.
55. On the question of Shakespeare's alleged Catholic sympathies, a thoroughgoing examination of the available evidence can be found in David Scott Kastan, *A Will to Believe: Shakespeare and Religion* (Oxford: Oxford University Press, 2014), especially pp. 15–81.
56. The phrase was popularly coined in James Bartholomew, 'The Awful Rise of "Virtue Signalling"', *The Spectator* (18 April 2015), <https://www.spectator.co.uk/2015/04/hating-the-daily-mail-is-a-substitute-for-doing-good/> (last accessed 14 March 2017).
57. See also Bayne, 'Religion', pp. 58–9. For more recent readings along these lines, see A. D. Nuttall, *Shakespeare: The Thinker*, pp. 242–7, 265–76.
58. See Max Weber, *The Protestant Ethic and the Spirit of Capitalism*, trans. Talcott Parsons (1958; Kettering, OH:

Angelico Press, 2014); Ernst Troeltsch, *Protestantism and Progress: A Historical Study of the Relation of Protestantism to the Modern World*, trans. William Montgomery (London: Williams & Norgate, 1912); and Robert K. Merton, 'Science, Technology and Society in Seventeenth Century England', *Osiris*, 4 (1938), pp. 360–632.

59. See Christopher Hill, *Intellectual Origins of the English Revolution* (Oxford: Oxford University Press, 1965); Hugh Trevor-Roper, 'Review of *Intellectual Origins of the English Revolution* by Christopher Hill', *Theory and History*, 5:1 (1966), pp. 61–82, and 'The Religious Origins of the Enlightenment', in *Religion, the Reformation and Social Change, and Other Essays* (London: Macmillan, 1967), pp. 193–236. See also John Robertson, 'Hugh Trevor-Roper, Intellectual History and "The Religious Origins of the Enlightenment"', *The English Historical Review*, 124:511 (December 2009), pp. 1389–421.

60. See Landes, *The Wealth and Poverty of Nations*.

61. For an overview, see Gordon Marshall, *In Search of the Spirit of Capitalism: An Essay on Max Weber's Protestant Work Ethic Thesis* (London: Hutchinson, 1982), pp. 82–96; Malcolm H. MacKinnon, 'The Longevity of the Thesis: A Critique of the Critics', in *Weber's Protestant Ethic: Origins, Evidence, Contexts*, ed. Hartmut Lehmann and Guenther Roth (Cambridge: Cambridge University Press, 1993), pp. 211–43; and Mark D. Isaacs, *Centennial Rumination on Max Weber's* The Protestant Work Ethic and the Spirit of Capitalism (Boca Raton: Dissertation.com, 2006), pp. 164–86.

62. See Werner Sombart, *The Jews and Modern Capitalism*, trans. M. Epstein (1911; New York: E. P. Dutton, 1913).

63. See R. H. Tawney, *Religion and the Rise of Capitalism: A Historical Study* (1926; New Brunswick, NJ: Transaction, 1998).

64. See H. M. Robertson, *Aspects of the Rise of Economic Individualism: A Criticism of Max Weber and His School* (1933; New York: Kelly & Millan, 1959). See also Talcott Parsons, 'H. M. Robertson on Max Weber and His School', *Journal of Political Economy*, 43:5 (October 1935), pp. 688–96.

65. Hugh Trevor-Roper, 'Religion, the Reformation and Social Change', in *Religion, the Reformation and Social Change, and Other Essays* (London: Macmillan, 1967), pp. 1–45.
66. Fernand Braudel, *Civilization and Capitalism, 15th–18th Century*, 3 vols, trans. Siân Reynolds (Berkeley: University of California Press, 1993), vol. 3: *The Wheels of Commerce*, p. 570.
67. See Liah Greenfeld, *The Spirit of Capitalism: Nationalism and Economic Growth* (Cambridge, MA: Harvard University Press, 2001), pp. 4–6.
68. G. R. Elton, *Reformation Europe 1517–1559* (New York: Meridian Books, 1964), p. 315n, 317, 312–18.
69. Weber, *The Protestant Ethic*, p. 38.
70. Greenfeld, *The Spirit of Capitalism*, p. 20.
71. Donald McIntosh, 'The Modernity of Machiavelli', *Political Theory*, 12:2 (May 1984), p. 186.
72. See Markku Peltonen, *Classical Humanism and Republicanism in English Political Thought, 1570–1640* (Cambridge: Cambridge University Press, 1995), pp. 198–200.
73. Rupp, 'Luther and the German Reformation to 1529', p. 70.
74. Weber, *The Protestant Ethic*, p. 48.
75. Greenfeld, *The Spirit of Capitalism*, pp. 24, 41–2.
76. Giovanni Botero, *A Treatise, Concerning the Causes of the Magnificencie and Greatnes of Cities, Devided into Thre Books*, trans. Robert Peterson (London, 1606), pp. 11, 14, 48–50.
77. See Craig Muldrew, 'Interpreting the Market: The Ethics of Credit and Community Relations in Early Modern England', *Social History*, 18:2 (May 1993), pp. 163–83. See also Jill Phillips Ingram, *Idioms of Self-Interest: Credit, Identity, and Property in English Renaissance Literature* (New York and London: Routledge, 2006), pp. 7–10. Both authors argue that the early modern economy was built as much on bonds of 'communal trust' as it was on self-interest.
78. John Wheeler, *A Treatise of Commerce* (London: John Harison, 1601), p. 7.
79. Tawney, *Religion and the Rise of Capitalism*, is excellent on this. See also R. H. Tawney, 'The Damnable Sin of Usury', in

Thomas Wilson, *A Discourse Upon Usury by Way of Dialogue and Orations* . . . (1572), ed. R. H. Tawney (London: G. Bell & Sons, 1925), pp. 106–21.

80. Walter Raleigh, *A Cleare and Evident Way for Enriching the Nations of England and Ireland and for Setting Very Great Numbers of Poore on Work* (London: T. M. & A. C., 1650), pp. 4–5.
81. Smith, *The Wealth of Nations*.
82. Haidt, *The Righteous Mind*, p. 150.
83. Weber, *The Protestant Ethic*, pp. 28, 36.
84. Ibid. p. 102.
85. Ibid. p. 28.
86. On Machiavelli as Nietzschean 'master morality', see Raymond Angelo Belliotti, *Niccolò Machiavelli: The Laughing Lion and the Strutting Fox* (Langham, MD: Lexington Books, 2009), pp. 59–60.
87. Friedrich Nietzsche, *On the Genealogy of Morality*, ed. Keith Ansell Pearson, trans. Carol Diethe (1887; Cambridge: Cambridge University Press, 2006), pp. 154–6.
88. See E. K. Chambers, *William Shakespeare: A Study of Facts and Problems*, 2 vols (Oxford: Clarendon, 1930), vol. 1, pp. 57–91. See also Jayne Elisabeth Archer, Howard Thomas and Richard Marggraf Turley, 'Reading Shakespeare with the Grain: Sustainability and the Hunger Business', *Green Letters: Studies in Ecocriticism*, 19:1 (2015), pp. 8–20.
89. For the former, see, for example, Burton Hatlen, 'Feudal and Bourgeois Concepts of Value in *The Merchant of Venice*', in *Shakespeare: Contemporary Critical Approaches*, ed. Harry R. Garvin (Lewisburg: Bucknell University Press, 1980), pp. 91–105; for the latter, see Ivo Kamps (ed.), *Shakespeare Left and Right* (New York and London: Routledge, 1991). For a neo-Randian take, see Ingram, *Idioms of Self-Interest*. Overviews of work on Shakespeare and capitalism can found in Peter F. Grav, 'Taking Stock of Shakespeare and the New Economic Criticism', *Shakespeare*, 8:1 (2012), pp. 111–36; and, from a Marxist perspective, David Hawkes, *Shakespeare and Economic Theory* (New York and London: Bloomsbury, 2015).

90. David C. Rose, *The Moral Foundation of Economic Behaviour* (Oxford: Oxford University Press, 2011), pp. 19, 20.
91. I discussed this scene at greater length in Neema Parvini, *Shakespeare and Cognition*, p. 20.

Part II

Shakespeare's Moral Compass

CHAPTER 5

PAST REFLECTIONS ON SHAKESPEARE AND MORALITY

Postmodern criticism, with its propensity to reduce all ideas to ideology in the service of power, has had precious little to say about morality in Shakespeare's plays. Indeed, the relentless narrowness of its vision is such that 'it's difficult to avoid the conclusion that a model that's unable to distinguish between a Stalin and a Gandhi is of limited value' to moral questions.[1] But that does not mean that Shakespeare criticism more generally has not had a great deal to say about the playwright's moral imagination, even if many of the books on this theme have fallen into neglect or been forgotten to time. In this chapter, I will survey the major studies on Shakespeare and morality from 1775 to 1964. There have been several useful studies written since 1964, which I reference elsewhere in this book.[2] In focusing on older criticism here my aim is threefold: first, I wish to build an understanding of how critics from the past have typically thought about and approached the question of morality in Shakespeare's plays. Second, I will be on the lookout for valuable critical insights that I might retain for this study moving forward, especially if patterns of such insight recur across the generations. Third, in the researching of this book I have found that no such survey on this topic exists, so I hope this will be of significant use and benefit to later scholars.

The first major study on Shakespeare and morality was *The Morality of Shakespeare's Drama Illustrated* (1775) by Elizabeth Griffith, the Irish novelist, playwright and bluestocking. She had collaborated with David Garrick on her successful comedy, *The School for Rakes* (1769), and accordingly her Shakespearean study is dedicated to him with a prefatory note. Griffith took her cue from Elizabeth Montagu's defence of Shakespeare against Voltaire's attacks, *An Essay on the Writings and Genius of Shakespeare* (1769) – incidentally, the first book of Shakespeare criticism – in which she wrote, 'we are apt to write Shakespeare only as a poet; but he is certainly one of the greatest moral philosophers who ever lived'.[3] Griffith's method consists chiefly in approaching each of the plays in turn and outlining what she determines as the underlying didactic moral message. The shortcoming of this approach to Shakespeare reveals itself when she reaches *Measure for Measure* and starts by confessing 'I cannot see what moral can be extracted from the fable of this Piece.' Her chief thesis, however, is broadly consistent with what later generations of critics have concluded – that Shakespeare's gifts are to show and not tell: 'the dramatic moralist possesses a manifest advantage over the doctrinal one . . . mere descriptions of virtue do not strike us as strongly as the visible representations of them . . . [which] avail us more than Tully's offices or Seneca's Morals'.[4] None the less, Griffith's imagination was such that she assumed at all times that there *must* be an intended 'moral' for each 'fable'.

Much of the subsequent century of Shakespeare criticism, however, proceeded in a different direction, focusing less on Shakespeare the moral philosopher and more on Shakespeare the psychologist and master of characterisation. In *The Characters of Shakespear's Plays* (1817), William Hazlitt successfully synthesised the contributions of other great Shakespeareans such as August Wilhelm Schlegel and Samuel Taylor Coleridge to produce a strain of character criticism that would culminate at the end of the Victorian era in the work of A. C. Bradley. There is none the less in Hazlitt the lingering quest for moral meaning, which often becomes a matter of which characters arrest the audience's sympathies and which repel them. Like Griffith, he too seemed defeated on this front by *Measure for Measure*, in which he found 'our sympathies are repulsed and defeated in all directions'. But he is content, as I quoted in Chapter 1, to see the playwright's 'fellow-feeling' for his characters and, by extension, for other people in the real world.[5]

Other nineteenth-century publications devoted to Shakespeare and morality were restricted chiefly to compilation volumes aimed at the contemporary Victorian readership with selections of 'moral quotations' from Shakespeare. These were not unlike the books of filleted quotations one might easily find on any trip to Shakespeare's Globe or the gift shops of Stratford-upon-Avon today. These publications include *The Wisdom and Genius of Shakespeare, Comprising Moral Philosophy* ... (1839) with selections by Reverend Thomas Price, and *Shakespeare's Morals: Suggestive Selections* ... (1880) with the selections made this time by Arthur Gilman. According to Price, the wide range of moral wisdom to be found in the lines penned by Shakespeare provides 'evidence of his mind having been deeply imbued with the pure morality of the Gospel'.[6] Gilman, meanwhile, suggests that the 'greatest value' of Shakespeare's morals, by which he means maxims spoken by individual characters in the plays and stripped from their original contexts, 'will be found in the truths they convey and the practical wisdom they express'.[7] Although both Price and Gilman seem at pains to point out that disseminated parts of Shakespeare cannot hope even to glimpse the whole, there seems to be an uneasy tension between the experience of actually watching and reading Shakespeare and the purposes of moral instruction into which they are attempting to press his service. This was in no small part because of their assumption that Shakespeare conformed to orthodox Reformation

Protestant belief, which was common in the period. This was the argument, for example, put forth by Charles Wordsworth, Bishop of St Andrews, in *On Shakespeare's Knowledge and Use of the Bible* (1864),[8] and echoed by Charles Knight in *Studies of Shakespeare* (1868).[9]

At the turn of the twentieth century this view began to be challenged along the lines I began to outline in Chapter 4. Not only was it unlikely for a non-specialist in Shakespeare's time to be an 'orthodox protestant', but also it was not exactly clear what it would mean to be one in the 1590s. Chief among those who led the charge against this view was Richard Simpson, whose manuscript writings on Shakespeare were collected by Henry Sebastian Bowden and published as *The Religion of Shakespeare* (1899). As Bowden outlines, in Simpson we find 'an endeavour is made to show that Shakespeare, so far from being the product of his times, or the voice of his times, was in direct antagonism to his time'. The concluding chapter of this collection is called 'Shakespeare's Ethics', which is a sustained argument that Shakespeare's moral philosophy was broadly Catholic in the virtue ethics tradition and explicitly anti-Calvinist. The argument emphasises the role of free will in moral agency as against Calvinist notions of predestination and providence. On this Simpson (as well as Bowden, for it is not possible to know who wrote which parts) is quite convincing:

> And indeed if each character were necessarily determined by the moral principle within, or by circumstance, or by both, the whole interest, power, and pathos of Shakespeare's plays would be gone. If Iago were a villain, Henry V a hero, Isabel pure, and Cressida stained, solely by necessity, how could any measure of praise or blame be attributed to them? They would be no more responsible for their moral conduct than for the height of their stature or the colour of their hair. Virtue and vice would be meaningless. But Shakespeare's aim was to show 'virtue her own feature, scorn her own image', and virtue and vice with him have a real meaning. Their very notion consists in the fact that the agent in each

case might have done the opposite. Isabella's purity is admirable because she voluntarily preferred her own honour to her brother's life. Cressida lashes Troilus to desperation because she was voluntarily forsworn. She 'is and is not Cressida'.[10]

It is a striking insight. Shakespeare often seems at pains in plays to provide a sense of contingency and real alternative. We find characters in two minds with alternative paths clearly signposted: not only in the most famous examples, such as when Macbeth chooses to pursue the plot to kill Duncan, persuaded by Lady Macbeth against his own instincts, but also in easily forgotten or incidental passages. One such passage can be found in 2 *Henry VI*, in a polaroid negative of Macbeth's judgement, when Humphrey, the Duke of Gloucester, ignores his wife's goading to make a play for the crown himself (I, ii, 62–7).[11] Humphrey *could* have become king of England just as Macbeth *could* have remained thane of Cawdor. It is remarkable that in both cases Shakespeare's own historical account shows that much bloodshed might have been averted if the men in question had decided differently. While it is plain to see, then, that Simpson and Bowden are correct to highlight Shakespeare's emphasis on moral responsibility, it is not entirely clear that he did so with a fixed idea of good and evil. Humphrey made the opposite call to Macbeth but the outcome was similar. Does Shakespeare's moral vision encourage us to consider only intentions or does it encourage us to think also about consequences? Bowden and Simpson insist that Shakespeare is always clear that morality speaks – through God – in the conscience of his characters. For them,

> Shakespeare knows nothing of man's evolution from a brute, and he is wholly a stranger to the doctrine of Professor Huxley, that 'the cunning and brutal instincts of the ape or tiger ancestors must at times break out in any human being'. Man can with God's help keep all God's law, and be ever chaste, true, loyal, and just.[12]

This view is in stark contrast to W. J. Birch's earlier study, *An Inquiry into the Philosophy and Religion of Shakspere* (1848), which argued that Shakespeare's moral thinking was 'interwoven in the nature of things': 'His philosophy went to paint morality as independent of religious considerations. With him the laws of morality were written with sufficient plainness on the tablets of the human heart.'[13] Birch even goes so far as to suggest Shakespeare was an atheist. Thus, broadly speaking, by 1900 there were at least three different visions of Shakespeare's moral thinking: the first, following Griffith, and then Knight and Bishop Wordsworth, is that his values are straightforwardly Protestant, even if the audience must sometimes do some mental work to 'find the message'. This view foregrounds notions of divine providence in Shakespeare's thinking. Second, following Bowden and Simpson, his values are Catholic, built on the notions of moral responsibility, conscience, vices and virtues. Third, following Hazlitt and Birch, his vision is primarily secular and centred on the nature of human beings, despite their obvious shortcomings. For the sake of shorthand convenience and clarity I will label these traditions of thinking about Shakespeare's treatment of morality as follows:

1. The Protestant tradition foregrounding divine providence (Elizabeth Griffith, Charles Knight, Charles Wordsworth).
2. The Catholic tradition foregrounding moral conscience (Henry Sebastian Bowden, Richard Simpson).
3. The secular–humanist tradition foregrounding human nature (William Hazlitt, W. J. Birch).

As we shall see, studies focused on Shakespeare's moral philosophy in the twentieth century did much to refine these three different visions, but they did little to overturn them. Indeed, even the present study can be viewed as a hybrid between the Catholic and secular–humanist traditions, although with significantly updated scientific knowledge and the advantage of another 168 years of historical hindsight. Although Birch was a contemporary of Darwin's, he does not mention him. One critic who does mention Darwin, if only in passing, is Frank Chapman Sharp, whose book, *Shakespeare's Portrayal of the Moral Life* (1902), draws some strikingly similar conclusions. He points out that 'certain of Shakespeare's characters who, cheered by no sure faith either in personal reward or the ultimate triumph of the good cause, deliberately ranged themselves on the side of right, and hold their allegiance in defeat as in victory'. In a stunning passage, Sharp fleshes out his argument:

> Such men, Shakespeare saw, are facts. He was, furthermore, convinced that their judgements of value would still remain sound, the ends they pursued worth attaining, even if the universe should turn out to be nothing better than a lifeless machine. For if his tragedies are studies in failure, failure does not consist for him, as it does and must for Dante and Bunyan, in losing the chance of heaven, whether through the omission of some rite, through entanglement in a plausible heresy, or through death in the midst of unrepented and unexpiated sin. Just as little does it consist in disobedience to a supersensible law, or failure to prepare for some higher mode of existence. The tragedy of life, in his eyes, is that men do not know how to gain the best in life itself, or that knowing, they have not the power to guide will by insight, or that knowing and willing, they may be cut off from attainment by forces beyond their art to control.[14]

This appears to anticipate something like the existential uncertainty found in Jan Kott's *Shakespeare Our Contemporary* (1964): 'In Shakespeare's world there is a contradiction between the order of action and the moral order. This contradiction is human fate. One cannot get away from it.'[15] In other words, Shakespeare put forward some version of the constrained or 'tragic' vision in which there are no solutions, only trade-offs. Virtuous deeds are not necessarily rewarded, evil ones not necessarily punished, and answers from the void fail to materialise.

Just a year after Sharp's book came another great study of Shakespeare and morality, *The Moral System of Shakespeare* (1903) by Richard G. Moulton. This imagines Shakespeare running a great 'zoological experiment':

> Humour is often occupied with the ways of human nature. Zoology gravely studies the ways of animals: not merely the structures of their skeletons as an element in comparative anatomy, but the lightest turn of habit and custom, as that one spider spreads a web, another lives in a box with a lid to it. The ways of the animal man have a similar interest, even the infinite variations of individuality: how the carriers talk with ostlers in free slang; how a tavern hostess adapts herself to impracticable guests; distracted drawers flinging 'anons' in every direction; what permutations of the human scarecrow can be mustered into Falstaff's company of soldiers; what combination of social absurdities can hold revel in Shallow's orchard.[16]

This is a similar idea to the game scenarios I outlined in Chapter 1. However, unlike Sharp's, Moulton's vision is not a secular one and strikes some Protestant notes: 'These moral accidents are sudden openings into the unknown, giving us scattered intimations of a supreme Power behind the visible course of things, overruling all.'[17] This makes the moral world of Moulton's Shakespeare 'a system', as indicated by his title, rather than one of free agents as we find in Bowden or Birch.

The next major study on Shakespeare and morality came in the form of *The Shakespeare Symphony: An Introduction to the Ethics of Elizabethan Drama* (1906) by Harold Bayley, conceived largely as a corrective to Edward Dowden's claim that the period is 'for the most part absolutely devoid of a conscious purpose',[18] and claims made by Schlegel and Emerson that Shakespeare is unique among its writers. This is a largely historicist study that reveals some interesting points of crossover to demonstrate commonplace ideas about morality in the 1590s and early 1600s. For example, Shakespeare's line 'Thought is free' (*Twelfth Night*, I, iii, 63, and *The Tempest*, III, ii, 116) is also found in Heywood, Randolph, Beaumont and Fletcher, Martson, and Webster and Rowley. Bayley reminds us that 'When these sentiments were uttered Thought was not free: it was cribbed, cabined and confined. When it attempted to flutter from its prison it was struck down by the relentless claws of Authority.'[19] But passages of insight such as these are relatively few and far between. While Bayley is still useful as a repository of information, the study contents itself with the trivial little questions from which this book set out to escape.

To an almost comical extent, the opposite is true of Harold Ford's *Shakespeare: His Ethical Teaching* (1922), which is written in a style so generalised and overwrought that the 'intangible, impalpable something' for which it is looking never seems to arrive.[20] One is tempted to dismiss it entirely as empty bardolatry, but Ford does eventually stumble on something approaching a thesis:

> Shakespeare, though he offers no solution of the vexed problem of good and evil, yet recognises the moral constitution of nature, by insisting on the supremacy of moral goodness, and the ultimate defeat of evil; that the unbridled passions of men when uncontrolled by the law of man's higher nature lead inevitably to damnation and death; that though wickedness may seem temporarily to have dethroned the good, yet goodness still reigns supreme in the moral world. The good remains good, and goodness is the more radiant because of the gloom which cannot extinguish it.[21]

This is precisely the opposite conclusion to that drawn by Sharp in 1902. It is also demonstrably untrue. Where is the goodness that reigns supreme in the moral worlds of *Hamlet* or *Measure for Measure*? If there are shimmering beacons of radiant goodness emanating from these plays, I must have missed them. Ford continues:

> No one whoever came into contact with the arch-villain, Iago, or the Gorgons, Regan and Goneril, was moved with admiration for such characters, much less by any impulse to emulate or imitate them. No, we instinctively repudiate them; our whole moral nature recoils from them as from something morally loathsome; and the more vividly such characters are portrayed on the stage, the intenser become our feelings of abhorrence.[22]

There is, I think, some truth to this. All three of these characters offend our moral intuitions, but at the same time, there is still something of a morbid curiosity about and fascination with them. We are somehow drawn closer as we are repelled. The same is true of the Macbeths or Richard III. Perhaps we are drawn in because we recognise in ourselves some potential in their behaviour? Even in the most extreme cases, such as Goneril or Regan, would anyone say with certainty that, granted land and wealth by an aged parent, we would be happy to acquiesce to their conditions (in this case, food and shelter for six months with a hundred men)? We do recoil from the villains, but I would warrant that we do so only because we see our own faces in the mirrors they hold back at us.

I think it is worth persevering with Ford because the simplicity of the straightforward moral lessons he draws from Shakespeare is so unsatisfactory. But why are these lessons so unsatisfactory? Let us consider one more passage:

> In *Hamlet* the tragedy springs from adultery in the past. In *Macbeth* it is criminal ambition. In *Othello* it is the poison of slander. In *Measure for Measure* it is the sin of sensuality. In *Antony and Cleopatra* it is illicit love. In *The Merchant*

of Venice it is religious bigotry. Thus, it is moral evil in one or other of its many Protean shapes that produces the pains and penalties which issue in the resultant tragedy.[23]

I cannot help but wonder if there was ever a theatregoer whose chief response to *Hamlet* was to draw the lesson that 'adultery is evil'. This level of reduction – so certain, so 'black and white' – seems entirely antithetical to Shakespearean thinking, moral or otherwise. Even in the 'sins' Ford lists, there are immediate questions. Does *Measure for Measure* condemn sensuality? Is the moral point of *The Merchant of Venice* really to highlight religious bigotry? One reason that so much has been written on Shakespeare is because his plays are uniquely resistant to exactly these sorts of readings.

In *Christ in Shakespeare: Ten Addresses on Moral and Spiritual Elements in Some of the Greater Plays* (1928), George H. Morrison's conclusions stand in stark contrast to Ford's and belong in the secular–humanist tradition. 'Shakespeare is the most intense of individualists', he argues:

> Christ was severe just as Shakespeare is. He proclaimed an inexorable law. He knew that sin is dead, and that as a man soweth, so shall he also reap. But side by side with that, in Christ, there is a hope of rescue for the vilest, which is not recognisable in Shakespeare.
>
> Macbeth shows no traces of repentance, even when he is told his wife is dead. Iago, to the last, has a heart as the nether-millstone. Regan and Goneril are never visited by any yearning to be right with God again – they pass on, hardened, to the night.
>
> That is to say you do not find in Shakespeare what thousands of sinful men have found – a power that can redeem, and save the vilest and most hardened heart.[24]

It is striking that a scholar from the 1920s, who set out to write a book about *Christ in Shakespeare*, found that the plays are notable not only for the fact that so many characters do not find redemption, but also because they do not even *look* for it. It is clear that the world of moral absolutes that Ford describes does not exist in Shakespeare's dramatic vision. There is no overriding ethical karma at work.

The next decade saw the publication of *Shakespearean Selves: Essays in Ethics* (1938) by Arthur Temple Cadoux, who was an English Congregational Church minister. Cadoux returns to the method of Elizabeth Griffith, turning to each play and teasing out the ethical interest, but he is a shrewd reader of Shakespeare and this study remains valuable. His key insight is that characters show us the limits of their own moral visions. Thus, of Angelo in *Measure for Measure* he writes, 'His scheme of life had no decent place for sex, and therefore no foothold from which to fight its indecencies.' Cadoux presents an elaborated version of the Bowden / Simpson thesis, although stripped of its Catholic implications. He stresses Shakespeare's emphasis on 'the working of more inward factors of destiny'. In this view, 'Shakespeare catches in his mirror the inmost cavities of the soul, and more than any other helps a man to know himself.' However, the reflection is 'distorted by self-bias', which 'was to Shakespeare the common root of human ruin'. As I outlined in Chapters 1 and 2, modern evolutionary psychology has found human thinking to be strewn with systematic confirmation bias and other heuristics that often render us blind to our own hubris. Cadoux recognises this in what he calls 'the dominance of self-regard'; but for him, if we give into this, we are 'heading for spiritual catastrophe'.[25]

This emphasis on character is developed in Alfred Harbage's *As They Liked It: A Study of Shakespeare's Moral Artistry* (1947), a study firmly in the secular–humanist tradition that stands in sharp contrast to the historicist work that dominated its decade, which was, of course, fixated on notions of divine providence. For Harbage, there is no way of discussing morality in Shakespeare's plays without recourse to characters who are 'the *foci* of moral interest'. He goes on to outline an earlier version of Michael Bristol's 'vernacular intuitions' argument, which I discussed in Chapter 1. Characters are perpetually on trial, and the audience's judgement is either 'a *sentence* – or else it is an accolade'.[26] Harbage is reluctant to attribute intentions to Shakespeare, and stresses that audiences are likely to see their own pre-existing notions of good and evil reflected in the plays: the playwright is moral without ever moralising. He also develops an idea that Shakespeare's gifts were primarily as artist rather than as a moral philosopher, as in the following characteristic passages:

> Shakespeare is a dramatic artist, and the relation of dramatic art to the moral nature of man is about that of wind to the surface of water. It keeps the surface agitated, spanking it into sunny little ripples or driving it into powerful surges, but it does not trouble the depths. Dramatic art neither raises nor lowers the level, and the business of the dramatic artist is to know the height of the surface upon which he works.[27]

> Certain words common in Shakespeare criticism have been avoided in the foregoing discussion: *indifference, impartiality, irony*. . . . The word *accommodating* would be preferable to any of them were it not for the ignobility of its suggestions. The best word of all, obvious but inevitable, is simply *artistic*. These plays are deft. We are the instruments, and Shakespeare knows our stops.[28]

His message is ultimately life-affirming: Shakespeare 'knows our stops' because he is one of us and writes ultimately in solidarity. He does not so much teach us anything new but shows us more clearly what we already know.

Harbage's most idiosyncratic and bizarre (and therefore most interesting) observation is that the plays tend to be populated in the majority by 'indubitably good' characters who throw the others into relief; this is 'the safe majority'. He calculates percentages by classifying 775 characters in the thirty-eight plays 'of whom we can form a moral estimate'. By this rough science, he works out 49 per cent (378) are 'indubitably good', 20 per cent (158) are 'good in the main', 14 per cent (106) are 'bad in the main' and 17 per cent (133) are 'indubitably bad'. I have tabulated some of his examples of classifications in Table 5.1.

Table 5.1

Indubitably good – 49 per cent (378)	Horatio, Cordelia, Orlando, Portia (wife of Brutus), Hamlet, Helena, Bottom, Anne Bullen
Good in the main – 20 per cent (158)	Lear, Friar Laurence, Emilia, Posthumus
Bad in the main – 14 per cent (106)	The Apothecary, King Lewis XI, Cleopatra, Mistress Quickly, Falstaff, Shylock
Indubitably bad – 17 per cent (133)	Richard III, Iago, Goneril, Joan la Pucelle, Andrew Aguecheek, Claudius, Macbeth

It will not have escaped keen observers that overall this puts the 'good' characters at 69 per cent (536) versus only 31 per cent (239) for the 'bad' characters. 'Considering that drama is focused on trouble spots, these figures are cheering,' quips Harbage breezily. 'Shakespeare's humanity works with the angels in the proportion of seven to three. This is his safe majority.' And he finds this rough 70–30 split broadly consistent across characters of upper, middle and low classes.[29]

While we might take genuine issue with the specifics of several of Harbage's classifications, I think his general point is broadly true: most people in the plays defined this loosely are 'good'. However, I think a more compelling statistic, given these broad norms, would be to see where Shakespeare focuses most of his attention. If one were to order all the characters in Shakespeare by their total number of lines, we could place relatively few of those in the top fifty in the 'indubitably good' category. Even if one follows Harbage in placing the likes of Hamlet and Helena there (which I would question), by my rough estimate at least half would find themselves in 'bad' categories, and this is even while giving the benefit of the doubt to characters such as Othello, Hal / Henry V, Duke Vincentio and Rosalind. There seems a strong and obvious correlation between the number of lines a character has and how 'indubitably good' they appear to us: the more lines, the less likely they seem like angels. Is it really the case, therefore, that the 'safe majority' *are* indubitably good, or rather that most of them are so out of focus that their moral flaws do not become apparent to us?

Perhaps influenced by Harbage (although he does not cite him), in *The Shakespearean Ethic* (1959), John Vyvyan makes a bold claim: 'Shakespeare is never ethically neutral. He is never in doubt as to whether the souls of his characters are rising or falling.' For Vyvyan, Shakespeare's moral standard is captured by Polonius's advice to Laertes: 'to thine own self be true' (I, iii, 80). He spots a recurring pattern in which characters give in to a temptation to choose certain principles over love or life and betray their 'true self'. Thus, Brutus in *Julius Caesar* 'puts politics before humanity', Hamlet's 'death-wish has triumphed over his love-wish', Isabella in *Measure for Measure* exalts 'chastity above life and humanity', and so on. Vyvyan's key insight is that the temptation is almost always followed by a period of inner conflict in which he see characters struggle with their 'true selves'; there will usually be a second temptation before the character makes their ultimate choice, for good or for ill. Eventually, this reveals itself as a rearticulating of the Catholic tradition à la Bowden and Simpson, foregrounding conscience: 'the tragic hero, who betrays his own Self' is akin to 'Judas, who betrays Christ'.[30] Thus, for Vyvyan, as for Bowden and Simpson, in Shakespeare there is always a choice, and moral agency leaves the door open for salvation.

Interestingly, in *Shakespeare and Christian Doctrine* (1963), Roland Mushat Frye draws quite a different conclusion: 'I find that an explicitly New Testament ethic is less relevant to Shakespeare's plays than an ethic of purely natural law, based equally in the Scriptures and the Greek and Latin classics.' As with George H. Morrison before him, Frye looks for an explicitly Christian message in Shakespeare and instead finds a humanist moral vision: 'the mirror of Shakespearean drama was held up to nature, and not to saving grace'. However, like Vyvyan, he foregrounds choice and agency as being integral to the Shakespearean ethic: 'Nowhere is the necessity for moral responsibility clearer than in the cases of Iago and Edmund. If these two great villains were not responsible for their actions, an audience could scarcely regard them as being, in any meaningful sense, villainous.' But if the mirror is held up to nature rather than to divine grace, by what moral authority can we tell what is villainous and what is virtuous? According to Frye, it comes down to basic humanity. For example, 'in general the family tie is basic to what is human in life', and so violence to that family tie – as we see in *King Lear* – offends nature and therefore Goneril and Regan are obvious villains.[31] Writing a year after Frye, in 1964, V. G. Kiernan similarly found Shakespeare's outlook 'profoundly humanistic' and 'profoundly unreligious': 'he was not interested, as some of the other dramatists were, in ropes to link human beings together that had to be slung over the pulley of a remote heaven'.[32]

In this survey, we have seen three broad traditions of thinking about Shakespeare and morality: first, the Protestant tradition, which emphasises an overarching cosmic system and concepts of divine or poetic justice. These include the studies by Elizabeth Griffith, Charles Knight, Bishop Wordsworth, Richard G. Moulton and Harold Ford, and they are implicitly endorsed by historicists, new or old, who broadly accept that Shakespeare and his audience were wedded to the Great Chain of Being. Second, there is the Catholic tradition, which emphasises the centrality of moral agency and conscience in a moral universe in which redemption is possible, if one chooses correctly. This strand of criticism includes Richard Simpson, Henry Sebastian Bowden, Arthur Temple Cadoux, Alfred Harbage and John Vyvyan; their inheritors, directly or indirectly, are David N. Beauregard, who (as we saw in Chapter 3) stresses the influences of Aristotle and St Thomas, and Michael D. Bristol, who (as we saw in Chapter 1) stresses the importance of moral agency. The third tradition is that of secular humanism, which views Shakespeare's moral sense as coming out of what is natural in humanity. Here there is no higher order, no cosmic justice, no final redemption, only an intuitive sense of what is right and wrong in lived experience. Advocates of this view include William Hazlitt, W. J. Birch, Frank Chapman Sharp, George H. Morrison, Roland Mushat Frye and V. G. Kiernan; their inheritors would include Jan Kott, Robin Headlam Wells and A. D. Nuttall.

Although these are three distinct strains in the criticism, there are naturally many points of similarity and crossover. Across virtually all these studies, we find a playwright sympathetic to individuals and unwilling to write off humanity. He is seldom despairing, even if his moral vision tends to look down at the groundlings rather than up at the sky for answers. He does not condemn or moralise, and he is suspicious of those who make exaggerated claims about their own virtuousness as a pretext to condemn others. Although it is not possible to locate adherence to any specific Christian doctrine in his works, Shakespeare's moral vision seems to echo Jesus on the Mount of Olives: 'He that is without sin among you, let him first cast a stone at her' (John 8: 7). We need to look inwards and judge ourselves, before we look outwards and judge others.

> **In summary**
> - A survey of Shakespeare criticism from 1775 to 1964 demonstrates that there are three main traditions of thinking about Shakespeare and morality: the Protestant tradition foregrounding divine providence (Elizabeth Griffith, Charles Knight, Bishop Charles Wordsworth, Richard G. Moulton and Harold Ford), the Catholic tradition foregrounding moral conscience (Richard Simpson, Henry Sebastian Bowden, Arthur Temple Cadoux, Alfred Harbage and John Vyvyan) and the secular–humanist tradition foregrounding human nature (William Hazlitt, Frank Chapman Sharp, George H. Morrison and Roland Mushat Frye).
> - Shakespeare stresses the importance of viable alternatives in ethical choices; as Richard Simpson and Henry Sebastian Bowden put it, 'the agent in each case might have done the opposite', and this is what makes the moral decisions in the plays meaningful.
> - Shakespeare's plays emphasise the psychological interiority of morality, what Arthur Temple Cadoux calls the 'inward factors of destiny'. We come to understand rights and wrongs 'from the inside out', rather than by external judgement.
> - Shakespeare has a positive view of humanity; in *As They Liked It: A Study of Shakespeare's Moral Artistry* (1947), Alfred Harbage argues there is a 'safe majority' of good characters in the plays.
> - It is not possible to pin Shakespeare down to any Christian doctrine, and it is not clear whether or not the worlds of his plays allow for redemption; his sinners seldom seek it.

Notes

1. Wells, *Shakespeare's Humanism*, p. 79.
2. I would include in their number: Beauregard, *Virtue's Own Feature*; Tzachi Zamir, *Double Vision: Moral Philosophy and Shakespearean Drama* (Princeton: Princeton University Press, 2007); Tilmouth, *Passion's Triumph of Reason*; Knapp,

Image Ethics in Shakespeare and Spencer; Bristol (ed.), *Shakespeare and Moral Agency*; Gray and Cox (eds), *Shakespeare and Renaissance Ethics*; and Anthony Raspa, *Shakespeare the Renaissance Humanist: Moral Philosophy and His Plays* (New York and London: Palgrave Macmillan, 2016).

3. Elizabeth Montagu, *An Essay on the Writings and Genius of Shakespeare* . . . (1769; London: Harding and Wright, 1810), p. 37.
4. Elizabeth Griffith, *The Morality of Shakespeare's Drama Illustrated* (London: T. Caddell, 1775), pp. 35, 526.
5. Hazlitt, *The Characters of Shakespear's Plays*, pp. 244, 247.
6. Thomas Price, *The Wisdom and Genius of Shakespeare: Comprising Moral Philosophy* . . . (Philadelphia: E. L. Carey & A. Hart, 1839), p. iii.
7. Arthur Gilman, *Shakespeare's Morals: Suggestive Selection* . . . (New York: Dodd, Mead & Company, 1880), p. ix.
8. Wordsworth, *On Shakespeare's Knowledge and Use of the Bible*.
9. Charles Knight, *Studies of Shakespeare* (London: Routledge, 1868).
10. Henry Sebastian Bowden, *The Religion of Shakespeare* (London: Burnes & Oates, 1899), pp. viii, 386.
11. For my full reading of this scene see Parvini, *Shakespeare's History Plays*, p. 108.
12. Bowden, *The Religion of Shakespeare*, pp. 407–8.
13. Birch, *An Inquiry into the Philosophy and Religion of Shakspere*, pp. 35, 40.
14. Frank Chapman Sharp, *Shakespeare's Portrayal of the Moral Life* (New York: Charles Scribner's Sons, 1902), pp. 223–4.
15. Jan Kott, *Shakespeare Our Contemporary* (1964; W. W. Norton, 1974), p. 17.
16. Richard G. Moulton, *The Moral System of Shakespeare: A Popular Illustration of Fiction as the Experimental Side of Philosophy* (New York and London: Macmillan, 1903), p. 201.
17. Ibid. p. 322.
18. Edward Dowden, *Shakespeare, His Mind and Art* (New York and London: Harper and Brothers, 1881), p. 8.

19. Harold Bayley, *The Shakespeare Symphony: An Introduction to the Ethics of Elizabethan Drama* (London: Chapman and Hall, 1906), pp. 68–9.
20. Harold Ford, *Shakespeare: His Ethical Teaching* (London: Smith's Printing Co., 1922), p. 20.
21. Ibid. p. 37.
22. Ibid. pp. 37–8.
23. Ibid. pp. 42–3.
24. George H. Morrison, *Christ in Shakespeare: Ten Addresses on Moral and Spiritual Elements in Some of the Greater Plays* (London: James Clarke & Co., 1928), pp. 43, 41–2.
25. Arthur Temple Cadoux, *Shakespearean Selves: Essays in Ethics* (London: Epworth Press, 1938), pp. 81, 159, 162.
26. Alfred Harbage, *As They Liked It: A Study of Shakespeare's Moral Artistry* (1947; New York: Harper Torchbook, 1961), pp. 16, 18, emphasis in original.
27. Ibid. p. 57.
28. Ibid. p. 113, emphasis in original.
29. Ibid. pp. 166–70.
30. John Vyvyan, *The Shakespearean Ethic* (1959; London: Shepherd-Walwyn, 2011), pp. 11, 12, 47, 65, 178.
31. Roland Mushat Frye, *Shakespeare and Christian Doctrine* (Princeton: Princeton University Press, 1963), pp. 94, 167, 158–9, 123.
32. V. G. Kiernan, 'Human Relationships in Shakespeare', in *Shakespeare in a Changing World*, ed. Arnold Kettle (London: Lawrence & Wishart, 1964), p. 50.

CHAPTER 6

AUTHORITY

In this chapter, I argue that Shakespeare's response to the moral foundation of authority is not located in the speeches of his political leaders because authority is not synonymous with power. Authority must be earned, whereas power is usually bestowed. Therefore, we must look to the relationships between characters of different social rank, especially between servants and their masters. In Shakespeare's plays these relationships often take the form of freely chosen employment as opposed to feudal oaths of fealty. This is because paid employment became the new norm as early capitalism flourished in the 1500s, and the last remnants of the old feudal order were swept away. Focusing on the relationship between Adam and Orlando in *As You Like It*, the contrast between Kent and Oswald in *King Lear*, and the relationship between Flavius the steward and Timon in *Timon of Athens*, I contend that in Shakespeare's plays virtuous authority entails reciprocal good service. Good service is found not in mere obedience but in a sense of duty, which might on occasion directly contradict the wishes of the master. In the ideal scenario, which is glimpsed in the relationship between Adam and Orlando in *As You Like It*, good leadership is rewarded with good service. However, sometimes – as in the cases of Kent and Lear, and Flavius and Timon – poor leaders are rewarded with good service, which (as bad leaders) they fail to recognise. Even so, good servants seem to derive a sense of meaningful purpose from their duty, while characters who fail to transcend self-interest find only existential despair. In virtually all cases, if authority is mistaken for oppressive power, and if liberty is mistaken for subversion, tyranny follows.

Few topics have been as thoroughly mined out as that of Shakespeare's depiction of power, which was an obsession of new historicist and cultural materialist critics from the 1980s to the mid-2000s. I have analysed the strengths and shortcomings of these two schools elsewhere at length.[1] New historicists tended to see Shakespeare's plays as being complicit with power, while cultural materialists tended to see them as working to expose the ideological contradictions in power structures. However, despite their sustained focus on power, neither of these approaches can tell us very much about the nature of authority in Shakespeare's plays. Their view of power is almost always corrosive and oppressive: something that is, by its very nature, harmful and even immoral. They can understand power structures only as shibboleths to be brought down. The baby boomer generation did not like anyone telling them what to do: the kids are alright. This overwhelmingly negative view of power is because, although they differed on many issues, new historicists and cultural materialists were united politically on the left, and in some cases, even on the far left. As per Jonathan Haidt's *The Righteous Mind*, those on the left tend to be morally blind to the foundation of authority because they process the world almost exclusively through the lens of care, fairness and liberty.[2] To such a mindset, power and oppression often appear to be synonyms, which is especially ironic, given that the same people often show a remarkable faith in the ability of government to solve social problems – if only it were the *right sort* of government, invariably the sort with their anointed philosopher kings *du jour* in key positions of power.

By contrast, in the 1960s, various voices from the right, including the Conservative Member of Parliament, Enoch Powell, arguably 'the most popular politician of his time',[3] viewed Shakespeare as being straightforwardly patriotic and, with perhaps a touch of jingoism, celebrated his apparent love of order. For Powell, Shakespeare sounded 'the chord of patriotism: the romantic self-consciousness of national identity as against the rest of mankind'.[4] This was the mainstream British Broadcasting Corporation (BBC) version of the thesis put forward by E. M. W. Tillyard about twenty years earlier.[5] At that time it was to drum up a sense of social cohesion and national spirit during World War II; in the 1960s it was bound up with questions of what it meant to be British in a rapidly changing society. Generally, those insisting on a Patriotic Bard make the keynote speeches in the history plays do much work. And it was this version of Shakespeare that the cultural materialists had initially set out to correct before encountering its modern update in the form of new historicism.[6]

From my vantage point, these old debates reveal more about the readers and watchers of Shakespeare's plays than they do about the playwright. Each of them seems to create Shakespeare in their own image or to serve their own ends. It should not surprise us that a staunch Conservative such as Enoch Powell should see his own patriotism reflected in Shakespeare, while radical leftists such as Alan Sinfield and Jonathan Dollimore see the same plays exposing the limits and ideological fractures of such patriotism. In both cases, we can see the real effects of confirmation bias. The Shakespeare play is a Rorschach test: where I am prone to see a butterfly, you are prone to see a bat. It is Richard II's mirror smashed into tiny pieces, reflecting our own faces. One reason for this, as T. J. B. Spencer argued, is because of the playwright's deliberate sophistry: his ability to argue for the wrong side brilliantly. In many cases, we do not and cannot know which side Shakespeare thought 'wrong'.[7]

It is therefore easy to become swayed by the virtuosity of his characters' speeches or else recognise views with which we agree in them, assuming in the excitement that Shakespeare is on 'our side'. Because of this, I do not think we can locate Shakespeare's attitude towards authority in these moments of rhetorical flourish. For example, it has been commonplace to take Ulysses' speech on the nature of degree in *Troilus and Cressida* as emblematic of the playwright's idealised vision of social order:

> How could communities,
> Degrees in schools, and brotherhoods in cities,
> Peaceful commerce from dividable shores,
> The primogenity and due of birth,
> Prerogative of age, crowns, scepters, laurels,
> But by degree stand in authentic place?
> Take but degree away, untune that string,
> And hark what discord follows. (I, iii, 97–104)

Taken in isolation and out of the context of the rest of the play, this might seem a straightforward endorsement of Plato's *Republic* and a proto-Hobbesian warning against the possibility of lapsing into the state of nature. But *Troilus and Cressida* is a play in which seemingly every point is debated endlessly, and on which many different speakers hold forth on a variety of topics. Rather than a straightforward endorsement, the play facilitates 'a conversation between Shakespeare and Platonism'.[8] Because of this quality of Shakespeare's politicians, I do not think that we can find a specifically *moral* response to authority through politics, and especially not through rhetorical flourishes. Instead, it seems to me that we might detect an underlying attitude to authority in the *relationships* between characters of different social ranks. Authority in Shakespeare is not located in power and governance, but in service and dependency.

For all the talk of the Great Chain of Being, feudalism had been in permanent decline in England from the end of Richard II's reign in 1399. To understand the nature of service in the 1590s and early 1600s, it is necessary to grasp drastic changes in economic relationships from feudalism to nascent pre-industrial capitalism.

> [I]n the thirteenth century, demesnes were managed by lords' officials for the lords' own table and profit, most of which was allocated for nonprofitable expenditure on display and warfare. The profits from the produce from demesnes can only be seen to have been invested profitably in feudal terms – that is, in the ability to further extra-economic ends. In the fifteenth century the demesnes were farmed by wealthy peasants producing in competition, an unprecedented step. So when the demesnes were leased to wealthier peasants in the fifteenth century, a novel dynamic of competitive production was set in train.⁹

Initially, these peasant farmers, who either held a copyhold or (increasingly) leased their demesnes wholesale from absentee *rentier* landlords, were mostly at subsistence level: 'In the early sixteenth century, around 80 per cent of farmers were only growing enough food for the needs of their family household.' But as the 1500s wore on the trend was towards increased productivity and profit, a long trend that would continue until 1850.¹⁰ As an example, Richard Shakespeare, William's grandfather on his father's side, was making a good living as a yeoman tenant famer in Stratford in the 1520s. His landlord was not an aristocrat but landed gentry: specifically, Robert Arden, William's grandfather on his mother's side. England's post-feudal, pre-industrial economy saw 'between 70 and 80 per cent of the occupied population . . . primarily engaged in agriculture, though of course many of them must have pursued secondary occupations in industry and trade'. It was a 'predominantly rural, family-based economy'.[11] It is crucial to recognise that, by the end of the sixteenth century, the manor – the bedrock of the old feudal system – 'had become an anachronism'.[12] Manorial lords, who for over a century had largely collected rents in absentia, for financial reasons started selling their lands on the open market. James I himself sold Crown lands in the 1610s to raise extra funds: for example, in 1614, he sold copyholds in the West Country for a total of £11,928. Between 1560 and 1620, land transactions in England doubled. Who was buying this land? In some cases, it was nobles or the gentry. In others, tenants would buy the land to convert their existing copyhold or leaseholds into freeholds. In Yorkshire, for example, 'roughly 40 per cent of all transactions in the later sixteenth century were "downwards transmissions"', from either nobility or gentry to yeomen.[13]

These economic changes effectively created new socio-economic classes comprising enterprising landowners and paid employees. Of those who received a working wage for a living – a 'shepherd to another man', as Corin in *As You Like It* puts it (II, iv, 70) – it is useful to make a distinction between those who 'lived out' and those who 'lived in'. Those employees who did not live in the households of their employers would usually makes ends meet working at a variety of different casual jobs as supply and demand dictated (although, as the statistics quoted above suggest, the vast majority of these jobs were in agricultural labour). Those who lived in consisted of apprentices, who would usually take training in lieu of payment, and domestic servants, who, as well as earning cash, might also take payment in the form of 'board', political privileges or even land. Around 29 per cent of households in England had live-in servants of various ranks and duties, typically aged between ten and thirty, with older servants such as stewards often having their own dwellings.[14]

This relatively new set of economic arrangements in the sixteenth century produced at least two interesting features for us to consider as regards authority. First, there is a yawning chasm between the political theory – of the Great Chain of Being variety that E. M. W. Tillyard made do so much work in *The Elizabethan World Picture* (1942),[15] which maintained something approximating the old feudal order – and the economic reality on the ground. To focus entirely on the official doctrine as Tillyard did, and, it must be said, as new historicists often did, is to ignore these 'new emerging forces which seemed to threaten cherished ideals'.[16] As I argued in Chapter 1, Shakespeare's moral vision plays out in the realm of lived experience rather than philosophical systems, and hence his concern here is with the economic reality rather than the political theory. Second, and perhaps easy to miss, is the fact that while forms of hierarchy and obedience are theoretically still in effect, *in practice* a servant, as a paid employee, is not bound to work for only one master for life, and likewise the master has no obligation to keep the employee in service beyond the terms of their contract. This means that service itself was something approaching a free market.

This topic, once neglected in Shakespeare studies, has been treated in three book-length studies, all of which were published in 2005: Linda Anderson's *A Place in the Story: Servants and Service in Shakespeare's Plays*, Judith Weil's *Service and Dependency in Shakespeare's Plays* and David Evett's *Discourses of Service in Shakespeare's England*. These monographs all make it clear that service was not only an ideal of early modern life in England, but also a practical and social necessity, for many of the same reasons that Shakespeare's Ulysses outlines. Anderson points out that recent critics have paid disproportionate attention to rebellious or subversive servants at the expense of the larger numbers of obedient ones because they seem more interesting. As I have noted, this should come as no surprise because cultural materialism, which valued subversion highly, was all the rage in the 1980s and 1990s.

> Servants who fail to rebel, who do as they are commanded, who flatter their employers, who remain loyal even at the expense of their own self-interest, are harder to incorporate into our narrative of subversion. We may acknowledge that they are too oppressed, but their failure openly to resist their oppression makes them less interesting, though potentially more disturbing, to us than the rioters and outlaws.[17]

Anderson's use of 'us' is interesting here. Who is 'we'? I would warrant it is certainly not Enoch Powell. The 'us' in this passage refers to Shakespeare critics on the liberal left, to whom the very notion of 'service' automatically translates into 'oppression'. To use Haidt's phrase, this is a 'WEIRD' response.[18] Evett addresses it head on, seeking to liberate us from the 'bleak vision of the materialists'. 'We postmoderns', he says with a touch of sarcasm, cannot process 'servants and other subordinates, expressing love and respect for their social and economic superiors' and so must explain this away as 'false consciousness' by relying on 'the materialist emphasis on *ressentiment*'.[19] Anderson goes on to argue that critics have been too quick to dismiss the more obedient servants as 'nose-picking halfwits' in Shakespeare's plays because of a 'desire for neatness of pattern rather than genuine engagement',[20] but then she seems to look for the *subversive* potential in these 'good' servants as possible comments on or judgements of their masters. This is to see these servants through WEIRD eyes. It is less an attempt at subversion and more a lived understanding of how authority works in the real world. As Weil argues, we should avoid 'narrow, utopian prejudices against subordination in general and work in particular'.[21] It is a basic fact of life, not only in Shakespeare's time but also in our own. Any mature response to the nature of service in the plays, and the moral foundation that underlies it, must move beyond the gaze of the wide-eyed revolutionary.

One obvious example is Adam in *As You Like It*, who, in an act of incredible selflessness, gives Orlando his life savings with a pledge: 'let me be your servant' (III, ii, 46). As Mark Thornton Burnett notes, although we think of Adam primarily as a *loyal* servant, 'in order to follow Orlando, Adam must be unfaithful to Orlando, which suggests that loyalty, a quality to be earned, can never be taken for granted'.[22] It seems to me that the relationship between Adam and Orlando primarily leans on the moral foundation of authority, rather than loyalty. Anderson picks up on this without naming it as such: Adam '*chooses* to serve his old master's virtuous son, rather than his villainous son, a choice Shakespeare surely must have meant us to applaud.'[23] The fact that Adam makes a free choice to follow Orlando is significant. Since it is Adam who gives his money to Orlando in aid, it cannot be for financial reasons – and the fact that he has such money in the first place tells us he was paid a wage. Adam is effectively a free agent after Oliver's dismissal of him at I, i, 78, and nothing obliges him to follow Orlando into the forest. The fact that he does so reveals a moment of authentic service in the name of authority. Evett goes further by suggesting that Orlando learns a sense of duty and how to serve from Adam:

> [T]he old servant's thematic role has been taken over by his new master, for the new Adam, Orlando, with the old Adam as his model, serves Adam as Adam has served him . . . ministering to him like a nurse to a child. More fully yet, we see that in Orlando, the concept of service has come to extend all elements of his life. . . . By the play's end he arrives at the center of a network of servitudes. . . . Despite the wrongs done him by his brother Oliver, Orlando freely chooses to serve the latter at the risk of his own life, saving him from the lion and the snake. . . . And even more than Adam, he freely chooses to do these things.[24]

This sense of duty, freely chosen when less risky choices are available, is the beating heart of the moral foundation of authority. Adam's dutiful service is repaid in kind by the fact that Orlando himself dutifully serves.

However, this curiously sentimental and romantic picture of reciprocal service in *As You Like It* is not reflected in every play. Let us substitute Orlando for Lear, and old Adam for Kent. What happens to the picture? Where there is a reciprocity in Orlando's relationship with Adam, those who follow Lear 'are touched by servility through their one-sided relations with him'.[25] Jonas A. Barish and Marshall Waingrow articulated this view in 1958:

> Service, for our purposes, may be thought of as the formalization of relationships between individuals of different social or political rank. So much is implicit in the doctrine of hierarchy. An individual obeys or ministers to his superior in the social scale, and that superior ministers to his superior. But an essential thing about this relationship in Lear is its *feudal* character: ideal service works two ways; it implies rights as well as duties, on each side. The reciprocity suggested by the term 'bond', where privileges are granted at the same time that duties are imposed, is the condition that justifies service in principle; in practice, it is precisely the denial of reciprocity that is the first of Lear's tragic violations. By refusing to honour the reciprocal force of the bond tying him to his inferiors, Lear cuts the bond, 'cracks' it, and so lets loose the forces of disorder, division, and disservice that are to overwhelm the kingdom.[26]

One key difference between Adam's bond to Orlando and Kent's to Lear is that the former, as we have seen, is freely chosen, whereas the latter has a feudal basis. Kent is no less devoted a servant than is Adam, but crucially Orlando has earned his authority, which is subsequently reciprocal, whereas Lear's rests on his status as king. It is fair to say that

Authority

Lear wields power but, at least as we see him in the play, he does not seem to have authority. It is valid to ask, therefore, what motivates Kent to keep following him? I will return to this question shortly.

At the start of the play Kent has a different understanding of service from his King, who seems to expect complete obedience from his subjects. This is revealed in one of his tirades against Goneril's steward, Oswald:

> Such smiling rogues as these,
> Like rats, oft bite the holy cords atwain
> Which are too intrinse t'unloose; smooth every passion
> That in the natures of their lords rebel,
> Bring oil to fire, snow to their colder moods;
> Renege, affirm, and turn their halcyon beaks
> With every gale and vary of their masters,
> Knowing naught (like dogs) but following. (II, ii, 79–86)

Kent berates Oswald for being servile in service. For Kent, a bad servant, such as Oswald, panders to their master's every whim like 'dogs'. To adapt Haidt's metaphor of the intuitive elephant and the rational rider (see Chapter 1), if the master's elephant – 'passions', as Kent puts it – seems to lurch wildly left or right, the bad servant, much like the rider, swiftly takes whatever actions are necessary to extenuate them. The bad servant sees their master in a hot temper ('fire') and, being a snivelling and submissive sycophant, thinks only to fuel it, and likewise bring 'snow to their colder moods'. The implication of Kent's attack is that good service in each of these cases would be to try to steer the elephant to a more rational course. The good servant, then, should not tell his master what he wants to hear, but in some cases must challenge him.

Barish and Waingrow argue that Shakespeare depicts Oswald as the epitome of the bad servant: he is little more than Goneril's 'puppet'. They go so far as to speak of 'the total immolation of his will in hers'; he is remarkable for 'his failure to exist at all except as her creature'.²⁷ In fact, so total is Oswald's subservience that in his first eight spoken lines of dialogue, more than half make explicit reference to his 'madam' (I, iii, 3; I, iii, 11; I, iii, 17; I, iv, 307) or 'lady' (I, iv, 71), and this continues throughout the play. In fact, he says 'madam' a total of ten times in Act IV alone (IV, ii, 3; IV, ii, 29; IV, iv, 1; IV, iv, 2; IV, iv, 5; IV, iv, 15; IV, iv, 17; IV, iv, 22; IV, iv, 27; IV, iv, 39). The repetition is too marked for this to be sketchy characterisation; Shakespeare deliberately makes Oswald as obsequious as possible – and a skilled actor could wring comic potential from the sliminess of his 'madam'. It is perhaps no coincidence either that his final utterance should start with the word 'slave' (IV, v, 238). Shakespeare makes it abundantly clear that there is nothing morally good in servility. Even in a feudal hierarchy, an excessive willingness to please one's superiors offends the moral foundation of authority.

Of course, Oswald finds his opposite in Kent himself, who has already demonstrated his philosophy of good service by speaking truth to power in the opening scene of the play:

> Think'st thou that duty shall have dread to speak
> When power to flattery bows? To plainness honour's bound
> When majesty falls to folly. Reserve thy state,
> And in thy best consideration check
> This hideous rashness. Answer my life my judgment:
> Thy youngest daughter does not love thee least,
> Nor are those empty-hearted whose low sounds
> Reverb no hollowness. (I, i, 144–52)

Even in the feudal bond, good service is not mere obedience or submission to power; the line of duty sometimes calls for disobedience. This is the rationale, for example, of Edward IV's lament regarding his subjects in *Richard III* after he discovers

Clarence has been killed: 'Who sued to me for him? Who, in my rage, / Kneeled at my feet and bade me be advised?' (II, i, 104–5). In *King* Lear, it is obvious that Cordelia has done nothing wrong and that Lear has acted in 'hideous rashness' in banishing her. As Weil observes, it results from his 'failure to recognize the difference between daughters and followers'.[28] Lear also fails to recognise that in openly speaking out against his foolish decision, Kent is the model of good service. As Richard Strier puts it, in his 'behaviour ... the theme of virtuous, morally mandated disobedience, even interference, is fully articulated'.[29] After Lear banishes Kent, he once again disobeys him by donning his disguise as Caius and living out the very opposite of banishment. What is interesting here is that, with banishment, Kent is effectively released from service as a feudal retainer, and yet he freely chooses to follow the King regardless. Since Lear has shown virtually no signs of being a good leader thus far in the play, why should this be? It is possible that he was once a good leader that has only momentarily lapsed into madness, but his two elder daughters are hardly good adverts of that possibility. In fact, we can infer from the one-sided nature of Goneril's relationship with Oswald – dominant mistress and toadying steward – not to mention her own skill in flattering Lear himself, that he was always a poor role model. It seems more likely that Kent's unswerving devotion to his King is a facet of his moral character rather than any direct response to Lear's leadership. It is unambiguous, I think, that Shakespeare views good service – of the kind that Kent embodies – as a moral virtue. Lear plainly does not deserve a servant like Kent, but England is better for it in the end that he is blessed with one.

We see a parallel example of this in *Timon of Athens*, a play that has often been paired with *King Lear*. Flavius, Timon's steward, is a servant who brings snow rather than oil to fire, much like Kent. In that play there is little doubt that Flavius stands at moral centre as the sole bastion of good service in a seemingly bankrupt world. The similarities between Flavius and Kent are too numerous to be accidental. Surely, then, the vision of good service they represent is morally ingrained in Shakespeare's imagination. Like Kent in Lear's court, we are supposed to laud Flavius's plainness in speaking the truth while Timon is surrounded by vapid or cynical flatterers. A. D. Nuttall describes the obvious similarities between Lear and Timon:

> Lear expects reciprocal gratitude after his gift of the kingdom to his three daughters at the beginning of the play. Goneril and Regan are like Timon's false friends. They profess love but are insensible of any ethical obligation. They simply hang on to whatever they can get. Lear's folly, we could say (as we said of Timon's), 'asked for it'.[30]

Authority must be earned and cannot be bought; Kent and Flavius alike are keenly aware of this fact.

There are further similarities: like both Adam in *As You Like It*, and Kent, Flavius follows his master *after* the point at which he can gain from the relationship personally: in this case, when Timon has lost all his money and leaves Athens in IV, i. In the following scene, Flavius demonstrates extraordinary altruism in dividing his own money between his fellow servants. This is an especially virtuous act because we know from the play that he is frugal, someone who knows the price of money. Yet, like Adam, he is willing to give of his own resources in good service until they are extinguished. After this, he resolves to find his old master, even though at this point Timon has nothing:

> He's flung in rage from this ingrateful seat
> Of monstrous friends.
> Nor has he with him to supply his life,
> Or that which can command it.
> I'll follow and inquire him out.
> I'll ever serve his mind with my best will;
> Whilst I have gold, I'll be his steward still. (IV, ii, 45–51)

Note that Flavius persistently emphasises that he follows Timon for his 'mind', not because of his social status. He finds Timon near his cave and articulates a pure vision of good service: 'That which I show, heaven knows, is merely love, / Duty, and zeal to your unmatched mind' (IV, iii, 507–8). As with Lear, Timon has been profligate and plainly does not deserve this level of good service, but as we have seen, the moral foundation of authority is about not only the leaders but also the followers. Perhaps, in the indefatigability of servants like Adam, Kent and Flavius, Shakespeare acknowledges the sorts of people who hold the fabric of society together in the real world. The people who keep things from falling apart are not those like Lear or Timon, but those like Kent or Flavius.

> For any benefit that points to me,
> Either in hope, or present, I'd exchange
> For this one wish: that you had power and wealth
> To requite me by making rich yourself. (*Timon of Athens*, IV, ii, 511–14)

Such sentiments bring to mind John Calvin's notion of the 'calling' (see Chapter 4). Flavius *wants* to be useful. He seems to see his calling in the world as being a steward, and specifically *Timon's* steward. If there is any aspect of the good service we see in Adam, Kent and Flavius that is not wholly selfless, it is the fact that all three of them draw their sense of purpose and meaning from their duty. One has the sense that, denied of their mission, they would be faced with an existential crisis. Their sense of meaning derives from serving something or someone beyond themselves. Timon, by contrast, loses any sense of meaning beyond himself. Alone, bitter and misanthropic in his cave, he loses any sense of purpose. As Arthur Temple Cadoux eloquently puts it,

> his scheme of life is shattered. He has no ground to which to retreat from the blow, for he has no value for other virtue than his own or that which he respects as a response to his own. . . . self-regard by its dominance wrecks the self.[31]

Like Macbeth, with nothing to serve beyond his own interests, life becomes 'a tale / Told by an idiot, full of sound and fury, / Signifying nothing' (*Macbeth*, V, v, 26–8). Why should Adam, Kent and Flavius derive meaning from serving others, but Timon and Macbeth find only existential despair in serving themselves?

In *Man's Search for Meaning*, Viktor E. Frankl, a survivor of the concentration camps of Nazi Germany, argues that humans possess a deep-seated psychological need to serve:

> A public-opinion poll was conducted a few years ago in France. The results showed that 89 percent of the people polled admitted that man needs 'something' for the sake of which to live. Moreover, 61 percent conceded that there was something, or someone, in their own lives for whose sake they were even ready to die.[32]

In *The Righteous Mind*, Jonathan Haidt has some insights from recent studies in human biology and evolution as to why this might be. The answer lies in the '10 percent bee' component of his formulation that humans are '90 percent chimp and 10 percent bee' (see Chapter 2). While mostly selfish, we are also inextricably social and groupish. Haidt describes a 'hive switch', which needs to be activated to bring about a sense of fulfilment and happiness: 'We have the ability (under special conditions) to transcend self-interest and lose ourselves (temporarily and ecstatically) in something larger than ourselves. That ability is what I'm calling the *hive switch*.'[33] It is a moment at which 'individualism' is replaced with more 'communal feelings': in other words, when we 'turn ... into team players'.[34] When describing his experiences of seeing his students' engage in such group activities in his years of researching this, Haidt says:

> They put on plays, compete in sports, rally for political causes, and volunteer for dozens of projects to help the poor and the sick in Charlottesville and in faraway countries.

I see them searching for *a calling*, which they can only find as part of a larger group. I see them striving and searching on two levels simultaneously, for we are all *Homo duplex*.[35]

It is interesting to note the Calvinist turn of phrase here. The 'calling' is to serve something beyond the individual self. Viewed in this way, Adam, Kent and Flavius are the ultimate team players, whose concern for their social bonds outstrips their individual needs and wants. Timon and Macbeth, meanwhile, have effectively lost their teams, the individual self without a calling necessarily struggles to generate meaningful purpose. The moral foundation of authority rests on an intuitive recognition of this fact. When religions and ideologies build social structures of authority into their doctrines, they are engaged in the *post hoc* justification and description of a more natural process to which most people respond as if by instinct.

Let us return to *King Lear* and its contrast between the bad and good servants, Oswald and Kent. There is no better measure of a *moral* response to a situation or person than visceral outrage. In order to have such a reaction to the difference between Oswald and Kent, one's moral taste buds must be responsive to the foundation of authority. Samuel Johnson, for example, had no such reaction. Indeed, he wondered, 'I know not well why Shakespeare gives the Steward, who is a mere factor of wickedness, so much fidelity.'[36] Dr Johnson apparently could not distinguish between good and bad service, and so his response to Oswald is not moral, but one of intellectual confusion. This response contrasts sharply with another great Shakespearean, Samuel Taylor Coleridge, who registers his full moral outrage in his notes on *King Lear*. For Coleridge, especially vehement on this point, Kent is, 'perhaps, the nearest to perfect goodness in all Shakespeare's characters'. In juxtaposition, he describes Oswald as 'the only character of utter irredeemable baseness in Shakespeare'.[37] It is worth pausing on the strength of

Coleridge's sentiments here: even within the confines of the play, he ranks Oswald below Goneril or Regan or Edmund. In terms of the whole canon, he is arguing that Oswald is more irredeemably base than the likes of Iago, the Macbeths, Richard III or, say, Tamora, Demetrius, and Chiron in *Titus Andronicus*. After all, from a certain point of view, Oswald's only crime is in following the orders of his superiors in an obsequious manner. He does not kill anybody, even though he might have killed Gloucester, and yet in Coleridge's estimation his complete obedience to Goneril makes him more irredeemably base than schemers, murderers, torturers and rapists. This is quite revealing of Coleridge's moral compass; for him, it appears that abject servility is a worse sin than mere cruelty, but is it possible that Shakespeare shares this?

In traditional virtue ethics, servility is viewed as evil. Thomas Aquinas addresses the question in the *Summa Theologiae* under the article 'Is Servile Fear Good?':

> There is an element of evil in servile fear, namely its very servility. Servitude, after all, is the denial of liberty, and if a free man is a *cause unto himself*, as Aristotle observes at the beginning of the *Metaphysics*, it follows that a slave is one who is not himself the source of his own activity, but is rather subject to coercion. Now if we take the case of someone acting out of love, he acts as it were, on his own, because the only impetus to activity comes from within himself. Consequently to act out of love is incompatible with the meaning of servility; this is only to say that servile fear, under the aspect precisely of servility, stands opposed to charity.[38]

He invokes Augustine to contrast 'love for justice' with 'fear of punishment'. For Aquinas, servility is evil chiefly because it offends the principles of liberty and free will. He is not wrong. However, as I have shown in this chapter, it *also* offends the principles of good leadership and service necessary for authority because they ultimately rest on what individuals in a hierarchy freely choose to do. For those with a liberal WEIRD mindset, liberty and authority *appear* to be in tension because liberty's opposite is oppression and authority's is subversion, and these four concepts *seem* interlinked. We can show this as in Table 6.1.

Table 6.1

| Authority | Oppression |
| Subversion | Liberty |

But we should *not* equate subversion with liberty or authority with oppression. As in the cases of Adam and Orlando, or Kent's service to Lear, authority – which is not power, but the upholding of principles of good leadership and justice – is *commensurate* with liberty, whether it is the servant or the master who is working to maintain it. Social hierarchy, even in feudal conditions, does not mean total obedience. It is a mistake common not only to Lear and to Oswald, but also to plenty of modern scholars. Perhaps they do not understand this principle because, as in the case of Samuel Johnson, it is in their moral blind spot. By the same token, subversion is *not* freedom; it is the wilful undermining of an existing social order. Thus, even in his total obedience to Goneril (oppression), by carrying out her orders Oswald is still guilty of undermining existing hierarchies (subversion).

This fundamental misunderstanding of the nature of authority is common to revolutionaries and tyrants alike. Perhaps Coleridge understood this better than most because in his own lifetime he saw the French Revolution – which mistook liberty for subversion and authority for power – turn into the Reign of Terror and very quickly saw a fledging republic succumb to tyranny. He had read John Milton, of course, who saw the same fate befall his own utopian dreams under Oliver Cromwell in the 1640s. Idealists of various stripes during the twentieth century must have experienced similar disappointment as socialist regimes on every continent – from the Soviet Union to China to Cuba to Zimbabwe – fell quickly into the hands of despots. The outcome of such drastic misunderstandings of the nature of liberty and authority is virtually always authoritarianism: a state where true authority is subverted and liberty is oppressed. While we cannot say if Shakespeare shared Coleridge's view of Oswald as the basest of his characters and Kent as the most virtuous, he undoubtedly grasped these crucial distinctions between authority and oppression, and liberty and subversion. When they are misaligned, as is very often the case in his plays, tyranny follows.

> **In summary**
> - The moral foundation of authority cannot be found in the political rhetoric of Shakespeare's characters, but rather in relationships between characters of different social rank.
> - The most common bonds of service in Shakespeare's England were not feudal in nature but freely chosen contracts of employment, which means that, in practice, real social relations bore little resemblance to the political theory outlined by the Great Chain of Being.
> - The ideal model of good service and authority is found in *As You Like It*, where Adam freely chooses to serve Orlando, who repays his duty reciprocally by performing his own dutiful service later in the play.
> - In *King Lear*, Shakespeare diametrically opposes Kent, as a model of good service, which is rooted in a sense of duty rather than mindless obedience, and Oswald as a model of bad service, which is rooted in servility.
> - We find a strong parallel to Kent in Flavius, the steward in *Timon of Athens*, another model of good service, whose sense of duty leads him to speak truth to power, and freely to give up his own time, money and efforts to serve Timon, even as he can see his master has gone astray.

- Through Jonathan Haidt's concept of the 'hive switch' – the ability to transcend our own self-interest to lose ourselves in something larger than ourselves – we can see why Adam, Kent and Flavius all derive a profound sense of purpose from their duty, while characters such as Timon and Macbeth, stuck only with self-interest, give way to misanthropy and existential despair.
- To understand the difference between Kent and Oswald in *King Lear* morally – as Samuel Johnson seemingly cannot but as Samuel Taylor Coleridge can – we must respond to the moral foundation of authority.
- Those who are blind to the moral foundation of authority frequently confuse it for oppression, the opposite of liberty, and likewise mistake authority's opposite, subversion, for liberty itself. In Shakespeare, and indeed in the real world as observed throughout history, the result of this fatal misunderstanding is virtually always tyranny.

Notes

1. See Neema Parvini, *Shakespeare's History Plays*; *Shakespeare and Contemporary Theory: New Historicism and Cultural Materialism* (New York and London: Bloomsbury, 2012); 'Cultural Materialism', in *The Edinburgh Companion to Critical Theory*, ed. Stuart Sim (Edinburgh: Edinburgh University Press, 2016), pp. 363–82; and *Shakespeare and New Historicist Theory*.
2. Haidt, *The Righteous Mind*.
3. Patrick Cosgrave, 'Obituary: Enoch Powell', *The Independent* (9 February 1998), <http://www.independent.co.uk/news/obituaries/obituary-enoch-powell-1143867.html> (last accessed 10 August 2017).
4. Enoch Powell, 'Politics in Shakespeare', in *Shakespeare: The Comprehensive Soul* (London: British Broadcasting Corporation, 1965), p. 24.
5. See E. M. W. Tillyard, *Shakespeare's History Plays* (London: Chatto & Windus, 1944).

6. See especially Jonathan Dollimore and Alan Sinfield, 'History and Ideology, Masculinity and Miscegenation: The Instance of *Henry V*', in *Faultlines: Cultural Materialism and the Politics of Dissident Reading* (Oxford: Clarendon Press, 1992), pp. 109–42.
7. T. J. B. Spencer, 'The Sophistry of Shakespeare', *English Studies Today: Fourth Series*, ed. Ilva Cellini and Giorgio Melchiori (Rome: Edizioni di Storia e Letteratura, 1966), pp. 169–85.
8. Alex Schulman, *Rethinking Shakespeare's Political Philosophy: From Lear to Leviathan* (Edinburgh: Edinburgh University Press, 2014), p. 30.
9. Spencer Dimmock, *The Origin of Capitalism in England, 1400–1600* (Leiden and Boston, MA: Brill, 2014), p. 135.
10. Mark Overton, *The Agricultural Revolution in England: The Transformation of the Agrarian Revolution 1500–1850* (Cambridge: Cambridge University Press, 2010), p. 8.
11. Phyllis Deane and W. A. Cole, *British Economic Growth 1688–1959: Trends and Structure* (Cambridge: Cambridge University Press, 1962), p. 3.
12. R. W. Hoyle, 'Tenure and the Land Market in Early Modern England: Or a Late Contribution to the Brenner Debate', *Economic History Review*, 43:1 (February 1990), p. 2.
13. Ibid. pp. 13–14, 16.
14. Mark Thornton Burnett, *Masters and Servants in English Renaissance Drama and Culture: Authority and Obedience* (Basingstoke: Macmillan, 1997), pp. 3–5.
15. Tillyard, *The Elizabethan World Picture*.
16. Burnett, *Masters and Servants*, p. 4.
17. Linda Anderson, *A Place in the Story: Servants and Service in Shakespeare's Plays* (Newark: University of Delaware Press, 2005), p. 23.
18. Haidt, *The Righteous* Mind, p. 129; for a brief definition of 'WEIRD', see Chapter 1.
19. David Evett, *Discourses of Service in Shakespeare's England* (New York and London: Palgrave Macmillan, 2005), pp. 153, 151.
20. Anderson, *A Place in the Story*, p. 26,

21. Judith Weil, *Service and Dependency in Shakespeare's Plays* (Cambridge: Cambridge University Press, 2005), p. 1.
22. Burnett, *Masters and Servants*, p. 84.
23. Anderson, *A Place in the Story*, p. 123, emphasis mine.
24. Evett, *Discourses of Service in Shakespeare's England*, pp. 153–4.
25. Weil, *Service and Dependency in Shakespeare's Plays*, p. 110.
26. Jonas A. Barish and Marshall Waingrow, '"Service" in *King Lear*', *Shakespeare Quarterly*, 9:3 (Summer 1958), p. 348, emphasis mine.
27. Ibid. p. 349.
28. Weil, *Service and Dependency in Shakespeare's Plays*, p. 111.
29. Richard Strier, 'Faithful Servants: Shakespeare's Praise of Disobedience', in *The Historical Renaissance: New Essays on Tudor and Stuart Literature and Culture*, ed. Heather Dubrow and Richard Strier (Chicago: University of Chicago Press), p. 113.
30. Nuttall, *Shakespeare: The Thinker*, p. 317.
31. Cadoux, *Shakespearean Selves*, pp. 145–6.
32. Viktor E. Frankl, *Man's Search for Meaning* (1959; London: Rider, 2004), p. 105.
33. Haidt, *The Righteous Mind*, p. 258.
34. Ibid. pp. 269–70.
35. Ibid. p. 270.
36. Samuel Johnson, *Johnson on Shakespeare: Essays and Notes*, ed. Walter Raleigh (London: Henry Frowde, 1908), p. 158.
37. Samuel Taylor Coleridge, *Coleridge's Essays and Lectures on Shakespeare: And Some Other Old Poets and Dramatists*, ed. Ernest Rhys (London: J. M. Dent & Sons, 1907), pp. 130–1.
38. Thomas Aquinas, *Summa Theologiae* (*Vol. 33: Hope*) [2a2ae. 17–22], ed. W. J. Hill (London: Eyre & Spottiswoode, 1969), question 19, article 4, p. 55.

CHAPTER 7

LOYALTY

Evolutionary theory expects to find that kin loyalty is stronger than group loyalty, which, in turn, is stronger than loyalty to all of mankind (see Chapter 2). Shakespeare seems to have had a special interest in the tension between loyalty to one's family and loyalty to the group or the nation. We can see this most violently in a play such as *Titus Andronicus*. It is striking, then, that Shakespeare's most loyal characters pledge their allegiance to *neither* kin *nor* country, but instead to their friends. 'Friendship always meant much to him.'[1] Studies in both psychology and sociology have found that while men tend to value group-level social relations within a hierarchy, women tend to value their individual relationships more highly. It is therefore interesting to find that when Shakespeare deals with loyalty, he focuses on individual relationships, as opposed to groups. This renders his friendships, and by extension his concept of loyalty, 'feminine', even though the friendships he depicts are between both men and women. In this chapter, I will approach the topic primarily through the lens of Antonio's devotion to Bassanio in *The Merchant of Venice* and Celia's to Rosalind in *As You Like It*. I argue that although these pairs of friends are differently gendered, they are structurally very similar, and marked by their total imbalance. Both Antonio and Celia demonstrate exceptional selflessness in their loyalty, despite the fact that neither Bassanio nor Rosalind comes close to ever repaying their kindness. I suggest our difficulty in processing these disproportionate relationships is because they upset the moral foundation of fairness, but loyalty is not transactional. It seems, rather, that Shakespeare's notion of friendship rested partly on the Christian (Thomist) virtue of charity.

We can divide Shakespeare's most loyal characters into two types: first, faithful servants such as Adam in *As You Like It*, Kent in *King Lear*, or Flavius in *Timon of Athens*. As I argued in Chapter 6, I believe that these bastions of good service respond primarily to the moral foundation of authority rather than that of loyalty. In the second category of Shakespeare's most loyal characters we find the devoted friends. As Kate Emery Pogue has shown convincingly in *Shakespeare's Friends* (2006), Shakespeare's obvious and deep interest in friendship as a structuring principle in his plays is rooted in his real-life relationships. While there is a still a great deal we will never know about Shakespeare's life, it does seem likely that he was a social man who maintained life-long friendships, both personal and professional.[2] Arthur Temple Cadoux lists some of the many friendships in Shakespeare's plays:

> Friendship is a chief feature of the plays written in the years from 1595 to 1601. We have here Valentine and Proteus [in *Two Gentlemen of Verona*], Antonio and Bassanio [in *The Merchant of Venice*], Beatrice and Hero [in *Much Ado About Nothing*], Brutus and Cassius [in *Julius Caesar*], Mistress Ford and Page [in *Merry Wives of Windsor*], Rosalind and Celia [in *As You Like It*], Hamlet and Horatio [in *Hamlet*].[3]

We might also add Antonio and Sebastian from *Twelfth Night*. A central feature of these relationships is how one-sided many of them seem to be. Mistresses Page and Ford are perhaps the most equal of the pairings, but beyond them each friendship appears to be lop-sided. Valentine forgives Proteus despite his treachery in thwarting his attempts with Silvia and then attempting to rape her. Antonio is willing to risk a pound of his own flesh for Bassanio to secure him a loan of 3,000 ducats, despite the fact that Bassanio already owes him money. Beatrice and Hero perhaps have a more equal relationship, but Hero risks her reputation and even her life for the friendship, while Beatrice risks only her blossoming courtship with Benedick. The hard pragmatism of Cassius allows him to outmanoeuvre his idealist friend, Brutus. In leaving the safety of her family home, Celia gives up much more for Rosalind than vice versa. Horatio is a constant friend to Hamlet, who offers him virtually nothing in return. And, finally, Antonio risks his life for Sebastian's with seemingly little recompense.

I will return to the question of one-sidedness in these friendships presently, but before so doing, it seems significant that Shakespeare locates his concept of loyalty here. Indeed, 'there are forty-one friendships in Shakespeare, and thirty-nine ties of loyalty; the two things tend more and more to merge, as he searches for a new moral cement to take the place of crumbling feudal associations'.[4] By focusing on individual friendships, he departs from the notion that loyalty is a bond between an individual and his or her group. Instead, he seems to foreground a view of loyalty as a bond between two people. In *The Righteous Mind*, Jonathan Haidt emphasises the predominantly tribal nature of the moral foundation of loyalty.

> The Loyalty / betrayal foundation is just part of our innate preparation for meeting the adaptive challenge of forming cohesive coalitions. The original trigger for the Loyalty foundation is anything that tells you who is a team player and who is a traitor, particularly when your team is fighting with other teams.[5]

This is the principally *male* view of loyalty, as seen, for example, in team sports. However, following recent research on gender differences by Roy F. Baumeister and Kirsten L. Sommer, Haidt adds that 'the objects of loyalty tend to be teams and coalitions for boys, in contrast to two-person relationships for girls'.[6] Psychological and sociological studies have long found that women seem to value their social relationships more than men:

> There is evidence that relationships are more central to women's lives than to men's, as reflected in women's greater tendency to have an interdependent self-concept, to report greater commitment in relationships, and to engage in more relationship maintenance behaviours.[7]

However, Baumeister and Sommer set out to counter the conventional wisdom that men are less social than are women by showing how apparent male independence is, in fact, a form of status-seeking within a hierarchy.

> Independence, by definition, means to be free of connection with other people, and this is readily elaborated into a desire for autonomy and social separation. We have proposed, in contrast to this view, that men are conditioned by both culture and nature to seek social attachments within a broader sphere than are women and that such a quest requires men to compete for an advantageous place within a hierarchy of power and status.[8]

Some have argued that this is because of the higher average propensity of males towards the Machiavellian personality type, as opposed to empathy.[9] Hence we can speak loosely of *masculine* loyalty (to the group) and *feminine* loyalty (between two individuals).

Shakespeare provides us with numerous examples of masculine loyalty. To take an extreme one, we might think of the shocking moment in *Titus Andronicus* in which Titus kills his own son, Mutius (I, i, 294), to demonstrate his loyalty to the newly crowned Saturnus. This cold Roman stoicism – which puts country before family, and group allegiance before individual bond – feels alien in Shakespeare's canon. Another example, less shocking but just as extreme, is Hotspur in *1 Henry IV*: perhaps the living embodiment of masculine loyalty. His passion for fighting the traitorous enemy is such that he gives it greater priority than having sex with wife. He has no time for individual relationships and thus, as per Baumeister and Sommer, *seems* independent. Hotspur's is a hyper-masculine world defined by tribal conflict:

> This is no world
> To play with mammets and to tilt with lips.
> We must have bloody noses and cracked crowns (II, iii, 84–6)

But here, as seemingly everywhere in his works, Shakespeare's overwhelming interest is not in this hyper-masculine world, but in the feminine loyalty between individuals. As much as the political battles rage in the background of the *Henriad*, surely the key dramatic – and, indeed, *moral* – concern in these plays is the friendship between Hal and Falstaff. Is there a more crushing moment of personal betrayal in Shakespeare than 'I know thee not, old man' (*2 Henry IV*, V, v, 45)? The fat knight fails virtually every test of the honour system that binds homosocial group hierarchies in the play – a man who thinks honour is a 'mere scutcheon' (*1 Henry IV*, V, i, 139) has no place in Hotspur's world – yet Shakespeare gives Falstaff's relationship with Hal vital importance in his retelling of this passage of history. Furthermore, and perhaps tellingly, Falstaff's catechism on honour is vindicated: he survives the battle, while Hotspur is killed. Through his friendship with Hal, Falstaff claims the glory of the kill: 'For my part, if a lie may do thee grace / I'll gild it with the happiest terms I have' (V, iv, 151–2). Individual loyalty seems to trump group loyalty in *1 Henry IV*, which is perhaps why it is so devastating when it breaks down in *2 Henry IV*.

However, the fact that he emphasised feminine, two-person loyalty over masculine group loyalty in this way does not mean that Shakespeare's concept of loyalty is individualistic.

V. G. Kiernan's essay of 1964, 'Human Relations in Shakespeare', remains one of the most compelling treatments of this topic. It outlines how the plays are full of what Kiernan calls, echoing William Hazlitt, 'a golden readiness of fellow-feeling for the world'.[10] Here characters are never wholly disconnected from other people but inextricably constituted by their individual relations:

> Shakespeare-criticism, growing up in days of fully-fledged individualism, was apt to fix its attention on characters as separate units, 'portraits', each a work of art in itself. Some of Shakespeare's own words show him thinking rather of the individual as the sum of his relationships, actual or possible, with his fellows. Brutus has to see himself in the mirror of Cassius's mind before his duty becomes clear to him. . . . Shakespeare was concerned with men in combination, interacting, entering into one another's lives, becoming part of one another.[11]

For Kiernan, Shakespeare fears not so much the breakdown of social hierarchies, as is so commonly suggested, but rather the disintegration of the bonds of friendship:

> It has been often enough or too often said that Shakespeare had a horror of anarchy, of social disorder; what really horrified him was not any breakdown of 'order' in the policeman's understanding of the word, but something more fundamental, the destruction of men's faith in one another that is always liable to accompany the break-up of an old social pattern whether authority remains intact or not. . . . Disloyalty and ingratitude are two of the sins he condemns most eloquently, and if he so habitually censures men by comparing them with brute beasts, what he has against the animals is, surely, their incapability of fellow-feeling.[12]

Indeed, as I argued in Chapter 6, it seems that Shakespeare's concept of authority is tied closely with this notion of 'fellow-feeling', as manifest in mutual good service between servant and master.

However, the ethics of friendship differ from the ethics of good service because there is no hierarchy as is implied by the terms 'master' and 'servant'. Aristotle dedicates two books of the *Nicomachean Ethics* to friendship.[13] In his characteristic manner, Cicero duly Romanised Aristotle's ideas, focusing on practice rather than theory in his treatise on the topic, *De Amicitia* ('On Friendship').[14] Shakespeare would undoubtedly have encountered this standard Latin text in his schooldays at Stratford. Aristotle ranks three levels of friendship:

1. Utility: the useful friend is someone we can rely on when we need something.
2. Pleasure: the pleasurable friend is someone who can make us laugh or otherwise entertain us.
3. Complete friendship: someone for whom you wish good things for their own sake, and for no other reason.

Clearly, we should aim for the third: in everyday parlance, we would say that the first two are merely on the level of acquaintance, and only the third is 'true friendship'. The Aristotelean–Ciceronian view of friendship is predicated on an equal partnership between 'good men'; without virtue it cannot exist. However, such an arrangement in its purest form is rarely achieved, to the extent that Cicero can name only four examples in history. In its most ideal incarnation, *amicitia perfecta* ('perfect friendship'), it becomes a necessary condition for the *summum bonum* or highest good. Literary historians have long pointed out that Cicero's concept of ideal friendship became something of a craze in sixteenth-century England; it was a cultural phenomenon that peaked during the late Elizabethan era. The classic study is Laurens J. Mills's *One Soul in Bodies Twain: Friendship in Tudor Literature and Stuart Drama* (1937), but the topic has received greater attention in the past two decades in major scholarly studies.¹⁵ Of these, the most useful for our purposes is Tom MacFaul's *Male Friendship in Shakespeare and His Contemporaries* (2007), not only because it deals directly with Shakespeare's plays, but also because of its clear-eyed distinction between the fantasy of the classical ideal – especially the notion that friendships should be equal – and the imperfect reality of actual friendships.

And so we return to a persistent feature of many of Shakespeare's friendships: their one-sidedness. They fail the 'preliberal utopian' ideal of equality in every respect at the first hurdle.¹⁶ Why does Antonio give so much of himself to Bassanio in *The Merchant of Venice* while receiving so little in return? It is a question that has puzzled critics for many years. In Tom MacFaul's reading, the mismatch occurs because Antonio tries to transcend the mercantile norms of Venetian society:

> Venice is a mercantile society, in which too much idealism about love or other matters cannot thrive. Antonio nevertheless tries to rise above his station within this society. Bassanio, in contrast to this, is fully adjusted to the mercantile world. His ideas regarding love and friendship are all bound up with money. . . . It is beyond his imagination to see friendship as more than a matter of give-and-take.¹⁷

As Tzachi Zamir puts it, Antonio's dream of idealised friendship is 'contaminated by financial dependency'.¹⁸ Bassanio not only sees the relationship in transactional terms, but also runs up a deficit – monetarily and emotionally – with seemingly no intention of settling the balance. And, as if to underline the stark imbalance of the relationship, Antonio does not even expect him to settle.

Such is the level of this imbalance that it has driven some critics to incredulity. Arthur Temple Cadoux, for example, cannot take Antonio at face value. He views him as little more than a poser, of a 'histrionic bent', full of 'self-deception'.[19] Cadoux seemingly cannot process the idea that Antonio's generosity could be for real. The opposite extreme is found in J. A. Bryant's view, which elevates him to a Christ-like figure.[20] In the year of 1960–1, *Essays in Criticism* staged some interesting exchanges on this topic, taking a more sympathetic view of the character. Graham Midgley advanced the idea that 'Antonio is an outsider because he is an unconscious homosexual in a predominantly, and indeed blatantly, heterosexual society.'[21] In this reading, Antonio is Shylock's mirror – he is to the world of love and marriage as the Jew is to Venetian society – both men are studies in loneliness. Naturally, this gained purchase in subsequent years: for example, A. D. Nuttall concludes that such is the inequality of their relationship that it must reveal Antonio's 'profound homosexual love' for Bassanio.[22] Midgley found swift rebuke from M. G. Deshpande, who, in the historicist–corrective mode, argued that the private and quiet loneliness he attributes to Antonio is 'typically modern; the concept of any individual as an outsider was not within the general consciousness of the Renaissance'.[23] This was enough to stir E. M. W. Tillyard, at this point in his seventies and one year from his death, who weighed in on Midgley's side with common sense: 'To say that Shakespeare was incapable of picturing such a contrast because the average Elizabethan was incapable of doing so is as great an error as to fashion him in the form of a twentieth-century intellectual.'[24] It turns out Elizabethan people could get lonely too. As Alan Bray has shown since, there is much evidence of same-sex love in the period.[25] Harold Bloom, meanwhile, postulated that Antonio's selflessness has less to do with his homosexuality than it has with his 'sadomasochism'.[26] Kenneth Muir insisted that these psychological readings are a 'distortion' of the play: 'we need to remember that Elizabethan friendships were frequently passionate, though usually platonic'. And, in any case, Antonio's melancholy is purely a function of the drama, 'to prepare the audience for disaster'.[27] These explanations, though not implausible, still somehow seem strangely unsatisfactory. It seems as if the critics personally struggle to make sense of Antonio's selfless behaviour and so generate *post hoc* rationalisations for it.

I think that one reason for this is that Bassanio seems such a shallow and vapid young man and critics feel that he is unworthy of Antonio's affections and efforts. As J. A. Bryant put it, 'Criticism has struggled with Bassanio for a long time, the problem being to justify the interest that Antonio and Portia take in him.'[28] His fecklessness is difficult to ignore, and few are taken in by his blustery promise during Shylock's trial:

> Antonio, I am married to a wife
> Which is as dear to me as life itself;
> But life itself, my wife, and all the world
> Are not with me esteemed above thy life.
> I would lose all – ay, sacrifice them all
> Here to this devil – to deliver you. (IV, i, 280–5)

Does anyone believe this? There seems a marked gap between what Bassanio says and what he actually does. Nuttall certainly does not believe him. He is especially disdainful of Bassanio's 'moral thinness' and wonders, as if out loud, 'How can Portia, who could have had anyone (including that very nice Prince of Morocco), love Bassanio?'[29] Similarly, Bloom seems at a loss to explain what anyone sees in Bassanio, who, though 'not a bad fellow', has little else to recommend him. 'If you compare Portia's Bassanio to Rosalind's Orlando, obviously you will prefer the amiable young wrestler of *As You Like It*.'[30]

Bloom compares Bassanio and Orlando because they are both male, but structurally, the more natural comparison point is between Bassanio and Rosalind. In both plays, a friend helps the romantic lead pursue the object of their affection, and does so through love. It just so happens that the romantic lead of *As You Like It* is a woman with a female friend pursuing a man, while in *The Merchant of Venice* it is a man with a male friend pursuing a woman. To make the structural similarity as plain as possible, I have constructed Table 7.2.

Table 7.2

Friend	Romantic lead	Object of affection
Antonio	Bassanio	Portia
Celia	Rosalind	Orlando

It does not occur to critics as regularly to ask what Celia or Orlando sees in Rosalind as they ask what Antonio or Portia sees in Bassanio. It is not difficult to see why: she dazzles the stage and dominates the action. But if we are studying what friendship means to Shakespeare, the *worth* of the friend subjectively evaluated by a critic should not matter. Is Rosalind somehow more worthy of devotion than Bassanio because the likes of Nuttall and Bloom do not like him? It seems to me that the moral concepts of friendship and loyalty cannot work like this. We must try to get beyond our own judgements of individual characters. Even so, if Bassanio were more like Rosalind, would we better understand Antonio's devotion to him?

We scarcely need to imagine this because Shakespeare runs exactly this variable with Celia in the place of Antonio.

> You know my father hath no child but I, nor none is like to have; and truly when he dies, thou shalt be his heir; for what he hath taken away from thy father perforce, I will render thee again in affection. (*As You Like It*, 1.2.16–19)

I do not think Antonio is any more devoted or any more selfless than is Celia. She not only abandons her father for Rosalind, but also pledges her future inheritance to her. If anything, this is a bigger price than that Antonio was prepared to pay because we should remember that he expected his ships to return:

> Why, fear not man: I will not forfeit it.
> Within these two months – that's a month before
> This bond expires – I do expect return
> Of thrice times the value of this bond. (*The Merchant of Venice*, I, iii, 149–53)

When Antonio agrees to the conditions of the loan, he does not expect that he is really wagering a pound of his own flesh, whereas when Celia pledges herself to Rosalind, she *is* really sacrificing her own fortune for her. If there is a question of whether Celia is really Antonio's moral equal, in the material terms of self-sacrifice the advantage is in Celia's favour. But it seems to me that in both cases, Shakespeare intended for us to take these as morally good characters because of their loyalty and devotion in friendship.

By insisting on reading Shakespeare's friendships through the lenses of gender and sexuality, it appears that some scholars may have missed the fact that very little separates Antonio and Celia. They are both ready to lose everything for a friend who may never repay them in kind. As I have suggested, this is because loyalty between friends in Shakespeare invariably takes a 'feminine' form – that is, centred on a bond between two people, as opposed to the bond between individual and group – regardless of whether the friends are male or female. Back in 1903, Richard G. Moulton argued that Antonio must be understood as 'the most ideal of characters . . . not simply a Christian . . ., but a supremely noble Christian . . . a combination of dignified strength with *almost womanly tenderness* towards his young friend'.[31] Within the world of the play, Antonio stands apart from the groupish male bonding we see in the laddish banter of his and Bassanio's mutual friends: Lorenzo, Graziano, Salerio and Solanio. These characters, the 'masquing mates' (II, vi, 60), form a pack in the play, between them representing something like the whole of Venetian society. As Marianne Novy puts it, they are 'sufficiently uncharacterized that they may represent the dominant biases of the play's Venice'.[32] They firmly establish a sense of an in-group and an out-group. We see them bullying Shylock (III, i, 17–43), which triggers his famous 'Hath not a Jew eyes?' speech (III, i, 44–60). Although Shylock is a proud man, the logic of his speech is to focus on the common humanity and similarities between the Christian in-group and the Jewish out-group. This has been commented on many times but how quickly it falls on deaf ears. No sooner has he finished than Solanio reinforces his status as a member of the out-group: 'Here comes another of the tribe; a third cannot be matched unless the devil himself turn Jew' (III, i, 64–5).

Hence there is an uneasy tension in *The Merchant of Venice* between these masculine social bonds of group loyalty and the feminine bonds of two-person loyalty. Antonio is firmly a member of the in-group, but in choosing to focus on loyalty in its more feminine form, he stands apart and, as per those who see him as a figure of loneliness, outside that group – 'a tainted wether of the flock' (IV, i, 113). We can also glimpse this effect when Jessica disguises herself as a boy and escapes her father's claustrophobic control by running away with Lorenzo. Graziano foregrounds the societal contexts of their impending union: 'Now by my hood, a gentle and no Jew' (II, vi, 52). But Lorenzo immediately refocuses attention to the two-person bond:

> Beshrew me, but I love her heartily;
> For she is wise, if I can judge of her;

> And fair she is, if that mine eyes be true;
> And true she is, as she hath proved herself. (II, vi, 53–6)

It is as if feminine two-person bonds pose a kind of existential threat to the bonds of masculine group loyalty. Although Jessica travels with the group disguised as a boy, and Graziano symbolically embraces her as a new member of the in-group ('a gentle, and no Jew'), Lorenzo, by insisting on her individual qualities and their special two-person bond, just as quickly places her (and indeed himself) apart from the group.

This tension between masculine in-group social bonds and feminine two-person bonds is perhaps even more marked in *As You Like It*. Paul A. Kottman spots it in his analysis:

> By offering 'in affection' what Duke Frederick would render by paternal authority, Celia aims to bind herself to Rosalind independently of preexistent kinship or political ties – and, thus, her affection is perceived as a threat to the durability and viability of those other ties.[33]

Celia explicitly rejects kin loyalty in favour of friendship: the bond between her and Rosalind is stronger than that between father and daughter. And, in the end, this bond is enough to bring down Duke Frederick, restore Duke Senior and reconcile Orlando and Oliver. In *As You Like It*, feminine two-person loyalty trumps masculine group loyalty.

However, we have not yet got to the bottom of the inequality problem, which makes characters like Antonio and Celia apparently so difficult for us to grasp. Even a perceptive observer of morality in Shakespeare such as Alfred Harbage complains of Shakespeare's frequent 'failure to reward the good' characters and puts it down to 'sheer forgetfulness' or 'irresponsibility' on the playwright's part.[34] Harbage seems to be operating under the expectations of literary convention and genre. But as we saw in Chapter 5, generations of critics who have turned to the playwright looking for divine or cosmic justice have been disappointed. As Stephen Greenblatt points out, 'Shakespeare did not think that one's good actions are necessarily or even usually rewarded.'[35] In Shakespeare's moral universe, there is no reason to expect characters, whether good or evil, to get their just deserts. In the constrained or tragic vision, life is frequently unfair, and to criticise Shakespeare's plays for reflecting this is to judge them against a utopian ideal (see Chapter 2). However, at the same time, it seems to me that many of our struggles with the inequities between Antonio and Bassanio, and Celia and Rosalind, come from an emotional and moral place. Intuitively, we feel something is not quite right. This is because the disproportionate nature of these friendships offends the moral foundation of fairness. Is Bassanio taking advantage of Antonio? Is Rosalind taking advantage of Celia? This nagging feeling will not leave us.

I think the key tension here is between the Christian concept of charity manifested as friendship, and what evolutionary theorists call reciprocal altruism (see Chapter 1). While the recent studies I discussed earlier in this chapter have concentrated on the early modern vogue for classical ideals of friendship, they neglect the most important Christian interpreter of Aristotle, Thomas Aquinas.[36] In *Virtue's Own Feature* (1995), David N. Beauregard argues that Shakespeare often depicts Aristotelian–Thomistic triads of virtues and vices in his plays. For example, in *The Merchant of Venice*, he thinks Antonio represents the virtue of liberality while Bassanio and Shylock represent the vices of prodigality and avarice, respectively.[37] I disagree: this surely makes Shakespeare more didactic and moralising than he is. There is scant evidence in the play that Bassanio is some sort of warning against prodigality, and Shakespeare's depiction of liberality elsewhere – *Timon of Athens* most obviously – suggests that his view of the supposed virtue is much more pessimistic than that of Aquinas. Instead, I posit that the chief virtue embodied in Antonio (and also Celia) is charity.[38]

In the *Summa Theologiae*, Aquinas answers the question 'is charity a friendship?'

> According to Aristotle, not all love has the character of friendship, but that only which goes with well wishing, namely when we so love another as to will what is good for him. For if what we will is our own good, as when we love wine or a horse or the like, it is not a love of friendship but of desire. It makes no sense of somebody being friends with wine or a horse.[39]

As I outlined above, Aristotle made a distinction between relationships based on utility or pleasure, and 'complete friendship' based only on goodwill for the other. Plainly, Aquinas does not consider the former types of relationship to be friendship at all. He continues:

> Yet goodwill alone is not enough for friendship for this requires a mutual loving; it is only with a friend that a friend is friendly. But such reciprocal good is based on something in common. . . . Now the love which is based on this sort of fellowship is charity.[40]

This is very similar to V. G. Kiernan's concept of 'fellow-feeling'. Although 'mutual loving' implies a certain reciprocity, note that Aquinas insists neither upon equality between friends, nor that the recipient of charity should repay any favours in kind. In fact, he widens the scope of charity and friendship to an extraordinary degree:

> Friendship goes out to another in two ways. When he is loved in himself, and such friendship is only for a friend; and when he is loved of another person, as when for the sake of a friend you love those belonging to him, be they children, servants or anyone connected with him at all,

even if they hurt or hate us, so much do we love him. In this way, the friendship of charity extends even to our enemies, for we love them for the sake of God who is principal in our loving. . . . In a friendship of true worth we love principally a man of virtue, though out of regard for him we love all who belong to him, even if they are not virtuous. In this way, charity, which above all is friendship, reaches out to sinners whom we love for God's sake.[41]

Here the 'fellow-feeling' between two friends extends to include practically all of mankind. As we saw in Chapter 2, although evolutionary theorists are currently divided on the human capacity for true altruism, virtually all of them would reject the idea that we could operate on this universal level. Advocates of reciprocal altruism would object to the idea that charity without some sort of *quid pro quo* payback could get us very far in non-kin relations. Advocates of group- or multi-level selection would maintain that, while altruism is possible, it is naïve, bordering on reckless, to think that it can transcend the in-group.

Shakespeare is perhaps too much the realist to expect any characters to live up to Aquinas's ideals of universality. For example, although Antonio shows Bassanio outstanding love and charity, he stops short of extending these to Shylock, who quite obviously stands outside his in-group. In *As You Like It*, Celia clearly makes herself and Rosalind an exclusive in-group, with her own father placed outside of it. Indeed, she inculcates a kind of siege mentality – those two against the world – pledging that they will 'love no man in good earnest' (I, ii, 22–3). Just as in the evolutionary theory of group selection, friendship and charity do not transcend the in-group in Shakespeare. However, *within* those boundaries, he appears to inherit Aquinas's ideal of friendship *as* charity wholesale. This is somewhat in keeping with what Haidt would expect:

Whatever Christ said about the good Samaritan who helped an injured Jew, if religion is a group-level adaptation, then it should produce *parochial* altruism. It should make people exceedingly generous and helpful toward members of their own moral communities, particularly when their reputations will be enhanced. And indeed, religion does exactly this.[42]

Whatever Shakespeare's attitude toward Shylock, in the world of *The Merchant of Venice* good Samaritans do not tend to help injured Jews, even though examples of parochial altruism abound in the play. However, as we have seen, what is remarkable about Shakespeare's treatment of parochial altruism is that it does not seem to play out on a group level. He fractures 'moral communities' into two-person relationships. We find characters such as Antonio and Celia acting in exceedingly generous ways towards their friends, but this is not based on (masculine) group loyalty but on (feminine) individual relationships.

In this chapter, we have seen that Shakespeare's notion of loyalty is unusually nuanced. He persistently emphasises two-person relationships based on 'fellow-feeling', as opposed to the relationship between individual and group based on power or status. In his plays, individual friendships frequently retain the capacity to trump family bonds. From Aristotle and Cicero, he takes the notion of 'complete friendship', but loses the ideals of equality and reciprocity. From Aquinas, he takes the notion of friendship as charity, but loses the ideal of extending this to all people, including the enemies of loved ones or members of out-groups. The price of loyalty may be that it results in unfair relationships with disproportionate levels of give and take. But despite this, it is obvious that Shakespeare sees loyalty – understood in this way, and as embodied in characters such as Antonio in *The Merchant of Venice* and Celia in *As You Like It* – as being unconditionally good.

> **In summary**
> - Psychological and sociological studies have found that men tend to prioritise group-level relations for power and status while women put place greater emphasis on two-person relationships.
> - Shakespeare roots his concept of loyalty in feminine two-person relationships as opposed to the masculine group level.
> - His two-person friendships are often imbalanced, with one person (the loyal friend) appearing to give more to the relationship than the other, and in so being fail the classical ideals of equality and reciprocity in friendship outlined by Aristotle and Cicero.
> - Critics have struggled to account for why Antonio gives so much of himself to Bassanio in *The Merchant of Venice*. In trying to justify this, they have cast Antonio variously as an attention-seeking poser, a Christ-like saviour, a lonely homosexual, a sadomasochist and a mere function of dramatic plot.
> - The relationship between Celia and Rosalind in *As You Like It* mirrors that between Antonio and Bassanio. Like Antonio's, Celia's selflessness in her loyalty to Rosalind is remarkable.
> - In both plays, feminine two-person loyalty presents an existential threat to, and perhaps even trumps, masculine group loyalty.
> - The unbalanced nature of Shakespeare's friendships offends the moral foundation of fairness, but the selfless loyalty of Antonio and Celia seems to appeal to the Christian concept of charity, as outlined by Thomas Aquinas, even if they do not fully live up to its ideals of universal inclusivity.
> - Loyalty, defined as a selfless and charitable yet exclusive commitment to a friend, is undoubtedly a key point on Shakespeare's moral compass.

Notes

1. Kiernan, 'Human Relationships in Shakespeare', p. 60.
2. Kate Emery Pogue, *Shakespeare's Friends* (Westport, CT, and London: Praeger, 2006).
3. Cadoux, *Shakespearean Selves*, p. 62.

4. Kiernan, 'Human Relationships in Shakespeare', p. 59.
5. Haidt, *The Righteous Mind*, p. 163.
6. Ibid. p. 162.
7. Emily A. Impett and Letitia Anne Peplau, '"His" and "Her" Relationships? A Review of the Empirical Evidence', in *The Cambridge Handbook of Personal Relationships*, ed. Anita L. Vangelisti and Daniel Perlman (Cambridge: Cambridge University Press, 2006), p. 287.
8. Roy F. Baumeister and Kirsten L. Sommer, 'What Do Men Want? Gender Differences and Two Spheres of Belongingness: Comment on Cross and Madson', *Psychological Bulletin*, 122:1 (July 1997), p. 43.
9. For an overview, see Minna Lyons and Sue Aitken, 'Machiavellian Friends? The Role of Machiavellianism in Friendship Formation and Maintenance', Journal of Social, Evolutionary, and Cultural Psychology, 4:3 (2010), pp. 194–202.
10. Kiernan, 'Human Relationships in Shakespeare', p. 47.
11. Ibid. p. 48.
12. Ibid. p. 62.
13. See Aristotle, *The Nicomachean Ethics*, ed. Lesley Brown (Oxford: Oxford University Press, 2009), books VIII and IX, pp. 1155–73.
14. Cicero, 'On Friendship', trans. Frank O. Copely, in *Other Selves: Philosophers on Friendship*, ed. Michael Pakaluk (Indianapolis: Hackett, 1991), pp. 77–116.
15. Laurens J. Mills, *One Soul in Bodies Twain: Friendship in Tudor Literature and Stuart Drama* (Bloomington: Principia Press, 1937); Reginald Hyatte, *The Arts of Friendship: The Idealisation of Friendship in Medieval and Early Renaissance Literature* (Leiden: E. J. Brill, 1994); Laurie Shannon, *Sovereign Amity: Figures of Friendship in Shakespearean Contexts* (Chicago: University of Chicago Press, 2002); Alan Bray, *The Friend* (Chicago: University of Chicago, 2003); Tom MacFaul, *Male Friendship in Shakespeare and His Contemporaries* (Cambridge: Cambridge University Press, 2007); Will Tosh, *Male Friendship and Testimonies of Love in Shakespeare's England* (New York and London: Palgrave Macmillan, 2016).

16. Shannon, *Sovereign Amity*, p. 10.
17. MacFaul, *Male Friendship in Shakespeare and His Contemporaries*, pp. 162–3.
18. Zamir, *Double Vision*, p. xi.
19. Cadoux, *Shakespearean Selves*, pp. 53, 55.
20. See J. A. Bryant, Jr, *Hippolyta's View: Some Christian Aspects of Shakespeare's Plays* (Lexington: University of Kentucky Press, 1961), pp. 33–51.
21. Graham Midgley, 'The *Merchant of Venice*: A Reconsideration', *Essays in Criticism*, 10:2 (April 1960), p. 125
22. Nuttall, *Shakespeare: The Thinker*, p. 256.
23. M. G. Deshpande, '"Loneliness" in *The Merchant of Venice*', *Essays in Criticism*, 11:3 (July 1961), p. 369.
24. E. M. W. Tillyard, '"Loneliness" in *The Merchant of Venice*', *Essays in Criticism*, 11:4 (October 1961), p. 488.
25. See Bray, *The Friend*.
26. Harold Bloom, *Shakespeare: The Invention of the Human* (New York: Riverhead Books, 1998), p. 179.
27. Kenneth Muir, *Shakespeare's Comic Sequence* (Liverpool: Liverpool University Press, 1979), p. 60.
28. Bryant, *Hippolyta's View*, p. 44.
29. Nuttall, *Shakespeare: The Thinker*, pp. 258, 259.
30. Bloom, *Shakespeare: The Invention of the Human*, p. 179.
31. Moulton, *The Moral System of Shakespeare*, pp. 314–15, emphasis mine.
32. Marianne Novy, *Shakespeare and Outsiders* (Oxford: Oxford University Press, 2013), p. 23.
33. Paul A. Kottman, *Tragic Conditions in Shakespeare: Disinheriting the Globe* (Baltimore: Johns Hopkins University Press, 2009), p. 32.
34. Harbage, *As They Liked It*, p. 47.
35. Stephen Greenblatt, *Shakespeare's Freedom* (Chicago: University of Chicago Press, 2010), p. 85.
36. I am referring to MacFaul, *Male Friendship in Shakespeare and His Contemporaries*, and Tosh, *Male Friendship and Testimonies of Love in Shakespeare's England*, neither of whom even mentions Aquinas. Hyatte, *The Arts of Friendship*, perhaps

owing to its focus on the late medieval and early Renaissance periods, devotes considerably more attention to Aquinas, especially pp. 43–9.
37. Beauregard, *Virtue's Own Feature*, pp. 87–103.
38. Some scholars subsume what I am calling 'charity' into the more general virtue of 'love'; see, for example, Martha Nussbaum, *The Fragility of Goodness: Luck and Ethics in Greek Tragedy and Philosophy* (1986; Cambridge: University of Cambridge, 2001), especially her discussion of *Antigone*, pp. 51–82.
39. Thomas Aquinas, *Summa Theologiae* (*Vol. 34: Charity*) [2a2ae. 23–33], ed. R. J. Batten (London: Eyre & Spottiswoode, 1969), question 23, article 1, p. 7.
40. Ibid. p. 7.
41. Ibid. p. 9.
42. Haidt, *The Righteous Mind*, p. 308.

CHAPTER 8

FAIRNESS

Fairness concerns itself with proportionality, not equality. It is a question of reciprocity – 'just desserts', what one *deserves* – rather than egalitarian distribution. Imagine you are working on a project with two colleagues, P and Q. P puts in a lot of effort, appearing to work beyond what would be expected in order to get the job done; Q appears to contribute very little to the project, is frequently missing from meetings, misses internal deadlines, and takes days off in the middle of the week to concentrate on their leisure activities. P, it seems to you, puts in just as much work as you do, if not more, whereas Q is not at all pulling their weight. Eventually, perhaps because of the efforts of P, and despite the efforts of Q, the project achieves its goals and attention turns to the question of remuneration. Is it fair that Q should be paid the same amount as you and P? To most people, it is not fair, and feelings of injustice or being wronged in some way are both natural and universal.[1] This chapter will focus on how Shakespeare tends to depict such feelings as a key motivation for revenge and, if unchecked, a possible route to villainy, evil and even societal collapse. This is because the desire for revenge fuels selfish or self-seeking behaviour – the antithesis of fairness – and thus unfairness begets unfairness. Human groups that lack any sense of fairness and in which individuals have become wholly selfish cannot flourish. I will focus chiefly on Richard III's primary motivation for revenge, Hamlet's refusal to kill Claudius when he is praying, the Duke's pardon of Angelo in *Measure for Measure*, and Edmund's motivations in *King Lear*.

In a robust study, which cites over a hundred books and papers on fairness and equality from across psychology, sociology and evolutionary studies, Christina Starmans, Mark Sheskin and Paul Bloom have shown that, when all other factors are equal, human beings show a preference for equality of outcome, but this is almost always trumped by the principle of proportional fairness. Indeed, this strong propensity towards and sensitivity to fairness, as opposed to equality, is an evolutionary trait in humans, developed to reward and punish good and bad actors for the benefit of the group:

> For cooperation and prosociality to evolve, there has to be some solution to the problem of free-riders, cheaters, and bad actors. The usual explanation for this is that we have evolved a propensity to make bad behaviour costly and good behaviour beneficial, through punishment and reward. That is, we respond differently to individuals based on what one can see as their 'deservingness' – responses that are present even in infants. It's possible that fairness intuitions more generally develop from this moral foundation.[2]

The rewards and punishment are not only material but also social. Selfish individuals are shunned, whereas cooperative individuals are included. However, because we are human beings and not, say, ants or termites, there must be a trade-off between altruism and self-interest.

> [C]ooperative individuals gain benefits from being included and selfish individuals lose out on those benefits by being shunned. But individuals who are too cooperative – too generous – run the risk of being taken advantage of by others. So a balance must be struck. To treat everyone equally would entail penalization of more productive individuals

when they collaborate with less productive individuals relative to highly productive individuals. In contrast with equality, fairness allows individuals with different levels of productivity to share the benefits of their collaboration proportionately. This focus on fairness is particularly important for humans (compared with even our closest evolutionary relatives), due to the critical importance of collaboration in human hunting and foraging.[3]

Either extreme, pure selfishness or pure altruism, is more likely to lead to net negative material and social outcomes than net benefits, and in the worst cases will result in the individual being killed. Such findings would not have been surprising for Niccolò Machiavelli, who advised a pragmatic balance between the two.[4]

One interesting finding is that just as proportionality is a central feature of fairness, disproportionality is a central feature of selfishness:

> [P]eople have selfish motivations, but ... these desires are not always for increasing one's absolute amount, but are often for increasing one's standing relative to others. For example, studies of income and happiness have revealed that, once a basic level of wealth is achieved, relative wealth is more important for overall happiness. Similarly, a vast body of research in social psychology finds that people engage in constant comparison of themselves with others.... Five-year-olds often reject equal payouts of two prize tokens for themselves and two prize tokens for another child, and choose instead only one token for themselves, if that means that the other child will get none.[5]

We typically think of such behaviour as spiteful and 'unfair', which is an intuitive *moral* response to a behaviour that seems rooted in our constrained natures. In this way, unfairness is defined, above all else, by selfishness.

Where Shakespeare evokes unfairness, villainy usually follows. Experience has not been 'fair' to Richard III, Aaron in *Titus Andronicus*, Shylock in *The Merchant of Venice*, Malvolio in *Twelfth Night* or Edmund in *King Lear*, and all of them are determined to prove themselves villains. Shakespeare depicts fairness almost always from the individual, psychological perspective, as opposed to the cosmic or disinterested third-party view. Thus, in *As You Like It*, despite Louis Montrose's famous arguments to the contrary,[6] we are not led to dwell too deeply on the disproportionate treatment of Oliver and Orlando by their father because Orlando himself does not articulate much in the way of grievance. Contrast this with King Lear's reaction to his treatment at the hands of Goneril and Regan when they refuse to host a hundred of his retinue, and quite a different story emerges.

> I gave you all . . . Made you my guardians, my depositaries,
> But kept a reservation to be followed
> With such a number. (*King Lear*, II, iii, 244, 246–8)

Lear feels that it is unfair that his daughters are not maintaining the conditions he had outlined when he gave them his lands, and very quickly seeks justice in the form of revenge:

> I will have such revenges on you both
> That all the world shall – I will do such things –
> What they are, yet I know not, but they shall be
> The terrors of the earth. (*King Lear*, II, iii, 274–7)

Lear's revenge is motivated by a sense of injustice. Similarly, Malvolio, who 'hath been most notoriously abused' (*Twelfth Night*, V, i, 365) by Sir Toby, Feste and Maria – far in excess of his actual wrong-doings – is last seen swearing 'I'll be revenged on the whole pack of you' (V, i, 364). And Shylock seeks to 'feed' his 'revenge (*The Merchant of Venice*, I, iii, 45) because he feels that Antonio has treated him terribly unfairly: 'He hath disgraced me and hindered me half a million, laughed at my losses, mocked at my gains, scorned my nation, thwarted my bargains, cooled my friends, heated mine enemies, and what's his reason? I am a Jew' (I, iii, 45–9). In each case, unfairness drives spite and revenge.

To my knowledge, the two most thoroughgoing recent studies on Shakespeare and fairness are Tzachi Zamir's *Double Vision: Moral Philosophy and Shakespearean Drama* (2007), which has a long chapter focusing on 'A Case of Unfair Proportions' in *Richard III*,[7] and Linda Woodbridge's *English Revenge Drama: Money, Resistance, Equality* (2010), which provides a detailed historical overview of attitudes to fairness in the early modern period.[8] Although they do not reference any of the psychological material from which I have been drawing – or, indeed, each other – both authors are acutely aware of the link between unfairness and revenge. However, in my view, neither of them captures Shakespeare's tragic sense of the continuity between unfairness and selfishness: if our sense of fairness is offended, the desire for revenge and the welling up of emotions invariably give sway to our worst instincts of self-interest and self-preservation.

In a nuanced and penetrating argument, Zamir concludes that *Richard III* confronts its central character's 'radical ethical skepticism', which turns out to be little more than 'a deficiency in knowing'.[9] Richard misperceives the motives of others and fails to see the real complexity of the world. Zamir correctly points out that Richard does not even entertain the *possibility* that Anne could really love him, although I would reject his claim that Anne's 'positive response to Richard's wooing is [so] outrageously unmotivated' that it might be explained by a 'sexual pull' towards him.[10] As I argued in a previous study, Anne's reaction is best understood as her reaching out for a brief respite from suffering, a momentary relief.[11] Let us look again at Richard's primary motivation:

> I, that am curtailed of this fair proportion,
> Cheated of feature by dissembling nature,

> . . . And therefore, since I cannot prove a lover
> I am determinèd to prove a villain. (*Richard III*, I, i,
> 18–19, 28, 30)

Zamir notes that, like Edmund in *King Lear* and Iago in *Othello*, Richard's 'villainy is vindictive', but unlike theirs, his 'vengeance seems to be general' rather than directed at a particular person. The charge that 'nature' is 'dissembling' reveals that Richard thinks beauty is a false mask that covers up the true (evil) nature of human beings. However, ultimately, this philosophising is just a 'superficial excuse', what in the terms of the present study we might call a *post hoc* rationalisation, because '*his* [real] preoccupation is with *his* ugliness'.[12] Zamir's suggestion is that so much of what drives Richard is his own paranoia, what he *imagines* others think of him, as opposed to the reality of the situation, which is one in which Anne might really have felt some attraction to him. While it is no doubt true that Richard is, or at least has become, paranoid, I see no reason for such an optimistic view of 'reality'. Richard – at least the man that Shakespeare imagines, as opposed to the historical King – probably *was* treated differently for most of his life, and, as I suggested, very likely did not possess a sexual allure for Anne.

If there is a moral point being made at all by Richard's villainy, it is that life is *not* fair and we must, if we are to live the good life, make peace with that fact. How might the world be corrected to make it fairer for Richard? Should all the ugly people be subjected to corrective surgery to make them better-looking, while all the most beautiful people are somehow disfigured to take away their unfair advantage? I am reminded of L. P. Hartley's dystopian novel, *Facial Justice*, which takes such a premise as its plot.[13] This is a nightmarish egalitarianism for which no sane person would wish. Individuals are not created with entirely equal traits, and this is something everyone must live with for the greater good. In this realisation lies the heart of the tragic, or constrained, vision I outlined in Chapter 2. In *Measure for Measure*, Claudio recognises this, echoing Paul in Romans 9: 15:

> Thus can the demigod Authority
> Make us pay down for our offense by weight.
> The words of heaven; on whom it will, it will,
> On whom it will not, so; yet still 'tis just. (I, i, 109–12)

As I discussed when outlining John Calvin's theology in Chapter 4, God's grace touches some people but not others, just as some people are good-looking and others 'cheated of feature'. This is obviously 'not fair' but it is still 'just', because to rail against this is to go the way of Richard III: a directionless revenge that can resolve only in empty self-interest and preservation. Justice is not a levelling egalitarianism; it is the proportionate relationship of one thing to another, as suggested by the title *Measure for Measure*.

Once again, we can turn to Thomas Aquinas and natural law for a definition of justice that would have been embedded in early modern society:

> The proper characteristic of justice, as compared with the other moral virtues, is to govern a man in his dealings towards others. It implies a certain balance of equality, as its very name shows, for in common speech things are said to be adjusted when they match evenly. Equality is relative to another. The other moral virtues, however, compose a man for activities which befit him considered in himself. So then that which is correct in their working and which is the proper object of their bent is not thought of save in relation to the doer. Whereas with justice, in addition to this, that which is correct is constituted by a relation to another, for a work of ours is said to be just when it meets another on the level, as with the payment of a fair wage for a service rendered.[14]

This idea of justice is based firmly on the fairness of proportionality, not on egalitarianism. Richard might feel that he is the victim of an unjust and cruel world, but based on this definition, he has no justification for seeking revenge on it.

But what if someone had a just reason to seek revenge? We might think of *Hamlet*. Surely, here, where Claudius has taken the life of Old Hamlet, based on this idea of proportional fairness, his son has just cause for vengeance? Here is Aquinas:

> Vengeance is accomplished by some punishment being inflicted upon one who has given offence. In vengeance, therefore, the attitude of the avenger must be considered. Should his intention be centred chiefly upon the evil done to the recipient and is satisfied with that, then the act is entirely unlawful. Taking delight in evil done to another is in fact a type of hatred, the opposite of that charity with which we are bound to love all. Nor is there any excuse just because the evil is intended towards one who has himself unjustly inflicted injury, even as there is no excuse for hating someone who already hates us. A person has no right to sin against another because the other first sinned against him; this is to be overcome by evil, which St. Paul forbids, *Be not overcome by evil, but overcome evil by good.*[15]

Based on these criteria, Hamlet is on dubious moral grounds because, while he plainly does not take 'delight' in his revenge mission to kill Claudius, he purposely wishes to do it in the most hateful and spiteful manner possible. He does not wish to murder Claudius while he is at prayer, not out of any respect for the sanctity of the Church, but because the idea of Claudius being forgiven for his sin and gaining admittance to Heaven sickens him. He prefers to wait instead for a time:

> When he is drunk asleep, or in his rage,
> Or in th'incestuous pleasure of his bed,
> At game, a-swearing, or about some act

> That has no relish of salvation in't.
> Then trip him that his heels may kick at heaven
> And that his soul may be as damned and black
> As hell whereto it goes. (*Hamlet*, III, iii, 89–95)

Hamlet's 'intention' is focused 'chiefly upon the evil done to the recipient' and hence, at least according to Aquinas, his revenge is 'unlawful' in the eyes of God.

But as the theologian goes on to say,

> Vengeance, however, can be lawful – so long as all proper conditions are safeguarded – if the intention of the avenger is aimed chiefly at a good to be achieved by punishing a wrongdoer; thus, for example, at the correction of the wrongdoer, or at least at restraining him and relieving others; at safeguarding the right and doing honour to God.[16]

To find an example of this in Shakespeare, we must turn to one of his least emotionally satisfying instances of justice: when the Duke seems to punish Angelo at the end of *Measure for Measure* only by ensuring he stays married to Mariana. For the theatre audience, this certainly *feels* unsatisfactory because Angelo has been such a despicable hypocrite throughout the play, and so ready to execute other characters for lesser crimes; this is scarcely a punishment at all, especially given that Mariana loves him. It seems to us that he gets off very lightly:

> By this Lord Angelo perceives he's safe:
> Methinks I see a quick'ning in his eye.
> Well, Angelo, your evil quits you well.
> Look that you love your wife, her worth worth yours.
> I find an apt remission in myself. (*Measure for Measure*, V, i, 496–502)

But Angelo has been exposed and shamed in public and subject to what Aquinas calls, drawing on Cicero's eight types of penalty in law, '*disgrace* (the ruin of his reputation)'.[17]

Incidentally, the other seven types are: death, flogging, retaliation, bondage, chains, exile and damages. If one assesses the net damages inflicted by Angelo on Claudio – he made him suffer the indignity of the experience of being arrested, being jailed, and desperately begging his sister, Isabella, to compromise her sacred vows to save his life – then the punishment seems more proportionate. Claudio suffered disgrace and loss of reputation, perhaps permanently with his sister, and this is what Angelo also receives: the scales of justice are in balance. In Aquinas's terms, we witness 'the correction of the wrongdoer': not only justice but also rehabilitation. And this would not have been possible with the harsher sentence that hot-headed vengeance would dictate. This is a judicial model of mercy, forgiveness and personal growth, and a restoration of true Christian justice after the tyrannical corruption of Angelo's abuses of power.

In rejecting any impulses in Shakespeare towards egalitarianism, I find myself at odds with Linda Woodbridge's *English Revenge Drama*. While this is a valuable work of scholarship on fairness in the early modern period, at times – perhaps in the pursuit of a politically radical thesis – Woodbridge seems to mistake the fairness of proportionality for a levelling egalitarianism. She recognises that fairness concerns itself with proportions. For example, she suggests that 'revengers are often embittered over unrewarded merit', and reflected feelings that were widespread in Shakespeare's audience:[18]

> Unfairness was like the weather: everyone talked about it. But revenge plays did something about it. Many revengers are disempowered people, unjustly treated, who step up and take control. . . . But rather than viewing revenge through a lens of individual psychology, I suggest that the fairness fixation and relish of vigilantism reveal widespread resentment of systemic unfairness – economic, political, and social – as the Renaissance witnessed severe disproportion between crime and punishment, between labor and its rewards.[19]

But, here, in creeps a utopian element to Woodbridge's analysis that is at odds with the sensibilities of the 1590s and early 1600s. She seems to think that Shakespeare and his contemporaries anticipate the *égalité* of Jean-Jacques Rousseau and the French Revolutionaries, who were later influenced by his philosophy:

> In three electrifying speeches by Shylock, Emilia, and Edmund, Shakespeare extends the radical thinking of his age into the realms of religious affiliation, ethnicity, gender equity, and legitimacy. Our blinkered dismissal of vengefulness castrates their radicalism. If we truly listen to these speeches, we'll find that the urge to *get even* harbored the germ of the idea that all men are created equal.... With its book-balancing devotion to equality, revenge fed into the broad stream of Renaissance egalitarianism. Revenge was never pleasant or morally uplifting. But audiences understood it and emotionally validated it. And I propose that the ubiquitous Renaissance writings about revenge, the audience zest for revenge, are inextricable from the political, economic, and social radicalism of the age.[20]

I am not persuaded of any such 'social radicalism' in these speeches.[21] They powerfully register characters who *feel* that they have been unfairly treated, but the plays neither endorse revenge nor call for revolution. Shakespeare's moral mode does not lend itself to the literature of political protest, and here, it seems, Woodbridge is projecting her own modern, progressive, perhaps even socialistic sensibilities on to the past. The inherited wisdom in Shakespeare is closer to that cautioned by Ulysses in *Troilus and Cressida*: 'Oh, let not virtue seek / Remuneration for the thing it was' (III, iii, 167–8).

Let us look briefly at just one of these speeches, Edmund's in *King Lear*:

> Thou, Nature, art my goddess; to thy law
> My services are bound. Wherefore should I
> Stand in the plague of custom and permit
> The curiosity of nations to deprive me,

> For that I am some twelve or fourteen moonshines
> Lag of a brother? Why 'bastard'? Wherefore 'base',
> When my dimensions are as well compact,
> My mind as generous and my shape as true
> As honest madam's issue? Why brand they us
> With 'base'? With 'baseness', 'bastardy'? Base? Base?
> Who, in the lusty stealth of nature, take
> More composition and fierce quality
> Than doth within a dull, stale, tired bed
> Go to th' creating a whole tribe of fops
> Got 'tween a sleep, and wake? Well, then,
> Legitimate Edgar, I must have your land.
> Our father's love is to the bastard Edmund
> As to th' legitimate. Fine word: 'legitimate'!
> Well, my legitimate, if this letter speed
> And my invention thrive, Edmund the base
> Shall to th' legitimate. I grow. I prosper.
> Now, gods, stand up for bastards! (*King Lear*, I, i, 1–22)

If Edmund anticipates a political philosopher here, it is assuredly not Rousseau, for whom all men are created equal, because he hints that in some ways he might be Edgar's *superior*, not only because of the way he was conceived (in a 'lusty' as opposed to 'dull, stale, tired bed'), but also because of the merits of his 'invention'. And to an extent this is borne out as Edmund continually tricks his naïvely trusting brother in the next couple of scenes. In outlining this case, based on the 'law' of 'Nature', Edmund echoes Machiavelli[22] and anticipates Thomas Hobbes. Indeed, in 1949, John F. Danby 'maintained that Hobbes is Edmund's philosopher'.[23] Andrew Moore makes the most recent and fully articulated case for this:

> Edmund is the prime example of a character who subscribes to the idea we are no different from animals, that we prioritize self-preservation and bodily satisfaction over all else, and are essentially governed by instinctual processes beyond our control. Edmund has made a 'goddess' of this emergent nature (1.2.1). Consequently, he is completely self-interested. Morality and religion have no hold over him.[24]

Yet, he remains a villain because 'Shakespeare recognises in our innate desire for security and felicity the simultaneous presence of communal and antisocial drives, and so anticipates the tension in Hobbes's *Leviathan* between our natural passions and natural law.'[25] Finding a 'plague of custom' that would hold him down because of a quirk of his birth, Edmund feels that the world is grossly unfair and so, filled with vengeance, he becomes the pure agent of self-seeking behaviour. In Edmund's new order – which temporarily overthrows Lear's old order – we are in the world of the ruthless Chicago gangsters that Richard Dawkins imagines in *The Selfish Gene*:[26] in other words, the Hobbesian state of nature. As evolutionary psychology maintains, however, pure selfishness, just like pure altruism, cannot subsist for long and, accordingly, Edmund's successes are short-lived. In *Why Nations Fail* (2012), Daron Acemoglu and James A. Robinson argue that nations cannot prosper without fair rules of cooperation and mutual trust under the rule of law,[27] and in *The Moral Foundations of Economic Behaviour* (2011), David C. Rose makes a similar case.[28] A society with a complete absence of fair play, filled with ruthlessly selfish cheaters such as Edmund, Goneril, Cornwall and Regan, is doomed.

In this chapter, I have argued that fairness is concerned with proportionality, not a levelling egalitarianism, and that this is mirrored in Shakespeare's treatment of the theme across several plays. In Shakespeare's moral vision, when codes of fairness break down, revenge and rampant selfishness, as manifest in villainy, are not far behind. A society in which a sense of fairness has given way to complete selfishness risks complete collapse. However, to some extent, to ward against this risk for the greater good, we must also accept that life is 'not fair': we are not born equal in looks, talents, wealth and so on. The worst villains cannot accept this. Shakespeare's depiction of fairness, as contrasted with selfishness, seems at once compatible with the view we find in a wide range of other sources, including Aquinas, Machiavelli, Hobbes, evolutionary psychology, and the constrained vision I outlined in Chapter 2.

> ### In summary
> - The moral foundation of fairness responds to proportionality, not equality. It is a question of *deserving*, of reward or punishment at an appropriate level.
> - Studies from across psychology, sociology and evolutionary studies have found that fairness developed chiefly to counter free-riders, cheaters and bad actors prone to ruthless and self-seeking behaviour. Despite this, human beings still show a selfish preference for increasing their own standing relative to others.
> - In Shakespeare, unfairness usually results in a desire for revenge, which leads to ruthless selfishness; we can see this in *King Lear* (Edmund, Lear himself), *Twelfth Night* (Malvolio), *Richard III* and *Hamlet*.
> - Following the tragic or constrained vision, Shakespeare cautions that we must accept that life is seldom fair, lest we become a Richard III.
> - His conception of justice seems to follow Thomas Aquinas in looking for moderately proportional punishments emphasising mercy and rehabilitation (the Duke's pardon of Angelo in *Measure for Measure*) rather than vengeance (Hamlet not killing Claudius at prayer out of spite).
> - There is no socially levelling or egalitarian strain in Shakespeare's conception of fairness, and it would be a mistake to take Edmund in *King Lear* as a political revolutionary, since the plays wholly condemns his self-seeking behaviour, which would result in complete societal collapse if taken to its logical endpoint (the Hobbesian 'state of nature'). In the absence of fairness, selfishness reigns, and it is a model that cannot subsist.

Notes

1. See Trivers, 'The Evolution of Reciprocal Altruism', pp. 35–57; Haidt, *The Righteous Mind*, pp. 158–61.
2. Christina Starmans, Mark Sheskin and Paul Bloom, 'Why People Prefer Unequal Societies', *Nature Human Behaviour*, 1:82 (April 2017), p. 4.
3. Ibid. p. 4.
4. Belliotti, *Niccolò Machiavelli*, pp. 17–18.
5. Starmans, Sheskin and Bloom, 'Why People Prefer Unequal Societies', p. 4. For the study on five-year-olds, see Mark Sheskin, Paul Bloom and Karen Wynn, 'Anti-Equality: Social Comparison in Young Children', *Cognition*, 130:2 (February 2014), pp. 152–6.
6. Louis Adrian Montrose, '"The Place of a Brother" in *As You Like It*: Social Process and Comic Form', *Shakespeare Quarterly*, 32:1 (Spring 1981), pp. 28–54.
7. Zamir, *Double Vision*, pp. 65–92.
8. Linda Woodbridge, *English Revenge Drama: Money, Resistance, Equality* (Cambridge: Cambridge University Press, 2010).
9. Zamir, *Double Vision*, pp. 89, 90.
10. Ibid. pp. 79–80.
11. Parvini, *Shakespeare and Cognition*, pp. 30–2.
12. Zamir, *Double Vision*, pp. 70, 71.
13. L. P. Hartley, *Facial Justice* (1960; London: Penguin, 2014).
14. Thomas Aquinas, *Summa Theologiae* (*Vol. 37: Justice*) [2a2ae. 57–62], ed. Thomas Gilby (London: Eyre & Spottiswoode, 1969), question 57, article 1, p. 5.
15. Thomas Aquinas, *Summa Theologiae* (*Vol. 41: Virtues of Justice in the Human Community*) [2a2ae. 101–22], ed. T. C. O'Brien (London: Eyre & Spottiswoode, 1969), question 108, article 1, p. 117, emphasis in original.
16. Ibid. p. 117.
17. Ibid. question 108, article 3, p. 125.
18. Woodbridge, *Revenge Drama*, p. 84.
19. Ibid. pp. 6–7.
20. Ibid. p. 270, emphasis in original.

21. As regards Shylock's and Emilia's speeches, I have made an argument to this effect before now: see 'What Did Shakespeare Understand About the Human Mind?', *The View of Life* (*The Evolution Institute*) (April 2016), <https://evolution-institute. org/article/what-did-shakespeare-understand-about-the-human-mind/> (last accessed 8 October 2017).
22. Robin Headlam Wells, *Shakespeare's Politics: A Contextual Introduction*, 2nd edn (1986; New York and London: Continuum, 2009), p. 174.
23. John F. Danby, *Shakespeare's Doctrine of Nature: A Study of King Lear* (London: Faber & Faber, 1949), p. 46.
24. Moore, *Shakespeare Between Machiavelli and Hobbes*, p. 68.
25. Ibid. p. 69.
26. Dawkins, *The Selfish Gene*, p. 5.
27. Daron Acemoglu and James A. Robinson, *Why Nations Fail: The Origins of Power, Prosperity, and Poverty* (London: Profile Books, 2012).
28. Rose, *The Moral Foundation of Economic Behaviour*, pp. 19–20.

CHAPTER 9

SANCTITY

In her classic study, *Shakespeare's Imagery and What It Tells Us* (1935), Caroline Spurgeon points out that, in Shakespeare's plays, evil and images of dirtiness and disease are strongly correlated:

> Evil in Shakespeare's imagination is dirty, black and foul, a blot, a spot, a stain; and some sixty examples could be quoted of this, as well as many of the reverse and rather more obvious uses of spotless, stainless, and so on. . . . Shakespeare also thinks of evil as a sickness, an infection, a sore and an ulcer.[1]

She also adds that evil, thus manifested, appears to be contagious, infecting all that are touched by it: 'the idea also that one evil leads to another is ever present with Shakespeare'.[2] This concept of evil rests on the moral foundation of sanctity. In this chapter, I will examine the link between sin and dirtiness, disease or contagion in Shakespeare by looking at some key examples in *King Lear, Timon of Athens, Othello, Richard III, Hamlet, Othello* and *Macbeth*. I will also compare Shakespeare's sometimes gruesome descriptions of degradation with those found in the Protestant theology of Richard Hooker and John Calvin, who each provide dark visions of human impurity. I will also cross-reference Catholic teachings on sin as embodied in Thomas Aquinas. In the process, I will attempt to discover what was sacred to Shakespeare.

It has been the fashion in recent years to think about Shakespeare's many images of disease in the context of 'a precise historical and medical moment'. For example, while Eric Langley is alert to 'connotations of contagion: interaction becoming infection; communication becoming communicative; sympathy facilitating contagion', in focusing so squarely on the early modern understanding of medicine, he appears to miss the moral dimension, even though this accounts for much of the process he describes.[3] Likewise, Jonathan Gil Harris does a superb job of tracing contagion and disease in the discursive concepts of the emerging nation-state and mercantilism (especially as regards xenophobia), but he too never seems to think of his subject as a moral matter.[4] Of course, one reason for this is that neither Langley nor Harris was writing books about Shakespeare and morality as I am. Another reason is that it simply would not occur to either of them that in writing about disease and contagion in Shakespeare, they were in fact dealing with a morally charged subject. Of the six moral foundations, sanctity / degradation is perhaps the one to which modern Westerners are least attuned to thinking of in a *moral* sense, even though it still has great purchase in our culture.

Jonathan Haidt adapts the concept from his mentor, Richard A. Shweder, who calls it the 'ethics of divinity'.[5] It is primarily concerned with notions of the sacred or 'purification', which, if violated, result in feelings 'of stain' and 'pollution',[6] activating moral revulsion and disgust. Psychological studies have found that disgust is not only unique to humans (animals do not reject food because of what else might have touched it), but also universal across cultures, with a readily recognisable facial expression (picture a child tasting a bitter lemon or grapefruit).[7] We have particularly visceral responses to objects associated with disease that might contaminate food. Humans experience:

> Revulsion at the prospect of (oral) incorporation of an offensive object. The offensive objects are contaminants; that is, if they even briefly contact an acceptable food, they tend to render that food unacceptable. . . . Disgusting items have the capacity to contaminate and are usually animals or animal products, with feces being a universal disgust object among adults.[8]

It is obvious that this deeply primeval response evolved to help us avoid pathogens. However, it extends beyond food into the moral realm whenever a community holds a sacred creed.

In *The Righteous Mind*, Haidt gives an example:

> The current triggers of the Sanctity foundation ... are extraordinarily variable and expandable across cultures and eras. A common and direct expansion is to out-group members. Cultures differ in their attitudes toward immigrants, and there is some evidence that liberal and welcoming attitudes are more common in times and places where disease risks are lower. Plagues, epidemics, and new diseases are usually brought in by foreigners – as are many new ideas, goods, and technologies – so societies face ... [a] dilemma, balancing xenophobia and xenophilia.[9]

It is a dilemma that became a reality in the summer of 2017 in the United States. Haidt wrote a piece in *The Atlantic* after President Donald Trump was criticised by many commentators for failing to condemn neo-Nazis sufficiently at a white nationalist rally in Charlottesville:

> Taboo and sacredness are among the most important words needed to understand Charlottesville and its aftermath.

> Taboo refers to things that are forbidden for religious or supernatural reasons. All traditional societies have such prohibitions – things you must not do, touch, or eat, not because they are bad for you directly, but because doing so is an abomination, which may bring divine retribution. But every society also makes some things sacred, rallying around a few deeply revered values, people, or places, which bind all members together and make them willing to sacrifice for the common good. The past week brought violent conflict over symbols and values held sacred – and saw President Trump commit an act of sacrilege by violating one of our society's strongest taboos.[10]

He continues by describing Trump's press conference of Tuesday, 15 August 2017, and especially his claim that there were 'very fine people' on both sides.

> Taboo violations are contagious. They render the transgressor 'polluted', in the language of anthropology, and the moral stain rubs off on those who physically touch the transgressor, as well as on those who fail to distance themselves from the transgressor. When people march with Nazis and Klansmen, even if they keep their mouths closed when others are chanting, and even if they don't personally carry swastika or Klan flags, they acquire the full moral stain of Nazis and Klansmen. By saying that some of these men were 'very fine people', the President has taken that stain upon himself.[11]

In this way, the moral transgression of a sacred creed becomes like a contagious disease. This is readily captured in the phrase 'guilt by association'. Of course, in logical argumentation, this is a variant of the *ad hominem* informal fallacy; it is fundamentally irrational, an appeal to emotion. Moral responses are seldom, if ever, rational.

Shakespeare gives us many examples of characters being totally irrational while leaning on the sanctity foundation.

For instance, let us take Lear's revolting verbal assault on Goneril:

> But yet thou art my flesh, my blood, my daughter,
> Or rather a disease that's in my flesh
> Which I must needs call mind. Thou art a boil,
> A plague sore, or embossèd carbuncle
> In my corrupted blood. (*King Lear*, II, iv, 215–19)

Lear is plainly disgusted at his daughter. She has transgressed that which is sacred to him, which in this case was her complicity in putting Kent (disguised as Caius) into the stocks (see Chapter 6) and her complicity with Regan in refusing to house his full retinue of a hundred knights (see Chapter 10). From Lear's point of view, moral culpability spreads rapidly in this scene. At first, he is angry only with Goneril, the source of the 'disease', but by the end of the scene Regan, Cornwall and Oswald all become tainted and untouchable to him as well. He begins by symbolically injecting the 'serpent-like' (II, iv, 154) Goneril with poison:

> You nimble lightnings, dart your blinding flames
> Into her scornful eyes. Infect her beauty,
> You fen-sucked fogs, drawn by the pow'rful sun
> To fall and blister. (II, iv, 158–61)

The sun was said to suck poisonous vapours from the marshy ground. Even though she has not yet entered the scene, Goneril is already polluted in mind. Thus, when Oswald enters, Lear immediately lashes out at him: he has guilt by association, and is therefore also untouchable:

> This is a slave whose easy borrowed pride
> Dwells in the sickly grace of her he follows.
> Out, varlet, from my sight. (II, iv, 177–9)

Later, after his daughters talk him down from a hundred men to just one, Regan catches Goneril's disease and seemingly, by extension, so do all women. Hence Lear will not let 'women's weapons, water drops, / *Stain* his man's cheeks' (II, iv, 72–3, emphasis mine). Having transgressed his sacred values, his daughters are now 'unnatural hags' (II, iv, 73). The castle itself has become contagious and so Lear forces himself out into the storm to contend with the 'fretful elements' (III, i, 4). His daughters have become so poisonous to him that he would rather spend the night raging at the weather than acquiesce to their requests to entertain fewer of his men. One critic has argued that Lear does not achieve 'purification' from the taint of this perceived evil until his final interview with Cordelia, in a mirror of Virgil's reunification with Beatrice in *The Divine Comedy*.[12] Even though the play depicts an essentially pagan world, this purification is possible because so much is animated – at least within Lear's own mind – by the moral foundation of sanctity.

In Shakespeare's plays, perceived spiritual and moral degradation nearly always manifests itself in the physical. Sin infects every aspect of a person's being, rendering 'diseased conditions of mind and body'.[13] For example, in *Timon of Athens*, as Timon – like Lear – comes to see himself as 'more sinned against than sinning' (*King Lear*, III, ii, 59), he paints those around him as physically degrading:

> Consumptions sow
> In hollow bones of man, strike their sharp shins,
> And mar men's spurring! Crack the lawyer's voice
> That he may never more false title plead,
> Nor sound his quillets shrilly. Hoar the flamen
> That scold'st against the quality of flesh
> And not believes himself. Down with the nose,
> Down with it flat, take the bridge quite away
> Of him that his particular to foresee
> Smells from the general weal. Make curled-pate ruffians bald,
> And let the unscarred braggarts of the war
> Derive some pain from you. Plague all,

>   That your activity may defeat and quell
>   The source of your erection. There's more gold,
>   Do you damn others, and let this damn you,
>   And ditches grave you all. (*Timon of Athens*, IV, iii, 151–66)

The imagery in this passage is horrific: here 'consumption' probably represents either syphilis or leprosy, and the effects of these diseases are chilling. It causes bone degeneration until the marrow is hollowed out. An ulcer grows in the larynx to 'crack' the voice. The bridge of the nose collapses ('Down with nose, / Down with it flat'). The contaminated man also experiences hair loss ('bald') and 'pain', and eventually loses his sexual functions ('erection'). Timon, at this point the complete misanthrope, embodies moral decay in this imagined disease-riddled and rotting character, a terrifying figure who would not be out of place in a modern zombie film. However, as in Lear, so much of this is projection from Timon: *he* perceives a morally bankrupt world gone to rack and ruin, and describes it in terms of disease, as if evil is a contagion or pathogen slowly destroying everyone around him. The fact that so many of these images of sickness and decay are *psychologically* generated is significant because we cannot straightforwardly align Shakespeare's morals with those of his characters. We can plainly see that a link between moral and physical degradation is hard-coded in his imagination, but that does not necessarily mean that he agrees with, for example, Lear or Timon on what counts as evil.

In fact, it seems that, no matter *who* is speaking, the logic of sin consistently works in the same contagious way in Shakespeare's universe. Thus, when Richard II predicts 'ere foul sin, gathering head, / Shall break into corruption' (*Richard II*, V, i, 58–9), the disease spreads not only into the next play but into the *one after that*: King Henry quotes him almost verbatim in 2 *Henry IV* (III, i, 76–7). The same logic is at play in *Othello*. We see Iago plotting to taint

Desdemona's purity: 'So will I turn her virtue into pitch' (*Othello*, II, iii, 331), and from there he can keep spreading his evil. Othello himself thinks of sin in this way – 'the slime / That sticks on filthy deeds' (*Othello*, V, ii, 143–4) – as something disgusting and sticky, something that contaminates once touched. Alexander G. Gonzalez has demonstrated how sin works in a close reading of the play, in which he finds a 'pattern of transfer' from one character to another: 'There exists in the play what amounts to a spread of evil from Iago to other characters and . . . Shakespeare has given us cues in the play's language that aid us in following the contamination's progress.'[14] It is a broadly convincing view of how evil functions in the play, and entirely consistent with what we have seen in other plays.

We also find similar language of corruption in cases where characters belie their guilt for sinful deeds they have freely chosen to commit, but here the images turn from diseases to staining: for example, when Richard III tells Buckingham

> But if black scandal or foul-faced reproach
> Attend the sequel of your imposition,
> Your mere enforcement shall acquittance me
> From all the impure blots and stains thereof. (*Richard III*, III, vii, 209–12)

Richard is playing his coquettish façade here; he must be seen to be reluctant to take the throne, but even in the process we know, as well as Buckingham, that his moral copybook is already covered in 'blots and stains'. Take Claudius too, in his pivotal confession scene in *Hamlet*:

> Oh, my offense is rank, it smells to heaven;
> It hath the primal eldest curse upon't –
> A brother's murder. Pray can I not:
> Though inclination be as sharp as will,
> My stronger guilt defeats my strong intent

> And like a man to double business bound
> I stand in pause where I shall first begin,
> And both neglect. What if this cursèd hand
> Were thicker than itself with brother's blood—
> Is there not rain enough in the sweet heavens
> To wash it white as snow? Whereto serves mercy
> But to confront the visage of offense? (*Hamlet*, III, iii, 35–47)

Images of defilement pile up. His offence is 'rank' and 'smells'. He cannot wash the stain of blood from his hands. Sanctity has been desecrated. The image is, of course, biblical:

> And when you shall stretch out your hands, I will hide mine eyes from you: and though ye make many prayers, I will not hear: for your hands are full of blood. Wash you, make you clean: take away the evil of your works from before mine eyes: cease to do evil. . . . though your sins were as crimson, they shall be made white as snow: though they were red like scarlet, they shall be as wool. (Isaiah 1: 15–18)[15]

It seems this passage was deeply ingrained in Shakespeare's imagination because he returns to it again in *Macbeth*:

> Will all great Neptune's ocean wash this blood
> Clean from my hand? No, this my hand will rather
> The multitudinous seas incarnadine,
> Making the green one red. (*Macbeth*, II, ii, 63–6)

Macbeth speaks these lines but the sin of the deed also infamously stains his wife and accomplice: 'Out, damned spot!' (V, i, 31). The stain seems permanent: her 'hands [will] ne'er be clean' and 'all the perfumes of Arabia will not sweeten' the odious smell of the blood (V, i, 37, 44–5). The doctor admits 'This disease is beyond my practice' because 'More needs she the divine than the physician' (V, i, 52, 67).

Of all the aspects of Shakespeare's moral compass we have explored so far, his mode of depicting sanctity and degradation in terms of disease, contamination and staining has the most overtly Christian overtones. However, as Francis Fergusson points out:

> [T]o recognize Shakespeare's dependence on medieval Christianity, as one must, does not require us to suppose that he was an orthodox believer. . . . he sometimes even wished to de-emphasize the Christianity of his scheme. There is very little reference to the Church in *Hamlet* or *Macbeth*, and *Lear* is ostensibly set in pre-Christian Britain.[16]

In closing this chapter, I would like to take some space to discern how Shakespeare's depiction of sanctity and degradation differs from what we find in theology. As we saw in Chapter 4, during the Reformation, Protestant teachings leaned heavily on the moral foundation of sanctity. Roland Mushat Frye describes 'how the theologians treated man's universal depravity': 'Sin exists as a disease in man; the disease may be controlled by the medicine of grace, but if it is not, it will destroy men in one way or another.'[17] In this view, mankind is already in a state of sickness or moral decay; the only cure comes from divine grace. We can see this plainly in Richard Hooker's theology:

> So, that which is nature once made a disease, the continuance of that disease hath made it nature; for even that light, which man whilst he wanteth liveth in perpetual darkness, is a light by our weakness not possible to be attained unto; and those paths, which in our blindness we grope after with so much desire, they are 'ways' not possible, by man's weakness, to be found out. For there is 'a cloud and darkness which are round about him', and thick mists to cover him[.][18]

Here human nature is 'made a disease', which has the consequence of shrouding us in perpetual darkness; thus weakened and blinded, we are unable to see the divine light of God.

John Calvin gives us an even bleaker vision for humanity, and describes it in more visceral terms, in fact, closer to the language of Shakespeare:

> To man we assign only this: that he pollutes and contaminates by his impurity those very things which were good. For nothing proceeds from a man, however perfect he be, that is not defiled by some spot.[19]

In Calvin's view, humans are so inherently sinful that they contaminate all they touch, including that which is good – we are all Lady Macbeth, the spot will never come out. Indeed, without the grace of God, 'it is futile to seek anything good in our nature': 'Only damnable things come forth from man's corrupt nature.'[20] Referring to Psalms 5: 9, 140: 3 and 107: 7, Isaiah 59: 7 and Romans 3: 10–16, Calvin argues:

> With these thunderbolts [God] inveighs not against particular men but against the whole race of Adam's children. Nor is he decrying the depraved morals of one age or another, but indicating the unvarying corruption of our nature.... This defect, therefore, is necessarily found in all who have forsaken God. He adds that all have fallen away and have, as it were, become corrupt, that there is no one who does good.[21]

As in Hooker, we are in a permanent state of degradation, the hosts of a disease with no cure that we can administer ourselves.

> For the body, so long as it nourishes in itself the cause and matter of disease (even though pain does not yet rage), will not be called healthy, so also will the soul not be considered healthy while it abounds with so many fevers of vice.[22]

Here we see, similar to Shakespeare, that sin has a physical manifestation: if the soul is diseased, so is the body. But it is interesting that where Calvin emphasises the soul, Shakespeare seems to emphasise the mind or the will, as

L. C. Knights noted: 'Disease [in Shakespeare's plays] ... is associated with disorder originating in will.'[23] Perhaps this is why critics have struggled to find the redemptive impetus in Shakespeare's moral universe because sin is a psychological phenomenon rather than an affliction of the soul. It is either perceived (as in *Lear* and *Timon*), contracted through contagion (as in *Othello* and the histories) or chosen by will (as in the case of Iago himself, *Richard III*, *Hamlet* and *Macbeth*).

However, the most glaring difference between Shakespeare and these Reformation theologians is that, whereas in Hooker and Calvin individuals are already corrupted by sin, it seems that in Shakespeare – as we have seen in this chapter – characters start plays as nominally pure and, whether through their own actions or by contagion, become contaminated by sin. In other words, in Hooker and Calvin, human beings are fundamentally bad until they are touched by goodness (divine saviour), but in Shakespeare human beings are fundamentally good until they are touched by evil. This is made most obvious in *Macbeth*, where we can trace a descent into sin from the 'milk of human kindness' (I, v, 15) to being 'in blood / Stepp'd in so far' (III, iv, 135–6) that it can never be washed away. We watch Lady Macbeth wish the taint of poison into her breasts:

> Come, you spirits
> That tend on mortal thoughts, unsex me here,
> And fill me from the crown to the toe top-full
> Of direst cruelty! . . . .
> Come to my woman's breasts
> And take my milk for gall, you murd'ring ministers,
> Wherever in your sightless substances
> You wait on nature's mischief. (I, v, 39–48)

And yet we know she cannot be wholly evil, the stain of sin has not yet fully stuck, because she retains some 'milk of human kindness' in the form of compassion for her father. Lady Macbeth gives this as the reason that she cannot kill

Duncan herself: 'Had he not resembled / My father as he slept, I had done't' (II, ii, 12–13). Perhaps this is what William Hazlitt meant when he said – as I quoted him in Chapter 1 – that Shakespeare maintains 'some soul of goodness in things evil'.[24] It seems that characters are nominally good until contaminated by evil. Therefore, it follows that 'in things evil' there must be some vestige of goodness as a kind of residue. This would also account for Alfred Harbage's findings, which I summarised in Chapter 5, that a 'safe majority' of his characters are good.[25]

Shakespeare's view of humanity thus seems diametrically opposed to the Protestant idea of total depravity. In the Protestant view, all mankind is 'already diseased', whereas in Shakespeare's it appears that characters start with a clean bill of health. Therefore, it stands to reason that they must also differ in the *source* of purity (or sanctity). In Hooker and Calvin, this is most obviously God, who is all sanctity as mankind is all degradation. But in Shakespeare, it seems individuals provide their own sanctity, and spread their own degradation. Naturally, this locates him firmly in the secular–humanist tradition. This is so striking that some, such as W. J. Birch in 1848 or, more recently, Eric S. Marlin, have suggested that Shakespeare was not a Christian.[26] This seems very unlikely to me because, in using the very language of sin as something that can 'stain' individuals, he is working within a recognisably Christian framework. It is certainly true, though, that God is somewhat out of focus, while human beings are in focus. If we were to presume to find God anywhere on Shakespeare's moral compass, it would be here, on the sanctity foundation (otherwise known as the 'ethic of divinity') – but where we expect God to be, we find only humans.

There are, however, some similarities to be found between Shakespeare's view of sanctity / degradation and Catholic teachings, especially those of Thomas Aquinas, who devotes a question in the *Summa Theologiae* to 'The Stain of Sin':

> In its literal sense the word 'stain' refers to physical objects, as is the case where one bright object – e.g. a garment or some gold or silver item – loses its lustre by rubbing against another object. It is by simile with this use that the term should be applied to spiritual realities. The human soul has a twofold radiance: one from the refulgence of the natural light of reason, by which its acts are guided; the other from the refulgence of the divine light of wisdom and grace, which also empower man to act well and nobly. When through love the soul cleaves to certain things it is as though it were touching them; where sin is involved, the soul as it were rubs against certain things that go against the light of reason and of divine law. The impairment of the soul's radiance resulting from such a contact is described metaphorically as a stain of soul.[27]

This view of 'the stain of sin' seems to me perfectly compatible with what we have seen in Shakespeare. In the same way that characters can be contaminated or stained by sin in the plays, here the human soul, which is in a condition of 'radiance', can be tainted when it 'rubs' against evil. This does raise the question of original sin. How can individuals take on the additional stain of sin when they are, in effect, already stained? Where, in Hooker and Calvin, the stain of original sin seems to be totalising, covering everyone and everything in darkness, Aquinas views it as being more like the capacity to do evil at all than something inherent: the privation of original justice rather than explicit wrongdoing on every sinner's part. In other words, original sin is that which makes sin *in general* possible. Babies are born with original sin, transmitted from their parents and down the generations from their ultimate origin in Adam and Eve, but to all intents and purposes they are still 'innocent' in the Fallen sense that they have yet to commit any wrongdoing of their own will.[28] Aquinas gives much greater scope for moral agency to humans than do the Reformers. Even if divine grace 'empowers' us to do good, the 'light of reason' grants us a certain independence from God in our ability to *act at all*. Here the Thomistic insistence on free will is sharply at odds with Hooker and Calvin, but entirely in keeping with Shakespeare. Even though England in the 1590s and early 1600s was nominally Protestant, in practice, the actual belief on the ground is closer to Catholicism. They may not have thought of themselves as Catholics in the sense of being ruled from Rome or respecting the Pope, but on such a fundamental issue as how original sin and mortal sins function, a writer like Shakespeare – probably representative of his audience – is far closer to the Catholic view than he is to the Protestant one. As I argued in Chapter 4, it seems likely to me that this was very common. Shakespeare and others might have belonged to the Anglican Church, but that does not mean that they swallowed the latest teachings of Hooker or Calvin wholesale; in fact, it seems as if they persisted in the older mainstream Christian beliefs as inherited from Aquinas. It takes a long time for new ideas to filter through to the populace at large.[29]

In this chapter, I have argued that the moral foundation of sanctity is fundamental to Shakespeare's depiction of good and evil. The idea that sin is a stain, contamination or disease that can be spread through contagion is deep-rooted in his imagination and recurs across the plays. His conception of evil undoubtedly has a Christian basis, but he consistently emphasises human action and free will rather than the divine, and the psychological rather than the spiritual. His view of sin is thus closer to Catholic theology, derived from Thomas Aquinas, than it is to Protestant notions of original sin outlined by Richard Hooker and John Calvin. This can be seen in the fact that he often shows characters becoming infected by or stained by sin – a journey from sanctity to degradation – which is in stark contrast to the doctrine of total depravity in Reformed theology. If God is sacred to Hooker and Calvin, then humanity is sacred to Shakespeare.

> **In summary**
> - Psychological studies have found that the disgust response to contaminated food is unique to humans and universal across all known cultures. This is the evolutionary root of the sanctity moral foundation. Degradation functions like a contagion, which infects or stains all it touches.
> - Shakespeare consistently depicts evil and sin as a disease, contamination or stain, and it functions like a pathogen: it can be transferred from one person to another. There are examples across the plays, including in *King Lear, Timon of Athens*, the history plays, *Othello* and *Macbeth*. Shakespeare emphasises the psychological effects of sin through metaphors of physical degradation or staining.
> - This way of thinking about evil is rooted in biblical imagery, but Shakespeare imagines the stain of sin in a radically different way from Protestant theologians of the Reformation, such as Richard Hooker and John Calvin.
> - Where Hooker and Calvin see humans as being stained by sin from birth, Shakespeare's characters start from a clean bill of health and become contaminated during a given play, whether by their own actions or through contagion. Sanctity in Protestant theology is God himself, whereas in Shakespeare it appears to be in mankind.
> - Shakespeare's view of moral degradation is similar to and perfectly compatible with that outlined by Thomas Aquinas, who also emphasises free will and an essential human 'radiance' in the *Summa Theologiae*.

Notes

1. Caroline Spurgeon, *Shakespeare's Imagery and What It Tells Us* (1935; Cambridge: Cambridge University Press, 1979), pp. 158–9.
2. Ibid. p. 160.
3. Eric Langley, 'Plagued by Kindness: Contagious Sympathy in Shakespearean Drama', *Medical Humanities*, 37 (2011), p. 103.

4. See Jonathan Gil Harris, *Sick Economies*.
5. Richard A. Shweder, Nancy C. Much, Manamohan Mahapatra and Laurence Park, 'The "Big Three" of Morality (Autonomy, Community, Divinity) and the "Big Three" Explanations of Suffering', in *Morality and Culture*, ed. Jerome Kagan and Sharon Lamb (Chicago: University of Chicago Press, 1997), p. 147.
6. Haidt, The *Righteous Mind*, p. 171.
7. For a comprehensive overview of this topic, see Paul Rozin and April E. Fallon, 'A Perspective on Disgust', *Psychological Review*, 94:1 (1987), pp. 23–41.
8. Ibid. pp. 23–5.
9. Haidt, *The Righteous Mind*, p. 173.
10. Jonathan Haidt, 'Trump Breaks a Taboo – and Pays the Price', *The Atlantic* (21 August 2017), <https://www.theatlantic.com/politics/archive/2017/08/what-happens-when-the-president-commits-sacrilege/537519/> (last accessed 4 September 2017).
11. Ibid.
12. See Darwin T. Turner, '*King Lear* Re-examined', *College Language Association Journal*, 3 (1959), pp. 27–39.
13. Campbell, *Shakespeare's Tragic Heroes*, p. 79.
14. Alexander G. Gonzalez, 'The Infection and Spread of Evil: Some Major Patterns of Imagery and Language in Othello', *South Atlantic Review*, 50:4 (November 1985), pp. 37, 35.
15. Lillback (ed.), 1599 *Geneva Bible*.
16. Francis Fergusson, *Shakespeare: The Pattern in His Carpet* (New York: Delacorte Press, 1970), p. 168.
17. Frye, *Shakespeare and Christian Doctrine*, p. 253.
18. Richard Hooker, *The Ecclesiastical Polity and Other Works of Richard Hooker*, 3 vols, ed. Benjamin Hanbury (1594; London: Holdsworth and Ball, 1830), vol. 2, p. 500.
19. Calvin, *Institutes of the Christian Religion*, 3.15.3, pp. 790–1.
20. Ibid. 2.3.1, pp. 291, 289.
21. Ibid. 2.3.1, p. 291.
22. Ibid. 2.3.1, p. 291.
23. L. C. Knights, *Some Shakespearean Themes: And An Approach to Hamlet* (Stanford: Stanford University Press, 1966), p. 51.
24. Hazlitt, *The Characters of Shakespear's Plays*, p. 246.

25. See Harbage, *As They Liked It*, pp. 166–70.
26. See Birch, *An Inquiry into the Philosophy and Religion of Shakspere*; Eric S. Marlin, *Godless Shakespeare* (New York and London: Continuum, 2007).
27. Thomas Aquinas, *Summa Theologiae* (Vol. 27: *Effects of Sin, Stain and Guilt*) [1a2ae.86–9], ed. T. C. O'Brien (London: Eyre & Spottiswoode, 1969), question 86, article 1, p. 5.
28. See Thomas Aquinas, *Summa Theologiae* (Vol. 26: *Original Sin*) [1a2ae.81–5], ed. T. C. O'Brien (London: Eyre & Spottiswoode, 1969). See also Jeremy Cohen, 'Original Sin as the Evil Inclination: A Polemicist's Appreciation of Human Nature', *Harvard Theological Review* 73:3 (July to October 1980), pp. 505–6.
29. I should note that in claiming both that the populace at large was not especially Calvinist and that the imagery of original sin in Shakespeare aligns him with Aquinas as opposed to the Reformers, I am at odds with John Gillies, 'The Question of Original Sin in *Hamlet*', *Shakespeare Quarterly*, 64:4 (Winter 2013), pp. 396–424. Gillies points to Calvinist turns of phrase, such as 'special providence' (*Hamlet*, V, ii, 191), as evidence that, at the very least, the play is a 'compatibilist check upon, or rather correction and modification to, the Calvinist consensus preeminent in Shakespeare's day' (p. 164). My own thought is that we have seen in our own time how wide the gap between the intellectual elites of the universities and the general populace can grow, and I see little reason to believe that the people were any more receptive to radical new ideas in Shakespeare's day than they are now. Of course, in making this claim I am implicitly putting Shakespeare on the side of 'the people' as opposed to the 'intellectual elites': it was his job to know his audience.

CHAPTER 10

CARE

In the previous four chapters, aspects of Shakespeare's moral vision have become clearer. He values the duty and reciprocal good service necessary for *authority*; this helps to give people a sense of meaning and purpose in their lives. He values two-person friendships held together by *loyalty*, which depends on love and charity. He values *fairness* as a measure of proportionality. However, he cautions against the selfishness and vindictiveness that can result from the feeling that the world is 'unfair' because people are not equally good-looking, talented or wealthy – a fact with which individuals must make their peace, lest they become a Richard III. When these values are violated (*sanctity*), there is mental and physical degradation, as sin moves like a contagion infecting all it touches. In each case, care and harm are symptoms or by-products, and invariably this comes either from selfless and altruistic gestures towards fellow human beings, or from selfish and hateful behaviour driven by spite. A subject providing good service, or a leader who is true to the principles of authority, performs a duty of care. Those that do not invariably bring harm to others and eventually themselves. The abandonment of friendship, love and charity leads inevitably either to their opposites – enmity, hatred and selfishness – or else to a Timon-like loneliness in misanthropy and self-exile; the net effects bring harm to those involved. When fairness gives way to selfishness, society descends into a dog-eat-dog death spiral. And when moral decay in the form of degradation, disease and contamination taints all it touches, the obvious consequences are physically and psychologically harmful. In this chapter, I will assess the extent to which this is true by focusing on plays in which moral order seems to break down completely, and the *dramatis personae* revert to the Hobbesian state of nature and unspeakable cruelty: *Titus Andronicus*, *3 Henry VI*, *Richard III* and *King Lear*. In the constrained or tragic vision, when there are no institutions with which to reinforce the morals that bind people together (authority, loyalty, fairness, sanctity), the worst aspects of humanity – as embodied in the tiger – are granted their fullest expression. However, in Shakespeare's version of this vision, human nature provides the seeds of its own rebirth.

The word 'tiger' occurs sparingly in Shakespeare's works: only fifteen times, and one of them is the name of an inn (*Comedy of Errors*, III, i, 95). In almost all other cases, including eight times in plural form, the tiger seems to represent solitary self-seeking and inhuman aggression in its rawest manifestation. Despite this sparse use, it still seems a peculiarly Shakespearean image, not only because his name will be forever connected with 'his Tiger's heart wrapped in a Player's hide', in Robert Greene's famous attack,[1] but also because, elsewhere in Renaissance and early modern writings, tigers are an endangered species. Niccolò Machiavelli, usually so fond of animal metaphors, mentions tigers neither in *The Prince* nor in *Discourses on Livy*. In this, Thomas Hobbes, his chief inheritor in political theory, follows him, finding no place for tigers in *Leviathan*. In the major theology of the period, tigers are seldom, if ever, mentioned. For example, Thomas Aquinas makes no reference to tigers in the entirety of the *Summa Theologiae* and, likewise, John Calvin's *Institutes* is tigerless.[2] Geoffrey Chaucer makes several references to 'tigres', which are said to be 'crueel' (*Knight's Tale*, 1657), 'ful of doublenesse' (*Squire's Tale*, 543) and 'swyfte' (*Boece*, 3.8.29).³ The chief source for Chaucer's usage is Statius's *Thebaid*, in which the two tigers that pull Bacchus's chariot break free and kill three men; the Argives kill the tigers in retaliation, thereby restarting the war between Argos and Thebes.⁴

However, tigers remain relatively scarce in English literature for the next 200 years. Ben Jonson makes no reference to them.⁵ In Christopher Marlowe's *Edward II*, shortly before his death the King laments 'Inhuman creatures, nursed with tiger's milk' (V, i, 71) and warns against leaving his son with Mortimer because 'More safety is there in a tiger's jaws (V, i, 116).⁶ Marlowe also mentions the 'tigers of Hyrcania' in *Dido* (V, i, 159). Both are references to Virgil's *Aeneid*, in which Dido says to Aeneas, 'The sharp-rocked Caucasus / Gave birth to you, Hyrcanian tigers nursed you' (4.466–7).⁷ This is the chief literary source for tigers in the period, and they are often connected with Hyrcania, an area to the southwest of the Caspian Sea in modern-day Iran. Tigers were abundant around Iran and the Caspian Sea in antiquity, although they are now extinct in the area.⁸ It is seemingly these tigers, rather than those that drew Bacchus's chariot, to which Shakespeare refers most often. Consider, for example, in *Macbeth*, when he sees Banquo's ghost and likens it to 'th' Hycran tiger!' (III, iv, 103) or 'th' Hycranian beast' in *Hamlet* (II, ii, 372). In *3 Henry VI*, York lambasts the cruel Margaret for being 'more inhuman, / more inexorable / Oh, ten times more than tigers of Hycrania' (I, iv, 154–5).

I am lingering on the image of tigers because they seem to have taken on almost mythical quality in the extent of their savagery, and Shakespeare appears to reserve it for only the most extreme cases – as if it is the most cruel and fierce thing he can evoke. One possible reason for this is that tigers have a long history of hunting and killing human beings, and, unlike lions, hunt alone rather than in packs and so bring the element of surprise. Since they were so exotic to England, rumours travelling down the trade routes and across the seas, and the imagination, must have buttressed this fearsome reputation. It is doubtful that anyone in London would have seen a real tiger, although the *Issues of the Exchequer* does record that, on 5 July 1613, Giovanni Perundini was 'sent from the Duke of Savoy to his majesty [James I] with the present of a tiger, the sum of 76*l*. 13*s*. 4*d*'.[9] However, Caroline Grigson, an expert in the history of exotic animals in England, thinks that this was likely to have been a leopard, not a tiger. Incidentally, in the early eighteenth century, when the vogue of bringing menageries of exotic animals to England started in earnest, the tiger lived up to its notoriety by claiming its first victim in 1703: Hannah Twynnoy, a barmaid from Malmesbury.[10] In Shakespeare's imagination, then, the tiger was an emblem of inhuman cruelty, a creature almost from another world.

As *Titus Andronicus* starts, Rome is already 'a wilderness of tigers' (III, i, 54). The play has long been met by critics with 'howls of disapproval' as 'an aberrant, "barbarous" work'.[11] Indeed, one theatre critic fainted when reviewing a production for *The Independent*. It was during a run at the Globe in London in 2014. She was not alone: 'more than 100 people either fainted or left the theatre after being overcome by on-stage gore – making it a strong candidate for the most potent show in British history'.[12] Why does this play, a box-office blockbuster during Shakespeare's own life, elicit such responses from us 'modern milksops'?[13] There is no reason to believe that early modern theatregoers did not have strong emotional responses to what they saw ('What's Hecuba to him?', *Hamlet*, II, ii, 478), but also there are no reports of them fainting at performances of *Titus Andronicus*. The answer lies in attachment theory, which explains how humans evolved to meet the adaptive needs of protecting and caring for children, and is now fundamental to developmental psychology.[14] When most people see a baby or, let us say, a puppy with big doe eyes, it induces a 'cuteness response', which is a 'releaser of parental instincts'.[15] Now imagine someone wielding a sledgehammer and threatening to bring it down on the head our doe-eyed puppy. Even the *thought* of such a brazen act of cruelty sends off signals in our brains and triggers an emotional response. The scope of what counts as 'cute' varies across cultures and history, and can widen or narrow. The trend in Western culture has been for this to widen: one need only think of the noun 'Disneyfication' to recognise this. Accordingly, the extent to which we recoil at violence has increased – although it may be hard for some to believe, given the daily news cycles – and the extent to which we are violent has decreased.[16] This may explain why Shakespeare's own audience could cope better with the gratuitous violence in *Titus Andronicus*, when today it sends some viewers into shock and even overwhelms them into fainting. However, the play is so extreme that it always threatens to teeter over from horror into absurdity; as the actor David Bradley, who once played Titus, put it, we might also respond with 'Tarantino-esque laughter'.[17] This is another coping strategy that puts us at an emotional post-ironic distance from the subject matter.

The question remains: why is Shakespeare's early tragedy so full of nihilistic cruelty? Even from the beginning, its characters have already morphed into 'tigers'. Revenge has become endemic and endlessly cyclical. As the play starts, Titus has defeated the Goths, yet ignores Tamora's pleas for mercy because he lost sons in the brutal ten-year war that precedes the play. Instead, Titus orders that Tamora's son, Alarbus, be executed to atone for his dead sons. As per my analysis in Chapter 8, this form of vengeance is not real justice according to natural law and Aristotelian–Thomist virtue ethics. Thus Titus, rather than defusing the bonfire of revenge, pours fresh fuel on to it, and gives Tamora and her remaining sons every reason to wish to get their own back. The new Emperor, Saturninus, declares his intention to marry Titus's daughter, Lavinia, who is already betrothed to Bassianus, Saturninus's younger brother. Shortly after this, moral order breaks down almost totally in Rome. Out of a sense of Roman stoicism (group loyalty, see Chapter 7), Titus sides with Saturninus, and in the ensuing scuffle kills his own son, Mutius. This unnatural act shows at a stroke that, in this imagined late Roman period, degradation has reached saturation point. It offends Shakespeare's sense of authority: Titus does not demonstrate good service in unquestioningly pledging himself to an arbitrary and tyrannical ruler such as Saturninus, who, in turn, shows no signs of good leadership. It also offends Shakespeare's sense of loyalty: Titus chooses masculine group-level allegiance to the kingdom over the feminine two-person bond with his own son. This is a kin-level relationship, the strongest bond in nature and, of course, the one on which the moral foundation of care and harm, which evokes the 'parental instinct response' is based. For a father to kill his own son for so slight a reason offends evolution itself, nature itself. To top it all off, Saturninus immediately reduces the gesture to nothing, by reneging on his pledge to marry Lavinia and proposing to Tamora instead – not only Titus's mortal enemy, but also an enemy of the Roman state. This grossly violates the moral foundation of fairness: Saturninus has cheated Titus, and negated any sense of justice and the rule of law. By the completion of the first act, we are already approaching Hobbes's vision of perpetual war: 'it is manifest that during the time men live without a common power to keep them all in awe, they are in that condition which is called war; and such a war, as is of every man, against every man'.[18]

In such a 'wilderness of tigers', Tamora promptly repays her new husband by cuckolding him with her lover, Aaron. He hatches a plan to murder Bassianus and pin the blame on another two of Titus's sons, Quintus and Martius. Acting on Aaron's orders, Tamora's sons, Demetrius and Chiron, murder Bassianus, trap Quintus and Martius in a pit, and then rape and mutilate Lavinia. They cut out her tongue and chop off her hands. In a bid to save his sons from execution, Titus has his own hand cut off by Aaron in exchange, but, of course, this agreement means nothing and the sons are killed anyway. Titus exacts his revenge by killing Demetrius and Chiron, baking them into a pie and feeding it to Tamora and Saturninus. For his sins, Aaron is buried alive up to his chest and left to starve. Titus performs a mercy killing on Lavinia before taking his own life. It is a lurid scene. Throughout all of this, Shakespeare constantly evokes tigers. When Lavinia is pleading for her life she says to Demetrius, 'When did the tiger's young ones teach the dam? / Oh, do not learn her wrath! She taught it thee. / The milk thou suck'st from her did turn to marble (II, iii, 142–4). In order to make sense of what is happening, she can only imagine that this is learned behaviour: the idea that Demetrius and Chiron are naturally *this* cruel is unconscionable. Yet, they seem to be. In the final scene, Lucius calls Aaron a 'ravenous tiger' (V, iii, 5), and repeats the epithet – 'ravenous tiger' (V, iii, 194) – when declaring that Tamora should not be granted funeral rites.

This is the constrained or tragic vision pushed to its breaking point. In the absence of any meaningful institutions to uphold a rule of law, to incentivise good behaviour and to punish bad and undesirable behaviour, Rome is turned to a living hellscape. It might appear that Shakespeare's view of humanity is bleak here: there are only a few checks and balances keeping us from turning into 'tigers'. But this is not entirely the case, and this is perhaps where Shakespeare departs from Machiavelli or Hobbes – it is also, to come back to the question I trailed in Chapter 1, as to whether William Hazlitt's optimism is well placed. Shakespeare includes a single beam of hope in the play: Aaron, in all other ways a despicable villain without a shred of moral decency, still shows he *cares* for his newly born son. He will not let Demetrius or

Chiron kill the baby (IV, ii, 80), and swiftly kills the nurse rather than risk its discovery (IV, ii, 144). One is reminded here of Emmanuel Levinas's 'face-to-face encounter' and what he sees as the infinite ethical responsibility for the other, which in various ways seems to parallel Shakespeare's view of good service in authority (Chapter 6), and charity and loyalty in friendship (Chapter 7).[19] As we saw in Chapters 5 and 9, in Shakespeare's moral universe, human beings are good or innocent until proven otherwise: and here, this child – born to abominable parents, and in a society so morally depraved it has reached the point of self-immolation – is still an innocent, and still, somehow, protected by a father who cares for him. In a poetic way, too, Aaron rights the wrong of Titus killing his own son, Mutius. It is not a divine or cosmic justice, or even a redemptive one, but it does offer some hope for rebirth and growth: a consolation for the future of our sorry species.

This basic template is repeated in *3 Henry VI* and *Richard III*. After the tumultuous events of the first two plays in the trilogy, moral order has broken down in England almost totally. Promises and oaths mean nothing, and wanton cruelty without mercy has become the rule rather than the exception. It is not enough for Margaret simply to kill York; she must humiliate him, forcing him to wear a paper crown (*3 Henry VI*, I, iv, 94). In one of the most senseless acts of cruelty in Shakespeare, Clifford slaughters the adolescent Rutland at the site of his birth. The boy begs for his life, appealing to common decency, and evoking Clifford's own son in the hope it might spark some human recognition: 'Thou hast one son, for his sake pity me' (I, iii, 40). Clifford responds robotically with an abstract and inhumane logic: 'Thy father slew my father; therefore die' (I, iii, 46).[20] The escalating cycle of revenge is not only endless but also now impersonal, routine and self-fulfilling, practically without real motivation. After Margaret and Clifford kill York in I, iv, his sons Edward and Richard immediately vow to avenge his death.

This crisis of intensifying immorality reaches its symbolic peak when Henry VI, the ailing and by this point truly pathetic King, watches a son who has killed his father carry away the body, and likewise, a father who has killed his son dispose of the corpse. It is as if the horror for the watching Henry is too much to bear, and the scene may signal his nervous breakdown. The crime is the same as that of Titus: murder of a kin-relation, the starkest transgression against natural law. But unlike in *Titus Andronicus*, where it is just another moment of madness in the spiralling chaos, here it takes on a more melancholy tone. The father recognises his crime: 'I have murdered where I should not kill' (II, v, 122). Henry is racked by 'more than common grief' (II, v, 94). Henry himself is later cruelly stabbed multiple times by Richard, even after he has already died (V, vi, 67). Margaret has to suffer, witnessing the murder of the only thing in the world she still cares about: her son Edward. She begs to follow him: 'Oh, kill me too' (V, v, 41). The scorpion whiplash of revenge comes back to sting her, as Richard and George leave her to live – in a cruel irony, where she showed York no mercy, his sons do show her mercy and it is a form of torture. But by not killing her, they also fail to halt the revenge cycle, which lingers on as Margaret drifts almost ghost-like into *Richard III*.

And yet, when we reach that play, after years of this circle of violence repeating itself, and as moral degradation intensifies further, we still get a moment of human recognition. Richard has sent a pair of assassins to murder his brother, Clarence (George). Again, this the murder of a kin-level relation, and a crime against nature itself. As one of the assassins sees Clarence sleeping, he hesitates: 'What, shall I stab him as he sleeps?' (*Richard III*, I, iv, 91). What follows is a kind of moral panic attack: 'The urging of the word "Judgement" hath bred a kind of remorse in me' (I, iv, 98–9). The second executioner fears that he will be damned for killing another human being as he sleeps. We must remember the backdrop to this moment. England has been torn by political violence and civil war for years at this point, as depicted in three plays by Shakespeare (*Henry VI Parts 1–3*); or, if we imagine he always intended to write the second tetralogy (*Richard II*, *Henry IV Parts 1 and 2*, and *Henry V*) next, this is the culmination of *seven* plays' worth of bloody history. We have seen fathers and sons murder each other, great warriors and politicians humiliated and killed, innocent children slain without mercy: as close to the Hobbesian state of nature as we see in Shakespeare, at least on a par with *Titus Andronicus*. And yet, this individual, whose *chosen profession* is in the dark art of murder, still experiences a pang of human feeling: 'some certain dregs of conscience are yet within me' (I, iv, 110–11).

The pattern in *King Lear* is similar. Albany calls Goneril and Regan 'Tigers, not daughters ... most barbarous and degenerate' (4.2.32.10, 13) shortly after we witness Cornwall and Regan plucking out Gloucester's eyes. This is a society on a downward spiral: soon Goneril and Regan are at each other's throats in their attempts to seduce Edmund, whose rapid advancement in wealth and military strength suddenly makes him a prize asset in their self-interested calculation. But while the effects of such degradation are physically and mentally corrosive, they cannot completely quash human decency from welling up in the kingdom. For example, as Cornwall is plucking out Gloucester's eyes, one of the servants, a bastion of good service, objects:

> Hold your hand, my lord.
> I have served you ever since I was a child,
> But better service have I never done you
> Than now bid you hold. (III, vii, 73–6)

This servant feels strongly enough to draw his sword and attack Cornwall, fatally wounding him. Of course, Regan and Cornwall – understanding authority only as oppression (see Chapter 6) – cannot understand this, and Regan promptly grabs her husband's sword and kills this 'peasant' (III, vii, 80). Yet, despite the cruelty to which society has succumbed in this play, a kind of compassion still wins out. Edmund is 'moved' (V, iii, 191) when he sees Edgar again. He seeks reconciliation if not redemption. His dying wish is to do 'Some good ... Despite of mine own nature' (V, iii, 218–19). Lear also comes 'To be tender-minded' (V, iii, 32) in his brief reconciliation with Cordelia before her death. In Coppélia Kahn's iconic reading, Lear makes 'some progress toward acceptance of the woman in himself'.[21] What this means in practice is exercising mercy, empathy and the ethics of care.

These moments of human decency in the otherwise brutal worlds of *Titus Andronicus*, the first tetralogy (*Henry VI Parts 1–3* and *Richard III*) and *King Lear*, reveal two crucial aspects of Shakespeare's moral vision. First, as John Vyvyan put it, 'there is always a choice':[22] no matter how endemic revenge or violence seems, individuals always retain the capacity to do *otherwise*. This is the theme of the next and final chapter. Second, even though human beings are corruptible to the extent that whole societies can degenerate and collapse, such moral degradation is never total and is seldom, if ever, lasting. Even those we would imagine to be ostensibly 'lost' to ruthless self-interest – in these cases, a self-described villain and a professional hitman – do not lose the capacity for 'fellow-feeling'.[23] This 'fellow-feeling' is not socially conditioned – how could such hellish societies, dictated by survivalist self-interest, produce such feelings? – but rather something that comes from within, that instinctually 'wells up in his characters'.[24] Even if Albany is often proven correct when he says 'Humanity must perforce prey on itself / Like monsters of the deep' (*King Lear*, 4.2.32.19–20), so too is Polixenes in *The Winter's Tale* when he says:

> Yet nature is made better by no mean
> But nature makes that mean. So over that art

> Which you say adds to nature is an art
> That nature makes. . . . We marry
> A gentler scion to the wildest stock
> And make conceive a bark of baser kind
> By bud of nobler race. This is an art
> Which does mend nature – change it, rather – but
> The art itself is nature. (IV, iv, 89–97)

Although 'humanity must . . . prey on itself', nature also gives us the tools with which to mend and grow. And this image of rebirth is not a utopian vision putting 'art' – that is, human invention or reason – above reality; 'the art itself is nature'. Interestingly, this aligns Shakespeare with advocates of group selection in modern evolutionary theory, who posit that cultural institutions themselves are evolutionary adaptations at a group level (see Chapter 2), and puts him at odds with Thomas Hobbes, who saw such institutions as 'utterly artificial'.[25]

In summary

- Care and harm manifest as consequences of the four moral foundations that 'bind' – authority, loyalty, fairness and sanctity; care results if they are respected, and harm (in the form of abject cruelty) results if they are offended.
- Tigers represent the ultimate symbol of cruelty in Shakespeare, the moment in which all human decency is lost, and we are returned to the 'state of nature' later described by Thomas Hobbes.
- In *Titus Andronicus*, *3 Henry VI*, *Richard III* and *King Lear* we witness the same pattern: society is reduced to a 'wilderness of tigers' as every moral foundation is offended.
- However, in each play, Shakespeare shows that even where moral degradation seems endemic, human nature still provides the tools for mending itself: individuals seem capable of empathy and care, even in the most extreme of circumstances, and even after the point where it appears that hope is lost.

Notes

1. Robert Greene, *Greene's Groat's-worth of Wit, Bought with a Million of Repentance* (London: William Wright, 1592), p. 19.
2. To compile my findings during this passage, I ran searches of various online databases, including <https://eebo.chadwyck.com/home> (last accessed 10 October 2017), and modern digitised versions of the texts, cross-checking where possible with older concordances.
3. Geoffrey Chaucer, *The Riverside Chaucer*, ed. Larry D. Benson (Oxford: Oxford University Press, 1988), pp. 47, 175, 428.
4. Statius, *Thebaid*, 2 vols, ed. and trans. D. R. Shackleton Bailey (Cambridge, MA: Harvard University Press, 2004), especially vol. 1, book 4, pp. 204–70.
5. Charles Crawford, *A Complete Concordance to the 1616 Folio of Ben Jonson's Works*, 5 vols (Microfilm; Ann Arbor: University of Michigan, 1923).
6. Marlowe, *Doctor Faustus and Other Plays*, pp. 383, 385.
7. Virgil, *The Aeneid*, trans. Sarah Ruden (New Haven, CT: Yale University Press, 2008), p. 80.
8. Patrick Humphreys and Esmail Kahrom, *Lion and Gazelle: The Mammals and Birds of Iran* (Abergavenny: Comma International Biological Systems, 1995), pp. 75–7.
9. Frederick Devon, *Issues of the Exchequer: Being Payments Made Out of His Majesty's Revenue during the Reign of King James I* (London: John Rodwell, 1836), pp. 166–7.
10. Caroline Grigson, *Menagerie: The History of Exotic Animals in England* (Oxford: Oxford University Press, 2016), pp. 20, 73.
11. R. S. White, '*Titus Andronicus* and *Romeo and Juliet*', in *Shakespeare: A Bibliographical Guide*, ed. Stanley Wells (Oxford: Oxford University Press, 1990), pp. 182–3.
12. Nick Clark, 'Globe Theatre Takes Out 100 Audience Members with Its Gory Titus Andronicus', *The Independent* (22 July 2014), <http://www.independent.co.uk/arts-entertainment/theatre-dance/news/globe-theatre-takes-out-100-audience-members-with-its-gory-titus-andronicus-9621763.html> (last accessed 10 October 2017).

13. Nuttall, *Shakespeare: The Thinker*, p. 246.
14. John Bowlby, *Attachment*, 2nd edn (1969; New York: Basic Books, 1983). See also Haidt, *The Righteous Mind*, pp. 153–8.
15. Gary D. Sherman and Jonathan Haidt, 'Cuteness and Disgust: The Humanizing and Dehumanizing Effects of Emotion', *Emotion Review*, 3:3 (2011), p. 1.
16. For a long and detailed study on this phenomenon, see Stephen Pinker, *The Better Angels of Our Nature: Why Violence Has Declined* (New York: Viking, 2011).
17. Quoted in Jonathan Bate and Eric Rasmussen (eds), Titus Andronicus *and* Timon of Athens*: Two Roman Plays* (Basingstoke: Macmillan, 2011), p. 127.
18. Hobbes, *Leviathan*, 1.13.8, p. 84.
19. Emmanuel Levinas, *Ethics and Infinity: Conversations with Philippe Nemo*, trans. Richard A. Cohen (Pittsburgh: Duquesne University Press, 1985), p. 95. For a direct application of Levinas to *Titus Andronicus* in particular, see Sean Lawrence, 'Listening to Lavinia: Emmanuel Levinas's Saying and Said in *Titus Andronicus*', in *Through a Glass Darkly: Suffering, the Sacred, and the Sublime in Literature and Theory*, ed. Holly Faith Nelson, Lynn R. Szabo and Jens Zimmermann (Waterloo, Ontario: Wilfrid Laurier University Press, 2010), pp. 57–69. There are some apparent similarities between Shakespeare's morality and Levinas's ethics, and this would make a good topic for a separate study for a motivated researcher. For various reasons this is not a direction in which I wanted to take this book. As per Chapter 2, it is difficult to reconcile the sort of pure altruism for which Levinas appears to call with what we know from evolutionary biology and psychology: human beings cannot reliably be called on for altruism. His thinking veers on the side of unconstrained or utopian vision, which is a framework, as I have said, that I must necessarily reject in drawing on evolutionary theory. That said, it does not follow that Levinas has nothing to say of value, only that the future he wishes for is unlikely ever to materialise, and what he describes is not the full picture of humanity. In Haidt's terms, we are only '10 percent bee'; Levinas seems to think we have the capacity

to become 100 per cent bee, but he none the less gives us some useful ways of thinking about what happens vis à vis human recognition and altruism.
20. For a longer reading of this passage, see Neema Parvini, *Shakespeare's History Plays: Rethinking Historicism* (Edinburgh: Edinburgh University Press, 2012), pp. 138–42.
21. Coppélia Kahn, 'The Absent Mother in *King Lear*', in *Rewriting the Renaissance: The Discourses of Sexual Difference in Early Modern Europe*, ed. Margaret W. Ferguson, Maureen Quilligan and Nancy Vickers (Chicago: University of Chicago Press, 1986), p. 46.
22. Vyvyan, *The Shakespearean Ethic*, p. 125.
23. Hazlitt, *The Characters of Shakespear's Plays*, p. 247.
24. James A. Knapp, 'A Shakespearean Phenomenology of Moral Conviction', in *Shakespeare and Moral Agency*, ed. Michael D. Bristol (New York and London: Continuum, 2012), p. 38.
25. Arnhart, *Darwinian Natural Right*, p. 61.

CHAPTER 11

LIBERTY

'There is always a choice':[1] John Vyvyan's maxim has been a consistent refrain in my consideration of Shakespeare's moral compass in Part II of this book. In Chapters 5–10, I have found that the plays emphasise individual free will as a prerequisite for both good and evil. I have argued that in Shakespeare there is no divine, cosmic or poetic justice; wrongdoers seldom look for a final redemption, and find it even less frequently. Characters are not born evil – we watch them choosing to sin, or else giving in to an emotional sense that they have been hard done by. A sense of contingency persists: it might have turned out differently if only people had made different choices. Edmund and Richard III did not have to prove themselves villains; Lear did not have to banish Cordelia; Titus did not need to kill his own son, Martius; Demetrius and Chiron did not need to rape and mutilate Lavinia, and so on. Likewise, the converse is true of good deeds: Adam did not have to sacrifice his savings and ultimately his life for Orlando; Kent did not have to follow Lear; Antonio need not have lent Bassanio the money; Celia need not have given up her inheritance and followed Rosalind into the woods, and so on. Thus, in Shakespeare, liberty – as defined by the ability of the individual to decide on their own course of action – is the engine room of morality. Without it, the entire vehicle grinds to a halt: without the ability to choose, we can travel in no moral direction at all. As I argued in Chapter 9 (see also Chapter 5), this emphasis on individual free will puts Shakespeare firmly in the secular–humanist and Catholic traditions, and at odds with Protestant Reformation thinking, which emphasises divine providence and predestination. Indeed, we have found, as Stephen Greenblatt has observed, that 'his work . . . is allergic to the absolutist strain so prevalent in his world'.[2]

In this study, which comes to its natural conclusion in this chapter, I have found all six of the moral foundations outlined in Jonathan Haidt's *The Righteous Mind* – authority, loyalty, fairness, sanctity, care and liberty[3] – registered in Shakespeare's plays, but they do not function independently of each other. Rather, they form an interlocking set of principles, which together we can call 'Shakespeare's moral compass'. In *Richard III*, when the Duchess of York sees her only surviving son, Richard, she offers him some moral counsel: 'put meekness in thy mind, / Love, charity, obedience, and true duty' (II, ii, 94–5). This represents a key with which to unlock the compass. It is plain that the Duchess is emphasising the moral foundations of authority and loyalty. As we have seen, sanctity / degradation and care / harm almost always come as the symptom or consequence of decisions and actions taken in the areas of authority and loyalty. Fairness, meanwhile, has functioned more as a catalyst or motivation. A sense of injustice tends to drive bad moral decisions and actions (subversion, betrayal) and therefore bad consequences (degradation, harm), whereas the just rule of law tends to give rise to good moral decisions and actions (authority, loyalty) and therefore good consequences (sanctity, care). To make this clearer, I have depicted these findings in Table 11.1.

Table 11.1

	Facilitator	Motivation	Decision / Action	Consequences
Moral Foundation (positive, good)	Liberty	Fairness	Authority, Loyalty	Sanctity, Care
Shakespeare's Usage	Choice, Free Will	Justice, Rule of Law, Proportionality	Good Service, Love, Charity, Friendship, Obedience, Duty, 'Fellow-feeling'	Innocence, Purity, Mercy, Empathy, Tenderness, Natural Rejuvenation, Humanity
Moral Foundation (negative, evil)	Oppression	Unfairness / Cheating	Subversion, Betrayal	Degradation, Harm
Shakespeare's Usage	Tyranny	Revenge, Vengeance	Servility, Hatred, Selfishness, Misanthropy, Disobedience, Treachery	Disease, Contamination, 'Wilderness of Tigers', Savagery, Cruelty, Inhumanity

In this way, Shakespeare's moral compass – for all its complex polyvocality, complications and outliers – provides us with an integrated view of human morality. While each of the moral foundations comes with its own set of instinctive intuitions and emotions, and the cultural *post hoc* rationalisations that have built up around them, the plays depict two distinct courses of actions:

1. Virtuous Circle: Liberty begets Fairness, which begets Authority and Loyalty, which result in Sanctity and Care.
2. Vicious Circle: Oppression begets Unfairness, which begets Subversion and Betrayal, which result in Degradation and Harm.

If we think through the examples of when the vicious circle manifests in Shakespeare's plays, it is in situations when the current ruler has used his relative autonomy to violate the stages of the virtuous circle. This happens in *Richard II*, in which the King's conduct 'can only be described as tyrannical'.[4] Richard condemns Thomas Mowbray to life exile largely for carrying out orders that he gave. He repays the good service of his uncle, John of Gaunt, not only by banishing his son, Bolingbroke, for six years, but also by seizing his estates and wealth after his death. In so doing, he tramples arbitrarily on the just rule of law. This is corruption: when good authority devolves into the mere exercise of power, which only ever results in tyranny and oppression. These actions by Richard birth the vicious circle: Bolingbroke feels he has been treated unfairly, which fuels a desire for revenge, and so we start the descent towards a 'wilderness of tigers' over the next seven history plays in the sequence. We see a near identical course of events in *Measure for Measure* during the period in which Angelo takes command (see Chapter 8), and in *Titus Andronicus* and *King Lear* (see Chapter 10): the arbitrary and tyrannical acts of the ruler set off a vicious circle. The sense of injustice fuels revenge and self-seeking behaviour, which result in abject cruelty and degradation.

But how does one break the vicious circle and restore the virtuous circle? As I showed in Chapter 8, one way, in a sense, is to let bygones be bygones. The Duke in *Measure for Measure* does not punish Angelo particularly harshly; he offers him a chance of self-improvement. This is not the justice of retribution, or even of forgiveness and redemption, but rather of natural rebirth and growth. However, I think a vital aspect of this judgement is that it is afforded by the person who has perhaps the greatest reason to seek vengeance: Isabella.

> Most bounteous sir,
> Look, if it please you, on this man condemned
> As if my brother lived. I partly think
> A due sincerity governed his deeds

> Till he did look on me. Since it is so,
> Let him not die. My brother had but justice,
> In that he did the thing for which he died.
> For Angelo, his act did not o'ertake his bad intent
> And must be buried but as an intent
> That perished by the way. Thoughts are no subjects,
> Intents but merely thoughts. (*Measure for Measure*, V, i, 446–56)

Here, even despite the fact that her brother, Claudio, is still alive as she says these words, Isabella shows compassion and mercy to a man she has every reason to hate. Rather than dwell in spite or bitterness towards Angelo, she instead shows great empathy in trying to understand things from his point of view: perhaps the most Shakespearean of ethics. This requires something of a leap of faith: to commit to a virtuous act for its own sake without worrying about possible consequences and without expecting any form of reward. In fact, each of the good deeds I have covered involves a character giving something freely of themselves without looking for recompense: Adam pledging his life savings to Orlando in *As You Like It*; Kent ensuring his King gets good service, even at the risk of angering him in *King Lear*; Flavius seeking out his old master while ensuring his colleagues are still paid in *Timon of Athens*; Antonio securing the loan for Bassanio in *The Merchant of Venice*; Celia giving up her inheritance and risking her life for Rosalind in *As You Like It*; and Aaron doing all he can to protect the life of his newborn son in *Titus Andronicus*. In order to have any chance of breaking the vicious circle and restoring the virtuous circle, an individual is required to put the needs of someone else ahead of their own needs. In other words, it takes an unconditional, 'no strings' act of altruism. In his morality, Shakespeare is closer to George Lakoff's concept of the 'Nurturant Parent', who foregrounds nurturance, empathy, self-development and growth, than he is to the

'Strict Father', who emphasises strength, authority (as defined by group hierarchy) and self-interest.[5]

Of course, Shakespeare is not an idealist: his plays show how frequently and how disastrously human beings fall short of this. This is the tragic vision: if nothing else is guaranteed, we can count on human beings – or at least a significant portion of them – to give in self-interest. Even within the same play as Isabella's display of compassionate mercy, her brother articulates the tragic vision:

> Our natures do pursue,
> Like rats that ravin down their proper bane,
> A thirsty evil, and when we drink we die. (I, ii, 117–19)

The 'vicious mole of nature' (*Hamlet*, I, iv, 24) tends to vice not virtue. Yet the strength to overcome it also comes from within. Nature destroys, but it also mends and grows.

Neither is Shakespeare a utopian visionary: he does not imagine or even wish for a time or place in which there is no conflict, no self-interest and no motivation for revenge. The best we can hope for is to keep these darker forces in abeyance for as long as we can by keeping the virtuous circle going through selfless moral choices. At the same time, he is not despairing or pessimistic: even in the direst circumstances – Hell-on-Earth scenarios such as those we glimpse in the first tetralogy, *Titus Andronicus* or *King Lear* – there is still an opportunity for the good moral actor to choose otherwise. Even if the self-sacrifice does not end the vicious circle there and then, the moral choice might still be enough to sow the seeds of future mending and replenishment. Even as human beings show a remarkable capacity to self-destruct, so we also show a perhaps even more extraordinary resilience and the ability to bounce back. As signalled most explicitly in *The Winter's Tale* (see Chapter 10),[6] it is likely that Shakespeare saw these two countervailing tendencies in human nature – towards self-interest, death and destruction on the one hand, and towards charity, growth and renewal on the other – as something akin to the changing seasons. John F. Danby called these two different faces of humanity 'The Benignant Nature' and 'The Malignant Nature',[7] but every individual has the capacity for both, and has agency to choose one course or another. Thus Shakespeare is less pessimistic than those who hold the most extreme variants of the tragic vision, such John Calvin or Thomas Hobbes, but at the same time he is less optimistic than unconstrained visionaries such as Jean-Jacques Rousseau or twenty-first-century Western progressives.

One of the most striking features of Shakespeare's moral compass is that his concern seems always geared towards the individual and their choices, actions and relationships with other individuals. Admittedly, this came as something of a surprise to me: I expected to find a writer from the 1590s and early 1600s more firmly committed to the idea of the group and more obviously communitarian in his impulses. To come back to a concept I have returned to many times since I introduced it in Chapter 1, in foregrounding the individual in this way, Shakespeare's morality is already in some ways 'WEIRD'.[8] However, it is not fully so because, unlike WEIRD people, who are supposedly blind to the moral foundations of authority and loyalty, as we have seen, these form the central pillars of Shakespeare's moral order – if they fall, the rest of society often collapses. But Shakespeare transmutes authority and loyalty from group-level concerns to individual-level concerns: the appeal of the 'band of brothers' (*Henry V*, IV, iii, 60) is quite different from the idea of good service predicated on a master–servant relationship or love and charity in friendship predicated on one-on-one relationships, and, as per Chapters 6 and 7, he foregrounds the latter. In insisting on these relations between individuals, as opposed to between individual and group, the importance and impact of moral choices are put at a premium. Individual choices matter to the extent that bad ones result in endemic degradation and cycles of cruelty, and, in the absence of any sense of divine or cosmic justice, good choices are the only path out of it. In one respect, Shakespeare's moral invocation seems relatively modest: we should try to get along without killing each other. In his view, merely existing without tearing each other's throats out for a while is a remarkable, tenuous, fragile accomplishment. But, as Patrick Gray reminds us, we live in a time in which we tend to see peace as the norm, whereas for the vast majority of human history – including Shakespeare's own time and, as some contend and despite perceptions, our own too – conflict and war have been the norm. Peace is fragile, and beyond that so are loving relationships between individuals.[9]

In closing, it is time to return to the question I asked at the start of the book: how can we characterise the moral vision of Shakespeare's plays? If I were to characterise the Shakespearean ethic beyond his emphasis on love, charity and friendship in authority and loyalty, it would be as follows:

1. There is always a choice; it is never too late to choose to do the right thing.
2. The responsibility ultimately stops with you because there is no divine or cosmic justice that will otherwise intervene; accordingly, do not expect rewards or recognition for your good deeds.
3. We should not write anyone off but rather make an effort to understand where they coming from, and try to see things from their point of view, because empathy and compassion are better than hatred, both morally and consequentially.
4. If we feel hard done by or slighted by unfairness, mercy is better than revenge, both morally and consequentially.

Despite the apparent simplicity of these moral instructions, in our current time of perpetual petty social media outrage, the prevalence of personality over character, a near-complete lack of intellectual charity, increasingly meaningless virtue signalling[10] – mere words that are seldom backed by actual virtue in the form of decisions and actions – and ever-mounting political and cultural polarisation, perhaps a little of the Shakespearean ethic would go a long way.

In summary

- Liberty, as manifested in individual free choice, facilitates the other five moral foundations.
- If liberty can be maintained through the just rule of law and the good choices of individuals, society can sustain a virtuous circle in which liberty begets fairness, which begets authority and loyalty, which result in sanctity and care.
- However, if oppression takes root, it breeds unfairness and individual bad choices, and society descends into a vicious circle in which oppression begets unfairness, which begets subversion and betrayal, which result in degradation and harm.
- To break the vicious circle and to maintain the virtuous circle takes a leap of faith on the part of the good moral actor: they must give freely of themselves and expect no reward.
- Shakespeare always foregrounds the individual (and their moral choices) over the group, yet authority and loyalty – as defined by individual rather than group relations – are of central importance in his moral compass.

Notes

1. Vyvyan, *The Shakespearean Ethic*, p. 125.
2. Greenblatt, *Shakespeare's Freedom*, p. 3.
3. Haidt, *The Righteous Mind*, pp. 150–79.
4. Wells, *Shakespeare's Politics*, p. 106.
5. George Lakoff, *Moral Politics: How Liberals and Conservatives Think*, 2nd edn (1996; Chicago: University of Chicago Press, 2002), pp. 65–142.

6. See also William B. Thorne, '"Things Newborn": A Study of the Rebirth Motif in *The Winter's Tale*', *Humanities Association Review*, 19:1 (1968), pp. 34–43.
7. Danby, *Shakespeare's Doctrine of Nature*, pp. 20–42.
8. See Haidt, *The Righteous Mind*, p. 129.
9. Patrick Gray, 'Shakespeare and War: Honor at the Stake', *Critical Survey*, 3:1 (Spring, 2018); I was kindly given an advance copy by the author. See also John Gray, especially *Straw Dogs* and *The Silence of Animals*. On the fragility of individual relationships, see Nussbaum, *The Fragility of Goodness*.
10. The phrase was popularly coined in James Bartholomew, 'The Awful Rise of "Virtue Signalling"'.

BIBLIOGRAPHY

Primary Sources

Aquinas, Thomas, *Commentary on the Nicomachean Ethics*, trans. C. I. Litzinger, 2 vols (Chicago: Henry Regnery Company, 1964).

—, *Summa Theologiae*, 60 vols (London: Eyre & Spottiswoode, 1969).

Aristotle, *The Nicomachean Ethics*, ed. Lesley Brown (Oxford: Oxford University Press, 2009).

Becon, Thomas, *The Governance of Vertue* (London: John Day, 1556).

Botero, Giovanni, *A Treatise, Concerning the Causes of the Magnificencie and Greatnes of Cities, Devided into Thre Books*, trans. Robert Peterson (London, 1606).

Calvin, John, *Institutes of the Christian Religion*, 2 vols, ed. John T. McNeil, trans. Ford Lewis Battles (1559; Philadelphia: Westminster Press, 1960).

Chaucer, Geoffrey, *The Riverside Chaucer*, ed. Larry D. Benson (Oxford: Oxford University Press, 1988).

Cicero, 'On Friendship', trans. Frank O. Copely, in *Other Selves: Philosophers on Friendship*, ed. Michael Pakaluk (Indianapolis: Hackett, 1991), pp. 77–116.

—, *Cicero on the Emotions: Tusculan Disputations 3 and 4*, trans. Margaret Graver (Chicago: University of Chicago Press, 2002).

—, *On Moral Ends*, ed. Julia Annas, trans. Raphael Woolf (Cambridge: Cambridge University Press, 2004).

—, *On Academic Scepticism*, trans. Charles Brittain (Indianapolis: Hackett, 2006).

—, *The Nature of the Gods*, ed. P. G. Walsh (Oxford: Oxford University Press, 2008).

Dante Alighieri, *The Divine Comedy of Dante Alighieri, Vol. 1: Inferno*, ed. Robert M. Durling (Oxford: Oxford University Press, 1996).

Darwin, Charles, *The Descent of Man: Selection in Relation to Sex* (1871; New York and London: Penguin, 2004).

Descartes, René, *Discourse on the Method of Correctly Conducting One's Reason and Seeking Truth in the Sciences*, trans. Ian Maclean (Oxford: Oxford University Press, 2008).

Devon, Frederick, *Issues of the Exchequer: Being Payments Made Out of His Majesty's Revenue during the Reign of King James I* (London: John Rodwell, 1836).

Diogenes Laërtius, *The Lives and Opinions of Eminent Philosophers*, trans. C. D. Younge (London: Henry G. Bohn, 1853).

Du Vair, Guillaume, *The Moral Philosophie of the Stoicks*, trans. Thomas James (London: Felix Kingston, 1598).

Farmer, Richard, *An Essay on the Learning of Shakespeare: Addressed to Joseph Cradock, Esq.* (Cambridge: W. Thurlbourn & J. Woodyer, 1767).

Fuller, Thomas, *The History of the Worthies of England who for Parts and Learning have been Eminent in the Several Counties: Together with an Historical Narrative of the Native Commodities and Rarities in Each County* (London: Thomas Williams, 1662).

Greene, Robert, *Greene's Groat's-worth of Wit, Bought with a Million of Repentance* (London: William Wright, 1592).

—, *Robert Greene's Planetomachia*, ed. Nandini Das (Aldershot: Ashgate, 2007).

Hall, Joseph, *Two Guides to a Good Life. The Genealogy of Vertue and the Nathomy of Sinne. Liuely Displaying the Worth of One, and the Vanity of the Other* (London: W. Iaggard, 1604).

—, *Meditations and Vowes, Diuine and Morall. Seruing for Direction in Christian and Ciuill Practise. Deuided into Two Bookes* (London: John Porter, 1605).

Hobbes, Thomas, *Leviathan*, ed. J. C. A. Gaskin (1651; Oxford: Oxford University Press, 2008).

Hooker, Richard, *The Ecclesiastical Polity and Other Works of Richard Hooker*, 3 vols, ed. Benjamin Hanbury (1594; London: Holdsworth and Ball, 1830).

Hume, David, *A Treatise of Human Nature* (1739; New York: Dover Publications, 2003).

Lillback, Peter A. (ed.), *1599 Geneva Bible* (Dallas, GA: Tolle Lege Press, 2006).

Lucretius, *On the Nature of the Universe*, trans. Ronald Melville (Oxford: Oxford University Press, 1997).

Luther, Martin, 'Disputation against Scholastic Theology', in *Martin Luther's Basic Theological Writings*, ed. Timothy F. Lull and William R. Russell, 3rd edn (1989; Minneapolis: Fortress Press, 2012), pp. 3–7.

Machiavelli, Niccolò, *Discourses on Livy*, trans. Harvey C. Mansfield and Nathan Tarcov (Chicago: University of Chicago Press, 1996).

—, *The Prince*, trans. James B. Atkinson (1976; Indianapolis: Hackett, 2008).

Marlowe, Christopher, *Doctor Faustus and Other Plays*, ed. David Bevington and Eric Rasmussen (Oxford: Oxford University Press, 1995).

Montaigne, Michel de, *Shakespeare's Montaigne: The Florio Translation of the Essays, A Selection*, ed. Stephen Greenblatt and Peter G. Platt, trans. John Florio (New York: New York Review Books, 2014).

Perkins, William, *A Golden Chain, Or The Description of Theologie, Containing the Order of the Causes of Saluation and Damnation, According to God's Word* (London: Edward Alde, 1591).

Petrarch, Francesco, *Letters on Familiar Matters, Vol. 1: Books I–VIII*, ed. Aldo S. Bernardo (New York: Italica Press, 2005).

Raleigh, Walter, *A Cleare and Evident Way for Enriching the Nations of England and Ireland and for Setting Very Great Numbers of Poore on Work* (London: T. M. & A. C., 1650).

Rousseau, Jean-Jacques, *'The Social Contract', and Other Political Writings*, ed. and trans. Victor Gourevitch (Cambridge: Cambridge University Press, 1997).

Seneca, *Moral and Political Essays*, ed. John M. Cooper and J. F. Procopé (Cambridge: Cambridge University Press, 1995).
—, *Dialogues and Essays*, trans. John Davie (Oxford: Oxford University Press, 2007).
—, *Selected Letters*, trans. Elaine Fantam (Oxford: Oxford University Press, 2010).
Sextus Empiricus, *Outlines of Scepticism*, ed. Julia Annas and Jonathan Barnes (Cambridge: Cambridge University Press, 2000).
Shakespeare, William, *The Norton Shakespeare*, 3rd edn, ed. Stephen Greenblatt, Walter Cohen, Suzanne Gossett, Jean E. Howard, Katharine Eisaman Maus and Gordon McMullen (New York: W. W. Norton, 2016).
Smith, Adam, *The Wealth of Nations*, ed. Edwin Cannan (1776; New York: Modern Library, 2000).
—, *The Theory of Moral Sentiments*, ed. Ryan Patrick Henley (1759; New York and London: Penguin, 2010).
Statius, *Thebaid*, 2 vols, ed. and trans. D. R. Shackleton Bailey (Cambridge, MA: Harvard University Press, 2004).
Valla, Lorenzo, 'Of the True and False Good', in *The Renaissance in Europe: An Anthology*, ed. Peter Elmer, Nick Webb and Roberta Wood (New Haven, CT: Yale University Press, 2000), pp. 72–87.
Virgil, *The Aeneid*, trans. Sarah Ruden (New Haven, CT: Yale University Press, 2008).
Wheeler, John, *A Treatise of Commerce* (London: John Harison, 1601).

Secondary Sources

Acemoglu, Daron, and James A. Robinson, *Why Nations Fail: The Origins of Power, Prosperity, and Poverty* (London: Profile Books, 2012).
Adams, Marylin McCord, 'The Structure of Ockham's Moral Theory', *Franciscan Studies*, 46 (1986), 1–35.
Adamson, Peter, 'Everybody Needs Somebody – Aquinas on Soul and Knowledge', *History of Philosophy Without Any Gaps*, 244 (3 January 2016), <http://historyofphilosophy.net/aquinas-soul-knowledge>.

Afary, Janet, and Kevin B. Anderson (eds), *Foucault and the Iranian Revolution: Gender and the Seductions of Islamism* (Chicago: Chicago University Press, 2005).

Allen, Don Cameron, 'The Rehabilitation of Epicurus and His Theory of Pleasure in the Early Renaissance', *Studies in Philology*, 41:4 (January 1944), 1–15.

Althusser, Louis, 'Philosophy as a Revolutionary Weapon', in *Lenin and Philosophy and Other Essays*, trans. Ben Brewster (1971; New York: Monthly Review Press, 2001), pp. 85–126.

Ames, Fisher, *Works of Fisher Ames: Compiled by a Number of His Friends* (Boston, MA: T. B. Wait & Co., 1809).

Anderson, H. R. D., *Shakespeare's Books: A Dissertation on Shakespeare's Reading and the Immediate Sources of His Works* (Berlin: George Reimer, 1904).

Anderson, Linda, *A Place in the Story: Servants and Service in Shakespeare's Plays* (Newark: University of Delaware Press, 2005).

Archer, Jayne Elisabeth, Howard Thomas and Richard Marggraf Turley, 'Reading Shakespeare with the Grain: Sustainability and the Hunger Business', *Green Letters: Studies in Ecocriticism*, 19:1 (2015), 8–20.

Arienzo, Alessandro, and Alessandra Petrina (eds), *Machiavellian Encounters in Tudor and Stuart England* (Farnham: Ashgate, 2013).

Arnhart, Larry, *Darwinian Natural Right: The Biological Ethics of Human Nature* (Albany: State University of New York Press, 1998).

—, 'Darwinian Conservativism', in *Darwinian Conservativism: A Disputed Question*, ed. Kenneth C. Blanchard, Jr (Charlottesville, VA: Imprint Academic, 2009), pp. 1–146.

Atkinson, James B., 'Introduction', in *The Prince*, trans. James B. Atkinson (1976; Indianapolis: Hackett, 2008), pp. 1–90.

Aurell, Jaume, 'Reading Renaissance Merchants' Handbooks: Confronting Professional Ethics and Social Identity', in *The Idea of Work in Europe from Antiquity to Modern Times*, ed. Josef Ehmer and Catharina Lis (Farnham: Ashgate, 2009), pp. 71–90.

Barish, Jonas A., and Marshall Waingrow, '"Service" in *King Lear*', *Shakespeare Quarterly*, 9:3 (Summer 1958), 347–55.

Barkan, Leonard, 'What did Shakespeare Read?', in *The Cambridge Companion to Shakespeare*, ed. Margareta de Grazia and Stanley Wells (Cambridge: Cambridge University Press, 2001), pp. 31–48.

Bartholomew, James, 'The Awful Rise of "Virtue Signalling"', *The Spectator* (18 April 2015), <https://www.spectator.co.uk/2015/04/hating-the-daily-mail-is-a-substitute-for-doing-good/>.

Bate, Jonathan, and Eric Rasmussen (eds), Titus Andronicus *and* Timon of Athens: *Two Roman Plays* (Basingstoke: Macmillan, 2011).

Baumeister, Roy F., and Kirsten L. Sommer, 'What Do Men Want? Gender Differences and Two Spheres of Belongingness: Comment on Cross and Madson', *Psychological Bulletin*, 122:1 (July 1997), 38–44.

Bayley, Harold, *The Shakespeare Symphony: An Introduction to the Ethics of Elizabethan Drama* (London: Chapman and Hall, 1906).

Bayne, Ronald, 'Religion', in *Shakespeare's England: An Account of the Life and Manners of His Age*, 2 vols, ed. C. T. Onions and Sidney Lee (Oxford: Clarendon Press, 1916), vol. 1, pp. 48–78.

Beauregard, David N., *Virtue's Own Feature: Shakespeare and the Virtue Ethics Tradition* (Newark: University of Delaware Press, 1995).

—, 'Shakespeare and the Passions: The Aristotlean–Thomistic Tradition', *The Heythrop Journal*, 54:6 (2013), 912–25.

Bell, Millicent, *Shakespeare's Tragic Skepticism* (New Haven, CT: University of Yale Press, 2003).

Belliotti, Raymond Angelo, *Niccolò Machiavelli: The Laughing Lion and the Strutting Fox* (Langam, MD: Lexington Books, 2009).

Berger, Jr, Harry, *Making Trifles of Terrors: Redistributing Complicities in Shakespeare*, ed. Peter Erikson (Stanford: University of Stanford Press, 1997).

Berlin, Isaiah, *Four Essays on Liberty* (Oxford: Oxford University Press, 1969).

Bett, Richard, 'Scepticism and Ethics', in *The Cambridge Companion to Ancient Scepticism*, ed. Richard Bett (Cambridge: Cambridge University Press, 2010), pp. 181–94.

Beuchot, Mauricio, 'Some Traces of the Presence of Scepticism in Medieval Thought', in *Scepticism in the History of Philosophy*, ed. Richard H. Popkin (Kluwer: Dordrecht, 1996), pp. 37–43.

Bevington, David, *Shakespeare's Ideas: More Things in Heaven and Earth* (Oxford: Blackwell, 2008).

—, 'The Debate about Shakespeare and Religion', in *Shakespeare and Early Modern Religion*, ed. David Loewenstein and Michael Witmore (Cambridge: Cambridge University Press, 2015), pp. 23–40.

Birch, W. J., *An Inquiry into the Philosophy and Religion of Shakspere* (London: C. Mitchell, 1848).

Bloom, Harold, *Shakespeare: The Invention of the Human* (New York: Riverhead Books, 1998).

Bouwsma, William, 'The Two Faces of Humanism: Stoicism and Augustinianism in Renaissance Thought', in *A Usable Past: Essays in European Cultural History* (Berkeley: University of California Press), pp. 19–73.

Bowden, Henry Sebastian, *The Religion of Shakespeare* (London: Burnes & Oates, 1899).

Bowlby, John, *Attachment*, 2nd edn (1969; New York: Basic Books, 1983).

Bradley, A. C., *Shakespearean Tragedy: Lectures on Hamlet, Othello, King Lear, Macbeth* (London: Macmillan, 1905).

Bradshaw, Graham, *Shakespeare's Scepticism* (Ithaca, NY: Cornell University Press, 1987).

Braudel, Fernand, *Civilization and Capitalism, 15th–18th Century*, 3 vols, trans. Siân Reynolds (Berkeley: University of California Press, 1993).

—, *A History of Civilizations*, trans. Richard Mayne (1987; New York and London: Penguin, 1993).

Bray, Alan, *The Friend* (Chicago: University of Chicago, 2003).

Brehm, Sharon S., and Jack W. Brehm, *Psychological Reactance: A Theory of Freedom and Control* (New York and London: Academic Press, 1981).

Bristol, Michael D., 'Confusing Shakespeare's Characters with Real People: Reflections on Reading in Four Questions', in *Shakespeare and Character Theory, History, Performance and Theatrical Persons*, ed. Paul Yachnin and Jessica Slights (New York and London: Palgrave Macmillan, 2009), pp. 21–40.

—, 'Macbeth the Philosopher: Rethinking Context', *New Literary History*, 42:4 (Autumn 2011), 641–62.

—, 'Is Shakespeare a Moral Philosopher?', in *Shakespeare and Moral Agency*, ed. Michael D. Bristol (New York and London: Continuum, 2012), pp. 1–14.

Brown, Alison, *The Return of Lucretius to Renaissance Florence* (Cambridge, MA: Harvard University Press, 2010).

—, 'Lucretian Naturalism and the Evolution of Machiavelli's Ethics', in *Lucretius and the Early Modern*, ed. David Norbrook, Stephen Harrison and Philip Hardie (Oxford: Oxford University Press, 2016).

Brown, Andrew, *The Darwin Wars: The Scientific Battle for the Soul of Man* (London: Simon & Schuster, 1999).

Bruckner, Pascal, *The Tyranny of Guilt: An Essay on Western Masochism*, trans. Stephen Rendall (Princeton: Princeton University Press, 2012).

Bryant, Jr, J. A., *Hippolyta's View: Some Christian Aspects of Shakespeare's Plays* (Lexington: University of Kentucky Press, 1961).

Burnett, Mark Thornton, *Masters and Servants in English Renaissance Drama and Culture: Authority and Obedience* (Basingstoke: Macmillan, 1997).

Cadoux, Arthur Temple, *Shakespearean Selves: Essays in Ethics* (London: Epworth Press, 1938).

Campbell, Lily B., *Shakespeare's Tragic Heroes: Slaves of Passion* (1930; London: Methuen, 1961).

Carroll, Joseph, 'Evolutionary Social Theory: The Current State of Knowledge', *Style*, 49:4 (2015), pp. 512–41.

Carroll, Joseph, John A. Johnson, Catherine Salmon, Jens Kjeldgaard-Christiansen, Mathias Clasen and Emelie Jonsson, 'A Cross-Disciplinary Survey of Beliefs about Human Nature, Culture, and Science', *Evolutionary Studies in Imaginative Culture*, 1:1 (2017), 1–32.

Carter, Thomas, *Shakespeare and the Holy Scripture with the Version He Used* (London: Hodder and Stoughton, 1905).

Cave, Terence, *Thinking with Literature: Towards a Cognitive Criticism* (Oxford: Oxford University Press, 2016).

Cessario, Romanus, *Short History of Thomism* (Rome: Catholic University of America Press, 2005).
Chambers, E. K., *The Elizabethan Stage*, 4 vols (Oxford: Clarendon Press, 1923).
—, *William Shakespeare: A Study of Facts and Problems*, 2 vols (Oxford: Clarendon, 1930).
Chesterton, G. K., *St. Thomas Aquinas* (London: Hodder & Stoughton, 1933).
Citti, Francisco, 'Seneca and the Moderns', in *The Cambridge Companion to Seneca*, ed. Shadi Bartsch and Alessandro Schiesaro (Cambridge: Cambridge University Press, 2015), pp. 303–18.
Clark, Nick, 'Globe Theatre Takes Out 100 Audience Members with Its Gory Titus Andronicus', *The Independent* (22 July 2014), <http://www.independent.co.uk/arts-entertainment/theatre-dance/news/globe-theatre-takes-out-100-audience-members-with-its-gory-titus-andronicus-9621763.html>.
Cohen, Jeremy, 'Original Sin as the Evil Inclination: A Polemicist's Appreciation of Human Nature', *Harvard Theological Review*, 73:3 (July to October 1980), 495–520.
Coleridge, Samuel Taylor, *Coleridge's Essays and Lectures on Shakespeare: And Some Other Old Poets and Dramatists*, ed. Ernest Rhys (London: J. M. Dent & Sons, 1907).
Colman, Andrew M., 'Race Differences in IQ: Hans Eysenck's Contribution to the Debate in the Light of Subsequent Research', *Personality and Individual Differences*, 103 (2016), 182–9.
Copleston, F. C., *The History of Philosophy, Vol. 3: The Late Medieval and Renaissance Philosophy, Part II: The Revival of Platonism to Suarez* (Westminster, MD: Newman Press, 1952).
—, *Aquinas* (New York and London: Penguin, 1955).
Cosgrave, Patrick, 'Obituary: Enoch Powell', *The Independent* (9 February 1998), <http://www.independent.co.uk/news/obituaries/obituary-enoch-powell-1143867.html>.
Costa, Paul T., and Robert R. McCrea, 'Four Ways Five Factors are Basic', *Personality and Individual Differences*, 13:6 (1992), 653–65.
Cox, John D., *Seeming Knowledge: Shakespeare and Skeptical Faith* (Waco, TX: Baylor University Press, 2007).

Crawford, Charles, *A Complete Concordance to the 1616 Folio of Ben Jonson's Works*, 5 vols (Microfilm; Ann Arbor: University of Michigan, 1923).

Damasio, Antonio, *Descartes' Error: Emotion, Reason and the Human Brain* (New York: Putnam, 1994).

Danby, John F., *Shakespeare's Doctrine of Nature: A Study of King Lear* (London: Faber & Faber, 1949).

Davies, Brian, *Thomas Aquinas's Summa Theologiae: A Guide and Commentary* (Oxford: Oxford University Press, 2014).

Dawkins, Richard, *The Selfish Gene* (1976; Oxford: Oxford University Press, 2016).

De Grazia, Margareta, Maureen Quilligan and Peter Stallybrass (eds), *Subject and Object in Renaissance Culture* (Cambridge: Cambridge University Press, 1996).

de Waal, Frans, *The Age of Empathy: Nature's Lessons for a Kinder Society* (New York: Harmony Books, 2009).

Deane, Phyllis, and W. A. Cole, *British Economic Growth 1688–1959: Trends and Structure* (Cambridge: Cambridge University Press, 1962).

Dennett, Daniel, *Darwin's Dangerous Idea: Evolution and the Meanings of Life* (New York and London: Penguin, 1995).

Deshpande, M. G., '"Loneliness" in *The Merchant of Venice*', *Essays in Criticism*, 11:3 (July 1961), 368–9.

Diamond, Jared, *Guns, Germs, and Steel: The Fates of Human Societies* (New York and London: W. W. Norton & Co., 1997).

Dickens, A. G., *The Marian Reaction in the Diocese of York, Part II: The Laity* (York: St Anthony's Press, 1957).

DiLorenzo, Thomas J., *The Problem with Socialism* (Washington, DC: Regnery Publishing, 2016).

Dimmock, Spencer, *The Origin of Capitalism in England, 1400–1600* (Leiden and Boston, MA: Brill, 2014).

Doherty, Kevin F., 'St. Thomas and the Pseudo-Dionysian Symbol of Light', *The New Scholasticism*, 34 (1960), pp. 170–89.

Dollimore, Jonathan, and Alan Sinfield, 'History and Ideology, Masculinity and Miscegenation: The Instance of *Henry V*', in *Faultlines: Cultural Materialism and the Politics of Dissident Reading* (Oxford: Clarendon Press, 1992), pp. 109–42.

Donaldson, Ian (ed.), *Ben Jonson* (Oxford: Oxford University Press, 1985).

Dowden, Edward, *Shakespeare, His Mind and Art* (New York and London: Harper and Brothers, 1881).

Durkheim, Émile, *The Elementary Forms of Religious Life* (London: George Allen & Unwin, 1915).

Elton, G. R., *Reformation Europe 1517–1559* (New York: Meridian Books, 1964).

Elton, W. R., 'Aristotle's *Nicomachean Ethics* and Shakespeare's *Troilus and Cressida*', *Journal of the History of Ideas*, 58:2 (April 1997), 331–7.

Enterline, Lynn, *Shakespeare's Schoolroom: Rhetoric, Discipline, Emotion* (Philadelphia: University of Pennsylvania Press, 2012).

Evett, David, *Discourses of Service in Shakespeare's England* (New York and London: Palgrave Macmillan, 2005).

Fergusson, Francis, *Shakespeare: The Pattern in His Carpet* (New York: Delacorte Press, 1970).

Floridi, Luciano, 'The Diffusion of Sextus Empiricus's Works in the Renaissance', *Journal of the History of Ideas*, 56 (1995), 63–85.

Floyd-Wilson, Mary, 'English Epicures and Scottish Witches', *Shakespeare Quarterly*, 57:2 (Summer 2006), 131–61.

Ford, Harold, *Shakespeare: His Ethical Teaching* (London: Smith's Printing Co., 1922).

Foucault, Michel, *The Order of Things: Archaeology of the Human Sciences* (1966; London: Routledge, 2002).

Frankl, Viktor E., *Man's Search for Meaning* (1959; London: Rider, 2004).

Freehafer, John, 'Stoicism and Epicureanism in England, 1530–1700', *PLMA*, 88:5 (October 1973), 1180–2.

Friedman, Milton, *Capitalism and Freedom* (Chicago: University of Chicago Press, 1962).

—, 'Is Capitalism Humane?', lecture delivered at Cornell University, Ithaca, NY (27 September 1977).

Frye, Roland Mushat, *Shakespeare and Christian Doctrine* (Princeton: Princeton University Press, 1963).

Fukuyama, Francis, *The Origins of Political Order: From Prehuman Times to the French Revolution* (London: Profile Books, 2011).

Garrett, Aaron, 'Seventeenth-Century Moral Philosophy: Self-Help, Self-Knowledge and the Devil's Mountain', in *The Oxford Handbook of the History of Ethics*, ed. Roger Crisp (Oxford: Oxford University Press, 2013), pp. 229–79.

Getlin, Larry, 'Inside Modern Iran, where Porn and Prostitution are Rampant', *New York Post* (30 August 2014), available at <https://nypost.com/2014/08/30/inside-modern-iran-where-porn-and-prostitution-are-rampant/>.

Gillies, John, 'The Question of Original Sin in *Hamlet*', *Shakespeare Quarterly*, 64:4 (Winter 2013), 396–424.

Gilman, Arthur, *Shakespeare's Morals: Suggestive Selections, With Brief Collateral Readings and Scriptural References* (New York: Dodd, Mead & Company, 1880).

Gonzalez, Alexander G., 'The Infection and Spread of Evil: Some Major Patterns of Imagery and Language in Othello', *South Atlantic Review*, 50:4 (November 1985), 35–49.

Goodhart, David, *The Road to Somewhere: The Populist Revolt and the Future of Politics* (London: Hurst & Co., 2017).

Gordin, Michael D., 'How Lysenkoism became Pseudoscience: Dobzhansky to Velikovsky', *Journal of the History of Biology*, 45:3 (Fall 2012), 443–68.

Gowarty, Patricia Adair (ed.), *Feminism and Evolutionary Biology: Boundaries, Intersections, and Frontiers* (New York and London: Chapman & Hall, 1997).

Grady, Hugh, *Shakespeare, Machiavelli, and Montaigne: Power and Subjectivity from Richard II to Hamlet* (Oxford: Oxford University Press, 2002).

Grav, Peter F., 'Taking Stock of Shakespeare and the New Economic Criticism', *Shakespeare*, 8:1 (2012), 111–36.

Gray, John, *Straw Dogs: Thoughts on Humans and Other Animals* (London: Granta, 2003).

—, *The Silence of Animals: On Progress and Other Modern Myths* (New York and London: Penguin, 2013).

Gray, Patrick, 'Shakespeare and War: Honor at the Stake', *Critical Survey*, 3:1 (Spring 2018), 1–25.

—, and John D. Cox, 'Introduction: Rethinking Shakespeare and Ethics', in *Shakespeare and Renaissance Ethics*, ed. Patrick

Gray and John D. Cox (Cambridge: Cambridge University Press, 2014), pp. 1–34.
Greenblatt, Stephen, *Will in the World: How Shakespeare Became Shakespeare* (New York: W. W. Norton, 2004).
—, *Shakespeare's Freedom* (Chicago: University of Chicago Press, 2010).
—, *The Swerve: How the World Became Modern* (New York: W. W. Norton, 2011).
—, 'Shakespeare's Montaigne', in Michel de Montaigne, *Shakespeare's Montaigne: The Florio Translation of the Essays, A Selection*, ed. Stephen Greenblatt and Peter G. Platt, trans. John Florio (New York: New York Review Books, 2014), pp. ix–xxxiii.
Greene, Joshua, *Moral Tribes: Emotion, Reason, and the Gap Between Us and Them* (London: Atlantic Books, 2014).
Greenfeld, Liah, *The Spirit of Capitalism: Nationalism and Economic Growth* (Cambridge, MA: Harvard University Press, 2001).
Greenslade, Roy, 'Newspapers Draw on Shakespeare to Report Gove's Knifing of Johnson', *The Guardian* (1 July 2016), <https://www.theguardian.com/media/greenslade/2016/jul/01/newspapers-draw-on-shakespeare-to-report-goves-knifing-of-johnson>.
Griffith, Elizabeth, *The Morality of Shakespeare's Drama Illustrated* (London: T. Caddell, 1775).
Grigson, Caroline, *Menagerie: The History of Exotic Animals in England* (Oxford: Oxford University Press, 2016).
Haidt, Jonathan, 'The New Synthesis in Moral Psychology', *Science*, 316:5827 (18 May 2007), 998–1001.
—, *The Righteous Mind: Why Good People Are Divided by Religion and Politics* (New York: Random House, 2012).
—, 'The Ethics of Globalism, Nationalism and Patriotism', *Minding Nature*, 9:3 (September 2016), 18–24.
—, 'Why Universities Must Choose One Telos: Truth or Social Justice' (21 October 2016), <http://heterodoxacademy.org/2016/10/21/one-telos-truth-or-social-justice/>.
—, 'Trump Breaks a Taboo – and Pays the Price', *The Atlantic* (21 August 2017), <https://www.theatlantic.com/politics/archive/2017/08/what-happens-when-the-president-commits-sacrilege/537519/>.

Haidt, Jonathan, and Joseph Craig, 'Intuitive Ethics: How Innately Prepared Intuitions Generate Culturally Variable Virtues', *Daedalus*, 133:4 (Fall 2004), 55–66.

Haigh, Christopher, *English Reformations: Religion, Politics, and Society Under the Tudors* (Oxford: Clarendon Press, 1993).

Hamilton, W. D., 'The Genetic Evolution of Social Behaviour', *Journal of Theoretical Biology*, 7:1 (1964), 1–52.

Hammer, Paul E. J., 'Lord Henry Howard, William Temple, and the Earl of Essex', *Huntington Library Quarterly*, 79:1 (Spring 2016), 41–62.

Harbage, Alfred, *As They Liked It: A Study of Shakespeare's Moral Artistry* (1947; New York: Harper Torchbook, 1961).

Harris, Jonathan Gil, *Sick Economies: Drama, Mercantilism, and Disease in Shakespeare's England* (Philadelphia: University of Pennsylvania Press, 2003).

—, *Untimely Matter in the Time of Shakespeare* (Philadelphia: University of Pennsylvania Press, 2008).

Harris, Sam, *The Moral Landscape: How Science Can Determine Human Values* (London: Bantam Press, 2010).

Hartley, L. P., *Facial Justice* (1960; London: Penguin, 2014).

Hatlen, Burton, 'Feudal and Bourgeois Concepts of Value in *The Merchant of Venice*', in *Shakespeare: Contemporary Critical Approaches*, ed. Harry R. Garvin (Lewisburg: Bucknell University Press, 1980), pp. 91–105.

Hauser, Marc D., *Moral Minds: How Nature Designed Our Universal Sense of Right and Wrong* (New York: HarperCollins, 2006).

Hawkes, David, *Shakespeare and Economic Theory* (New York and London: Bloomsbury, 2015).

Hay, Denys, 'The Background to the Reformation', in *The Reformation Crisis*, ed. Joel Hurstfield (London: Edward Arnold, 1965), pp. 8–20.

Hazlitt, William, *The Characters of Shakespear's Plays* (1817; London: J. M. Kent & Sons, 1912).

Heinemann, Margot, *Puritanism and Theatre: Thomas Middleton and Opposition Drama during the Early Stuarts* (Cambridge: Cambridge University Press, 1980).

Herman, Arthur, *The Cave and the Light: Plato Versus Aristotle and the Struggle for the Soul of Western Civilization* (New York: Random House, 2013).

Highet, Gilbert, *The Classical Tradition: Greek and Roman Influences on Western Literature* (1949; Oxford: Oxford University Press, 1976).
Hill, Benjamin, 'Thomas of Vio (Cajetan)', in *Encyclopedia of Medieval Philosophy: Philosophy Between 500 and 1500, Vol. 1*, ed. Henrik Lagerlund (New York and London: Springer, 2011), pp. 1295–1300.
Hill, Christopher, *Intellectual Origins of the English Revolution* (Oxford: Oxford University Press, 1965).
Hillier, Russell M., 'Hamlet the Rough-hewer: Moral Agency and the Consolations of Reformation Thought', in *Shakespeare and Renaissance Ethics*, ed. Patrick Gray and John D. Cox (Cambridge: Cambridge University Press, 2014), pp. 159–85.
Hinch, Jim, 'Why Stephen Greenblatt Is Wrong – and Why It Matters', *Los Angeles Review of Books* (1 December 2012), <https://lareviewofbooks.org/article/why-stephen-greenblatt-is-wrong-and-why-it-matters/>.
Hodgen, Margaret T., 'Shakespeare and Montaigne Again', *Huntington Library Quarterly*, 16:1 (November 1952), 23–42.
Holbrook, Peter (ed.), *The Shakespearean International Yearbook, 6: Special Section, Shakespeare and Montaigne Revisited* (Aldershot: Ashgate, 2006).
Hooker, Elizabeth Robbins, 'The Relation of Shakespeare to Montaigne', *PMLA*, 17:3 (1902), 312–66.
Hoyle, R. W., 'Tenure and the Land Market in Early Modern England: Or a Late Contribution to the Brenner Debate', *Economic History Review*, 43:1 (February 1990), 1–20.
Humphreys, Patrick, and Esmail Kahrom, *Lion and Gazelle: The Mammals and Birds of Iran* (Abergavenny: Comma International Biological Systems, 1995).
Hunter, Joseph, *New Illustrations of the Life, Studies, and Writings of Shakespeare, Vol. 2* (London: J. B. Nichols and Son, 1845).
Hutton, Sarah, 'Platonism, Stoicism, Scepticism and Classical Imitation', in *A Companion to English Renaissance Literature and Culture*, ed. Michael Hattaway (Oxford: Blackwell, 2000), pp. 44–57.
Hyatte, Reginald, *The Arts of Friendship: The Idealisation of Friendship in Medieval and Early Renaissance Literature* (Leiden: E. J. Brill, 1994).

Impett, Emily A., and Letitia Anne Peplau, '"His" and "Her" Relationships? A Review of the Empirical Evidence', in *The Cambridge Handbook of Personal Relationships*, ed. Anita L. Vangelisti and Daniel Perlman (Cambridge: Cambridge University Press, 2006), pp. 273–92.

Ingram, Jill Phillips, *Idioms of Self-Interest: Credit, Identity, and Property in English Renaissance Literature* (New York and London: Routledge, 2006), pp. 7–10.

Inwood, Brad, 'The Will in Seneca', in *Reading Seneca: Stoic Philosophy at Rome* (Oxford: Oxford University Press, 2005), pp. 132–56.

Irwin, Terence, *The Development of Ethics, Vol. 2: From Suarez to Rousseau* (Oxford: Oxford University Press, 2011), pp. 1–69.

Isaacs, Mark D., *Centennial Rumination on Max Weber's* The Protestant Work Ethic and the Spirit of Capitalism (Boca Raton: Dissertation.com, 2006).

James, Scott M., *An Introduction to Evolutionary Ethics* (Oxford: Wiley-Blackwell, 2011).

James, William, *The Will to Believe, Human Immortality, and Other Essays in Popular Philosophy* (1897; New York: Dover Publications, 1956).

Jenkins, Jr, Holman W., 'Jonathan Haidt: He Knows Why We Fight', *The Wall Street Journal* (29 June 2012).

Jeschke, Thomas, 'John Caprelous', in *Encyclopedia of Medieval Philosophy: Philosophy Between 500 and 1500, Vol. 1*, ed. Henrik Lagerlund (New York and London: Springer, 2011), pp. 606–8.

John, Eileen, 'Caring About Characters', in *Fictional Characters, Real Problems: The Search for Ethical Content in Literature*, ed. Garry L. Hagberg (Oxford: Oxford University Press, 2016), pp. 31–46.

Johnson, Samuel, *Johnson on Shakespeare: Essays and Notes*, ed. Walter Raleigh (London: Henry Frowde, 1908).

Jones, Ann Rosalind, and Peter Stallybrass, *Renaissance Clothing and the Materials of Memory* (Cambridge: Cambridge University Press, 2001).

Joy, Lynn S., 'Epicureanism in Renaissance Moral and Natural Philosophy', *Journal of the History of Ideas*, 53:4 (October to December 1992), 573–83.

Kahn, Charles H., 'Discovering Will from Aristotle to Augustine', in *The Question of 'Eclecticism': Studies in Later Greek Philosophy*, ed. John M. Dillon and A. A. Long (Berkeley: University of California Press, 1988), pp. 234–59.

Kahn, Coppélia, 'The Absent Mother in *King Lear*', in *Rewriting the Renaissance: The Discourses of Sexual Difference in Early Modern Europe*, ed. Margaret W. Ferguson, Maureen Quilligan and Nancy Vickers (Chicago: University of Chicago Press, 1986), pp. 33–49.

Kahneman, Daniel, *Thinking Fast and Slow* (New York and London: Penguin, 2011).

Kamps, Ivo (ed.), *Shakespeare Left and Right* (New York and London: Routledge, 1991).

Kastan, David Scott, *A Will to Believe: Shakespeare and Religion* (Oxford: Oxford University Press, 2014).

Kiernan, V. G., 'Human Relationships in Shakespeare', in *Shakespeare in a Changing World*, ed. Arnold Kettle (London: Lawrence & Wishart, 1964), pp. 43–83.

King, Peter, 'Ockham's Ethical Theory', in *The Cambridge Companion to Ockham*, ed. Paul Vincent Spade (Cambridge: Cambridge University Press, 1999), pp. 227–44.

Kirk, Russell, *The Conservative Mind: From Burke to Eliot*, 7th edn (1953; Washington, DC: Gateway Editions, 2016).

Knapp, James A., *Image Ethics in Shakespeare and Spencer* (New York and London: Palgrave Macmillan, 2011).

—, 'A Shakespearean Phenomenology of Moral Conviction', in *Shakespeare and Moral Agency*, ed. Michael D. Bristol (New York and London: Continuum, 2012).

Knight, Charles, *Studies of Shakespeare* (London: Routledge, 1868).

Knights, L. C., *Some Shakespearean Themes: And An Approach to Hamlet* (Stanford: Stanford University Press, 1966).

Kohlberg, Lawrence, *The Psychology of Moral Development: The Nature and Validity of Moral Stages (Essays on Moral Development, Vol. 2)* (New York: Harper & Row, 1984).

Korda, Natasha, *Shakespeare's Domestic Economies: Gender and Property in Early Modern England* (Philadelphia: University of Pennsylvania Press, 2002).

Kornstein, Daniel J., 'A Comment on Prof. Halper's Reading of *Measure for Measure*', *Cardazo School of Law*, 13:2 (Fall 2001), 265–9.
Kott, Jan, *Shakespeare Our Contemporary* (1964; W. W. Norton, 1974).
Kottman, Paul A., *Tragic Conditions in Shakespeare: Disinheriting the Globe* (Baltimore: Johns Hopkins University Press, 2009).
Kraye, Jill, 'Moral Philosophy', in *The Cambridge History of Renaissance Philosophy*, ed. Charles B. Schmitt, Quentin Skinner, Eckhard Kessler and Jill Kraye (Cambridge: Cambridge University Press, 1988), pp. 301–86.
—, 'Philologists and Philosophers', in *The Cambridge Companion to Renaissance Humanism*, ed. Jill Kraye (Cambridge: Cambridge University Press, 1996).
Kreeft, Peter, *The Summa of the Summa* (San Francisco: Ignatius Press, 1990).
—, *Ethics: A History of Moral Thought* (Charlotte Hall, MD: Recorded Books, 2003).
Kruger, Daniel J., 'Evolution and Altruism: Combining Psychological Mediators with Naturally Selected Tendencies', *Evolution and Human Behavior*, 24 (2003), 118–25.
Lakoff, George, *Moral Politics: How Liberals and Conservatives Think*, 2nd edn (1996; Chicago: University of Chicago Press, 2002).
Landes, David S., *The Wealth and Poverty of Nations: Why Some Are So Rich and Some So Poor* (New York: W. W. Norton & Co., 1998).
Langley, Eric, 'Plagued by Kindness: Contagious Sympathy in Shakespearean Drama', *Medical Humanities*, 37 (2011), 103–9.
Lawrence, Sean, 'Listening to Lavinia: Emmanuel Levinas's Saying and Said in *Titus Andronicus*', in *Through a Glass Darkly: Suffering, the Sacred, and the Sublime in Literature and Theory*, ed. Holly Faith Nelson, Lynn R. Szabo and Jens Zimmermann (Waterloo, Ontario: Wilfrid Laurier University Press, 2010), pp. 57–69.
Levin, Harry, *The Overreacher: A Study of Christopher Marlowe* (London: Faber & Faber, 1952).

Levinas, Emmanuel, *Ethics and Infinity: Conversations with Philippe Nemo*, trans. Richard A. Cohen (Pittsburgh: Duquesne University Press, 1985).

Lines, David A., 'Humanistic and Scholastic Ethics', in *The Cambridge Companion to Renaissance Philosophy*, ed. James Hankins (Cambridge: Cambridge University Press, 2007), pp. 304–18.

Lyons, Minna, and Sue Aitken, 'Machiavellian Friends? The Role of Machiavellianism in Friendship Formation and Maintenance', Journal of Social, Evolutionary, and Cultural Psychology, 4:3 (2010), 194–202.

Lyotard, Jean-François, *The Postmodern Condition: A Report on Knowledge*, trans. Geoff Bevington and Brian Massumi (Manchester: Manchester University Press, 1984).

MacCulloch, Diarmaid, *All Things Made New: The Reformation and Its Legacy* (New York: Oxford University Press, 2016).

MacFaul, Tom, *Male Friendship in Shakespeare and His Contemporaries* (Cambridge: Cambridge University Press, 2007).

McGinn, Colin, *Shakespeare's Philosophy: Discovering the Meaning Behind the Plays* (New York: HarperCollins, 2006).

McGrath, Alister E., *Reformation Thought: An Introduction*, 4th edn (Chichester: Wiley–Blackwell, 2012).

McIntosh, Donald, 'The Modernity of Machiavelli', *Political Theory*, 12:2 (May 1984), 184–203.

MacKinnon, Malcolm H., 'The Longevity of the Thesis: A Critique of the Critics', in *Weber's Protestant Ethic: Origins, Evidence, Contexts*, ed. Hartmut Lehmann and Guenther Roth (Cambridge: Cambridge University Press, 1993), pp. 211–43.

Marcus, Gary, *The Birth of the Mind: How a Tiny Number of Genes Creates the Complexities of Human Thought* (New York: Basic Books, 2004).

Marlin, Eric S., *Godless Shakespeare* (New York and London: Continuum, 2007).

Martin, Clancy, *Moral Decision Making: How to Approach Everyday Ethics* (Chantilly, VA: The Great Courses, 2014).

Marius, Richard, *Thomas More: A Biography* (1984; Cambridge, MA: Harvard University Press, 1999).

Marshall, Gordon, *In Search of the Spirit of Capitalism: An Essay on Max Weber's Protestant Work Ethic Thesis* (London: Hutchinson, 1982).

Marshall, Peter, 'Choosing Sides and Talking Religion in Shakespeare's England', in *Shakespeare and Early Modern Religion*, ed. David Loewenstein and Michael Witmore (Cambridge: Cambridge University Press, 2015), pp. 40–56.

Martindale, Charles, and Michelle Martindale, *Shakespeare and the Uses of Antiquity: An Introductory Essay* (New York and London: Routledge, 1990).

Marx, Steven, *Shakespeare and the Bible* (Oxford: Oxford University Press, 2000).

Mayerfield, Jamie, *Suffering and Moral Responsibility* (Oxford: Oxford University Press, 1999).

Mayo, Thomas Franklin, *Epicurus in England (1650–1725)* (Dallas: Southwest, 1934).

Meek, Richard, and Erin Sullivan (eds), *The Renaissance of Emotion: Understanding Affect in Shakespeare and His Contemporaries* (Manchester: Manchester University Press, 2015).

Meloni, Maurizio, 'Moralizing Biology: The Appeals and Limits of the New Compassionate View of Nature', *History of the Human Sciences*, 26:3 (2013), 86–106.

Merton, Robert K., 'Science, Technology and Society in Seventeenth Century England', *Osiris*, 4 (1938), 360–632.

Midgley, Graham, '*The Merchant of Venice*: A Reconsideration', *Essays in Criticism*, 10:2 (April 1960), 119–33.

Miller, Christian B., *Character and Moral Psychology* (Oxford: Oxford University Press, 2014).

Mills, Laurens J., *One Soul in Bodies Twain: Friendship in Tudor Literature and Stuart Drama* (Bloomington: Principia Press, 1937).

Mohamed, Feisel G., *In the Anteroom of Divinity: The Reformation of the Angels from Colet to Milton* (Toronto: University of Toronto Press, 2008)

Monfasani, John, 'The Swerve: How the Renaissance Began', *Reviews in History* (July 2012), <http://www.history.ac.uk/reviews/review/1283>.

Montagu, Elizabeth, *An Essay on the Writings and Genius of Shakespeare, Compared with the Greek and French Dramatic Poets: With Some Remarks Upon the Misrepresentations of Mons. de Voltaire* (1769; London: Harding and Wright, 1810).

Montrose, Louis Adrian, '"The Place of a Brother" in *As You Like It*: Social Process and Comic Form', *Shakespeare Quarterly*, 32:1 (Spring 1981), 28–54.

Moore, Andrew, *Shakespeare Between Machiavelli and Hobbes: Dead Body Politics* (Lanham, MD: Lexington Books, 2016).

Morris, Ian, *Why the West Rules – For Now* (London: Profile Books, 2010).

Morrison, George H., *Christ in Shakespeare: Ten Addresses on Moral and Spiritual Elements in Some of the Greater Plays* (London: James Clarke & Co., 1928).

Moulton, Richard G., *The Moral System of Shakespeare: A Popular Illustration of Fiction as the Experimental Side of Philosophy* (New York and London: Macmillan, 1903).

Mousely, Andy, *Re-Humanising Shakespeare* (Edinburgh: Edinburgh University Press, 2007).

Muir, Kenneth, *Shakespeare's Comic Sequence* (Liverpool: Liverpool University Press, 1979).

Muir, W. M., 'Group Selection for Adaptation to Multiple-Hen Cages: Selection Program and Direct Responses', *Poultry Science*, 75 (1996), 447–58.

Muldrew, Craig, 'Interpreting the Market: The Ethics of Credit and Community Relations in Early Modern England', *Social History*, 18:2 (May 1993), 163–83.

Murray, Douglas, *The Strange Death of Europe: Immigration, Identity, Islam* (New York and London: Bloomsbury, 2017).

Nietzsche, Friedrich, *On the Genealogy of Morality*, ed. Keith Ansell Pearson, trans. Carol Diethe (1887; Cambridge: Cambridge University Press, 2006), pp. 154–6.

Novy, Marianne, *Shakespeare and Outsiders* (Oxford: Oxford University Press, 2013).

Nussbaum, Martha, *The Fragility of Goodness: Luck and Ethics in Greek Tragedy and Philosophy* (1986; Cambridge: University of Cambridge, 2001).

Nuttall, A. D., *A New Mimesis: Shakespeare and the Representation of Reality* (1983; New Haven, CT: Yale University Press, 2007).
—, *Shakespeare: The Thinker* (New Haven, CT: Yale University Press, 2007).
Overton, Mark, *The Agricultural Revolution in England: The Transformation of the Agrarian Revolution 1500–1850* (Cambridge: Cambridge University Press, 2010).
Palmer, Ada, 'Reading Lucretius in the Renaissance', *Journal of the History of Ideas*, 73:3 (July 2012), 395–416.
—, *Reading Lucretius in the Renaissance* (Cambridge, MA: Harvard University Press, 2014).
Parker, Patricia, *Shakespeare from the Margins: Language, Culture, Context* (Chicago: Chicago University Press, 1996).
Parsons, Talcott, 'H. M. Robertson on Max Weber and His School', *Journal of Political Economy*, 43:5 (October 1935), 688–96.
Partee, Charles, *The Theology of John Calvin* (Louisville, KY: Westminster John Knox Press, 2008).
Parvini, Neema, *Shakespeare and Contemporary Theory: New Historicism and Cultural Materialism* (New York and London: Bloomsbury, 2012).
—, *Shakespeare's History Plays: Rethinking Historicism* (Edinburgh: Edinburgh University Press, 2012).
—, 'The Scholars and the Critics: Shakespeare Studies and Theory in the 2010s', *Shakespeare*, 10:2 (2014), pp. 212–23.
—, *Shakespeare and Cognition: Thinking Fast and Slow Through Character* (New York and London: Palgrave, 2015).
—, 'Cultural Materialism', in *The Edinburgh Companion to Critical Theory*, ed. Stuart Sim (Edinburgh: Edinburgh University Press, 2016), pp. 363–82.
—, 'What Did Shakespeare Understand About the Human Mind?', *The View of Life* (*The Evolution Institute*) (April 2016), <https://evolution-institute.org/article/what-did-shakespeare-understand-about-the-human-mind/>.
—, *Shakespeare and New Historicist Theory* (New York and London: Bloomsbury Arden Shakespeare, 2017).
Pascucci, Margarita, *Philosophical Readings of Shakespeare: 'Thou Art the Thing Itself'* (New York and London: Palgrave Macmillan, 2013).

Patterson, Mary Hampson, *Domesticating the Reformation: Protestant Best Sellers, Private Devotion and the Revolution of English Piety* (Madison, NJ: Fairleigh Dickinson University Press, 2007).
Peltonen, Markku, *Classical Humanism and Republicanism in English Political Thought, 1570–1640* (Cambridge: Cambridge University Press, 1995).
Pinker, Steven, *The Blank Slate: The Modern Denial of Human Behaviour* (New York and London: Penguin, 2002).
—, *The Better Angels of Our Nature: Why Violence Has Declined* (New York: Viking, 2011).
—, 'The False Allure of Group Selection', *Edge* (6 June 2012), <https://www.edge.org/conversation/steven_pinker-the-false-allure-of-group-selection>.
Pirillo, David, 'Philosophy', in *The Cambridge Companion to the Italian Renaissance*, ed. Michael Wyatt (Cambridge: Cambridge University Press, 2014), pp. 260–75.
Pogue, Kate Emery, *Shakespeare's Friends* (Westport, CT, and London: Praeger, 2006).
Pope, Stephen J., 'Overview of the Ethics of Thomas Aquinas', in *The Ethics of Aquinas*, ed. Stephen J. Pope (Washington, DC: Georgetown University Press, 2002), pp. 30–53.
Popkin, Richard H., 'Introduction', in *The Philosophy of the 16th and 17th Centuries*, ed. Richard H. Popkin (London: Collier-Macmillan, 1966), pp. 1–22.
—, *The History of Scepticism from Erasmus to Spinoza* (Berkeley: University of California Press, 1979), pp. 18–41.
Price, Thomas, *The Wisdom and Genius of Shakespeare: Comprising Moral Philosophy – Delineations of Character– Paintings of Nature and the Passions – Seven Hundred Aphorisms – and Miscellaneous Pieces* (Philadelphia: E. L. Carey & A. Hart, 1839).
Powell, Enoch, 'Politics in Shakespeare', in *Shakespeare: The Comprehensive Soul* (London: British Broadcasting Corporation, 1965), pp. 23–38.
Pritchard, Duncan, 'Doubt Undogmatized: Pyrrhonian Scepticism, Epistemological Externalism and the "Metaepistemological" Challenge', *Principia*, 4:2 (2010), 187–214.

Prozorov, Sergei, *The Biopolitics of Stalinism: Ideology and Life in Soviet Socialism* (Edinburgh: Edinburgh University Press, 2016).

Raab, Felix, *The English Face of Machiavelli: A Changing Interpretation, 1500–1700* (London: Routledge & Kegan Paul, 1964).

Rahe, Paul, 'In the Shadow of Lucretius: The Epicurean Foundations of Machiavelli's Political Thought', *History of Political Thought*, 28:1 (2007), 30–55.

Raspa, Anthony, *Shakespeare the Renaissance Humanist: Moral Philosophy and His Plays* (New York and London: Palgrave Macmillan, 2016).

Redmond, Michael J., *Shakespeare, Politics, and Italy: Intertextuality on the Jacobean Stage* (New York and London, Routledge, 2009).

Reinhardt, Tobias, 'Introduction', in Seneca, *Dialogues and Essays*, trans. John Davie (Oxford: Oxford University Press, 2007), pp. vii–xxvii.

Robertson, H. M., *Aspects of the Rise of Economic Individualism: A Criticism of Max Weber and His School* (1933; New York: Kelly & Millan, 1959).

Robertson, John, 'Hugh Trevor-Roper, Intellectual History and "The Religious Origins of the Enlightenment"', *The English Historical Review*, 124:511 (December 2009), 1389–421.

Roecklein, Robert J., *Machiavelli and Epicureanism: An Investigation into the Origins of Early Modern Political Thought* (Lanham, MD: Lexington Books, 2012).

Rose, David C., *The Moral Foundation of Economic Behaviour* (Oxford: Oxford University Press, 2011), pp. 19, 20.

Rossiter, A. P., *Angels With Horns: Fifteen Lectures on Shakespeare* (1961; New York: Longman, 1989).

Rossiter, Clinton, *Conservativism in America: The Thankless Persuasion*, 2nd edn (1955; New York: Vintage Books, 1962).

Rossiter, William T., *Wyatt Abroad: Tudor Diplomacy and the Translation of Power* (Cambridge: D. S. Brewer, 2014).

Rowe, John, *Shakespeare and Machiavelli* (Cambridge: D. S. Brewer, 2002).

Rozin, Paul, and April E. Fallon, 'A Perspective on Disgust', *Psychological Review*, 94:1 (1987), 23–41.

Rupp, E. G., 'Luther and the German Reformation to 1529', in *The New Cambridge Modern History, Vol. 2: The Reformation*, ed. G. R. Elton (Cambridge: Cambridge University Press, 1958), pp. 70–95.

Russell, Bertrand, *History of Western Philosophy* (1946; New York and London: Routledge, 2004).

Saarinen, Risto, *Weakness of Will in Renaissance and Reformation Thought* (Oxford: Oxford University Press, 2011).

Schaeffer, Jean-Marie, *Why Fiction?*, trans. Dorrit Cohn (1999; Lincoln: University of Nebraska Press, 2010).

Schmitt, Charles B., *John Case and Aristotelianism in Renaissance England* (Montreal: McGill-Queen's University Press, 1983).

—, 'The Rediscovery of Ancient Skepticism in Modern Times', in *The Skeptical Tradition*, ed. Myles Burnyeat (Berkeley: University of California Press, 1983), pp. 225–51.

Schulman, Alex, *Rethinking Shakespeare's Political Philosophy: From Lear to Leviathan* (Edinburgh: Edinburgh University Press, 2014).

Scruton, Roger, *Fools, Frauds and Firebrands: Thinkers of the New Left* (New York and London: Bloomsbury, 2015).

Shannon, Laurie, *Sovereign Amity: Figures of Friendship in Shakespearean Contexts* (Chicago: University of Chicago Press, 2002).

Sharp, Frank Chapman, *Shakespeare's Portrayal of the Moral Life* (New York: Charles Scribner's Sons, 1902).

Sherman, Gary D., and Jonathan Haidt, 'Cuteness and Disgust: The Humanizing and Dehumanizing Effects of Emotion', *Emotion Review*, 3:3 (2011), pp. 1–7.

Sheskin, Mark, Paul Bloom and Karen Wynn, 'Anti-Equality: Social Comparison in Young Children', *Cognition*, 130:2 (February 2014), 152–6.

Shweder, Richard A., Nancy C. Much, Manamohan Mahapatra and Lawrence Park, 'The "Big Three" of Morality (Autonomy, Community, Divinity) and the "Big Three" Explanations of Suffering', in *Morality and Culture*, ed. Jerome Kagan and Sharon Lamb (Chicago: University of Chicago Press, 1997), pp. 119–69.

Sidgwick, Henry, *Outlines of the History of Ethics for English Readers* (1886; Cambridge: Cambridge University Press, 2011).

Simpson, Catherine, 'Shakespeare's World in 100 Objects: Number 74, a Knife and Fork Set', *Finding Shakespeare* (18 April 2003), <http://findingshakespeare.co.uk/shakespeares-world-in-100-objects-number-74-a-knife-fork-set>.

Smith, Craig A., and Richard S. Lazarus, 'Emotion and Adaptation', in *Handbook of Personality: Theory and Research*, ed. L. A. Pervin (New York: Guildford Press, 1990), pp. 609–37.

Smith, Neil G., 'Was Shakespeare a Theologian?', *Theology Today*, 21:4 (January 1965), 417–32.

Soellner, Rolf, 'The Four Primary Passions: A Renaissance Theory Reflected in the Works of Shakespeare', *Studies in Philology*, 5:4 (October 1958), 549–67.

Sohmer, Steve, *Shakespeare's Mystery Play: The Opening of the Globe Theatre 1599* (Manchester: Manchester University Press, 1999).

Sombart, Werner, *The Jews and Modern Capitalism*, trans. M. Epstein (1911; New York: E. P. Dutton, 1913).

Sowell, Thomas, *The Vision of the Anointed: Self-Congratulation as Social Policy* (New York: Basic Books, 1995).

—, *Migrations and Cultures: A World View* (New York: Basic Books, 1996).

—, *The Quest for Cosmic Justice* (New York: Simon & Schuster, 1999).

—, *A Conflict of Visions: Ideological Origins of Political Struggles*, rev. edn (1987; New York: Basic Books, 2007).

Spencer, T. J. B., 'The Sophistry of Shakespeare', *English Studies Today: Fourth Series*, ed. Ilva Cellini and Giorgio Melchiori (Rome: Edizioni di Storia e Letteratura, 1966), pp. 169–85.

Spurgeon, Caroline, *Shakespeare's Imagery and What It Tells Us* (1935; Cambridge: Cambridge University Press, 1979).

Starmans, Christina, Mark Sheskin and Paul Bloom, 'Why People Prefer Unequal Societies', *Nature Human Behaviour*, 1:82 (April 2017), 1–8.

Stewart, Stanley, *Shakespeare and Philosophy* (New York and London: Routledge, 2010).

Strier, Richard, 'Faithful Servants: Shakespeare's Praise of Disobedience', in *The Historical Renaissance: New Essays on Tudor and Stuart Literature and Culture*, ed. Heather Dubrow and Richard Strier (Chicago: University of Chicago Press), pp. 104–33.

Tadmor, Naomi, *The Social Universe of the English Bible: Scripture, Society, and Culture in Early Modern England* (Cambridge: Cambridge University Press, 2010).

Tawney, R. H., 'The Damnable Sin of Usury', in Thomas Wilson, *A Discourse Upon Usury by Way of Dialogue and Orations: For the Better Variety and More Delight of All Those That Shall Read This Treatise 1572*, ed. R. H. Tawney (London: G. Bell & Sons, 1925), pp. 106–21.

—, *Religion and the Rise of Capitalism: A Historical Study* (1926; New Brunswick, NJ: Transaction, 1998).

Thorne, William B., '"Things Newborn": A Study of the Rebirth Motif in *The Winter's Tale*', *Humanities Association Review*, 19:1 (1968), 34–43.

Tillyard, E. M. W., *Shakespeare's History Plays* (London: Chatto & Windus, 1944).

—, *The Elizabethan World Picture* (1942; London: Vintage, 1959).

—, '"Loneliness" in *The Merchant of Venice*', *Essays in Criticism*, 11:4 (October 1961), 487–8.

Tilmouth, Christopher, *Passion's Triumph of Reason: A History of the Moral Imagination from Spencer to Rochester* (Oxford: Oxford University Press, 2007).

Tooby, John, and Leda Cosmides, 'Letter to the Editor of *The New York Review of Books* on Stephen Jay Gould's "Darwinian Fundamentalism" (12 June 1997) and "Evolution: The Pleasures of Pluralism"' (26 June 1997), <http://cogweb.ucla.edu/Debate/CEP_Gould.html>.

Tosh, Will, *Male Friendship and Testimonies of Love in Shakespeare's England* (New York and London: Palgrave Macmillan, 2016).

Trevor-Roper, Hugh, 'Review of *Intellectual Origins of the English Revolution* by Christopher Hill', *Theory and History*, 5:1 (1966), 61–82.

—, *Religion, the Reformation and Social Change, and Other Essays* (London: Macmillan, 1967).

Trivers, Robert L., 'The Evolution of Reciprocal Altruism', *The Quarterly Review of Biology*, 46:1 (March 1971), 35–57.

Troeltsch, Ernst, *Protestantism and Progress: A Historical Study of the Relation of Protestantism to the Modern World*, trans. William Montgomery (London: Williams & Norgate, 1912).

Tucker, Shawn R., *The Virtues and Vices in the Arts: A Sourcebook* (Eugene, OR: Cascade Books, 2015).

Turner, Darwin T., '*King Lear* Re-examined', *College Language Association Journal*, 3 (1959), 27–39.

Tyacke, Nicholas, *Aspects of English Protestantism, c. 1530–1700* (Manchester: Manchester University Press, 2001).

Uberweg, Friedrich, *History of Philosophy: From Thales to the Present Time, Vol. 1: History of the Ancient and Medieval Philosophy*, trans. Geo. S. Morris (New York: Charles Scribner's Sons, 1890).

Vespa, Matt, 'Sanders Slams UC Berkeley's Anti-Free Speech Zealots: "It's a Sign of Intellectual Weakness"', *Townhall* (23 April 2017), <https://townhall.com/tipsheet/mattvespa/2017/04/23/sanders-slams-uc-berkeleys-antifree-speech-zealots-its-a-sign-of-intellectual-weakness-n2317054>.

Vyvyan, John, *The Shakespearean Ethic* (1959; London: Shepherd-Walwyn, 2011).

Walsh, Anthony, *Science Wars: Politics, Gender, and Race* (New Brunswick, NJ: Transaction Publishers, 2013).

Weber, Max, *The Protestant Ethic and the Spirit of Capitalism*, trans. Talcott Parsons (1930; Kettering, OH: Angelico Press, 2014).

Weil, Judith, *Service and Dependency in Shakespeare's Plays* (Cambridge: Cambridge University Press, 2005).

Wells, Robin Headlam, *Shakespeare's Humanism* (Cambridge: Cambridge University Press, 2005).

—, *Shakespeare's Politics: A Contextual Introduction*, 2nd edn (1986; New York and London: Continuum, 2009).

White, Peter, 'The Rise of Arminianism Reconsidered', *Past and Present*, 101 (November 1983), 34–54.

White, R. S., '*Titus Andronicus* and *Romeo and Juliet*', in *Shakespeare: A Bibliographical Guide*, ed. Stanley Wells (Oxford: Oxford University Press, 1990), pp. 181–200.

White, R. S., Mark Houlahan and Katrina O'Loughlin (eds), *Shakespeare and Emotions: Inheritances, Enactments, Legacies* (New York and London: Palgrave Macmillan, 2015).
Wilson, David Sloan, *Darwin's Cathedral: Evolution, Religion, and the Nature of Society* (Chicago: University of Chicago Press, 2002).
—, 'Richard Dawkins, Edward O. Wilson, and the Consensus of the Many', *This View of Life* (1 January 2015), <https://evolution-institute.org/article/richard-dawkins-edward-o-wilson-and-the-consensus-of-the-many/>.
Wilson, Edward O., *Sociobiology: The New Synthesis* (1975; Cambridge, MA: Harvard University Press, 2000).
—, *On Human Nature*, rev. edn (1978; Cambridge, MA: Harvard University Press, 2004).
Wood, Rega, 'Ockham's Repudiation of Pelagianism', in *The Cambridge Companion to Ockham*, ed. Paul Vincent Spade (Cambridge: Cambridge University Press, 1999), pp. 350–74.
Woodbridge, Linda, *English Revenge Drama: Money, Resistance, Equality* (Cambridge: Cambridge University Press, 2010).
Woodruff, Paul, 'The Pyrrhonian Modes', in *The Cambridge Companion to Ancient Scepticism*, ed. Richard Bett (Cambridge: Cambridge University Press, 2010), pp. 208–31.
Wordsworth, Charles, *On Shakespeare's Knowledge and Use of the Bible* (London: Smith, Elder & Co., 1864).
Wright, Robert, *The Moral Animal: Why We Are the Way We Are* (London: Abacus, 1994).
Zalloua, Zahi Anbra, *Montaigne and the Ethics of Skepticism* (Charlottesville, VA: Rookwood Press, 2005).
Zamir, Tzachi, *Double Vision: Moral Philosophy and Shakespearean Drama* (Princeton: Princeton University Press, 2007).

Other Media

Dylan, Bob, 'It's Alright Ma (I'm Only Bleeding), on *Bringing It All Back Home* (New York: Columbia Records, 1965).
Notorious B.I.G., The, 'Mo' Money, Mo' Problems', on *Life After Death* (New York: Bad Boy Records, 1997).

Rolling Stones, The, 'I'm Free', on *Out of Our Heads* (London: Decca, 1965).
Smith, Patti, 'Gloria', on *Horses* (New York: Arista, 1975).
Zeffirelli, Franco (dir.), *Jesus of Nazareth* (UK and Italy: ITC Films, 1977).

INDEX

Acemoglu, Daron, 258, 261
Adamson, Peter, 84, 130
Agrippa, 104–5
Alighieri, Dante, 114, 136, 187
Allen, Don Cameron, 31, 120–2, 137
Althusser, Louis, 4, 46, 67
altruism, 10, 13, 31, 56, 58, 68, 214, 238, 240–1, 247–8, 258, 260, 293–4, 299
Ames, Fisher, 15, 32
angelology, 109, 134, 149, 173, 194–5, 293
Antifa, 48
Aquinas, Thomas
   Summa Theologica, 76, 80–1, 83–4, 90–1, 128–9, 174, 218, 223, 239, 245, 260, 274, 277, 279, 281
   Thomism, 7, 72, 76, 84–5, 88, 97, 99, 114, 127, 130, 139, 163, 170, 225, 238, 276, 284
   vices, 21, 36, 76, 80–4, 90–1, 108, 114–15, 119, 124, 129, 156, 186, 238
      avarice, 36, 124, 164, 238
      covetousness, 81, 155
      cruelty, 53, 83, 218, 273, 281, 283–4, 287, 290–1, 297–8, 302
      curiosity, 83, 109, 190, 256
      despair, 81, 83, 89, 197, 202, 216, 221, 300
      gluttony, 81–2, 119–20
      greed, 36–7, 82, 113, 160
      intemperance, 83
      lust, 36, 81–2, 120–1, 257
      pride, 9, 36, 82, 84, 108, 155, 266
      prodigality, 238
      servility, 210, 212, 218, 220, 297
      sloth, 81–2, 114, 156
      vainglory, 81–2, 150
      vanity, 108, 133
      wrath, 82, 286
   virtues, 7, 10–12, 16, 21, 30, 51, 53–4, 74, 76–8, 80–3, 90–1, 93, 95–100, 107–8, 111, 113–15, 119, 122, 127–30, 139, 144, 157, 170, 174, 182, 184, 186, 198, 213, 215, 218, 225, 230, 238–40, 245, 252, 256, 260, 269, 284, 300, 303–4
      abstinence, 21, 81–2, 115
      charity, 81, 83, 161, 174, 218, 225, 238–42, 245, 253, 280, 287, 296–7, 301–3
      chastity, 54, 81–2, 195
      diligence, 82, 119
      fortitude, 53, 70, 80–1
      hope, 17, 36, 39, 57, 78, 80–3, 89, 106, 151, 181, 183, 191, 215, 223, 286–7, 291, 300
      humility, 82, 108
      justice, 10, 16, 40, 48, 57–8, 66, 68, 78, 80–1, 89, 154, 196–7, 218–19, 238, 246, 249, 251–5, 259–60, 275, 284–5, 287, 295–9, 302
      kindness, 10, 53, 64, 82, 225, 273, 277
      mercy, 81, 255, 259, 270, 284, 286–90, 297, 299–300, 302
      prudence, 78, 80–1, 83
      temperance, 78, 80–1, 83
      wisdom, 36–7, 77, 81, 83, 90, 92, 113, 115, 121, 151, 183, 199, 227, 256, 275

Aragon, Catherine of, 85, 88
Aristotle
   eudaimonia, 77, 90, 111
   habits (virtues), 12, 16, 23, 72, 76–7, 91, 188, 229
   ideal friendship, 23, 113, 224–6, 228–32, 234–5, 237–44, 280, 287, 297, 301–2
   Nicomachean Ethics, 12, 30, 76, 119, 128–30, 137, 230, 243
Arminianism, 147, 172
Arnhart, Larry, 32, 35, 65, 294
Augustine of Hippo, 36, 66, 74, 80, 96, 98, 132, 144–5, 148, 158, 218
Authority, Moral Foundation of, 7, 9–10, 18, 28, 39, 48, 53–4, 56, 70, 80, 85, 109, 125, 153, 159, 170, 189, 196, 201–5, 207–15, 217–23, 225, 229, 237, 252, 280–1, 285, 287, 289, 291, 296–8, 300–3
Avicenna, 39, 81

Bacon, Francis, 72, 103, 162
Barkan, Leonard, 73, 128
Barnes, Barnable, 125, 133, 142
Baumeister, Roy F., 227–8, 243
Bayne, Ronald, 172–4
Beauregard, David N., 76, 84, 89, 97, 128, 130, 197–8, 238, 245
Becon, Thomas, 140, 146, 154–7, 159, 171, 174
behaviourism, 11
Bell, Mellicent, 106–7, 134, 177
Belliotti, Raymond Angelo, 177, 260
Bentham, Jeremy, 15
Berger Jr., Harry, 22, 33
Berlin, Isaiah, 104, 134, 172
Bett, Richard, 133–4
Bevington, David, 67, 129, 132, 174
bias (cognitive), 14, 31–2, 46, 50, 192, 203, 236
Bible, The, 76, 80, 128, 142–3, 146, 148–9, 151, 153, 155, 158, 172, 174, 184, 199, 278
biblical, 128, 148–9, 174, 270, 277
Birch, W. J., 121, 137, 186–8, 197, 199, 274, 279
blindness (moral), 3, 11, 46, 61–2, 83, 192, 202, 219, 221, 266, 271, 301
Bloom, Harold, 232–4, 244, 247, 260
bonds (between individuals), 113, 176, 217, 220, 229, 236–7, 241

Borgia, Roderic (Pope Alexander VI), 142
Botero, Giovanni, 140, 163, 165–6, 169, 176
Bouwsma, William, 132, 173
Bowden, Henry Sebastian, 184–6, 188, 192, 195, 197–9
Bradley, A. C., 107, 134, 183, 284
Bradshaw, Graham, 106–7, 134
Braudel, Fernand, 55, 69, 161, 176
Bray, Alan, 232, 243–4
Bristol, Michael D., 22, 26–7, 33–4, 193, 197, 199, 294
Burke, Edmund, 36–7, 65
Buss, David M., 56
Buss, Leo, 56

Cadoux, Arthur Temple, 192, 197–8, 200, 215, 223, 225, 231–2, 242, 244
Cajetan, (Cardinal) Thomas de Vio, 75, 85–8, 91, 130
Calvin, John
   callings, 156–7, 159, 166, 169, 215–17, 245
   Calvinism, 7, 36, 66, 139–40, 145–56, 158–62, 166–7, 169–70, 173–4, 184, 215, 217, 252, 262, 272–9, 281, 301
   Geneva (under Calvin), 140, 146, 148, 155, 172, 174, 278
   Institutes of the Christian Religion, 139, 145, 154, 156, 173–4, 278, 281
   (opposition to) Pseudo-Dionysus the Areopagite, 149
   predestination, 145, 152–4, 158–9, 184, 296
   Protestant Work Ethic, 174–5, 177
   providence, 113–14, 126, 184, 186, 192, 198, 279, 296
   sola fide, 148–9, 152, 155, 158–9
   sola gratia, 148–9, 152, 158
   sola scriptura, 148, 155, 158–9
   Total Depravity, 271, 274, 276
Camden, William, 162
Campbell, Lily B., 74, 89, 128
capitalism, 7, 45, 66, 73, 76, 127–8, 139–41, 143–5, 147, 149, 151, 153, 155, 157, 159–63, 165–7, 169–71, 173–7, 201, 205, 222
Capréolus, John, 75, 85–6, 88, 91
Care, Moral Foundation of, 7, 10–11, 18–19, 26, 28, 48, 52–3, 60, 90,

94, 152–3, 166, 170, 202, 280–1, 283, 285, 287, 289–91, 293, 296–7, 303
Carneades, 75, 101–2, 110
Carroll, Joseph, 62–4, 67, 70
Case, John, 87–8, 91, 131, 250
Catholicism, 75, 83, 85–6, 102, 130, 141, 144, 147–9, 158, 160, 172, 174, 184, 186, 192, 195, 197–8, 263, 274, 276, 296
causation, 39, 57
Cave, Terence, 24, 33, 35, 60, 65–6
Chambers, E. K., 171, 177
character, 8, 16–18, 20–3, 25, 28, 31, 33, 51, 77, 79, 124, 159, 161, 182, 184, 192, 195, 210, 212–13, 217, 232, 239, 250, 257, 268–9, 299, 303
Chesterton, G. K., 80, 128
Christianity, 87, 98, 115, 123, 144–5, 153, 271
Cicero, Marcus Tullius, 36, 74–6, 79, 85, 89, 91–5, 100–2, 114, 117, 120, 127–8, 131, 133, 136, 230, 241–3, 254
cognition, 8, 22, 24, 31–3, 67, 178, 260
Coleridge, Samuel Taylor, 182, 217–21, 223
consequentialism, 124, 166
conservativism, 6, 9, 46–7, 62, 65, 147–8, 172, 203, 303
Copleston, F. C., 79–80, 128, 131
Cosmides, Leda, 56, 69
Coulter, Anne, 47
Cox, John D., 4, 22, 29, 33, 106–7, 134–5, 172, 199
Cranmer, Thomas, 146, 172
cultural scripts, 20, 28, 42, 63, 170
cuteness, 284, 293

Danby, John F., 257, 261, 301, 304
d'Aragona, Luigi, 142
Darwin, Charles, 13, 30–2, 51–4, 57–8, 60–1, 64–5, 68–70, 187, 278, 294
de Waal, Frans, 58, 69
degradation (moral), 10, 18–19, 26, 262–3, 267–8, 270–2, 274, 276–7, 280–1, 285, 288–91, 296–8, 302–3
demonology, 95, 149, 173
Dennett, Daniel, 12, 30–1, 56–8, 60, 69
deontology, 15, 77
Descartes, René, 31, 72, 103, 105, 134

Deshpande, M. G., 232, 244
Diamond, Jared, 55, 68–9
Dickens, A. G., 174
DiLorenzo, Thomas, 67
Diogenes Laertius, 75, 102, 107, 112, 116, 120, 135–6
Dionysus, 149
disincentives, 37, 42, 50
disloyalty, 229
disobedience, 53, 81, 83, 187, 212–13, 223, 297
disputation, 80, 88, 145, 171
Dollimore, Jonathan, 203, 222
Dowden, Edward, 188, 199
Durkheim, Émile, 13, 31, 62
Dylan, Bob, 112, 136

egalitarianism, 246, 251–3, 255–6, 258–9
Eldredge, Niles, 56
Elizabeth I, Queen of England, 146–7, 172, 182
Elton, G. R., 129, 161, 171, 176
empiricism, 35, 45–6, 48, 50, 58–60, 64–5, 243
Enlightenment, 61, 160, 175
Enterline, Lynn, 24, 32–3
envy, 81–2
Epicurus, 7, 36, 71, 75–6, 111–27, 132, 136–9, 153, 157, 170
equality, 40, 231, 239, 241–2, 246–8, 250, 252, 256, 259–60
Erasmus, Desiderius, 86, 130, 133, 160
ethos, 12
Evett, David, 207–9, 222–3
evolution, 6–8, 10, 13, 30–1, 35, 37, 39–41, 43, 45–7, 49–51, 53–65, 67–70, 138, 185, 192, 216, 224, 238, 240, 243, 247–8, 258–61, 277, 285, 291, 293

Fairness, Moral Foundation of, 7, 10–11, 18, 28, 40, 48, 56, 58, 153, 170, 202, 225, 238, 242, 246–51, 253, 255, 257–9, 261, 280–1, 285, 291, 296–7, 303
Farmer, Richard, 73, 128
fatalism, 152
fealty, 201
fellow feeling, 17, 58, 183, 214, 229, 233, 239–41, 280, 290, 297
Fergusson, Francis, 271, 278
feudalism, 205

Floyd-Wilson, Mary, 121, 137
folly, 83, 90, 212, 214
Ford, Harold, 173, 189–92, 196, 198, 200, 225
forgiveness, 83, 148, 153, 226, 253, 255, 298
fornication, 151, 155
fortune, 51, 97–8, 111, 123, 235
Foucault, Michel, 15, 44, 46, 66–7
Foxe, John, 146, 177
Frankl, Viktor E., 216, 223
freedom, 66, 73, 93, 97, 128, 219, 244, 303
Friedman, Milton, 36, 42, 66, 73, 128
Frye, Roland Mushat, 196–8, 200, 271, 278
Fukuyama, Francis, 55, 68
Fuller, Thomas, 86, 98, 132

Galbraith, John Kenneth, 38, 45
Galen, 74, 89
game simulations, 24–5, 27–8, 165, 168, 188, 253
Geertz, Clifford, 15
gender, 29, 66, 68, 224, 227, 235, 243, 256
genes, 13, 30, 59, 64
Genesis, 155
Gilman, Arthur, 183, 199
Godwin, William, 38
Goodhart, David, 29
Gould, Stephen Jay, 56–8, 69
Gove, Michael, 5–6, 30
Grady, Hugh, 107, 134, 138
Gray, Patrick, 4, 22, 29, 33, 172, 199, 302, 304
Great Schism, the, 141
Greenblatt, Stephen, 118–20, 122–3, 126, 135, 137, 238, 244, 296, 303
Greene, Joshua, 61–2, 64, 70
Greene, Robert, 120–2, 137, 281, 292
Greenfeld, Liah, 176
Griffith, Elizabeth, 182–3, 186, 192, 196, 198–9
Grigson, Caroline, 283, 292
group selection, 9–10, 13, 46, 48, 54, 56–60, 63–4, 70, 216–17, 224, 226–8, 235–7, 240–2, 247, 264, 285, 291, 300–1, 303
groupishness, 13, 40, 48, 53, 55–6, 60–1, 64, 110, 216, 224, 236, 241, 246

Guicciardini, Francesco, 125
guilt, 9, 29, 50, 94, 129, 151, 219, 265–6, 269, 279

Hagberg, Garry L., 22, 33
Haidt, Jonathan
  elephant (metaphor), 14, 16, 46, 79, 211
  Moral Foundation Theory (MFT), 7, 10–11, 16–19, 26–8, 30, 40, 48, 53–4, 56, 60–4, 70, 102–3, 105, 118, 127, 153, 159, 168, 170, 178, 201–2, 209–10, 212, 215, 217, 220–1, 225–6, 238, 242, 247, 259, 261–5, 267, 271, 274, 276–7, 285, 291, 296–7, 301, 303
  Moral Foundations, 7–8, 18, 32, 50, 90, 138, 258
  rider (metaphor), 14, 16, 46, 79, 211, 223
  telos, 47–8, 68
  The Righteous Mind, 9, 16, 30–1, 41, 56, 61–2, 64, 66, 69, 177, 202, 216, 221–3, 226, 243, 245, 260, 264, 278, 293, 296, 303–4
  WEIRD, 9–10, 23, 40, 48, 54, 61, 64, 208, 219, 222, 301
Hall, Joseph, 30, 67, 75, 98–100, 132–3, 200
Hamilton, Alexander, 36, 40
Hamilton, W. D., 51, 68
Harbage, Alfred, 192–5, 197–8, 200, 237, 244, 274, 279
Harris, Jonathan Gil, 29, 263, 278
Harris, Sam, 60–2, 64, 70
Hartley, L. P., 251, 260
Hauser, Marc, 70
Hay, Denys, 141, 144, 171
Hayek, F. A., 36
Hazlitt, William, 16–17, 32, 182–3, 186, 197–9, 229, 274, 278, 286, 294
hedonism, 111–12, 120, 126, 166
Henry VIII, King of England, 85, 87–8, 157
Herman, Arthur, 35, 39, 60, 65–6
heuristics, 14, 31, 192
hierarchy, 38, 54, 149, 156, 164, 207, 210, 212, 219, 224, 227, 230, 300
Highet, Gilbert, 73, 127
Hill, Christopher, 130, 160–1, 175, 223

Index

Hippocrates, 74, 89
historicism, 4, 18, 29, 34, 106, 134, 189, 192, 196, 202–3, 207, 221, 232, 294
Hitchens, Christopher, 60
Hobbes, Thomas, 36, 55, 69, 72, 138, 204, 257–9, 261, 281, 285–6, 289, 291, 293, 301
Holmes, Oliver Wendall, 36
homosexuality, 232, 242
Hooker, Richard, 89, 109, 135, 147, 262, 271–8
humanism, 86, 122, 132–4, 139, 173, 176, 197–8
Hume, David, 15, 32
Hus, Jus, 142

incentives, 37, 42–3, 50, 168, 286
inequality, 232, 237
Iran, 43–4, 46, 66, 282, 292
Iraq, 46
Irwin, Terence, 72, 127

James, Scott M., 11, 30
James, William, 5, 29
Jesus, 8, 65, 143, 156, 197
John, Eileen, 23, 33
Johnson, Boris, 5
Julius Caesar, 5, 97, 195, 225

Kahneman, Daniel, 14, 31, 67
Kant, Immanuel, 15, 32
Kastan, David Scott, 174
Khan, Coppélia, 290, 294
Khomeini, Ayotollah Ruhollah, 66
Kirk, Russell, 36–7, 65
Knapp, James A., 18–20, 22, 32, 79, 198, 294
Kohlberg, Laurence, 15, 31
Korda, Natasha, 29
Kott, Jan, 187, 197, 199
Kraye, Jill, 120, 128, 133, 135–7
Kreeft, Peter, 6, 30, 129
Kruger, Daniel J., 31

Lakoff, George, 299, 303
Landes, David S., 55, 68, 160, 175
Langely, Eric, 263, 277
Lazarus, Richard, 14, 31
Lenin, Vladimir, 39, 67
Lévinas, Emmanuel, 287, 293
Lewontin, Richard, 56

liberalism, 6, 9, 11, 54, 61–2, 64, 104, 167, 208, 219, 264, 303
liberality, 82, 238
Liberty, Moral Foundation of, 7, 9–11, 18, 28, 48, 70, 118, 134, 153, 170, 202, 218–21, 295–7, 299, 301, 303
Locke, John, 36, 38, 65, 72
Loyalty, Moral Foundation of, 7, 10, 16, 18, 28, 41, 48, 54, 56, 70, 122, 153, 170, 185, 208–9, 224–9, 231, 233–7, 239, 241–3, 245, 280–1, 285, 287, 291, 296–7, 301–3
Lucretius, 75, 111, 113, 117–23, 126–7, 136–8
Luther, Martin, 72, 85–6, 102, 140, 143, 145–6, 158, 160, 171, 176
Lyotard, Jean-Francois, 46, 67
Lysenko, Trofim, 46, 67

MacCulloch, Diarmaid, 139, 147, 171–3
MacFaul, Tom, 231, 243–4
McGinn, Colin, 26–7, 34
McGrath, Alister, 150, 152, 156, 171, 173–4
Machiavelli, Niccolò, 36, 75, 102, 111, 123–6, 134, 138, 142, 162, 166–7, 169–70, 176–7, 248, 257, 259–61, 281, 286
Machiavellianism, 5, 25, 125, 138, 162, 166, 169, 227, 243
Malthus, Thomas, 36
Marcus, Gary, 11, 30
Marlowe, Christopher, *Doctor Faustus*, 82, 129, 148, 292
Martin, Clancy, 6, 30
Martindale, Charles, 97, 132
Martindale, Michelle, 97, 132
Marxism, 15, 27, 39, 45–7, 128, 167, 172, 177
Mary I, Queen of England, 121, 137, 146, 148–9, 173
mercantilism, 29, 165, 168–70, 231, 263
Midgley, Graham, 232, 244
Miller, Christian B., 21, 33
misanthropy, 17, 132, 215, 221, 268, 280, 297
money, 15, 112, 136, 142–3, 159, 165–9, 209, 214, 220, 226, 231, 250, 260, 295
Montagu, Elizabeth, 182, 199

Montaigne, Michel de, 72, 75, 101, 103, 106–10, 125, 134–5, 138
Morris, Ian, 55, 68, 129
Mousely, Andy, 107, 135
Muir, Kenneth, 232, 244
Muir, W. M., 59, 70
Murray, Douglas, 29

nationalism, 41, 54, 66, 162, 164, 176, 264
naturalism, 12, 23, 138
Nietzsche, Friedrich, 167, 177
Nifo, Agostino, 114
nihilism, 17, 106, 152, 284
Notorious B.I.G., The, 112, 136
Novy, Marianne, 236, 244
Nussbaum, Martha, 245, 304
Nuttall, A. D., 22, 33, 174, 197, 214, 223, 232–4, 244, 293

Ockham, William of, 102, 144–5, 153, 171
oeconomics, 74

Paine, Thomas, 38
Palmer, Ada, 122, 127, 137
Parsons, Talcott, 159–60, 174–5
patriotism, 10, 66, 122, 203
Pelagianism, 145, 171
Perkins, William, 140, 146, 154–5, 159, 173
pessimism, 17, 39, 132, 167, 239, 300–1
Pinker, Steven, 35, 37, 41, 56, 58, 65, 70, 293
Plato, 15, 35, 39, 65–6, 74, 77, 80, 85, 89, 101, 123, 131, 134, 204, 233
positivism, 4–5, 161
Powell, Enoch, 203, 208, 221
pragmatism, 125–6, 138, 162, 226, 248
progressivism, 57, 256, 301
prostitution, 43, 66, 158
Protestantism, 7, 72, 76, 85–6, 102, 127, 140, 144–6, 148, 157, 159–61, 163, 169, 172–7, 184, 186, 188, 196, 198, 262, 271, 274, 276–7, 296
puritanism, 48, 146, 148–9, 157–60, 166, 170, 172, 174
Pyrrho of Elis, 101–8, 110, 134

Quintilian, 74

Raleigh, Walter, 84, 106, 140, 162, 164–7, 169, 177, 223
Rasmussen, Eric, 129, 293
Raspa, Anthony, 199
rationalism, 15, 31, 35, 37, 39, 48, 60–1, 64, 153, 162
reasoning, 14, 16, 18–20, 31, 39, 46, 61, 79
reciprocal altruism, 10, 13, 31, 59, 68, 105, 201, 210, 214, 220, 238–42, 246, 260, 280
Reformation, 7, 48, 72, 76, 85–6, 102, 127, 131, 139–41, 143–5, 147, 149, 151, 153, 155, 157–61, 163, 165, 167, 169, 171–7, 183, 271, 273, 277, 296
Renaissance, 4, 7, 29, 32, 72, 74–5, 81, 85–7, 94, 99–100, 109, 111, 114–15, 118–20, 122–3, 125–8, 130–4, 136–7, 139, 141, 153, 161, 172, 174, 176, 199, 222–3, 232, 243, 245, 255–6, 281, 294
repentance, 83, 191
Robertson, H. M., 160, 175
Rolling Stones, The, 30
Rousseau, Jean-Jacques, 37–9, 65, 127, 256–7, 301
Rumsfeld, Donald, 46
Rupp, E. G., 171, 176
Russell, Bertrand, 72, 109, 127

sadomasochism, 232
Sanches, Francisco, 75, 103
Sanctity, Moral Foundation of, 7, 10, 18–19, 26, 28, 48, 53–4, 56, 148, 153, 159, 170, 253, 262–5, 267, 269–71, 273–7, 279–81, 291, 296–7, 303
Sanders, Bernie, 47
Scepticism, 7, 17, 75–6, 93, 100–11, 123, 125, 127, 131–5, 139, 153, 170
Schaeffer, Jean-Marie, 24, 33
schism, 71
Scotus, Duns, 84–5, 144–5
Scruton, Roger, 38, 65, 67
Seneca, 36, 74–5, 79, 89, 91, 95–100, 111–13, 118, 120, 127, 131–2, 135–6, 182
service, 13, 18, 51, 88, 94, 142, 152, 158, 164, 181, 183, 201–2, 205, 207–15, 217–20, 225, 229–30, 252, 256, 280, 285, 287, 289, 298–9, 301

Index

Sextus Empiricus, 75, 101–7, 110, 133–4
Shakespeare, William
   All's Well that Ends Well, 90, 93–4, 129, 254, 257
   Anthony and Cleopatra, 174, 199
   As You Like It, 23, 41, 54, 183, 201, 206, 209–11, 214, 216, 220, 224–5, 233–4, 237, 240–2, 249, 260, 290, 299–300
   Cymbeline, 82
   Hamlet, 19, 32, 97, 134–5, 172, 189–91, 194–5, 225–6, 247, 253–4, 259, 262, 269–71, 273, 278–9, 282–3, 300
   Henry IV, Part 1, 25, 111, 157, 159, 168, 228–9
   Henry IV, Part 2, 228–9, 268
   Henry V, 184, 195, 222, 289, 301
   Henry VI, Part 2, 26, 134, 185
   Henry VI, Part 3, 26, 134, 185, 281–2, 287–91
   Henry VIII, 82, 88
   Julius Caesar, 5, 195, 225
   King John, 143
   King Lear, 17, 23, 84, 107, 116, 121, 134, 168, 194, 196, 201, 210–11, 213–15, 217, 219–23, 225, 247, 249, 251, 256–9, 261–2, 266–8, 271, 273, 277–8, 281, 289–91, 294–5, 298–300
   Macbeth, 22–3, 33–4, 121, 134, 168, 185, 190–1, 194, 216–18, 221, 262, 270–3, 277, 282
   Measure for Measure, 21, 23, 26, 34, 43, 109, 158–9, 182–3, 190–2, 195, 247, 252, 254, 259, 298–9
   Midsummer Night's Dream, 23
   Much Ado About Nothing, 225
   Othello, 32, 134, 168, 190, 195, 251, 262, 268–9, 273, 277–8
   Richard II, 24, 88, 203, 205
   Richard III, 17, 190, 194, 212, 218, 247–8, 250–2, 259, 262
   Romeo and Juliet, 86, 292
   The Comedy of Errors, 281
   The Merchant of Venice, 24, 162, 167, 177, 191, 224–5, 231, 234–6, 238, 241–2, 244, 249, 299
   The Merry Wives of Windsor, 225
   The Taming of the Shrew, 97
   The Tempest, 107, 189
   The Two Gentlemen of Verona, 225
   The Winter's Tale, 88, 279, 290, 300, 304
   tigers in, 185, 281–6, 289, 291, 297–8
   Timon of Athens, 17, 201, 213–15, 220, 225, 238, 262, 267–8, 277, 293, 299
   Titus Andronicus, 17, 218, 224, 227, 249, 281, 283–93, 295, 298–300
   Troilus and Cressida, 82, 84, 129, 184–5, 204, 256
   Twelfth Night, 43, 149, 157, 159, 189, 225, 249, 259
Sharp, Frank Chapman, 187–9, 197–9
Sheskin, Mark, 247, 260
Shweder, Richard, 263, 278
Sidgwick, Henry, 72, 127
sin, 8, 82–4, 125, 129, 145, 156–8, 164, 176, 187, 190–1, 197, 218, 253, 262–3, 267–77, 279–80, 295
Sinfield, Alan, 203, 222
situatedness, 19–21, 23, 27–8, 33, 63, 97, 100, 124, 141–2, 217, 251, 297
Smith, Adam, 36, 42, 44–5, 51, 67–8, 165, 168, 177
Smith, Craig A., 14, 30–2, 176
Smith, Patti, 8–9, 30, 105
socialism, 40, 45–7, 67, 167, 220, 256
Sombart, Werner, 160, 175
Sommer, Kirsten L., 227–8, 243
Sowell, Thomas
   A Conflict of Visions, 35, 41, 65–6, 68
   constrained vision, 11–12, 15, 35–45, 47, 49–51, 53, 55, 57, 59, 61, 63, 65–7, 69, 187, 238, 248, 252, 259, 281, 286
   unconstrained vision, 15, 35, 37–42, 44–5, 49–51, 56, 58, 60, 293, 301
   The Quest for Cosmic Justice, 40, 48, 66, 89, 145, 196–7, 238, 249, 287, 295, 302
   The Vision of the Anointed, 57, 62, 65–8, 70, 203
species selection, 37, 54, 56–8, 62, 281, 287
Spinoza, Baruch, 72, 133
staining (moral), 269, 271, 277
Stalin, Joseph, 46, 67, 181
Starmans, Christina, 247, 260
Stoicism, 7, 15, 38, 53, 71, 75–7, 79, 89, 91–102, 107, 111–15, 118, 121, 123, 127, 132, 134, 139, 153, 170, 227, 285

subversion, 10, 12, 18, 202, 207–8, 219–21, 296–7, 303
summum bonum, 77, 111, 153, 166, 230

Tarantino, Quentin, 284
Tawney, R. H., 160–1, 175–7
Thorne, William B., 304
Tillyard, E. M. W., 79, 89, 128, 131, 203, 207, 221–2, 232, 244
Tooby, John, 56, 69
Tosh, Will, 243–4
treachery, 6, 226, 297
Trevor-Roper, Hugh, 160, 175–6
Trivers, Robert L., 31, 51, 68, 260
Troeltsch, Ernst, 159, 175
Trump, Donald, 45, 165, 264–5, 278
Tunstall, Cuthbert, 87–8, 91
Tversky, Amos, 14
Tyacke, Nicholas, 147, 172
Tyndale, William, 172
tyranny, 12, 25, 29, 47, 167, 202, 219–21, 297–8

unfairness, 238, 241, 246, 248–51, 255–6, 258–9, 280, 297–8, 302–3
universality, 5–6, 8, 11, 18–19, 32, 70, 79, 103, 113, 170, 240, 242, 246, 263–4, 271, 277
utopian thinking, 15, 35, 37, 39, 43, 45–6, 48, 51, 60, 62, 64, 97, 208, 219, 231, 238, 256, 291, 293, 300

Valla, Lorenzo, 114–15, 136
value pluralism, 69, 104–5, 134, 138
Veblen, Thorstein, 38
vengeance, 251, 253–6, 258–9, 284, 297–8
villainy, 246, 248, 251, 258
vindictiveness, 251, 280

Virgil, 120, 267, 282, 292
Vyvyan, John, 195–8, 200, 290, 294–5, 303

Walsh, Anthony, 49, 68, 129, 136
wealth, 44, 67–8, 93, 112–13, 126, 160, 164–5, 169, 175, 177, 190, 205, 215, 248, 258, 280, 289, 298
Weber, Max, 140, 157, 159–62, 166–7, 169, 174–7
Webster, John, 142, 189
Weil, Judith, 207–8, 213, 223
welling up (of emotion), 20–2, 63, 79, 250, 289
Wells, Robin Headlam, 128, 134, 197–8, 261, 292, 303
Wheeler, John, 140, 163–6, 169, 176
White, Hayden, 4
wickedness, 115, 153, 157, 189, 217
Williams, Raymond, 4
Wilson, David Sloan, 56, 58–60, 63–4, 69–70
Wilson, Edward O., 47, 51, 56, 58–60, 63–4, 67–70, 137, 164, 177
Woodbridge, Linda, 250, 255–6, 260
Woodruff, Paul, 104, 134
Wordsworth, Charles, 184, 186, 196, 198–9
Wright, Robert, 56, 58, 66, 69, 199, 292
Wright, Thomas, 84
Wyatt, Thomas, 87, 130, 133
Wycliffe, John, 142

xenophilia, 264
xenophobia, 263–4

Zalloua, Zachi Anbra, 108, 135
Zamir, Tzachi, 198, 231, 244, 250–1, 260
Zeno of Citium, 38, 75, 93–4, 97, 100, 113